REGULAT
AND
THE REAGAN ERA

*For further information on the Independent Institute's program
and a catalog of publications, please contact:*

THE INDEPENDENT INSTITUTE
350 Sansome Street
San Francisco, CA 94104
(415) 434-2976

REGULATION AND THE REAGAN ERA

Politics, Bureaucracy and the Public Interest

Edited by
Roger E. Meiners and Bruce Yandle

FOREWORD BY ROBERT CRANDALL

Independent Studies in Political Economy

HM

HOLMES & MEIER
NEW YORK / LONDON

Published in the United States of America 1989 by
Holmes & Meier Publishers, Inc.
30 Irving Place
New York, N.Y. 10003

Book design by Dale Cotton

The paper used in this publication meets the requirements
of the American National Standard for Permanence of Paper
for Printed Library Materials, Z39.48-1984.

Library of Congress Cataloging-in-Publication Data

Regulation and the Reagan era : politics, bureaucracy, and the public
    interest / edited by Roger E. Meiners and Bruce Yandle : foreword
    by Robert Crandall.
        p. cm. — (Independent studies in political economy)
    Includes index.
    ISBN 0-8419-1174-6 (alk. paper). — ISBN 0-8419-1271-8 (pbk.
alk. paper)
        1. Trade regulation—United States.   2. Deregulation—United
States.   3. Privatization—United States.   4. United States—
Politics and government—1981–1989.   I. Meiners, Roger E.
II. Yandle, Bruce.   III. Series.
HD3616.U47R1435   1989
338.973′009′048—dc20   89-7594
                                                                    CIP

MANUFACTURED IN THE UNITED STATES OF AMERICA

Contents

Foreword
Robert W. Crandall

In the process of selecting Ronald Reagan's successor as President, the major campaign issues included the U.S. trade deficit, continuing budget deficits, Central American policy, and the decline in U.S. industrial supremacy. In all of the rhetoric that surrounded the presidential election, there was very little talk of regulation, deregulation, or regulatory reform.

There are a number of possible reasons for the virtual disappearance of regulation as a major national issue. First, and perhaps most important, the major economic problems of America's farmers, oil producers, or major manufacturing industries do not derive from excessive or misguided federal regulation. Weak prices for feed grains or petroleum products cannot be attributed to past exercises in wellhead price regulation or support and loan programs. If anything, these regulatory programs reduced output and raised prices. Nor is excessive health-safety regulation to blame for the declining fortunes of semiconductor, machine tool, home electronics, or farm-machinery producers. In fact, manufacturing productivity has recently been growing as rapidly as it did in the 1950s and 1960s.

Second, much of the "easy" deregulation occurred under the Carter Administration. The attempt to change financial, natural-gas, and even telephone regulation is much more difficult than the deregulation of airlines, trucks, and railroads because the potential losers from such deregulation are more widespread and have better political representation than the Teamsters or airline flight attendants.

Third, as the Reagan Administration learned most painfully, attempts to change regulatory policies that affect health and safety require considerable courage and the likely sacrifice of political capital. Ralph Nader's disciples are more powerful in stirring up fear of crass, pro-business Republicans at the helm of the Environmental Protection Agency, the Consumer Product Safety Commission, or the Occupational Safety and Health Administration than in improving health and safety when they head these agencies in a Democratic regime. Because of this populist opposition, the Reagan Administration essentially gave up on new initiatives to reform these health-safety policies in the first term.

When Reagan assumed office in 1981, "regulatory reform" was one of four pillars of a policy to rescue the U.S. from its economic abyss. As the years wore on, and the economy recovered from the 1982 recession, it was clear that changes in regulatory policy were not very important in rescuing the economy from the depths into which it had plunged after the inflationary 1970s. Tax cuts, sharp increases in defense spending, steady monetary policy, and (eventually) dollar depreciation were the government's tools for regenerating economic growth. Regulatory reform was quickly perceived as a set of actions consistent with the Administration's conservative philosophy, but not a program that would add noticably to GNP by 1984 or even 1988.

The limited political benefits of assaulting the government's regulatory policy inefficiencies were soon combined with the large potential costs of taking on the health-safety-environment monster. Controversy at OSHA and NHTSA combined with scandal at EPA in the first three years of the Administration, obviously cooling the ardor of Reagan's principal aides. The administrators of several of the larger agencies resigned, James Miller moved from OMB to the Federal Trade Commission, and regulatory reform essentially moved to the back burner.

Many of Reagan's appointees to positions in the regulatory agencies have obviously been disappointed by their failure to achieve reform even as rapidly as the Carter Administration. Licking their wounds, most now recognize that it is far from sufficient to have a good idea if one wants to overcome decades of regulatory folly. It is simply not enough to show that natural gas regulation has reduced natural gas supplies or that excessive EPA regulation of new power plants keeps the old, dirty ones alive. One must understand the political forces that create and perpetuate these seemingly foolish assaults on the welfare of American producers and consumers. And even with this understanding it may be impossible to fashion the coalitions that are required to effect major changes in these regulatory policies.

This book contains both contributions by scholars of regulation who have remained outside government and the reflections of several of those involved with the early struggles of Reagan reformers. Most have now returned to the academy or to private practice. Some remain to continue the fight. But their collected writings suggest a continuing concern for pressing ahead with reforms or reductions of federal regulatory practice.

In these chapters, one detects a struggle among those who believe that clever policymakers can assemble or manipulate political coalitions to obtain reform or at least uncover reform policies that will not be rendered stillborn by various private interest. Langenfeld and Walton, for instance, attribute the relative success of the Reagan FTC and OSHA and the failure of Reagan's EPA to different strategies pursued by the leaders of these agencies. Others, such as Nelson and Cohen view the politics of public-land management and foreign-trade protection as overwhelming any attempts at reform. Some people benefit from these policies and not surprisingly resist strenuously when the reformers arrive.

The first two chapters provide the reader with a review of the ample evidence—perhaps overstated—that regulation is merely the outcome of private interests lobbying for various types of government protection from competition or assaults on their competitors. The uninitiated reader may find this brief introduction either too cynical or too hopeless. On the one hand, how is it that some industries succeed so well in gaining government protection while others do not? On the other hand, what can any of us do to overcome the seemingly invulnerable political alliances that have provided generations of government protection to dairy producers, western cattle ranchers, or investment bankers?

We still do not have answers to these questions. Therefore, it is difficult to offer clever suggestions for undoing the evils of established regulatory policies or preventing new ones. This book does not offer much hope in this regard, and a few of the papers even counsel despair. McCormick tells us that private use of government's monopoly "police power" of regulation is inevitable. Shugart argues that administrative reforms are bound to be shortlived—that new political coalitions will form or the old ones will wait to reassert their power when administrations change. Nelson views progress in reversing generations of public land policies as necessarily slow if it occurs at all. Cohen despairs that ITC commissioners fail to use their offices, not for the impossible task of promoting free trade but just as "bully pulpits" to educate the public of the folly of any ITC regulation. Douglas and Metrinko fear that airline regulation will return through the back door at the Department of Transportation as engineers and bureaucrats at DOT succumb to arguments that economists would reject out of hand.

If these arguments seem to reflect despondency, later chapters suggest a more troubling aspect of regulation and government activity in general. Bureaucrats can use the mere threat of government intervention to pressure private interests into "voluntary" actions to avoid the embarrassment of hostile government action. Rogowsky details such possibilities at the CPSC, FTC, or the Antitrust Division. He might have added the broadcast-license renewal process at the FCC, which fortunately has been reformed substantially in the past five years. McChesney and Stroup offer an even more ominous thought—that legislators use their leverage as potential suppliers of taxation or regulatory costs to extract political support from private interest groups. From their perspective, no issue is ever settled because the legislator maximizes his potential campaign contributions, etc. by maintaining an "open mind" on most issues.

The fact that no political issue can be permanently settled should send chills up the spines of the deregulatory scholars represented in this volume. With the 1988 election there is some minor renewal of interest in government regulation. "Insider trading" and corporate takeovers are receiving the eager attention of the staff of the Senate Finance Committee. Reregulation of airlines is discussed in the pages of the *Washington Post* and *New York Times,* and before leaving, former Secretary Elizabeth Dole moved to increase the Department of Transportation's role in controlling airline schedules, advertising, and punctuality. The Congress has passed a bill requiring broadcasters to abide by the "Fairness Doctrine." And there is even some discussion of reregulation of railroads.

Is all of this analysis too defeatist—too willing to explain why the forces of right are not necessarily those of might? Why can Roosevelt or Johnson succeed in pursuing a New Deal or a Great Society while Reagan fails in his assault on excessive government? Why did Dunkirk turn into Waterloo? One has the feeling that more could have been done.

Perhaps the Reagan administration may have missed an historic opportunity to continue the deregulation movement begun by Presidents Ford and Carter. On the other hand, it has held fast in preserving the gains won in the late 1970s and 1980. The public has had the opportunity to see how less regulated markets work. The populists have less to seize upon than they might have had if Reagan had taken on EPA and OSHA regulation in earnest. And because of the accumulated experiences of the scores of keen students of public choice who worked in the Reagan Administration, we may begin to understand why politicians are so eager to squander the nation's precious resources in so many little ways that add up to a sizable burden on their constituents.

Brookings Institution
Washington, DC

Notes on Contributors

Roger E. Meiners is Director of the Center for Policy Studies and Professor of Law and Economics at Clemson University. He served as Director of the Atlanta office of the Federal Trade Commission and has been a member of the faculty of the University of Miami, Emory University, and Texas A & M University.

Bruce Yandle is Alumni Professor of Economics and Senior Research Scholar, Center for Policy Studies, Clemson University. Yandle served as Executive Director of the Federal Trade Commission from 1982 to 1984.

Robert E. McCormick is Professor of Economics and Senior Research Scholar, Center for Policy Studies, Clemson University. McCormick was previously a faculty member at the Graduate School of Business, Rochester University, and has been a consultant to several federal agencies.

Thomas F. Walton, Ph.D. University of California at Los Angeles, is Director of Policy Analysis at General Motors Corporation and former Federal Trade Commission official.

James Langenfeld is Deputy Assistant Director, Bureau of Economics, at the Federal Trade Commission. He has held other positions at the Federal Trade Commission and at General Motors.

William C. MacLeod is Director, Bureau of Consumer Protection, at the Federal Trade Commission. He has held other positions at the Federal Trade Commission as well as in private law practice.

Robert A. Rogowsky, Ph.D. University of Virginia, is a former Executive Assistant to the Chairman at the International Trade Commission and is Deputy Director, Bureau of Consumer Protection, at the Federal Trade Commission.

William F. Shughart II is Professor of Economics at the University of Mississippi. He was previously at the Public Choice Center of George

Mason University, on the economics faculty at Clemson University, and a former Federal Trade Commission economist.

John T. Wenders is Professor of Economics at the University of Idaho. He taught previously at the University of Arizona and has extensive experience in telecommunications.

Robert H. Nelson, Ph.D. Princeton, is a research economist at the Department of Interior. He previously taught at City College, The City University of New York, and was with the Twentieth Century Fund.

Lloyd R. Cohen, Associate Professor of Law at California Western School of Law, is a lawyer-economist who served as attorney adviser to a commissioner at the International Trade Commission.

George W. Douglas, Ph.D. Yale, is a private consultant in Austin, Texas, and former Commissioner, Federal Trade Commission.

Peter Metrinko is attorney adviser to a commissioner at the Federal Trade Commission.

Fred S. McChesney is Robert Thompson Professor of Law at Emory University. He is former Associate Director of the Bureau of Consumer Protection at the Federal Trade Commission and has taught at the University of Chicago Law School.

Richard L. Stroup is Professor of Economics at Montana State University and Senior Associate of the Political Economy Research Center. He was the director of the Office of Policy Analysis at the U.S. Department of Interior.

Daniel K. Benjamin is Professor of Economics and Senior Research Scholar at the Center for Policy Studies at Clemson University. He is former Chief of Staff of the U.S. Department of Labor and was a member of the economics faculty at the University of Washington.

Alan Rufus Waters is Professor of Economics at California State University—Fresno and former Chief Economist of the U.S. Agency for International Development.

REGULATION
AND
THE REAGAN ERA

Part I

REGULATION AND DEREGULATION

1

Regulatory Lessons from the Reagan Era: Introduction

Roger E. Meiners and Bruce Yandle

The "Reagan revolution" officially began in November 1980, when Ronald Reagan swept Jimmy Carter out of the White House and the Republican party made unexpectedly large gains in Congress. This political strength was maintained through 1984, but it seems clear that the 1986 elections that returned the Senate to the Democratic party spelled the end of that revolution. With the Reagan revolution behind us, we can now begin not only to evaluate its relative successes and failures, but to see what lessons can be learned from these added years of observation of our political economy at work.

The purpose of this book is to bring together the views of professional economists and legal scholars who have devoted much of their careers to studying government and the regulatory process. The contributors to this volume generally favor either deregulation or regulation that embodies a greater degree of economic rationality. While the authors would not necessarily characterize themselves as supporters of the Reagan administration, most are sympathetic to the general economic goals it originally professed. Indeed, most worked for the federal government during part of the Reagan years, some because they had explicit hopes that they could help rationalize policy making and the regulatory process.

Looking back at November 1980 and the general expectations that were commonly discussed, some of us are a bit chagrined by the overly optimistic expectations we held early in the administration. Economists who understood, or even contributed to, the economic theory of regulation described by Robert McCormick in chapter 2 should have known that rapid change is unlikely. They should have known, too, that the sage advice of even the most eminent economists would not lead members of Congress to act against their own interests. Nevertheless, there was talk about abolishing numerous agencies, such as the Department of Education, the Department of Energy, and a host of lesser agencies that had been attacked as imposing unnecessary burdens on individuals and the productivity of U.S. business.

Now, with the regulatory reform of the Reagan administration finished, not one major agency has been abolished. The real estate market in Washington, D.C., did not collapse; the federal government still employs hundreds of thousands of career employees to run the same agencies they ran before the advent of the Reagan administration. Nevertheless the world today is different from what it was when Ronald Reagan took office, and so is federal regulation.

This collection of papers helps evaluate how the world of regulation has changed. The volume is not intended to be an indictment of, or paean to, the regulatory record of the Reagan administration, nor will the volume comment on other economic policies undertaken since 1981. Drawing on the experiences of people who were there, we wish to provide comments on successes and failures and to discover the reasons for what occurred. It is our hope that such an understanding will enable us to make better predictions of what is likely to happen in the future.

To help put the contents of this volume in perspective, the rest of this chapter will provide a review of the general state of regulatory development in recent years. An overview of the content of each chapter follows. The style of various chapters differs, and substantially different approaches to the issues are taken. Some address specific policy development in particular areas. Others are concerned with a better understanding of the workings of the bureaucracy. And still others further our still developing economic theory of regulation. While each chapter bears the mark of its author, we find a common theme runs through the volume: People make a difference. Just how much difference they make in effecting changes in regulation will be discovered as each chapter is read.

A Perspective on the Economic Theory of Regulation

When James Buchanan was awarded the Nobel Memorial Prize in Economic Science in 1986, he was cited for his work in developing public-choice theory, which concerns the application of economic theory to political institutions. The media commonly described Buchanan's contribution as the "discovery" that politicians and bureaucrats work to further their own self-interest. Shallow-minded political commentators (and some narrow-minded economists) attempted to belittle Buchanan's work by commenting to the effect that any idiot knows that people act in their own self-interest. Actually, economists for years talked, and most political scientists today talk, as if elected and appointed officials do not operate in their self-interest. The economic theory of regulation and the public-choice approach to government processes is a relatively new development. The seminal works on public-choice theory have all been written in the last thirty years, and it is only during the past two decades that the economic theory of regulation has been developed and applied to studies of legislation and regulation.

As recently as 1964, one of the first economic analyses of the impact of a regulatory agency was produced. That year, Nobel laureate George Stigler published an article about the consequences of Securities and Exchange Commission (SEC) regulation of securities markets.[1] Prior to the publication of his article, there had been essentially no critical examination by economists of the reasons for the origins of the SEC or, more importantly, the impact of its regulations in practice. Rather, there was uncritical acceptance of the public-interest view that Congress, in its wisdom, had protected investors by creating the SEC and its assorted regulations. Stigler attempted to demonstrate empirically that SEC regulations did not enhance the efficiency of security markets. Given our understanding of regulations today, this hardly seems to be a startling conclusion. However, in 1964 this conclusion was nothing short of heresy.

In reply to Stigler, two professors of finance at the University of Pennsylvania defended the SEC as "a valuable and effective agency."[2] Further they claimed that Stigler's empirical analysis was a "triumph of ideology over scholarship." The "need" for the SEC was demonstrated by pointing to such evidence as the Pecora investigation, which Congress held prior to passage of the 1933 and 1934 SEC legislation. Were anyone to claim today that congressional investigations are unbiased and truly fact-finding in intent, they would be laughed at for naïveté, but in 1964, respected economists often made such statements. Other comments on Stigler's article, including one by a professor of finance at Columbia University, defended an SEC-commissioned study that Stigler had criticized as obviously being an excellent report because it was financed by public funds. Its preparation was entrusted to a public agency, it concerned financial institutions of vital importance to the public, "it was . . . a public document."[3]

This 1964 discussion reminds us of the level of the debate less than two decades before the advent of the Reagan administration. Today, no one, even if they believe that certain regulations are justified, would make statements, at least in an academic journal, that imply unqualified acceptance of a federal agency simply because it is a federal agency, nor do we see many economists assert that studies commissioned by federal agencies are somehow less biased and of higher quality than independently produced documents.

In the past two decades, students of the public policy and regulatory process have made substantial gains in understanding the development and impact of public institutions in our political economy. Nevertheless, we still find many occurrences difficult to explain, a sign that our economic theory of regulation is not fully developed. We think the papers in this volume will help contribute to a fuller understanding. The experiences with regulatory change described and recounted in later chapters do not represent the first plowing of a new field. The reform efforts of the 1980s were part of a continuous process that originated formally in the Ford administration.

Developments in the 1970s

In the mid-1970s, when economists and scholars of regulation were developing robust theories that claimed to explain regulation, their counterparts in the Ford administration were struggling to bring about change. Regulation of all forms had been expanded, especially those dealing with safety, health, the environment, and employment—the so-called social regulation. Using arguments based on economic efficiency, the much-in-vogue cost-benefit analysis, and just plain common sense, those first modern deregulators somehow affected the quantity and quality of regulations flowing from the *Federal Register* printing presses.

But not to be overlooked is the fact that the broader economy was ripe for change. The nation was reeling from the effects of inflation, the OPEC-inspired oil embargo, and the onerous wage price controls concocted to deal with those two problems. The combination of rapidly rising energy prices and archaic regulation of routes and rates for airlines, trucking, and rail transportation had become a heavy burden, even for the regulators. Rapidly rising interest rates were crippling financial institutions that were bound by rate regulations. Simply put, regulatory flexibility had to be introduced where it was missing.

Importantly, the Ford administration delivered legislation that altered rail and truck regulation; it set in motion the reform of financial institutions, and initiated hearings on airline deregulation. It saw repeal of the fair trade laws and established formal mechanisms in the White House for managing the regulatory process. Looking back, it seems only logical that regulation had to respond to the significant changes in the market. The U.S. economy was being restructured.

In some ways, the Carter administration played the hand dealt by the

Ford administration, but the focus of the effort was quite different. In fact, a kind of split personality is seen in the record for the period. Reforms of economic regulation, the kind produced by the Interstate Commerce Commission (ICC), Civil Aeronautics Board (CAB), and Federal Reserve Board, were remarkably successful. Again, inflation and rising energy prices played a major role. However, the output of regulations from the Occupational Safety and Health Administration (OSHA), Environmental Protection Agency (EPA), National Highway Traffic Safety Administration, Consumer Product Safety Commission, and other social regulators expanded at almost an explosive rate.

Still, during the Carter years the broad theme of regulatory reform was kept alive, and mechanisms for reviewing newly produced rules became even more elaborate. Heads of regulatory agencies formed a White House cartel and struggled over which new regulations might pass unscathed into the economy.

Regulatory reform was one of the major planks in Ronald Reagan's bid for the presidency. On assuming office, Reagan set out to deliver on his promises. But the hopes held by many Reagan appointees that somehow the regulatory stables would be cleaned once and for all overlooked several things, including the economic law of diminishing returns. It was somehow believed that the greatly expanded social regulatory agencies could be scaled back simply by applying the same energies and logic used successfully during the Ford years. It was to be learned again that incremental costs rise exponentially. The easiest reforms had already occurred.

Overlooked also was the fact that the regulation of the past was now woven securely into the fabric of the economy. Many industry spokesmen who initially opposed ardently the new and costly rules were found to be supporting those same devices. What first looked like a straightjacket now felt more like an old tweed suit. Indeed, life was much more comfortable for some surviving firms and industries with regulations than without them. Much more than cost-benefit analysis would be needed to knock down the remaining regulatory walls.

But while the Ford and Carter administrations had inflation generating a demand for regulatory change, the Reagan administration found support for change because of an economic recession. Regulatory relief was a battle cry for the Reagan deregulators. Budget reductions brought regulatory rollbacks, modifications in rules, and changes in the working relationships of some of the regulators and the regulated. Yet while reform continued and the screen for reviewing newly proposed rules became more difficult to pass through, little in the way of fundamental change can be reported. In fact, a reading of current regulatory budgets and activities strongly suggests that another wave of regulation is in the making.

Figure 1.1
A Decade-By-Decade Comparison of
Major Regulatory Legislation, Pre-1900–1979

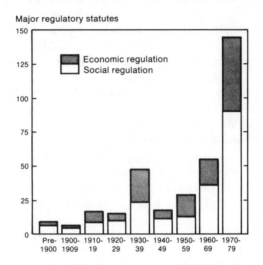

Major regulatory statutes

Source: Bruce Yandle, "The Evolution of Regulatory Activities in the 1970s and 1980s,"
Phillip Cagan, ed., *Essays in Contemporary Economic Problems, 1986* (Washington:
American Enterprise Institute, 1986), p. 111. Data from which the chart was developed are from Center for the Study of American Business, Washington University, St. Louis, Mo.

Figure 1.2
Antitrust Actions, Pre-1900–1983

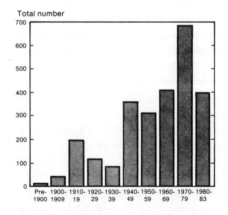

Total number

Source: Bruce Yandle, "The Evolution of Regulatory Activities in the 1970s and 1980s,"
Phillip Cagan, ed., *Essays in Contemporary Economic Problems, 1986* (Washington:
American Enterprise Institute, 1986, p. 112). Data for chart were taken from Rich-
ard A. Posner, "A Statistical Study of Antitrust Enforcement," *Journal of Law and
Economics,* 13, no. 2 (October 1970): 365–419, and from annual reports of the
Antitrust Division of the U.S. Department of Justice.

The Fourth Wave of Regulation

The historic expansion and contraction of federal regulation shown by patterns of legislation in Figure 1.1 form three waves that coincide with the Progressive period (for example, transportation regulation and antitrust laws), the New Deal (for example, financial markets, labor and agriculture regulations), and the social reform movements of the 1970s (for example, environmental, safety, and health controls). A somewhat similar pattern, shown in Figure 1.2, is observed for antitrust actions taken by federal agencies. Similar measures for the Reagan period would show a marked decline, but there is good reason to believe that counts of legislation and antitrust cases do not fully reveal important current dimensions of regulatory change.

First, past growth in federal regulation involved systematic take-overs of the work of state and local regulators by the federal government. We speculate that the amount of regulation encountered by business managers and citizens did not change, but the quality of regulation changed. It became uniform and all-encompassing across the national economy. Federal expansion reached the limit in the 1970s when virtually all forms of local regulation migrated to the federal level. In this sense, recent regulatory reform reflected an antifederalist reaction. Recent regulatory reform also reflected a problem with uniformity. Greater flexibility was needed if federal regulators were to hold on to their newly gained political powers. Interest groups, including industries and organized consumer groups, countered the reform efforts in cases where regulation by the federal government restricted output, reduced competition, and generated substantial gains, something that could not be accomplished by the uncoordinated efforts of fifty state governments.

The reforms in transportation and communications that occurred in the 1970s and 1980s returned some regulatory power to states while revising and shifting regulatory powers at the federal level. State telephone regulators became more important after the AT&T decision, as did their transportation counterparts after the revision of the ICC's powers. The demise of the CAB led to a concentration of regulatory powers in the Department of Transportation (DOT), and changes in the regulation of financial institutions were associated with a large expansion of the Federal Deposit Insurance Corporation (FDIC), the Federal Savings and Loan Insurance Corporation (FSLIC), and the SEC and actions by states to restrict the growth of interstate banking.

Second, regulation has become increasingly complex and subtle as the emphasis moved from rate making and entry control to the investigation and attempted control of such things as upper atmospheric chemistry, the psychological response of consumers to alternative forms of advertising, and competing technologies for broadcasting microwave signals. Specification of minute details of accounting and the management of highly complex financial transactions, instruments, and markets can have substantial economic effects on industries, interest groups, and economic performance, but not make headlines on the evening news.

Along with the all-encompassing nature of federal regulation in the 1970s came strong emphasis on risk reduction and the expansion of efforts to reduce safety, health, and environmental hazards. Implementation of the many rules that followed brought recognition that regulatory risk reduction was itself risky. Sometimes the risk added by the regulators was greater than the risk they sought to remove. This third qualitative feature of modern regulation is not necessarily reflected in counts of legislation and pages in the *Federal Register,* but continues to characterize rules produced by EPA, OSHA, the Food and Drug Administration (FDA), and the financial regulators.

Finally, regulation growth during the Reagan administration has featured protection of domestic industries from foreign competition. Monetary and fiscal policy that evolved in the 1980s strengthened the dollar and turned the tables on import-sensitive U.S. sectors, which had previously flourished when the dollar was weak. A long line of petitioners formed at the commerce department's International Trade Administration, and the International Trade Commission passed out protection as called for by the statutes that dictate the agency's action. The point is that regulation expanded, but few new laws and rules were put on the books.

For all these reasons, we argue that the fourth wave of regulation associated with the Reagan administration is far more complex and subtle than previous ones and resists assessment by any simple measuring rod. However, even traditional evidence, such as employment growth in regulatory agencies, suggests regulation is expanding in those areas related to the service sectors, which after all are the most vibrant part of the economy.

Any analysis of regulatory activities is an analysis of the behavior of people, their ideas, and efforts to effect change. The papers in this volume tell us about some of the people and some of the struggles. The collection does not attempt to present a complete story of what some might term the Reagan administration's major regulatory reforms and successes. Reading through the chapters will spur some thinking, shake some prejudices, and probably leave the reader feeling that reform is never simple and hardly ever completely successful.

Overview of This Volume

The papers that make up this collection are divided into three components. The first section consists of this introductory chapter and a paper by Robert McCormick that surveys developments in economic thought on regulation, why it occurs, and how outcomes might be predicted. McCormick's paper discusses the origins of the special-interest theory of government and what it has revealed when applied to a rich array of regulatory events. This chapter reviews the state of economic knowledge about regulation and bureaucracy that was understood by professional economists and economist-lawyers who went to work for the federal government during the Reagan administration. Rent-seeking behavior, the notion that politically interested individuals and groups will grapple in the democratic arena and use government to increase and maintain their wealth—a common theme in later papers—plays a major role in the research McCormick surveys.

The next section of the book contains seven papers that assess the performance of Reagan regulatory reform from the perspective of individual agencies and issues. The first paper, by Thomas F. Walton and James Langenfeld, formerly and currently on the staff of the Federal Trade Commission (FTC), examines the FTC, OSHA and EPA. Arguing that people who lead agencies do make the difference between success and failure, Walton and Langenfeld give a rather optimistic account of the record for the FTC and OSHA and then contrast that with the failure of Reagan's EPA appointees to generate reform. Their paper provides rich detail on cases, actions, and management reforms as they build their argument and report on the three case studies.

According to William MacLeod and Robert Rogowsky, authors of the second paper, one area in which there was a direct effort to repeal or modify regulatory activities of the past was in consumer protection at the FTC. MacLeod, who served as director of the Bureau of Consumer Protection, and Rogowsky, who has held various staff positions at the FTC also, detail consumer protection activities that had been built from almost nothing to an active agenda through the 1970s, particularly during the reign of Michael Pertschuk, chairman during the Carter administration. Reagan's first chairman, James Miller, clearly intended to reverse the trend. Some of the battles that were fought and the results of attempting to rationalize consumer protection with the use of economic analysis are discussed.

William Shughart's paper, which comes next, also focuses on the FTC but from a slightly different perspective and with a much less favorable conclusion than that of Walton and Langenfeld. Shughart was in the FTC's Bureau of Economics prior to Reagan's 1980 victory. He tells about expectations for change in antitrust enforcement, how change did occur, and then goes on to predict that a future FTC will have little difficulty in returning to its former regulatory habits. While noting successes and failures in the agency, Shughart leaves the reader with the admonition that the Reagan changes were associated with people—they were not substantive revisions in statutes and procedures that might be long lived.

The next chapter in this section looks at regulation and deregulation in the communication industry. John T. Wenders, a leading consultant to the communications industry during the past decade who has written extensively on the economics of communication regulation and worked with firms and regulators in understanding the effects of changes in regulation that take place, works through some of the key changes that have affected an industry radically changed by technological innovations.

Robert H. Nelson, a career employee in the Department of Interior and a specialist in the history of U.S. public land policy, recounts the expectations and controversies that surrounded privatization of Western land in the Reagan administration. Nelson goes back to the almost forgotten 1979 Sagebrush Rebellion and gives a detailed account of how that movement joined and then became separated from efforts to sell public land. Heated debates among special interests, public misperceptions, and the misconstrued but rather benign role of Interior Secretary James Watt are major themes in the chapter. From Nelson we learn that privatization, like most other reform efforts, has a continuous history, one that rises and falls with political action in the Western states.

Calling the International Trade Commission (ITC), the subject of the sixth paper, a regulatory agency may be a mistake according to author Lloyd Cohen, who was an attorney-adviser to an ITC commissioner. That being the case, we should not be disappointed that regulatory reform did not occur there. Stating clear and strong views regarding the purpose of, and social cost imposed by, the ITC—its purpose is protectionism, and the cost imposed is the largest of any agency—Cohen describes the tight legislation that constrains ITC behavior and the agency's recent behavior and offers only faint optimism regarding prospects for change. In Cohen's view, which is one that supports free trade, the Reagan record on protectionism is mixed at best, poor at worst. As Cohen sees the matter, hope for an improved ITC, one that protects consumers from higher tariffs and prices, will come when one or several ITC commissioners use the office as a pulpit for informing the U.S. public of the merits of open markets and the costs of protectionism.

In the final paper in this section, a former FTC commissioner, George Douglas, who was appointed by President Reagan, and FTC attorney-adviser Peter Metrinko focus on the sunset of the CAB and the associated struggle over the former agency's residual authorities. Here we see the backwash of regulatory reform that ended one agency while planting new seeds for industry regulation in another agency. Douglas and Metrinko discuss the regulatory habits and incentives of the FTC, the Department of Justice, and the DOT, the agencies slated to argue over the CAB's remains. They then describe the behavior of the DOT, the agency that became the regulator of commercial air transportation, and suggest that regulation may be on the rise again, this time in the guise of the Federal Aviation Administration.

The last section of the book contains five papers concerned with the operation of bureaucracies and their relationship to Congress. The first paper is by Robert Rogowsky, currently of the FTC but previously with the ITC and the Consumer Product Safety Commission. Based on his experiences in those agencies, he details how bureaucrats are often able to execute their own agenda of regulation regardless of the intent of Congress or the executive branch. The latitude in the Consumer Product Safety Commision and the FTC may be somewhat peculiar to agencies given broad and vague mandates by Congress compared to those with highly specific missions that are easier to monitor. Rogowsky does not contend that bureaucracy is "out of control," as many members of Congress like to assert when running for office, but that administrative procedures simply allow substantial flexibility to regulators, enabling them to impose costs on private parties that may or may not have been intended by the original legislation.

In contrast to Rogowsky, Fred McChesney develops the thesis that politicians have strong incentives to monitor the regulatory process closely. Not only do vote-seeking legislators have to make special-interest constituents happy, but they can use the regulatory process to earn political rents. That is, politicians can gain directly by "milking" potential victims of threatened regulations. Thus we observe the phenomenon of threatened regulations that appear to have no major constituency interested in organizing a campaign for their implementation. Perhaps for the same reason we observe Congress allowing regulators to pursue their own agenda, since the institution of new regulations benefits members of the legislature who can manipulate the final result.

Richard Stroup, who served as director of the policy analysis office of the Department of Interior, argues in the next chapter (in agreement with McChesney) that politicians have incentives not to be consistent in their positions. That is, if a member of a legislature is always guaranteed a vote on an issue, or if an agency head can always be expected to behave in a consistent manner with respect to various issues, then he has no political capital to sell. It is only by being flexible on issues that political agents can extract rents from those who stand to gain from their support on certain issues.

The two final chapters address more of the practical aspects of working in the bureaucracy. The first of these papers is by Daniel Benjamin, who served as Chief of Staff in the Department of Labor before returning to academia. Benjamin models the top management tier of a cabinet-level agency and explains the incentives of various officeholders. He focuses on power—who has it, how it can be identified, and how the official structure of agencies may not accurately depict the way things get done. Benjamin goes on to describe some of the difficulties encountered when officials seek to bring about change while simultaneously operating with smaller budgets.

The last paper is by the former Chief Economist of the U.S. Agency for International Development. Many economists consider the name of this agency a contradiction in terms; indeed Rufus Waters found it, in practice, to be largely so. Waters contends, after being frequently frustrated at an agency that ignores the economic basis for success in development, that to effect change one should take a "mad dog" approach to the agency. Such an approach may, it is true, limit one's future in Washington; however, unless one takes a hard line when confronted with economically senseless policies, one will be sucked into the endless politics of the moment that engulf all bureaus. His advice, then, is written for someone who intends to use government service as an opportunity to introduce some aspect of economic rationality, rather than to become part of the rent-seeking machine in Washington.

In sum, the papers offer insight, new theories, and many accounts of experiences with regulation during the Reagan years. If we sought ideal political conditions for bringing about regulatory reform, we would be hard pressed to find a better environment than that which existed during the first half of the decade of the 1980s. The president was committed to change; his party controlled the Senate; and there was strong popular and academic support for making major changes. Even so major reform efforts were frustrated. Strong personalities—people—made major differences in the successes that did occur.

Notes

1. George Stigler, "Public Regulation of the Securities Markets," *Journal of Business* 37, no. 2 (April 1964): 117–41.

2. Irwin Friend and Edward S. Herman, "The S.E.C. through a Glass Darkly," *Journal of Business* 37, no. 4 (October 1964): 382.

3. Sidney Robbins and Walter Werner, "Professor Stigler Revisited," *Journal of Business* 37, no. 4 (October 1964): 406.

2

A Review of the Economics of Regulation: The Political Process

Robert E. McCormick

Introduction

The early days of the Reagan administration brought a new breed of civil servant to Washington. Many of them were economists; that is nothing new, but these people were different. They were educated and well-versed in the new economic theory of regulation; they were public-choice scholars. They did not believe that government service was performed for the public good. They did not believe that for government to run properly, all that was necessary was to have the "right" people in office. Instead, these economists and lawyers saw the world in a different light: Politicians did things to garner votes; they were responsive to their electorate; they were not benevolent despots. To the newcomers, regulation was used to redistribute income, not to correct market failures costlessly and perfectly. Theirs was not a philosophical view, it was a hard-edged empirical approach to the world, and it was built on twenty-five years of exacting interdisciplinary academic research. The purpose of this paper is to review and explore that literature, which formed the background of many involved in shaping the Reagan administration's policy on the regulation front.

We start this discussion with predation, a venerable concept in the literature of industrial organization. In fact, few topics have received as much theoretical attention and so little empirical scrutiny. For example, see the exchanges between McGee (1980), Areeda and Turner (1975), and Williamson (1978). Basically, price predation is an economic unicorn de-

Thanks go to James Buchanan, Matt Lindsay, Michael Maloney, Roger Meiners, William Shughart II, and Mark Wasserman for help on an earlier draft. The usual caveat applies.

pending on whether you want it to be or not—there is no consensus of opinion on the matter. Therefore, it is a bit surprising that the theory of predation has actually grown into an area where there is considerable agreement. This is the strategic use of governmental processes to disadvantage consumers and rivals.[1] Predation works by manipulating government regulations and the court system rather than through price cutting. Malevolence can mean higher profits through reduced output and higher price. Regulation fashioned in this manner affords regulated firms several advantages: Services are often provided at less than factor cost, and the monopoly police power of the state offers a unique opportunity to adjust the behavior of rivals. Most prominently, cartel enforcement is made relatively inexpensive, and the scrutiny of antitrust authorities is avoided.[2] Lobbying and other vote-supplying activities are the price that must be paid. Whether the strategic use of regulation is profitable then becomes a capital budgeting problem not unlike most other decisions the firm has to make about purchasing inputs (Salop 1981).

The literature in economics on the strategic use of regulation is relatively new; however, in many respects, all analysis of government fits the description. Moreover, there is a growing literature on strategy in general.[3] To define the topic that broadly here would impose large digestion costs for which most readers have neither the time nor the demand. Hence, for tractability, I adopt a more narrow rent-seeking definition. The strategic use of regulation is any attempt by a firm or a collection of firms or others with similar interest to alter the political or legal structure of the economy to their advantage.[4] This approach purposely ignores the question of good and bad influence. Even more importantly, it does not require deliberate aggression. There are two advantages to ignoring motives: First, they are very hard to determine; and second, from an economic standpoint, only the effects are relevant.

Strategy may take the form of trying to coerce legislation, affecting a bureaucratic ruling, or instigating a law suit. However, from an analytical viewpoint, these actions are the same and serve one or more purposes: To restrict the entry of rivals, to prevent nonprice competition, to differentially impose costs on members of an industry, or to restrict the production of substitute goods and services. Whether these actions are legal is, for the most part, irrelevant from the point of view of economic analysis. That question has received considerable attention elsewhere and is interesting in its own right, but brevity requires that I ignore the issue here.

One of the themes in the literature on the strategic use of regulation is the importance of the self-interested politician. This contrasts with most analysis in industrial organization and predation in particular. Here the politician, his motives, and his constraints are often the center of attention.

Although the role is often subsumed, nonetheless the politician is there. And most importantly, he is not disguised as a public-spirited individual benevolently maximizing some well-behaved social welfare function. Instead, the politician like all other actors is a rational, self-interested, maximizing agent. Of course there are exceptions to this principle. Kelman (1981) is the polar case of ignoring economic incentives in regulatory rule making, and most analysis of antitrust law and enforcement takes a benevolent view of politicians and the law. For example, Easterbrook (1983, p. 24) says, "The antitrust laws, in contrast, are designed to preserve the functioning of competitive markets that, at least presumptively, produce allocative efficiency." The myth of the public spirited politician dies slowly.[5]

Incorporating politicians into the behavioral system adds an apolitical market to the analysis and makes regulations endogenous. This makes it easier to predict many aspects of regulation, such as its inception and the industries that will be affected. This is accomplished by focusing analysis on various groups in the economy; for example, consumers and producers and their competing interests. These groups supply votes and campaign contributions to politicians who in turn supply regulation. The outcome of this process ultimately turns on the relative organizational costs across groups, the structure of political institutions, and the extent of competition in the political market. This is the setting for the strategic use of regulation.

This chapter is divided into six sections. The section 2 briefly reviews the emerging theory of rent seeking and its application to regulation. Section 3 reviews the economic theory of regulation, with particular emphasis on standards and cost-imposing regulation. Section 4 highlights the importance of heterogeneous interest groups in affecting regulation— the regulatory triad. The emphasis is on the ability of some firms to disguise their private pursuits as public interest whether there is a legitimate market failure or not. In some cases mutual interests bring together the strangest bedfellows—the Sierra Club and Eastern coal-mining interests. Section 5 focuses on a relatively uncharted area, the strategic use of antitrust laws to prevent competition. The chapter closes with some suggestions for the direction of future research.

Rent Seeking

The economic analysis of rent seeking was recently surveyed by Tollison (1982). The theory has important implications for the analysis of the strategic use of regulation—especially normative analysis. Tullock's (1967) seminal article demonstrates that transfers are typically not a zero-sum event. For this reason the economic cost of many activities is often far greater than conventionally assumed.

The normative problem arises because it is impossible to differentiate rent seeking from profit seeking except in the context of a normative model. On the one hand, rent seeking refers to (wasteful) competition for rents created by gifts, grants, or government transfer activities. Profit seeking, on the other hand, refers to those activities that are by definition efficient: Research and development expenditures, piano practice, or committing resources to enter an industry where price exceeds average cost are examples of behavior that create value. By contrast, standing in line for free cheese, taking a politician to lunch in hopes of securing his vote on a bill that provides a subsidy, or arguing before the ICC with an eye toward receiving a certificate are examples of behavior that simply consume rents artificially created by government. That is, rent-seeking activities produce nothing real or consumable, these only result in a transfer. Behaviorally the two are indistinguishable, and it is only morally that these can be made distinct.[6]

This approach has important implications for the strategic use of regulation because it can be viewed in the same light. Consider the case of some vertical restraint on trade, such as the prohibition on resale price maintenance (RPM). Suppose that one accepts the agency cost or public good explanation for RPM; that is, RPM is a device used by manufacturers to force retailers to provide complimentary goods, such as service and information, at the point of sale that they would not otherwise rationally offer. In this case, if a firm brings a law suit or lobbies Congress for a change in the law to allow RPM, then it can be argued that this strategic use of regulation is value increasing *even* if it happens to disadvantage some rivals.[7] In this case the strategic use of regulation increases the real output of society. It is not difficult to construct other examples where the opposite conclusion is reached. Based on this approach, it is imperative to know the firm's motives in order to judge its actions—a difficult chore at best.

The problem is pervasive. Spence (1977) makes a similar point in the context of firm size and capacity decisions. He argues that it is hard to tell which capacity decisions are predatory—designed to limit entry—and which are efficient—driven by competition. Courts have faced the problem in terms of influencing the political process and made their judgment, which has been labeled the Noerr-Pennington doctrine—firms may lobby the government even if it disadvantages their rivals. Fischel (1977) analyzes the antitrust implications of Noerr-Pennington and concludes that lobbying is legal (efficient?), while price conspiracy is illegal (inefficient?).[8] In the Pennington case the doctrine was extended to attempts to influence administrative agencies.[9] The economic theory of rent seeking posits that competition for rents will drive the expected value of the rents to zero at the margin. Moreover, this competition consumes (costs) the economic value of the rents.[10] Transfers are not free. Of course, there is also competition for profits. Therein lies the conundrum. Government action can create rents through regulation, laws, and court decisions. Firms seek these rents or profits in a variety of ways, most notably here, through attempts to influence government decisions. Whether this behavior is efficient or not is beyond the current state of the literature. It all depends on the nature of the regulation and whether or not the rents are artificially created by government.[11] It is fair to say that the economics of rent seeking implies that normative analysis of the strategic use of regulation is rendered virtually impotent, at least for the moment.

The Economic Theory of Regulation

Part one of this section briefly reviews the economic theory of regulation. Part two focuses on the empirical literature of regulation. Part three looks at heterogeneous interest groups within an industry and across industries.

ECONOMIC THEORIES

It is difficult to trace the evolution of the public-interest model of regulation, although Pigou certainly plays a prominent role.[12] This theory argues that regulation corrects market failures stemming from natural monopolies, externalities, economies of scale, public goods, informational asymmetries, or some other problem in property rights assignments. How this benevolence is accomplished through the political process is almost never addressed in public-interest theory. It is plausible that the public-interest theory of regulation was never meant to be descriptive but instead prescriptive. Nevertheless criticism of the public-interest theory of regulation argues that this do-good approach to the behavior of public officials is analytically embarrassing in light of the propensity of most people to pursue their self-interest. The theory can be partly rescued by realizing that alternatively, *constraints* on politicians' behavior can force them, in quest of votes and wealth, to design and implement laws with general welfare-improving characteristics. This is the spirit of Becker (1983) and to a lesser extent Barro (1973) and Becker and Stigler (1974).

Dissatisfaction with the paternalistic view of government implicit in the public-interest theory of regulation has led to the economic theory of regulation (Stigler 1971).[13] Regulation is demanded by special-interest groups to limit entry, raise price, or otherwise reduce output where the private costs of cartelization are too high. These laws are supplied by politicians. Subsequent contributions have emphasized cross-subsidization, Posner (1971), and the imperfections of such a cartel, Peltzman (1976). For the most part, industries are assumed to be homogeneous. The battle over rents is a simple struggle between consumers and producers. In the last part of this section, this simple one-on-one perspective is criticized and analysis of heterogeneous interest groups is presented.

The economic theory of regulation is descriptive. It attempts to predict the effects of regulation on price and output, the onset of regulation, the pattern of regulation, and deregulation.[14] For the most part, the theory is void of normative analysis, but there is the presumption, based on the considerable weight of the evidence, that regulation in practice bears little resemblance to the vision of Pigou. That is, regulation is industry-inspired and profitable. The moral connotations of this fact are usually left to the reader.

THE EMPIRICAL LITERATURE

The empirical literature on regulation has one predominant theme: Regulation is often beneficial to the regulated firms. This benefit accrues in one of several fashions. In the simplest form a regulatory agency, such as the ICC, acts as an (imperfect) cartel manager for members of the industry, disallowing entry, apportioning and policing output, regulating price, preventing nonprice competition, and regulating the provision of substitutes. It is widely held that in their original forms, the CAB and ICC were at least operated in this way, if not designed for that purpose. Recent research suggests that the story is more complicated. Boyer (1981) argues that the ICC engages in substantial redistribution of rents across modes of transportation. That is, some rules aid railroads at the expense of truckers and vice versa. Moore (1978) presents evidence that truck drivers benefit from ICC regulation through higher wages. He estimates that union members obtain rents on the order of $1 billion. Certificate owners receive transfers totaling about $2 billion primarily because of restrictions on entry of new firms. These numbers suggest that the strategic use of regulation can be a profitable enterprise.

Taxicab and jitney regulation appears to fit the same mold. Kitch, Issacson, and Kasper (1971) estimate the value of rents created by taxicab regulation in Chicago to be more than $40 million. Eckert and Hilton (1972) contend that jitney regulation was designed to eliminate competition with railroads in the mass transit markets; jitneys were a low-cost, high-quality substitute for railroad transportation, so trains "sought protection from municipal governments, which . . . proved unanimously willing to provide it" (p. 304).

The CAB regulation of airlines had the same characteristics: Entry was barred and price regulated. It is hard to control all margins of competition however. Nonprice competition from within the industry eroded much of the cartel profits. Airlines competed in scheduling and the number of flights by adding capacity to the point where expected profits were zero. Douglas and Miller (1974) argue that this process resulted in average load factors equaling break-even load factors. In turn this impled a " 'ratchet effect' of regulation and reaction, in which price increases, thought by the CAB as necessary to raise profits, only resulted in a new equilibrium with greater levels of excess capacity" (p. 55). Airlines also competed in terms of in-flight service. The CAB responded by regulating meals, flight attendants, and liquor service. What has not been adequately explained is why the CAB restricted these latter forms of nonprice competition but did not regulate the obviously more costly methods of competition through increased capacity or flights per day. One explanation is prominent: Excess capacity benefits airplane producers, pilots, engineers, and attendants, so that the political clout of these groups may have forestalled capacity constraints.[15] The strategic use of regulation implies that if entry is restricted, output is reduced, price is above cost, and nonprice competition sets in. Regulated firms will seek ways of preventing this nonprice competition. The degree to which they are successful depends on the impact of competition on input suppliers and diverse consumer groups.

In another area of long-standing government involvement, Jarrell (1978) presents evidence that state regulation of electricity production was sought to prevent competition where rivalry had brought low prices. In fact, regulation proceeded first in jurisdictions with the *lowest* prices—another nail in the coffin of the public-interest theory of regulation.[16]

It would be a mistake to think that the conventional, hands-on type of regulatory programs, such as electricity and transportation, are the only ones where the economic approach of supply and demand of political action are at work. Marvel and Ray (1983) argue that nontariff barriers to trade implemented after the Kennedy round of tariff agreements were primarily in industries that were vulnerable to foreign competition. Similarly, the literature on broadcasting maintains that regulation of cable television (CATV) has primarily been motivated to protect the interests of local over-the-air broadcast franchises. FCC Chairman Burch has said that CATV regulation could be translated "into the short-hand of protectionism for over-the-air broadcasting, but we feel that is a public interest consideration as well" (Besen 1974, p. 41). Greenberg (1967) and Besen (1974) support the view that the primary beneficiaries of regulation were television stations in the top fifty markets. Comanor and Mitchell (1971) argue that CATV regulations in 1966 and 1968 differentially impacted small firms and drove them out of business. A similar argument is made about antidumping laws: They are a means of preventing foreign competition. In one notable case Outboard Marine Corporation, the sole U.S. producer of golf carts, wanted the U.S. price to be used to determine whether a foreign producer was selling below cost.[17] That is, the corporation wanted it declared illegal for foreigners to sell below its own price— the ne plus ultra of the strategic use of regulation. In fact, they were unsuccessful.

These few examples are by no means the only types of regulation subject to strategic planning by firms.[18] However, most of the recent research in this area stresses the diversity of interests *within* a particular industry. This is the subject of the next section.[19]

HETEROGENEOUS INTERESTS

The economic theory of regulation falls into one of four analytical categories: Producers versus consumers, cross-subsidization, producers versus producers, and the regulatory triad—producers and an unrelated public-interest group against consumers.[20] The first two categories of analysis have not proven satisfactory in explaining regulation as a general phenomenon, although their usefulness is without doubt in such areas as transport regulation. The simple approach has been weak in its ability to explain why so many industries decry regulation. The answer seems to lie in the fact that industries are not human beings. They are a heterogeneous collection of firms and factors of production whose interests may radically diverge on a particular topic.

Since firms are not homogeneous, input price increases will not have symmetric effects. For example, let there be two different production technologies yielding the same minimum average cost. Let one be capital intensive and the other labor intensive. An increase in wage rates will cause average costs to increase more for the latter than the former (Williamson 1968). Some of the labor-intensive firms will leave the market until price is again equal to average cost. Since average cost for labor-intensive firms increased more than for their capital-intensive rivals, it follows that price increases more than average cost for capital-intensive firms. A profit potential exists if capital-intensive firms can somehow increase wage rates. Presumably labor-intensive firms cannot switch technologies for free.

Consider the simple case of an industry with specialized resources and different firm sizes. The industry supply curve will be positively sloped. Profits are zero at the margin, but inframarginal firms (specialized factors of production) earn rents. Again, suppose regulation imposes costs on *all* firms in the industry, but not symmetrically. The supply curve will shift upward. If costs are heaviest on the marginal firms (factors), then supply will become more inelastic, and price will increase more than cost for some firms. Price increases more than cost for some firms because some rivals are eliminated; therein lies the demand for regulation. There are many ways of achieving success (Salop and Scheffman 1983): Capital-intensive firms can join with a labor union to support an industrywide collective bargaining agreement and adopt a wage sufficiently high to exclude some rivals (Maloney, McCormick, and Tollison 1979). Alternatively, the capital-intensive firms can seek regulation to restrict the use of the input that will raise its price (Marvel 1977, Maloney and McCormick 1982, and Neumann and Nelson 1982). Thus the strategic use of regulation can be an effective means of increasing profits.

Examples of this principle in practice are common in the literature. Marvel (1977) argues that just such a scheme explains the English Factory Laws passed in the early 1800s. Water- and steam-powered mills had different costs of production. According to his argument, water-powered mills depended on abundant rainfall for operation. Laws restricting child labor imposed costs differentially on these water-powered mills because it became more costly for them to operate when the weather was right.[21] That is, steam-powered mills sought regulation as a means of reducing output, raising price, and increasing profits at the expense of their water-powered peers.

Maloney and McCormick (1982) make this argument about environmental quality laws. The current practice of regulating environmental quality through standards rather than emission fees is hard to explain without taking into account the interests of the regulated.[22] Moreover, many details of environmental quality regulation are best explained by noting the potential for intraindustry transfers, as described in Figure 1.1. In two examples of the theory using financial market analysis, cotton dust regulation and the PSD ruling, regulation was associated with large increases in value for some of the regulated firms.[23] Yandle (1980) reports that in the negotiating stages of miles-per-gallon (MPG) regulation, GM lobbied for a standard more stringent than was actually implemented. He also reports that the standard was expected to have differentially large costs on both Chrysler and AMC, especially the latter.

Horwitz and Kolodny (1981) argue that regulation of accounting standards is also the focus of strategic planning.[24] After 1975 the SEC and the FASB required research and development outlays to be expensed. Evidence is presented that large companies in high-technology industries benefited from this ruling because small high-tech companies reduced their R & D expenditures, and some were forced to exit.

Ippolito (1979) argues that insurance regulation appears to benefit small writers at the expense of large direct writers. In most cases, the large direct writers are out-of-state firms, such as Allstate, whereas the smaller American Agency firms are predominately locally owned and operated. It should come as little surprise that regulation is designed to favor local voters at the expense of foreign disenfranchised firms. In addition, there is an effective cross subsidy to high-risk drivers via assigned risk pools. Maurizi, Moore, and Shephard (1981) report that ophthalmologists and optometrists (especially the latter) have successfully used state regulation to eliminate competition from their optician rivals. The result has been higher prices for eyeglasses. Car prices are also higher because of state regulation of automobile franchises according to R. Smith (1982). He attributes the regulation to lobbying by in-state retailers who gain at the expense of out-of-state manufacturers. [25]

The story goes on. Schneider, Klein, and Murphy (1981) report evidence that the cigarette television advertising ban has actually increased the consumption of cigarettes (because warning ads were simultaneously dropped), and a relative price change has resulted. The cost of introducing new low-tar brands has increased, raising the value of existing brands. Higgins and McChesney (1986) find evidence that the FTC's ad substantiation doctrine benefits some large ad agencies presumably while harming other small ones. The costs imposed by ad substantiation fall more heavily on small ad agencies, who find it more difficult to substitute ads not subject to FTC review. The researchers also report that large firms are vocally opposed to deregulation. Linneman (1980) claims that the 1973 mattress safety standard had little impact on the average quality of mattresses because 80 percent of the mattresses produced already satisfied the standards. However, many small producers were adversely affected because of the increased costs of production. Some exited, and consequently "large, significant, and predictable income redistributions from small to large producers resulted from the 1973 flammability standard" (Linneman 1980, p. 478). He also claims that there was a cross subsidy from low-income to high-income families.

A few more examples should suffice to demonstrate that almost no area of regulation is free from strategic planning by firms to disadvantage rivals for higher profits. There is evidence that large textile producers in the United States not only profited from the OSHA-imposed cotton dust standard but supported its passage (Maloney and McCormick 1982, and McCormick 1983). Oster (1982) specifically argues that many regulatory programs "may be used by groups in the industry as a competitive weapon against other groups" (p. 604). Evidence is presented that this force was important in implementing generic drug laws at the state level. Landes (1980) presents evidence that laws passed in 1920 regulating maximum hours worked reduced the number of hours worked by women and their total employment. Moreover, the entry of foreign-born women was deterred: Unable to work long enough hours to make the trip profitable, many foreign women chose not to immigrate to the United States. Both of these had the effect of raising the wages of men. Federal regulation of financial institutions differentially disadvantages thrift institutions to the advantage of commercial banks (Tuccillo 1977). Consumer protection regulations at the state level are, in part, motivated by intraindustry transfers (Oster 1980). Johnson and Libecap (1982) discuss the conflict between onshore and offshore shrimp fishermen in the design of fishing regulations in Texas. Hours-of-operation regulation in Canada benefits small stores at the expense of large ones (Morrison and Newman 1983). Building codes restrict the entry of "foreign" labor and prevent use of efficient mass production techniques while increasing the demand for local labor (Oster and Quigley 1977). There is little doubt that whiskey-labeling regulation has been used by certain elements in that industry, bonded producers and Scotch importers, to prevent competition from blended products (Urban and Mancke 1972). Labeling requirements in fact deceived customers into thinking that domestic-blended whiskey had not been aged. On the subject of deregulation, Spiller (1983) presents evidence that there are substantially different effects across firms subject to CAB deregulation based on location and routes.

With a few exceptions, the literature does not claim or present evidence that firms actually sought regulation to hurt their rivals. As stressed earlier, most of this literature is positive or descriptive and looks primarily at the effects of regulation, but there is a growing body that takes a stronger stance (Oster 1982). These redistributional effects are not accidental: General Motors knew what it was doing when lobbying for a stringent MPG standard; Burlington was not stupid when supporting cotton dust standards; the Eastern coal-mining industry was not throwing money away when it lobbied Congress and the EPA for a standards-based approach to sulphur oxide emission reductions (Ackerman and Hassler 1981). However, not all take this view; for example, Noll and Owen (1983) cling to the notion that these redistributional effects are an unintended by-product of regulation.

One conclusion seems inescapable: With the abundant evidence presented, it is hard to argue that managers of firms do not anticipate some, if not most, of the effects of regulation. Rational expectations implies that they will, on average, be correct about the impact of regulation. Given the magnitude of the wealth estimated to be redistributed via regulation, job security implies that managers spend a nontrivial amount of time working a regulatory margin, not just to fight it off, but as an input to their production processes.

The Regulatory Triad

Regulation often brings together groups who have little in common. Yandle (1983) calls this the bootleggers and Baptist phenomenon, reminiscent of restrictions on the sale of alcohol in the South. Industry or a subset desires regulation to capture consumer wealth or disadvantage rivals. An independent group seeks regulation to correct what it perceives as a social ailment requiring government intervention. Private interest joins the public interest, and together they present a stronger political force pitted against the interests of consumers or rivals. In many cases only public interest generates sufficient political support to allow regulation to proceed.

The 1962 Drug Amendments were passed shortly after the Thalidomide incident, even though the bill had languished in committee for years. Peltzman (1974) argues that the amendments created a barrier to entry and raised the price of old drugs. Temin (1979) reports that the Food and Drug Act of 1938 was also passed following a drug accident. Elixir Sulfanilamide contained a poison that killed more than one hundred people in September 1937. Weiss (1964) notes that the 1906 meat inspection laws were passed five months after *The Jungle* was published. He, too, finds the industry in bed with the muckrakers: "I find that members of the industry . . . are as ready to recall the mythology of *The Jungle* as any group has ever been" (p. 120).

Maloney and McCormick (1982) and Ackerman and Hassler (1981) argue that environmental quality regulation is the product of a coalition between public-interest groups and industry. This suggests the potential for a whole new approach to the analysis of regulation. What are the private interests behind mandatory seat belt laws or air bags? What was the role of the U.S. airline industry in limiting U.S. landings of the Concorde? Clarkson, Kadlec, and Laffer (1979) claim that regulation was primarily to blame for Chrysler's recent financial difficulties; what was GM's role in this affair? Nuemann and Nelson (1982) argue that labor unions were a major force in implementing coal mine safety regulation, but not for the obvious reason. They claim that the purpose was to purge nonunion production (small mines) from the industry. Did the remaining firms, some of which gained from the regulation, join hands with the union to support the law? J. Smith (1982) rejects the public-interest theory of regulation of liquor stores. She claims that religious groups and others join with producers to effect regulation. Does this justify a different look at the Parker doctrine or licensing in general?

There is abundant evidence in the economics literature that when the flag of public interest is raised to support regulation, there is always a private interest lurking in the background. There is hardly a regulatory program anywhere that does not benefit some industry or subset, most often at the expense of rivals or consumers. Antitrust authorities are mistaken to assume that just because a legitimate public-interest group supports regulation there cannot be anticompetitive results.

ANTITRUST LAW

Given the volume of research on the importance of private interests in affecting government in general and regulation in particular, it is surprising that there remains one large research area still haunted by the ghost of Pigou. This is the analysis of antitrust law. For example, Posner (1982) links the passage of antitrust law with other public-interest laws, such as statutes against murder. According to Joskow and Klevorick (1979), "The primary objective of antitrust policy is to promote full and fair market competition and to reap the benefit that competition brings with it" (p. 220). But there is another side; McGee (1980) states: "It may pay competitors to complain that someone is preying on them" (p. 300). Earlier in his writing Posner (1976) does an about face saying that the antitrust law is used to "harass competitors that have lower costs and otherwise frustrate the fundamental goals of antitrust policies" (p. 27). He may mean that the law was intended for one purpose but used for another. This implies a mistake in judgment by the forces behind the law. Rational expectations will not allow this explanation to apply to all laws or regulatory programs. As Stigler (1971) notes, "The fundamental vice of such criticism is that it misdirects attention" (p. 17). Just because the law or its advocates say that the law was intended for some purpose does not mean that is the actual purpose. Survey data is notoriously unreliable. Courts have recognized the problem and adopted the public posture that competition is to be protected, not competitors. It remains to be seen whether that is the case or not.

Bork (1978) bites the bullet. Antitrust law is a fertile breeding ground for firms to sow anticompetitive seeds where free-market forces fail to do so. Stone (1977) claims that 80 to 90 percent of all FTC investigations are begun at the request of the public. It would be nice to know how many of these are brought by firms competing with the alleged violator.

In sum, the power of antitrust law can be used by firms to limit the behavior of their rivals. It has not yet been sufficiently demonstrated whether the bulk of antitrust cases are pro- or anticompetitive. Smith (1982) says, "Mounting evidence . . . suggests that the correspondence between the stated objectives of regulatory legislation and the actual effects is sufficiently weak to lead one to seek out an alternative model of regulation which stresses the gains and losses to plural special interest groups" (p.

319). There remains a great deal of research to be accomplished. Shughart and Tollison (1985) survey the positive analysis of antitrust, which is but a small first step in this direction.[26]

Conclusions

The first of two major themes in this chapter stresses that anticompetitive or strategic use of regulation is pervasive. There is a lot of wealth at stake, and managers would be remiss in their fiduciary responsibilities if they ignored profits available through (legal) manipulation of governmental processes. The decision to invest resources in lobbying to prevent the entry of rivals, to form a regulatory cartel, or to impose costs on existing rivals does not differ materially from other decisions managers make on a daily basis.

Secondly, even though one may want the law to accomplish a specific goal, in practice it frequently achieves a different one. More importantly, if the law repeatedly accomplishes something other than its avowed purpose, then it is time to abandon the pretense that people cannot rationally anticipate ultimate effects. It will no longer suffice to adopt the position that "prior to regulation, no interest group . . . existed. But regulation created such an interest, one that subsequently fought hard against deregulation" (Noll and Owen 1983, p. 35). Although this view may be correct in selected circumstances, it cannot provide a general explanation for regulation. Hardly anyone would claim that managers do not rationally forecast markets for their new products. Sometimes they are wrong, but on average they are correct. What is the nature of regulation that exempts it from this same principle?

This points the way for fruitful research. What is the role of the politician as a regulatory entrepreneur? Does he function as a leader throwing regulatory stones into the water, hoping to cast a ripple of wealth redistribution on some innocent bystanders who then surface and offer votes or other thanks? Or in contrast, do managers and politicians work hand-in-hand developing wealth redistributions? To be specific, what has been the role of coal and oil producers and existing electricity producers in regulating the production of nuclear power? Evidence in the economics literature leads me to believe that these interest groups have not quietly watched as the NRC has slowly but surely put nuclear power on the back burner in the United States. Instead, intuition suggests that they have played a much more active part in eliminating their rival, especially when they have such a strong political ally as the antinuclear movement.

In sum, the literature has an abiding theme: Real political clout is one of the most important, if not the most important, determinants of regulation. The reformers of regulation who came to Washington with newly elected President Reagan knew this, or at least they should have. The literature is compelling. This leaves us with one conclusion: As long as there is a monopoly on police power, there will be a strategic use of regulation. The original research presented in the rest of this volume helps answer some issues not previously addressed in the economics literature. While many of us may wish that more economically sensible policy changes had been made during the Reagan administration, at least we are all a bit wiser now in understanding the mechanisms at work.

Notes

1. I use the phrase strategic use of regulation only because it is used by so many others. I attach no special importance to strategic behavior as distinct from any other kind of behavior. In fact one of the main themes of this paper is to argue that there is no fundamental difference between the so-called strategic use of regulation and the day-to-day operations of the firm.

2. This is not always true. Whether regulation is outside the scope of antitrust enforcement depends on the regulation and who is doing the regulating. State regulation must meet certain procedural requirements as detailed in several Supreme Court decisions—Parker v. Brown, 317 U.S. 341 (1943) and California Retail Liquor Dealers' Association v. Midcal Aluminum, Inc., 445 U.S. 97 (1980), among others. Moreover, certain cartel arrangements are specifically excluded from scrutiny by legislative mandate. The FTC cannot expend resources to investigate agricultural cooperatives and Federal Marketing Orders, and labor unions are exempt by statute in the Clayton Act and the Norris-LaGuardia Act.

3. See Caves (1980) for a review of strategy and industry structure.

4. Compare this with Bork's definition of predation: "Predation may be defined, provisionally, as a firm's deliberate aggression against one or more rivals through the employment of business practices that would not be considered profit maximizing except for the expectation either that (1) rivals will be driven from the market, leaving the predator with a market share sufficient to command monopoly profits, or (2) rivals will be chastened sufficiently to abandon competitive behavior the predator finds inconvenient or threatening" Bork (1978, p. 144).

5. I take it as given that the reader is familiar with the public-choice literature and its cynical approach to politicians' behavior. Those who wish to become more acquainted with this literature can see Mueller (1976) for a survey. More recent work includes Landes and Posner (1975), Crain (1977), McCormick and Tollison (1978), and Becker (1983).

6. See Buchanan (1980) for a more thorough elaboration on this subject. The point can be made obvious with a simple example. Imagine two children who both spend time learning to spell and write. The first uses his skills to become a successful playwright. The second uses his skills as a lobbyist for the sugar industry, obtaining quotas on imported sugar. The first is profit seeking and the

second is rent seeking, but in the classroom the two activities are identical. Rent seeking as a cost turns on the individual's definition of waste.

7. The problem can be analyzed with externality theory but with a twist. Welfare analysis holds that pecuniary externalities do not disturb Pareto optimality. That is, my demand for cars, though it may affect the price you pay, does not cause price to diverge from its social cost. However, my demand for laws can harm you or help you, as in the case of tying arrangements, and the question of Pareto optimality depends on the effect of the law. In this case a pecuniary externality can disturb a Pareto optimality.

8. Eastern Railroad Presidents Conference v. Noerr Motor Freight, Inc., 365 U.S. 127 (1965). The court concluded that there was an "essential dissimilarity" between the two activities. This position appears to have been abandoned, or at least modified, in California Motor Transport Co. v. Trucking Unlimited, 404 U.S. 508 (1972).

9. United Mine Workers v. Pennington, 381 U.S. 657 (1965). The doctrine was extended even further to include such things as boycotts in NAACP v. Clairborne Hardware Co., 102 S. Ct. 3409 (1982). From a legal perspective the problem is compounded by the courts' indecisiveness on the antitrust character of state regulations. The Parker doctrine effectively exempts state regulations from antitrust scrutiny (Parker v. Brown, 317 U.S. 341 [1943]). However, recent decisions have altered this course and imposed necessary guidelines for exemption. For example see California Retail Liquor Dealers' Association v. Midcal Aluminum, Inc., 445 U.S. 97 (1980). Page (1981) analyzes the court's position.

10. Tullock (1980) addresses the question of whether the entire rent is consumed or not. However, his analysis is not based on rent seekers employing a Nash equilibrium strategy.

11. See also Anderson and Hill (1983). Their analysis further muddles the issue. Even competition for scarcity rents that are efficiently created can impose a social cost. This implies that what has previously been considered efficient enforcement of property rights by government may have hidden costs that make the efficiency claim suspect.

12. For example, see Pigou (1932).

13. See Posner (1974) for an old review of the economic theories of regulation and McGraw (1975) for a slightly more recent version.

14. For a sampler see Jarrell (1978), Pincus (1977), Guttman (1978), or any issue of the Journal of Law and Economics or the Rand Journal of Economics.

15. For additional analysis of the impact of regulation on the airline industry, see Keeler (1972), Jordan (1970), and La Mond (1976). La Mond analyzes airline regulation in the state of California. He concludes that the California Public Utility Commission behaved in much the same way as the CAB, protecting intrastate airlines from competition with one other.

16. Earlier research on electricity prices (Stigler and Friedland 1962) has reported no impact of regulation on prices. There is also a strand of the literature that looks at the political environment of regulation. That is, whether the method of selecting regulators has any impact. See Eckert (1973) on taxicabs and Crain and McCormick (1984) on utilities for example.

17. Outboard Marine Corp. v. Pezetel, 461 F. Supp. 384, 474, F. Supp. 168 (D. Del. 1978, 1979). See Schwartz (1980).

18. It is almost impossible to list all the research employing the economic theory of regulation, but two more examples should suffice to demonstrate that no quarter is given nor any asked. Benham and Benham (1975, p. 423) argue that regulations restricting the flow of information "may be one of the most effective politically acceptable methods available for constraining the behavior of suppliers and consumers in the desired direction [decreased competition and higher price]." Plott (1965) reports that the Oklahoma Dry Cleaning price-setting board works hand-in-hand with the industry trade association.

19. Not all of the empirical literature finds that regulation is profitable to the regulated firms. For example, Schwert (1977) reports that the value of New York Stock Exchange seats fell in the period preceding passage of the SEC Act in 1934. One explanation for this empirical anomaly is that a private cartel was already in place, but this begs the question of why regulation was ever passed in the first place. Tests of the public-interest theory of SEC regulation have not proved very successful.

20. For analysis of cross-subsidization, see Posner (1971) and Tuccillo (1977), among others. There is also the bureaucratic largesse approach to regulation as developed in Niskanen (1971) and Tullock (1965). These models of bureaucracy claim that regulation proceeds to maximize the size of the bureau.

21. Anderson and Tollison (1984) claim this is only part of the story. They argue that adult male laborers were the primary force behind, and beneficiaries of, the laws and that switching technologies for water-powered mills could be accomplished at low cost.

22. See also Buchanan and Tullock (1975).

23. For a description of the PSD ruling, see Alabama Power Co. v. Costle, 636 F. 2d 323 (1979) at 346. Schwert (1981) details the use of financial market analysis to assay the effects of regulation. Basically, according to the efficient markets hypothesis of modern finance theory, a security price incorporates at every moment all information available to the market. Therefore these prices, common stocks most notably, can be used as a benchmark to measure the impact of unexpected changes in regulation.

24. For a general theory of the setting of accounting standards that focuses on the strategic planning of firms, see Watts and Zimmerman (1978, 1979). Watts and Zimmerman (1979) report evidence that large accounting firms systematically support FASB rulings that will increase the wealth of their most important clients.

25. See Maloney, McCormick, and Tollison (1984) for more on this exportation effect of regulation. Easterbrook (1983) also discusses the problem in the context of federalism. He takes the view that state regulation should not be the concern of antitrust authorities because there is competition across states. His structuralist approach to competition does not allow for comparative advantage or immobile specialized resources across states.

26. See Clarkson and Muris (1981), Weingast and Moran (1983), and Stigler (1985) for instance.

References

Ackerman, Bruce A., and Hassler, William T. *Clean Coal/Dirty Air.* New Haven: Yale University Press, 1981.

Anderson, Terry L., and Hill, Peter J. "Privatizing the Commons: An Improvement?" *Southern Economic Journal* 50 (October 1983): 438–50.

Anderson, Gary M., and Tollison, Robert D. "A Rent-Seeking Explanation of the British Factory Acts." In *Rent Seeking and Appropriability,* edited by David Collander. Cambridge, Mass.: Ballinger Press, 1984.

Areeda, Phillip, and Turner, Donald F. "Predatory Pricing and Related Practices under Section 2 of the Sherman Act." *Harvard Law Review* 88 (1975): 679–712.

Barro, Robert T. "The Control of Politicians: An Economic Model." *Public Choice* 14 (Spring 1973): 19–42.

Becker, Gary S. "A Theory of Competition among Pressure Groups for Political Influence." *Quarterly Journal of Economics* 98 (August 1983): 371–400.

Becker, Gary S., and Stigler, George J. "Law Enforcement, Malfeasance, and Compensation of Enforcers." *Journal of Legal Studies* 3 (January 1974): 1–18.

Benham, Lee, and Benham, Alexandra. "Regulating Through the Professions: A Perspective on Information Control." *Journal of Law and Economics* 18 (October 1975): 421–48.

Besen, Stanley M. "The Economics of the Cable Television 'Consensus'." *Journal of Law and Economics* 17 (April 1974): 39–52.

Bork, Robert H. *The Antitrust Paradox.* New York: Basic Books, 1978.

Boyer, Kenneth D. "Equalizing Discrimination and Cartel Pricing in Transport Rate Regulation." *Journal of Political Economy* 89 (April 1981): 270–86.

Buchanan, James M. "Rent Seeking and Profit Seeking." In *Toward a Theory of the Rent-Seeking Society,* edited by J. M. Buchanan, R. D. Tollison, and G. Tullock. College Station: Texas A & M Press, 1980.

Buchanan, James M., and Tullock, Gordon. "Polluter's Profits and Political Response: Direct Controls versus Taxes." *American Economic Review* 65 (March 1975): 139–47.

Caves, Richard E. "Industrial Organization, Corporate Strategy, and Structure." *Journal of Economic Literature* 18 (March 1980): 64–92.

Clarkson, Kenneth W., Kadlec, Charles W., and Laffer, Arthur B. "Regulating Chrysler out of Business?" *Regulation* 3 (September/October 1979): 44–49.

Clarkson, Kenneth W., and Muris, Timothy J., eds. *The Federal Trade Commission Since 1970.* Cambridge: Cambridge University Press, 1981.

Comanor, William S., and Mitchell, Bridges M. "Cable Television and the Impact of Regulation." *Bell Journal* 2 (Spring 1971): 154–212.

Crain, W. Mark. "On the Structure and Stability of Political Markets." *Journal of Political Economy* 85 (August 1977): 829–42.

Crain, W. Mark, and McCormick, Robert E. "Regulators as an Interest Group." In *The Theory of Public Choice II,* edited by J. M. Buchanan and R. D. Tollison. Ann Arbor: University of Michigan Press, 1984.

Douglas, George W., and Miller, James C. III. *Economic Regulation of Domestic Air Transport Theory and Practice*. Washington, D.C.: Brookings Institute, 1974.

Easterbrook, Frank H. "Antitrust and the Economics of Federalism." *Journal of Law and Economics* 26 (April 1983): 23–50.

Eckert, R. D. "On the Incentives of Regulators: The Case of Taxicabs." *Public Choice* 14 (Spring 1973): 83–99.

Eckert, R. D., and Hilton, George. "The Jitneys." *Journal of Law and Economics* 15 (October 1972): 293–326.

Fischel, Daniel R. "Antitrust Liability for Attempts to Influence Government Action: The Basis and Limits of the Noerr-Pennington Doctrine." *University of California Law Review* 45 (Fall 1977): 80–123.

Greenberg, Edward. "Wire Television and the FCC's Second Report and Order on CATV Systems." *Journal of Law and Economics* 10 (October 1967): 181–92.

Guttman, Joel L. "Interest Groups and the Demand for Agricultural Research." *Journal of Political Economy* 86 (June 1978): 467–84.

Higgins, Richard, and McChesney, Fred. "Truth and Consequences: The Federal Trade Commission's Ad Substantiation Program." *International Review of Law and Economics* 6 (1986): 151–68.

Horwitz, Bertrand, and Kolodny, Richard. "The FASB, the SEC, and R & D." *Bell Journal* 12 (Spring 1981): 249–62.

Ippolito, Richard. "The Effects of Price Regulation in the Automobile Industry." *Journal of Law and Economics* 22 (April 1979): 55–90.

Jarrell, Gregg A. "The Demand for State Regulation of the Electric Utility Industry." *Journal of Law and Economics* 21 (October 1978): 269–98.

Johnson, Ronald N., and Libecap, Gary D. "Contracting Problems and Regulation: The Case of the Fishery." *American Economic Review* 72 (December 1982): 1005–22.

Jordan, William A. *Airline Regulation in America*. Baltimore: Johns Hopkins Press, 1970.

Joskow, Paul L., and Klevorick, A. K. "A Framework for Analyzing Predatory Pricing Policy." *Yale Law Journal* 89 (1979): 213–70.

Keeler, Theodore E. "Airline Regulation and Market Performance." *Bell Journal* 3 (Autumn 1972): 399–414.

Kelman, Steven. *What Price Incentives? Economists and the Environment*. Boston: Auburn House, 1981.

Kitch, Edmund, Issacson, Marc, and Kasper, Daniel. "The Regulation of Taxicabs in Chicago." *Journal of Law and Economics* 14 (October 1971): 285–350.

La Mond, A. M. "An Evaluation of Intrastate Airline Regulation in California." *Bell Journal* 7 (Autumn 1976): 641–57.

Landes, Elisabeth M. "The Effect of State Maximum-Hours Laws on the Employment of Women in 1920." *Journal of Political Economy* 88 (June 1980): 476–94.

Landes, William, and Posner, Richard. "The Independent Judiciary in an Interest-Group Perspective." *Journal of Law and Economics* 18 (December 1975): 875–901.

Linneman, Paul. "The Effects of Consumer Safety Standards: The 1973 Mattress Flammability Standard." *Journal of Law and Economics* 23 (October 1980): 461–80.

Maloney, Michael T., and McCormick, Robert E. "A Positive Theory of Environmental Quality Regulation." *Journal of Law and Economics* 25 (April 1982): 99–124.

Maloney, Michael T., McCormick, Robert E., and Tollison, Robert D. "Achieving Cartel Profits through Unionization." *Southern Economic Journal* 46 (October 1979): 628–34.

Maloney, Michael T., McCormick, Robert E., and Tollison, Robert D. "Economic Regulation, Competitive Governments, and Specialized Resources." *Journal of Law and Economics* 27 (October 1984): 329–38.

Marvel, Howard. "Factory Regulation: A Reinterpretation of Early English Experience." *Journal of Law and Economics* 20 (October 1977): 379–402.

Marvel, Howard, and Ray, Edward J. "The Kennedy Round: Evidence on the Regulation of International Trade in the United States." *American Economic Review* 73 (March 1983): 190–97.

Maurizi, Alex, Moore, Ruth L., and Shephard, Lawrence. "Competing for Professional Control: Professional Mix in the Eyeglass Industry." *Journal of Law and Economics* 24 (October 1981): 351–64.

McCormick, Robert. "The Cotton Dust Standard: The Private Interests." Unpublished, 1983.

McCormick, Robert E., and Tollison, Robert D. "Legislators as Unions." *Journal of Political Economy* 86 (February 1978): 63–78.

McGee, John S. "Predatory Pricing Revisited." *Journal of Law and Economics* 23 (October 1980): 289–330.

McGraw, Thomas K. "Regulation in America: A Review Article." *Business History Review* 49 (Summer 1975): 159–83.

Moore, Thomas G. "The Beneficiaries of Trucking Regulation." *Journal of Law and Economics* 21 (October 1978): 327–44.

Morrison, Steven A., and Newman, Robert J. "Hours of Operation Restriction and Competition among Retail Firms." *Economic Inquiry* 21 (January 1983): 107–14.

Mueller, Dennis C. "Public Choice: A Survey." *Journal of Economic Literature* 14 (June 1976): 395–433.

Niskanen, William A. *Bureaucracy and Representative Government.* Chicago: Aldine-Atherton, 1971.

Noll, Roger, and Owen, Bruce M. *The Political Economy of Deregulation.* Washington: American Enterprise Institute, 1983.

Nuemann, George R., and Nelson, Jon P. "Safety Regulation and Firm Size: Effects of the Coal Mine Health and Safety Act of 1969." *Journal of Law and Economics* 25 (October 1982): 183–200.

Oster, Sharon M. "An Analysis of Some Causes of Interstate Differences in Consumer Regulations." *Economic Inquiry* 18 (January 1980): 39–54.

Oster, Sharon M. "The Strategic Use of Regulatory Investment by Industry Subgroups." *Economic Inquiry* 20 (October 1982): 604–18.

Oster, Sharon M., and Quigley, John M. "Regulatory Barriers to the Diffusion of Innovation." *Bell Journal* 8 (Autumn 1977): 361–77.

Page, William H. "Antitrust, Federalism, and the Regulatory Process: A Recon-

struction and Critique of the State Action Exemption after Midcal Aluminum."
Boston University Law Review 61 (November 1981): 1099–1138.

Peltzman, Sam. *Regulation of Pharmaceutical Innovation.* Washington, D.C.: American Enterprise Institute, 1974.

Peltzman, Sam. "Toward a More General Theory of Regulation.," *Journal of Law and Economics* 19 (August 1976): 211–40.

Pigou, Arthur C. *The Economics of Welfare.* London: Macmillan, 1932.

Pincus, Jonathan J. *Pressure Groups and Politics in Antebellum Tariffs.* New York: Columbia University Press, 1977.

Plott, Charles R. "Occupational Self-Regulation: A Case Study of the Oklahoma Dry Cleaners." *Journal of Law and Economics* 8 (October 1965): 195–222.

Posner, Richard A. "Taxation by Regulation." *Bell Journal* 2 (Spring 1971): 22–50.

Posner, Richard A. "Theories of Economic Regulation." *Bell Journal* 5 (Autumn 1974): 335–58.

Posner, Richard A. *Antitrust Law: An Economic Perpsective.* Chicago: University of Chicago Press, 1976.

Posner, Richard A. "Economics, Politics, and the Reading of Statutes and the Constitution." *University of California Law Review* 49 (Spring 1982): 263–91.

Salop, Steven C., ed. *Strategy, Predation, and Antitrust Analysis.* Washington: Federal Trade Commission, 1981.

Salop, Steven C., and Scheffman, David T. "Raising Rivals' Costs." *American Economic Review* 73 (May 1983): 267–71.

Schneider, Lynne; Klein, Benjamin; and Murphy, Kevin. "Government Regulation of Cigarette Health Information." *Journal of Law and Economics* 24 (December 1981): 575–612.

Schwartz, Louis B. "American Antitrust and Trading with State-Controlled Economies." *Antitrust Bulletin* 25 (1980): 513–55.

Schwert, G. William. "Public Regulation of National Securities Exchanges: A Test of the Capture Hypothesis." *Bell Journal* 8 (Spring 1977): 128–50.

Schwert, G. William. "Using Financial Data to Measure Effects of Regulation." *Journal of Law and Economics* 24 (April 1981): 121–58.

Shughart, William F., II, and Tollison, Robert D. "The Positive Economics of Antitrust Policy: A Survey Article." *International Review of Law and Economics* 5 (July 1985): 39–57.

Smith, Janet K. "An Analysis of State Regulations Governing Liquor Store Licenses." *Journal of Law and Economics* 25 (October 1982): 301–20.

Smith, Richard L., II. "Franchise Regulation: An Economic Analysis of State Restriction on Automobile Distribution." *Journal of Law and Economics* 25 (April 1982): 125–58.

Spence, A. Michael "Entry, Capacity, Investment, and Oligopolistic Pricing." *Bell Journal* 8 (Autumn 1977): 534–44.

Spiller, Pablo T. "The Differential Impact of Airline Regulation on Individual Firms and Markets: An Empirical Analysis." *Journal of Law and Economics* 26 (October 1983): 655–90.

Stigler, George J. "The Theory of Economic Regulation." *Bell Journal* 2 (Spring 1971): 3–21.

Stigler, George J. "The Origin of the Sherman Act." *Journal of Legal Studies* 14 (January 1985): 1–12.

Stigler, George J., and Friedland, Claire. "What Can Regulators Regulate? The Case of Electricity." *Journal of Law and Economics* 5 (October 1962): 1–16.

Stone, Alan. *Economic Regulation and Public Interest: The Federal Trade Commission in Theory and Practice.* Ithaca: Cornell University Press, 1977.

Temin, Peter. "The Origin of Compulsory Drug Prescriptions." *Journal of Law and Economics* 22 (April 1979): 91–106.

Tollison, Robert D. "Rent Seeking: A Review." *Kyklos* 35 (1982): 575–602.

Tuccillo, John. "Taxation by Regulation: The Case of Financial Intermediaries." *Bell Journal* 8 (Autumn 1977): 577–90.

Tullock, Gordon. *Politics of Bureaucracy.* Washington, D.C.: Public Affairs Press, 1965.

Tullock, Gordon. "The Welfare Costs of Tariffs, Monopolies, and Theft." *Western Economic Journal* 5 (June 1967): 224–32.

Tullock, Gordon. "Efficient Rent Seeking." In *Toward a Theory of the Rent Seeking Society,* edited by J. M. Buchanan, R. D. Tollison, and G. Tullock, College Station: Texas A & M Press, 1980.

Urban, Raymond, and Mancke, Richard. "Federal Regulation of Whiskey Labelling: From the Repeal of Prohibition to the Present." *Journal of Law and Economics* 15 (October 1972): 411–26.

Watts, Ross L., and Zimmerman, Jerold L. "Towards a Positive Theory of Accounting Standards." *Accounting Review* 53 (January 1978): 112–34.

Watts, Ross L., and Zimmerman, Jerold L. "The Demand for and Supply of Accounting Theories: The Market for Excuses." *Accounting Review* 54 (1979).

Weingast, Barry R., and Moran, Mark. "Bureaucratic Discretion or Congressional Control?" *Journal of Political Economy* 91 (1983).

Weiss, Roger. "The Case for Federal Meat Inspection Examined." *Journal of Law and Economics* 7 (October 1964): 107–20.

Williamson, Oliver E. "Wage Rates as a Barrier to Entry: The Pennington Case." *Quarterly Journal of Economics* 82 (February 1968): 85–116.

Williamson, Oliver E. "On Predatory Pricing." *Yale Law Journal* 87 (1978): 1337–1668.

Yandle, Bruce. "A Cost-Benefit Analysis of the 1981–1984 MPG Standard." *Policy Analysis* 6 (Summer 1980): 291–304.

Yandle, Bruce. "Bootleggers and Baptists." *Regulation* 7 (May/June 1983): 12–16.

Part II

REGULATION AND THE REAGAN ERA

3

Regulatory Reform under Reagan—
The Right Way and the Wrong Way

Thomas F. Walton and James Langenfeld

Although it is too early to issue a final report card on the Reagan administration's regulatory reform efforts, it is clear that some agency heads achieved notably greater results than others. Much was accomplished at the Federal Trade Commission (FTC) and the Occupational Safety and Health Administration (OSHA). In addition, a number of deregulatory initiatives were completed, including several begun by the Carter administration. On the other hand, at least until the appointment of William Ruckelshaus, followed by Lee Thomas, efforts to make the Environmental Protection Agency (EPA) more effective and less of a drag on the competitiveness of domestic industry had been notably unsuccessful.

Do these results follow from the nature of the regulations involved? Are they mainly a function of the type of administrator appointed to head each agency? Or is the degree of success and failure determined by the vulnerability of specific agencies to pressures from special interest groups and their representatives in Congress? In this paper, we argue that improvements made under the Reagan administration were largely the result of the nature of agency heads and how they dealt with the issues. In addition, we argue that many of the administrative reforms will prove long-lasting, even though little or no new legislation was passed.

It is widely believed that the regulatory reforms were mainly limited to so-called economic regulations (regulations of prices and conditions of entry) and little was achieved in the area of social regulations (health,

The opinions expressed do not necessarily reflect those of GM or the FTC. The authors wish to thank George Eads, Martin P. Laurent, William Kovacic, Thomas Marx, Thomas N. O'Donnell, Brent Upson, and a referee for their comments. Any remaining errors are solely those of the authors.

safety, and the environment). Going further, some critics of the Reagan program contend that rigid adherence to a doctrinaire free-market approach is largely responsible for that failure. Others argue that politics determined the outcome. We believe that the explanation for success and failure is more straightforward. Where heads of agencies understood the institutional incentives with which they were dealing, embraced solid analytical procedures, and displayed a real commitment to achieving market-oriented reforms, progress was made. Where such an approach was lacking, politics reigned supreme and little was accomplished.

In section 1 we offer some general comments about the overall Reagan regulatory record. In sections 2 through 4 we provide case studies of three agencies in order to illustrate our chief argument that effective administrators and sound analytic tools are crucial to meaningful reform. Section 5 compares the pace of reform of social regulation to that of antitrust, pointing out that progress in both areas has resulted from the development of carefully constructed analytical arguments—and that neither occurred rapidly. We conclude that the rate of regulatory reform under the Reagan administration exceeds historical trends in the reform of antitrust and economic regulations in general. Section 6 addresses the implications for future regulatory reform.

The Impact of Reagan Reforms

Some critics of the Reagan reform program single out the regulation of health, safety, and the environment. They observe that progress in this area had been made by the Ford and Carter administrations through quiet support of market-based modifications of the regulatory apparatus—as opposed to outright deregulation. In their view, the Reagan reforms fell victim to a meat-axe budgetary approach and to rhetoric that mobilized the opposition by constantly proclaiming the virtues of unlimited reliance on the marketplace.[1] Others concerned about the effectiveness of the reforms include leading officials in the Reagan administration; for example, Christopher DeMuth, former head of the Office for Information and Regulatory Affairs of the Office of Management and Budget, stated: "[I]n three years we have not advanced a single detailed proposal of our own for reform of any of the major health, safety, or environmental regulatory statutes."[2]

We submit that such commentators underestimate the progress achieved in the area of social as well as economic regulation. The promulgation of additional, costly, and sometimes counterproductive, environmental, health, and safety regulations has been slowed. Some of the most costly and least effective of these regulations have been repealed and the administration now exercises tighter control over both the promulgation and enforcement of all such regulations.[3] This has been achieved without measurable diminution in the quality of the nation's environment, health, and safety. Overall air quality has probably continued to improve.[4] The bottom-line measure of health and safety in the nation's workplaces—the rate of lost workday cases due to injury and illnesses—appears to have reversed the upward trend of three previous administrations, falling 10 percent since 1980 and 16 percent since its peak in 1979. The bottom-line measure of highway safety—the death rate per 100 million vehicle miles traveled—has fallen by 26 percent since 1980 after rising by 5 percent from 1976 to 1980.[5]

In addition, completing the work begun by the Ford and Carter administrations, the Reagan administration has eliminated several counterproductive economic regulations. Initial indications are that the nation's consumers have realized considerable savings as a result. For example, following airline deregulation, average fares have fallen dramatically. Steven Morrison and Clifford Winston recently estimated that "under deregulation travelers have saved $6 billion annually through lower fares and better service and that airlines have improved their earnings by $2.5 billion annually."[6] According to the Department of Transportation (DOT), following (partial) trucking deregulation, the number of firms with Interstate Commerce Commission operating authority has increased from 18,000 in 1980 to 31,000 in 1984, and there has been as much as a $30 billion reduction in annual logistics expenditures for the nation's shippers and their customers.[7] To its credit, after some foot-dragging in the first Reagan term, under the new leadership of Elizabeth Dole, DOT is now pressing for the removal of all remaining Interstate Commerce Commission regulations, including termination of antitrust immunity for joint rate-setting. Other DOT efforts include the deregulation of intercity busing.

The Reagan administration also expedited decontrol of petroleum prices, begun by President Carter. Many opponents of decontrol predicted that prices would surge and reliance on unstable foreign sources would increase. For example, shortly after President Reagan issued the order for immediate decontrol in January 1981, Senator Howard Metzenbaum said, "Mr. President, I believe we will see $1.50 gas this spring, and maybe before. And it is just a matter of time until the oil companies and their associates, the OPEC nations, will be driving gasoline pump prices up to $2 a gallon." Shortly after President Carter began the process of decontrol in June 1979, Senator Dale Bumpers warned that "without rationing, gasoline will soon go to $3 a gallon." In January 1980 Ed Rothschild, director of Energy Action, stated that because of decontrol, "the [Carter] administration has placed the American economy, competition in the oil industry, and the public at the mercy of a handful of international oil companies and OPEC." Earlier his organization had predicted that following decontrol, petroleum prices "could range from at least $56 per barrel under the most optimistic assumptions, to about $870 per barrel under assumptions which many experts believe are realistic."[8]

Following decontrol, however, the price of crude oil and its derivatives has fallen substantially. Since 1980, the (nominal) price of regular unleaded self-serve gasoline has fallen by more than one-third. Although much of the decline is the result of other factors, it seems reasonable to attribute some of the reduction to oil price decontrol and the elimination of the entitlements program. For example, Kenneth Arrow and Joseph Kalt estimated that as of May 1979, the cost of petroleum price controls appeared to be "at least $2.5 billion per year." Elsewhere, Kalt estimated that from 1975 to 1980, the price controls and accompanying entitlements policies had increased imports by as much as 3 million barrels per day (or roughly 50 percent of the nation's present level of imports.).[10]

In addition to these achievements, there has been a small but noticeable reduction in the penalty imposed by social regulations on the nation's industrial competitiveness. Gregory Christiansen and Robert Haveman estimate that deregulation accounted for an increase of 0.2 percentage points in the growth of labor productivity from 1982 to 1983 in the private, nonfarm sector of the economy.[11] Elsewhere Christiansen and Haveman estimated that federal regulations accounted for 12 to 21 percent of the slowdown in labor productivity growth in the manufacturing sector between 1973 and 1977 as compared to 1958 to 1965.[12] Wayne Gray has estimated that in the 1970s, environmental and health and safety regulations may have accounted for as much as 39 percent of the slowdown in productivity growth in the manufacturing sector. In addition, it has been estimated that environmental regulation has had a significant adverse effect on the international competitiveness of domestic industries, especially in the manufacturing sector.[13] According to Joseph Kalt, this penalty is

> due to the *style,* rather than the stringency of U.S. regulation. The nation's environmental standards are about at the average for industrialized countries, but its costs of achieving these standards are near the very highest. This most fundamentally reflects the country's insistence on mandating abatement techniques, rather than mandating emissions levels and leaving polluters free to meet these levels by least-cost methods.[14]

To be sure, much more remains to be done, especially in the area of environmental regulation; nonetheless, there is much to be learned from the Reagan reform efforts. What accounts for the success of some and the failure of others? Why has there been relatively little progress in reforming environmental regulation? Is it inherently more difficult to modify social as opposed to economic regulations? In order to address these questions, we present three case studies of agencies widely regarded as the least effective and most disruptive in the 1970s—the FTC, OSHA, and EPA.

The Federal Trade Commission—Reordering Priorities and a Positive Agenda

Reforming the FTC was one of the Reagan administratoin's most positive accomplishments.[15] When Reagan took office in January 1981, the FTC was an agency besieged.[16] The *Washington Post* had dubbed it the "National Nanny" in response to the agency's "kid-vid" program, which purported to tell television sponsors what was and was not good for their underage viewers. The agency's seeming penchant for angering practically every interest group in the nation led Congress to rein in the agency's discretionary powers by enacting the FTC Improvements Act of 1980, which imposed limits on the FTC's rule-making authority (including a one-house veto over FTC rules) and forced the agency to respond to order modification requests within 120 days.[17]

Whatever the desirability of the goals of the pre-Reagan FTC, it was scarcely achieving its objectives. Between 1975 and 1978 nineteen rule-makings were initiated by the commission, while only five of these had resulted in final rules by 1981. Two of these were remanded at least in part by federal appeals courts, and one was vetoed by Congress in 1982.[18] Nor was the agency in tune with emerging trends in antitrust law.[19] The commission, consisting of a majority of pre-Reagan appointees, won only fifteen of thirty-five antitrust decisions appealed to the federal courts from 1977 to 1981, after winning twenty-one of twenty-four such appeals between 1970 and 1976.[20]

To refocus and reform the agency, President Reagan nominated James C. Miller, III, to be chairman. Miller, trained mainly as an academic econo-mist, had written extensively on the effects of airline regulation. He headed the president-elect's FTC transition team and had been instrumen-tal in formulating the team's proposed agenda for change at the commis-sion, so he was familiar with the structure of the agency and the laws it enforces. As past editor of *Regulation* magazine, he was aware of the agency's controversial history.

Miller began by replacing each bureau head with administrators who were willing to institute market-oriented reforms. Timothy Muris, a lawyer with an extensive background in economics, was appointed direc-tor of the Bureau of Consumer Protection. Muris also served as a member of the FTC transition team; he had previously worked at the commission, and published a book about the FTC. Miller appointed Thomas Campbell, a lawyer and Ph.D. economist, as director of the Bureau of Competition, and public-choice economist Robert Tollison to head the Bureau of Economics. All three were familiar with the agency's activities.

The Miller management team moved quickly to implement the plan developed by the transition team, but the commission's structure inhibited the speed of reforms. Miller had only one vote on the commission, and initially his colleagues were appointed by previous presidents. This structure made policy changes more difficult at the commission than most administrative agencies, because the chairman could be outvoted and inside critics could solicit congressional support or public opinion to block reform.

Despite the difficulties inherent in changing the commission, Miller initiated reforms in both areas of FTC jurisdiction: consumer protection and antitrust.[21] The commission's new policies and programs met with great hostility from special interest groups and their congressional allies. The critics brought to bear all the familiar emotional arguments used to support the status quo on social regulations.

Regarding consumer protection, the new administration pushed for reforms in four areas: rule-making standards, case selection, enforcement techniques, and the definition of unfair and deceptive practices. In order to determine whether a practice is widespread enough to justify an industrywide rule, the administration sought to require systematic evidence, such as consumer surveys and econometric analyses, rather than anecdotal evidence.[22] The administration also sought to require a "clear substantive theory that specified why regulation would solve the perceived problem whereas market forces would not."[23] Despite opposition from some of the pre-Reagan commissioners and staff, the rules were systematically analyzed and processed. Specifically, the commission required answers to four questions before a rule was adopted: (1) Is the act or practice prevalent? (2) Does a significant harm exist? (3) Will the proposed rule reduce that harm? And (4) will the benefits of the rule exceed its costs? Convincing the commissioners to decide rules on this basis was not easy, and two rules were passed over Miller's objections. Nevertheless, this process was eventually agreed to by all five commissioners in the Statement of Basis and Purpose of the Credit Practices Rule.[24] In practice, the FTC staff made particularly effective use of surveys and studies to determine if the action in question affected a large enough proportion of the industry to justify imposing regulatory costs on innocent as well as guilty firms. If these studies found that only a small portion of the firms committed the questionable act and compliance costs for the proposed rule would be significant, then case-by-case prosecution was often determined to be a more cost-beneficial remedy to the problem.

To improve its case selection and enforcement techniques, the Bureau of Consumer Protection's evaluation committee for new cases added economists from the Bureau of Economics. They now help the committee recommend cases where potential injury to consumers is the greatest, and the market is least likely to solve the alleged problems. For example, in one case a company decided that its lifetime service guarantee was too costly to honor in a time of inflation and unilaterally billed its customers for follow-up visits.[25] The individual bills were relatively small, and each customer lacked the incentive to sue the company because of the time and costs associated with a court proceeding. Arguably, the cumulative injury to a large number of customers with limited recourse was great enough to merit effective government intervention.

One example of the administration's innovative enforcement methods was its 1983 project to improve real estate credit advertisers' compliance with the Truth in Lending Act. Many advertisers improperly calculated annual percentage rates, making comparative shopping difficult. The commission's staff systematically reviewed newspapers and other advertisements, notified advertisers of violations, and provided pamphlets that explained in plain English how to comply with the law.[26] Compliance in the targeted cities rose from 13 to over 80 percent, without the delay and cost of litigation or formal proceedings. After the initial campaign, the FTC reduced its monitoring to spot checks, without finding a significant increase in violations.[27]

Defining unfair and deceptive practices probably posed the most challenging test for the Miller administration. Miller initially attempted to have Congress pass a definition of deception, so that advertisers would better know what constituted an illegal act and truthful advertisements would not be deterred. Specifically, he sought to clarify the guidelines by explicitly requiring consumer injury to be demonstrated; that a representation, omission, or practice should be likely to mislead consumers; and that the commission rely more on empirical evidence than its own expertise.[28] Fierce opposition from both the advertising industry and consumer advocacy groups ensued, based on fears that the concern not to deter truthful advertising might result in increased deception. Numerous congressional oversight hearings were held to condemn the Reagan FTC's alleged tolerance of increased deception in advertising practices. Eventually a majority of commissioners voted for the policy statement.[29] Although it could be changed in the future, the commission appended the statement to its decision in FTC v. Cliffdale Associates, Inc., et al., 103 FTC 110, 174-184 (1984). Unless this standard is overturned through appeal or changed by the commission itself, the statement will stand because it "became the legal standard which the Commission ha[s] to apply in all future decisions."[30]

Similar efforts to change the FTC's antitrust enforcement policy have also proven successful. Under Chairman Miller, the commission moved away from many of the previous administrations' controversial economic theories and unfocused, industrywide investigations to concentrate on areas where collusion and other generally agreed-on anticompetitive business practices threaten competition.[31] Miller and his administrators followed the transition team's recommendations by focusing resources on horizontal restraints to competition (that is, agreements and practices by competitors that directly reduce or prevent competition).[32] To a large degree, this process involved bringing the agency into line with the mainstream of antitrust analysis—that is, embracing emerging trends toward the efficiency school of industrial organization.[33]

The Miller commission also closed several unproductive investigations. It refused to reconsider decisions by administrative law judges dismissing questionable complaints, such as the "shared monopoly" case in the cereals industry.[34] Miller also challenged the majority of pre-Reagan commissioners, powerful interest groups in Congress, and certain segments of the business community by issuing lone dissents in such antitrust cases as *Russell Stover*,[35] *Ethyl*,[36] and *Borg-Warner*.[37] Each of these dissents was supported by the reviewing court. In *Russell Stover*, the Eighth Circuit Court of Appeals reversed the commission majority's decision to deny manufacturers the right to choose their retailers, as long as price-setting did not result from any of the agreements. Subsequently this stand was supported in the Supreme Court's holding in *Monsanto–Spray Rite*.[38] The Second Circuit Court of Appeals reversed the commission's opinion in *Ethyl*, agreeing with Miller that less than perfect structural conditions do not support an antitrust violation for price signaling without evidence of explicit collusion.

The Reagan FTC also substantially reduced the enforcement of anticompetitive, anticonsumer vertical price-setting cases—cases that tried to prevent firms from reducing prices to consumers because price reductions would harm competitors' profits. This policy was effectively carried out, despite fierce congressional resistance.[39] The commission also emphasized the legality of manufacturers' engaging in nonprice vertical restrictions that could be expected to increase consumer welfare. Finally, a number of decisions were issued that emphasized the necessity of showing the adverse economic effects of challenged industry practices before liability could be found.[40]

In addition to challenging cases initiated under previous administrations, Miller also implemented a positive agenda based on economic analysis. The evaluation committee of the Bureau of Competition expanded the role of economists in helping identify cases most likely to benefit consumers.[41] In an effort to clarify its policy toward mergers, the FTC issued a public statement on its policy at the same time the Department of Justice issued its 1982 Merger Guidelines, which deemphasized structural analysis and required a finding of entry barriers into the affected market before a merger would be challenged.[42] This reordering of priorities took some time, but by fall 1984, the commission began challenging horizontal restraints at a rate of about one a month.[43]

Partly as a result of economic studies, the commission continued to shift enforcement efforts from the manufacturing sector to the rapidly growing service sector.[44] A number of new initiatives were implemented in order to ferret out guildlike restrictions such as those condemned by Adam Smith. In particular, Miller expanded the commission's efforts to identify and prosecute restrictive practices in the health care and other professions, as well as trade associations. For example, it issued a complaint against a physician-controlled malpractice insurer refusing to extend coverage to physicians who supervised self-employed nurse-midwives, while continuing to insure physicians who supervised employee nurse-midwives. This practice effectively created a barrier to entry for self-employed nurse-midwives without a persuasive efficiency rationale.[45] Although such enforcement activities could be scaled back by future administrations, the Supreme Court's reversal of the Seventh Circuit's decision in *Indiana Federation of Dentists*[46] has upheld the authority of the commission to pursue such restrictions, even where a professional group attempts to hide anticompetitive practices under the cloak of efforts to maintain the quality of care.

Regarding trade associations, the commission emphasized investigations of industries not previously targeted.[47] For example, the commission obtained a consent agreement with a multiple-listing service that allegedly conspired to raise brokerage commission rates from 6 to 7 percent.[48] Despite such court decisions as *Town of Hallie* v. *City of Eau Claire*,[49] which may limit enforcement efforts in an area that "represents one of the most significant examples of the effective creation and maintenance of monopoly power in the U.S. economy,"[50] the FTC did increase antitrust enforcement involving anticompetitive practices partially sheltered by city and state laws. This included the controversial prosecutions of taxicab cartels in New Orleans and Minneapolis.[51] These efforts increased public awareness, which resulted in taxicab deregulation in such cites as Kansas City, Missouri, and Bloomington, Minnesota.[52] The ability of the FTC to bring such cases was threatened, however, by early versions of the so-called "City of Boulder" legislation.[53] Miller had to devote significant time and energy to prevent such blocking legislation, and he was successful.[54] Despite the political controversy associated with these initiatives, they were based on well-accepted economic theories.

The final aspect of the Miller administration's reorientation of the FTC involved making "competition advocacy" an integral part of the commission. Organizations were created in the two of three bureaus with explicit responsibility for arguing for competition and efficiency before state and federal regulatory bodies. This program has provided analysis of, and evidence on, many issues to a variety of bodies, such as the International Trade Commission and the Interstate Commerce Commission.[55]

Even though there has been little by way of legislative reform,[56] in our opinion the Reagan FTC has made that agency a much more effective advocate for consumers and competition.[57] The commission has withdrawn from areas of questionable merit to consumers and has not been afraid to enter areas where it believes efficiency and consumer welfare can be enhanced. Antitrust commentator Joe Sims, in fact, gave the Miller team an "A" on its first forty-two months in office.[58]

There are many reasons why these reforms should endure beyond 1988. First, the success of many of the initiatives will make it difficult for such powerful interest groups as the American Medical Association and others to avoid FTC oversight. Second, the analytic procedure used by Miller and the other economists at the FTC earned even the "grudging respect" of such activists as former chairman Michael Pertschuk, because the approach forced them to "think through" the implications of government intervention.[59] Such appreciation of the unintended results of government actions should prevent some of the excesses of the past, even if activists return to power. Third, so long as the appeals courts continue to uphold the Miller commission's rulings, future commissions will find it difficult to turn back the clock.

In sum, given the increasingly market-oriented make-up of federal judges, it is unlikely that a major reversal of the course charted by the Reagan FTC will occur any time soon. In that regard, the Reagan reforms are best viewed as evolutionary rather than revolutionary. Indeed, Sanford Litvack, assistant attorney-general for antitrust under President Carter, speaking on the trend of antitrust policies under the Reagan administration, said that "even in a Democratic Administration I just cannot foresee any major changes."[60]

OSHA—Focused Approach Achieves Results

OSHA provides another example of meaningful regulatory progress. Under Thorne Auchter OSHA replaced a highly adversarial command

and control approach with a more performance-oriented and less adversarial set of goals and enforcement procedures. In promulgating new regulations, Auchter put into place a protocol that uses risk assessment and cost effectiveness. A philosophy of inflexible enforcement of specifications has largely been replaced by a policy emphasizing worker-management codetermination and cost effectiveness. OSHA actively encourages employers and employees to work together to identify and eliminate those conditions most likely to lead to serious injuries and illnesses in the workplace. Enforcement efforts have been directed to those industries and firms whose rates of serious injury and illness exceed the national average. All these efforts have been consistent with both the letter and intent of the Occupational Safety and Health Act, which requires OSHA to "assure so far as possible every working man and woman in the Nation safe and healthful working conditions and to preserve our human resources."[61] Indeed, occupational injury and illness rates have fallen since 1980.[62]

At the outset in 1971, OSHA compiled codified volumes of detailed safety regulations based mainly on consensus standards of the American National Standards Institute (ANSI).[63] A majority of the ANSI standards were adopted, even though a U.S. Labor Department study in 1968 had reported that 60 percent of them were out of date and in need of revision. The weakness in this approach was identified as early as 1976 in a study for the Brookings Institution:

> The provision in the Occupational Safety and Health Act enabling the OSHA, during its first two years, to adopt as mandatory standards the exposure limits recommended by national consensus organizations illustrates the congressional desire for speed. When formulated, these standards were not meant to be made mandatory nor were they designed to be universally applicable nor were they expected to be permanent. The result of this approach to safety regulation is that the agencies have all too often set standards for what seem to be frivolous hazards.[64]

Arguably, many of those standards were so narrowly drawn that when enforced, they precluded advances in state-of-the art technology and ignored safe industry practices. Under the command and control approach followed by three successive administrations, it was assumed that strict compliance with detailed regulations was the best way of improving occupational safety. Yet it is not obvious that such a policy had any appreciable impact. As a casual inspection of Figure 3.1 suggests, there is a positive correlation between OSHA citations and worker injury rates: Injury rates tend to rise and fall with the number of serious citations issued.[65]

Of course, correlation does not prove cause and effect. It may be that

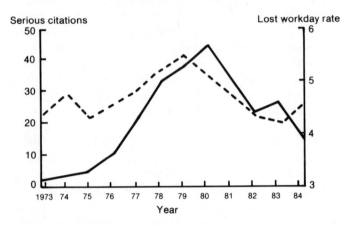

Figure 3.1
Citations & Injury Rate
Correlation Between the Series

Source: Bureau of Labor Statistics

changes in OSHA enforcement activities merely reflect changes in occupational injuries; that is, increased enforcement comes in response to an increased volume of worker complaints as a result of increased occupational hazards. Alternatively, the trends in occupational injury rates may be explained by underlying trends in demographic and economic variables. However, the latter interpretation is inconsistent with results from econometric studies of the impact of OSHA inspections on occupational injury rates, which seldom find evidence of beneficial effects. Where such effects have been found, they are extremely limited. For example, Ann Bartel and Lacy Glenn Thomas estimate that the costs of OSHA enforcement efforts are over $450 million per year compared to $6.4 million in benefits. They conclude that OSHA has misdirected the nation's health and safety resources and "[s]tepping up OSHA enforcement efforts would . . . not be an appropriate policy."[66] Another student of OSHA, John Morrall of the Office of Management and Budget, is even more critical; he states:

> My review of the studies of OSHA's impact on workplace safety finds almost unanimous agreement that there has been none . . . Lost workdays increased by 27 percent from 1973 to 1979. Over the last ten years, on the other hand, I estimate . . . that the incremental compliance cost due to OSHA safety rules has averaged between $50 million and $1.4 billion.[67]

One example of the ineffective if not counterproductive nature of command and control regulation is provided by OSHA's past enforcement of the occupational noise standard. Prior to 1981, OSHA's enforcement efforts were directed toward costly engineering and administrative controls, even where personal protection (ear plugs and ear muffs) could provide comparable if not superior protection at substantially lower cost. In several cases, businesses successfully appealed such requirements, arguing that the costs of these programs were unreasonable in relation to the benefits. In two cases, the OSHA Review Commission stressed that resources available to promote employee safety and health are limited and "should first go toward solving more hazardous (life-threatening) problems."[68] In another case a district court observed that requiring engineering controls might actually increase employee noise exposure, because the associated reduction in noise could mean that more effective personal protection would not be worn.[69]

The Auchter OSHA instituted a number of reforms, based on recognition that by and large, the expertise required to improve occupational safety and health lies not with administrators and enforcement officials in the agency, but with employees and employers in the workplace. OSHA now recognizes that employers, and not agency administrators, possess "site-specific" information on how their production processes and equipment operate and how they can best be modified to improve worker health and safety.

In the area of promulgation, Auchter adopted a four-step process, which requires the agency to (1) demonstrate significant risk, (2) "verify that the standard . . . would reduce that risk," (3) "set the most protective exposure limit . . . that is technologically and economically feasible," and (4) "find the most cost-effective way for employers to meet that limit,"[70] including personal protection as well as training and engineering controls. This approach is illustrated in the guidelines issued for compliance with the Noise Standard, which "allow employers to rely on personal protective equipment and a hearing conservation program, rather than engineering and administrative controls, when hearing protectors will effectively attenuate the noise received by the employee's ear to levels specified in tables G-16 and G-16a of the standard."[71] According to Thomas O'Donnell, director of OSHA relations for General Motors, another example is the hazard communication standard, which emphasizes worker notification, education, and cooperation. Unfortunately, OSHA has not been completely consistent in applying its cost-effectiveness criterion in promulgating regulatons. For example, it proceeded to require costly engineering controls under the Cotton Dust Standard, in spite of evidence that personal protection (respirators) could accomplish a similar level of protection at substantially lower cost. (See the discussion of *American Textile* that follows.) Nonetheless, the explicit consideration of risk assessment and cost-effectiveness is a major step forward.

Auchter also established a targeting program that focuses the agency's most exhaustive, or so-called "wall-to-wall", inspections on firms whose plants have a higher than average incidence of occupational injuries and illnesses.[72] In the process, it has redirected its limited agency resources from design-specific safety standards. Given the limited benefits from historical enforcement efforts regarding readily observable occupational safety issues and given the relatively greater potential from regulating the less well understood causes of occupational illnesses, such a policy seems more likely to yield worthwhile results. In addition, as a result of this approach, a number of industry and labor representatives have voluntarily formed joint committees to establish new methods and programs to address employee safety concerns and propose further improvements in the workplace.

Another example of more effectively allocating safety resources is OSHA's informal complaint procedure.[73] That procedure allows OSHA under certain clearly specified conditions to respond to complaints by sending a letter to plant management, instead of an inspector. Management posts the complaint, investigates the allegation, and must respond to OSHA in writing within a specified number of days about what was uncovered and what action, if any, is required or was taken to resolve the alleged problem. This procedure does not preclude OSHA's right to conduct an on-site inspection of the original complaint, or to undertake a follow-up inspection.

Auchter also restricted the historical use of the "General Duty" clause, which allowed enforcement officers to cite businesses for violations not spelled out in the law. Many businesses were especially aggrieved by what they felt were arbitrary and capricious citations. Under the new directive issued in 1982, the hazard must be "serious," and there must be a "feasible means of correcting the problem."[74]

In short, the Reagan administration has redirected a substantial amount of the agency's enforcement resources toward projects of greater impact on worker health and safety. Under OSHA's emphasis on voluntarism, compliance can often be achieved much more quickly and effectively than under the old system of command and control. To be sure, much of this progress can be halted by a new administration less disposed toward voluntarism and cost-effective promulgation and enforcement.[75] Yet to the extent that OSHA's efforts continue to be accompanied by improvements in occupational safety and health, it will be difficult to veer from the present course.

Importantly, the OSHA Review Commission and the courts have held that careful assessment of relevant costs and benefits of alternative enforcement and promulgation strategies is consistent with legislative intent. (See the preceding discussion of occupational noise cases.) For example, in

1979, the Sixth Circuit Court of Appeals noted that in the area of occupational noise, a "consensus is developing among the circuits that the term [feasibility] should encompass both technological and economic feasibility" and "[n]umerous cases have held that [OSHA] should weigh the estimated costs of compliance against the benefits reasonably expected therefrom when promulgating or enforcing a regulation."[76] The Supreme Court's decision in the Benzene case required showing "significant risk" when promulgating regulations.[77] Although its subsequent decision in *Cotton Dust* held that the agency is not required to use cost-benefit analysis when determining the level of stringency of a standard for toxic substances, the Supreme Court emphasized that it was not foreclosing use of cost-effectiveness analysis in determining the method of compliance.[78] In addition, the decision expressly allowed that cost-benefit analysis may be applicable to standards not involving toxic substances and even to the choice among alternative standards involving toxic substances.[79]

In fact, the Ninth Circuit Court of Appeals has held that *American Textile* does not apply to occupational noise, where once an employer documents the relative costs of engineering and administrative controls versus personal protection, "the burden of proof returns to the Secretary, who must establish that the benefit of the proposed engineering controls justifies their relative cost in comparison to other abatement methods."[80] Moreover, some legal scholars conclude that even in the case of toxic substances, *American Textile* does not preclude the use of cost-benefit analysis, but merely seeks to ensure that it is not abused in order to prevent the agency from achieving its mandate.[81]

In sum, the success of OSHA reforms is especially encouraging in light of the conventional wisdom that cost-effectiveness means eliminating vital safety programs. The OSHA experience has shown that reordering regulatory priorities in order to get maximum results from society's health and safety resources—that is, requiring cost-effective regulations—can diminish the adverse effects such regulations have on productivity and the competitiveness of domestic industry without interfering with efforts to improve health and safety.[82] Such evidence should go a long way toward ensuring the permanence of OSHA reforms.

EPA—Opportunities Lost and Reforms Delayed

Early in 1981, the time appeared ripe for reforms in environmental policy that could significantly reduce the substantial costs of these regulations without delaying progress toward a cleaner environment. The Clean Air Act's reauthorization deadline was September of that year, so air pollution policy ranked high on the political agenda. Studies showed that many existing command and control regulations left the EPA and businesses no discretion in selecting the means of controlling pollution and thus imposed unnecessary costs.[83] Indeed, under the command and control approach, new coal-fired plants had to reduce sulfur dioxide emissions by chemical treatment rather than by using lower sulfur coal. The Congressional Budget Office (CBO) estimated that by the year 2000, $3.3 billion could be saved each year by using low sulfur coal rather than chemical treatment to achieve the same level of control.[84] More generally the General Accounting Office estimated that a market-oriented system could reduce the costs of environmental control in some cases by 40 to 90 percent.[85]

In fact, a market-based plan to reform environmental policy was drawn up by President-elect Reagan's transition Task Force on the Environment in late 1980.[86] But the new administrator did not follow the plan that the team developed, choosing instead to pursue her own agenda. At the beginning of 1982, Robert Crandall quoted an article in *Automotive News* that summed up his and many others' opinion about the state of the EPA:

> In the ten-year history of EPA, there have been periods of turmoil, but none rivals what is happening now under the reign of Anne Gorsuch. What was a dynamic entity has shriveled to a gray shadow of its former self, wracked by internal dissension, run by people with little expertise in environmental issues, and dogged by a paranoia that has virtually brought it to a standstill.[87]

The agency not only failed to make effective administrative reforms during its first year, it also lost the opportunity for legislative reform. This frustration was perhaps best expressed by Thomas Gale Moore:

> Despite the high priority that should be assigned to amending the Clean Air Act, the [Reagan] administration has failed even to introduce a bill to do so. Early in the administration, a proposed set of amendments was prepared within the executive office of the president, but Gorsuch rejected them. Although individuals within the administration admit that the act inhibits economic growth and productivity, they claim that there is no possibility of securing passage of any amendments that would improve matters.[88]

When the Clean Water Act came up for reauthorization, the administration developed a sketchy proposal of fourteen changes, all of which were rejected by Congress. As Eads and Fix conclude, "Congressional response to the administration bill was cool at best; it had become apparent that administration influence over the legislative process—at least in the environmental area—had declined substantially."[89]

What accounts for these administrative and legislative failures? Part of the responsibility undoubtedly rests with an uncooperative Congress and powerful interest groups opposing change. However, such opposition to many of the reforms achieved by the administrators of OSHA and the FTC was just as intense. Instead, the major reason for the failures was the appointment of officials who were hostile to systematic analysis of regulations, had limited or no experience in the subject matter, lacked experience in management, and did not understand the regulatory institution. Reagan chose Anne Gorsuch (later Burford), a lawyer from Colorado, to head the agency. She was committed to reducing the excessive costs that environmental regulations imposed on business. Unfortunately she was not prepared for the economic, procedural, and managerial issues that she faced in administering the EPA's complex regulations and in guiding its 11,000 employees.[90] Her top staff also lacked experience in management and environmental programs and possessed a deep distrust of the career bureaucracy.[91] She and most other top officials of the agency relied on a small circle of confidants to make decisions, reducing the role of the regulatory analysis team. Indeed one of her top aides later stated that the EPA administrator equated disagreements on policy with personal disloyalty,[92] thus discouraging a free flow of ideas on the most effective way of solving problems.

Gorsuch initially opposed using economic incentives to improve the environment because they had been advocated by members of the Carter administration. To this end, she forced out a number of aides who worked for such market-incentive concepts as the "bubble" policy for air pollution.[93] Instead of a systematic approach to cost-effective regulation, the EPA administration seemed intent on granting relief without either analyzing the full impact on the environment or searching for less costly ways of controlling pollutants.

The EPA administration compromised its efforts to grant regulatory relief by not following rule-making procedures—and in some instances by engaging in conflicts of interest. One example of not following rule-making procedures was in part due to the agency's attempt to comply with Executive Order (E.O.) 12291 (which required cost-benefit and cost-effectiveness analyses where permitted by law) and in part to delays in appointing EPA officials. Prior to the appointment and confirmation of Gorsuch, the EPA had postponed President Carter's "midnight" pretreatment regulations in order to perform cost-benefit analysis as required by E.O. 12291. The U.S. Court of Appeals for the Third Circuit found the postponement a violation of the Administrative Procedures Act.[94] The resulting confusion significantly reduced the lead time for industry compliance with standards. Had the agency operated within the proper rule-making procedures, it could have avoided the costly delays and employed cost-effectiveness analysis.

Even more damaging were allegations of conflict of interest leveled against many of the top staff at EPA. These allegations resulted in twenty officials resigning or being fired in early 1983, and one going to jail.[95] The perception that those in charge were only interested in catering to business interests made Congress unwilling to trust the EPA administration with regulatory reform, even after William Ruckelshaus (the first administrator of the EPA) took Burford's place in 1983.[96] Burford's focus on providing industry relief led not only to allegations of impropriety, but also made the task of those who followed even more difficult. In fact, Congress eventually forced increases in the agency's budget to prevent the administration from cutting back on enforcement.[97]

As Eads and Fix observe, however, all was not lost. For example, despite the initial hostility of Gorsuch and her administration toward the "bubble concept," others in the Reagan administration and a group of career EPA officials were ultimately able to convince her of the merits of a market-incentive approach. In 1982 and 1983 EPA issued an aggressive, market-based emissions trading policy that included the bubble and related concepts.[98] Subsequently, in one application of emissions trading, the EPA has estimated emissions will be reduced by 3,000 tons per year compared to traditional command and control regulations, saving the firm $20 million per year and $500 million over the life of the plant.[99] Under Ruckelshaus and Thomas, the agency has increased its efforts to expand such trading to other EPA programs—even outside the clean air environment—within statutory limits on the procedures.

The bubble concept was dealt a major setback when the U.S. Court of Appeals for the District of Columbia invalidated the concept in nonattainment areas.[100] The court ruled that because these areas were not in compliance with existing standards, they could not engage in averaging across different areas within the plant. This delayed the implementation of market incentives until the Chevron Corporation won what may prove to be a landmark decision in *Chevron USA, Inc. versus Natural Resources Defense Council*.[101] In that case, the Supreme Court upheld what Eads and Fix call "nearly eight years of institutional commitment within the EPA to [legitimate] regulatory reform" by finding the "bubble policy" could be employed in nonattainment as well as attainment areas. According to Eads and Fix, "*Chevron* . . . may indeed have reinforced the agency's continuing practice of promulgating policies regarding the use of market mechanisms in the form of policy guidelines, rather than by statute, or by regulation."[102]

Despite the potential for expanding the use of market forces to achieve clean air in *Chevron,* the Court only confirmed the EPA's *discretion* to implement the bubble concept; it did not *require* EPA to do so. An internal debate ensued over whether the bubble concept was too complex to administer effectively. Ruckelshaus's successor at EPA, Lee Thomas, ended the debate by having the staff develop a set of guidelines to limit the use of the bubble in nonattainment areas without an EPA-approved state emissions improvement plan.[103] Since the EPA has been slow to approve such plans, further extensions of the bubble concept to many areas of the country could be limited by regulatory delays. Nevertheless, this modest gain is due to persistent efforts by the agency's regulatory reform staff, which has fought for the standard under three administrations. To a large degree they have prevailed because of their commitment to a cost-effective approach to regulation.

In sum, it is clear that reform at the EPA falls far short of the progress achieved at the FTC and OSHA. Indeed, at the outset the agency seemed bent on undoing substantive reforms begun under the Carter administration. The reform program was initially handicapped by administators who did not fully understand either the environmental laws themselves or the role that market incentives might play in reducing their cost and improving effectiveness. Nonetheless, there now appears to be some movement toward meaningful reform.

Economic Analysis and the Pace of Regulatory Reform

Why, then, were administrators at the FTC and OSHA more successful in reforming regulations than were those at the EPA? What are the implications for the future pace of regulatory reform? Without question, the relative difficulty of the regulatory challenge is part of the explanation. It is one thing to ensure that a potential antitrust initiative is analytically sound. It is quite another to apply economic and other systematic analyses to such emotional issues as protecting the environment or human life.

Some opponents of such regulatory reform are quick to raise the spectre of uncaring government administrators caving in to profit-hungry corporations and trading dollars for environmental improvements or lives. Consequently, businesses that do not wish to take the public relations heat from appearing cruel and indifferent to legitimate public goals are reluctant to speak out. In addition, they may be afraid that economic incentives can mean greater costs of compliance than the familiar command-and-control enforcement techniques. It has also been suggested that organized labor and established enterprises favor the existing system because it protects established firms and unions against potential competitors.[104] Still others suggest that the Clean Air Act was partly designed to discourage the migration of industry from urbanized areas to rural areas.[105]

Under this theory, congressional oversight committees opposed reforms because of strong hostility from those favoring the status quo and silence from those standing to gain from reform. Administrators are deterred from carrying out the intent of President Reagan's E.O. 12291, which requires that "regulations should be issued only on evidence that their potential benefits exceed their potential costs" and that where cost-benefit analysis is prohibited by statute, cost-effectiveness analysis should be used.

Such a theory has considerable appeal. However, it does not account for progress made at such agencies as OSHA and the FTC's Bureau of Consumer Protection. It also does not account for a number of highly successful economic regulation reforms since the mid-1970s, in spite of obstacles that seemed every bit as daunting when reform efforts began. There were powerful lobbies marshaled in favor of each of the economic controls eliminated in this period. Just ten years ago, commentators were explaining why trucking and airline regulations would never be repealed because of the clout wielded by the Teamsters Union, the Airline Pilots Association, and established firms in those industries. Petroleum price deregulation was widely denounced by many of the same congressmen who consistently support more stringent environmental controls. Yet as evidence from economic studies mounted on the benefits from regulatory reform, so did pressures for change. Indeed, many authors of such studies took administrative posts in the Ford, Carter, and Reagan administrations, as well as positions on key congressional committees, and helped speed the process along.

Antitrust reform evolved in a similar fashion, albeit at a much slower pace. As long ago as 1911, the Supreme Court found Standard Oil guilty of attempted monopolization of the petroleum market, even though the price of its primary product had fallen by nearly 90 percent in the previous fifty years.[106] In 1945, in a case with the precedential value of a Supreme Court decision, the Second Circuit found Alcoa guilty of monopolizing the sale of primary aluminum ingots because, in the words of now-Judge Richard Posner, "[I]t had tried to satisfy as much of the growth in demand for aluminum as possible by expanding its own capacity, instead of sitting back and letting its competitors, or new entrants, provide for the growth of the market."[107]

In 1966, the Supreme Court blocked an acquisition by *Von's Grocery,* even though (contrary to the argument of complaint counsel) it found that the merger would reduce consumer prices.[108] The decision was based on a finding that the three largest sellers would increase their combined penetration from 19 to 23 percent and concentration among the eight largest sellers would rise from 39 to 42 percent. In his biting dissent, Justice Stewart complained that the only thing for sure in merger cases was that the government always wins.[109]

It could be said that until at least the mid 1970s the outlook for antitrust reform was bleak—as bleak or bleaker than the present-day consensus outlook for reforming environmental regulation. Populist pressures prevented legislators from enacting meaningful reforms. Enforcement of the Robinson-Patman Act—which prohibits certain price discounts and other procompetitive marketing practices—was at its zenith. Yet agency policies and court decisions did finally come to reflect concerns for economic efficiency and consumer welfare and did so as better analysis of the problems evolved and was spread to the agencies and judiciary.[110]

In 1974, eight years after *Von's,* Justice Stewart authored a decision upholding the legality of an acquisition where the two leading coal producers would increase their combined share of sales from 44 to 53 percent.[111] In 1976, the Supreme Court reversed its own decision ten years earlier in *Schwinn,*[112] holding in *Sylvania*[113] that a manufacturer's restrictions on its resellers' marketing practices can be procompetitive—even though such restrictions limit the number of resellers in a given market. In 1980, the FTC found DuPont innocent of attempted monopolization charges, even though it was the leading firm in an industry with a four-firm concentration of over 80 percent.[114] In 1984, a unanimous Second Circuit, the same court that thirty-nine years earlier had issued the *Alcoa* decision, relied on the dissent of Chairman Miller, when it reversed the majority's decision in *Ethyl.*[115]

And in 1985, Commissioner George Douglas, a contributor to this volume, authored a unanimous commission decision approving an acquisition, even though there was a Herfindahl-Hirschman index of nearly 3000—well above the level that is supposed to trigger close scrutiny.[116]

Although there is debate about the permanence of each of these changes, most commentators doubt that antitrust will ever return to the days of *Von's Grocery.*[117] There can be little question that these trends have largely been the result of a number of articles and books as well as the active participation of legal and economic scholars in policy positions.[118]

More importantly, social regulation reform seems to be just as responsive to solid analytical work. Indeed, such reform appears to be proceeding more rapidly than past antitrust reforms and reform of economic regulations. A number of court decisions have already affirmed administrative decisions to use cost-effectiveness analysis and performance-oriented approaches in environmental and health and safety decisions. On the other hand, *DuPont* was decided some twenty-two years after McGee's seminal work on predation in the *Standard Oil* case. The overall reform of antitrust policies begun in the mid-1970s occurred several decades after the publication of works by von Mises, Schumpeter, and others challenging the basis for attacks on size and concentration. The Airline Deregulation Act of 1978 occurred some twenty-seven years after Lucile Keyes published the seminal work on the economic effects of airline regulation in 1951.[119] In each of these areas, progress was achieved only by the repeated application of economic and other systematic analyses that have convinced agencies and courts of the importance of assessing the efficiency and public welfare effects of their interpretations of legislative mandates.

Why, then, the frustration with the pace of reform under Reagan? Much of it probably reflects expectations that are unrealistically high. To us, the relevant standard is not some Platonic ideal of the perfect regulatory world but what is feasible given the public-choice environment in which government administrators, Congress, and the judiciary must operate. As Adam Smith observed, in the real world success often falls significantly short of absolute perfection.

> When a critic examines the work of any of the great masters in poetry or painting, he may sometimes examine it by an idea of perfection, in his own mind, which neither that nor any other human work will ever come up to; and as long as he compares it with this standard, he can see nothing in it but faults and imperfections. But when he comes to consider the rank which it ought to hold among other works of the same kind, he necessarily compares it with a very different standard, the common degree of excellence which is usually attained . . . and when he judges of it by this new measure, it may often appear to deserve the highest applause, upon account of its approaching much nearer to perfection than the greater part of those works which can be brought into competition with it.[120]

Indeed it was a full seventy years after publication of *The Wealth of Nations* that Britain repealed the Corn Laws, eliminating the anticompetitive trade restraints that were a central target of Smith's classic treatise.

Conclusion

Some critics argue that efforts by the Reagan administration to reform governmental regulation were undermined by administrators constrained by ideological inflexibility and a lack of willingness to take on the special interests—especially in the area of so-called "social regulation." However, in the face of intense political opposition, market-oriented administrators were able to reform two of the agencies that some have characterized as the least effective and most disruptive in the 1970s. Some meaningful reform now appears to be under way at a third, in spite of early frustrations and failures.

Such overall improvement suggests that where sound arguments for cost-effective and market-based regulatory approaches can be made, they will find their way into administrative practices and judicial interpretations, if not legislative revisions of existing statutes. The progress may be less than some would have liked and portions of the reforms might be reversed by future administrations, but this is to be expected in a pluralistic society that encourages competition among ideas. Indeed, the present pace of reform may well be optimal for a democratic system of government—a system that is, and should be, sensitive to the interests of everyone.

Notes

1. See for example Robert Crandall, "Has Reagan Dropped the Ball?" *Regulation* (September/October 1981): 15–18; and Paul Portney, "Natural Resources and the Environment: More Controversy Than Change," in John Palmer and Isabel Sawhill (eds.), *The Reagan Record* (Washington, D.C.: The Urban Institute, 1984), pp. 141–75.

2. *Dun's Business Month* (May 1984): 84.

3. See for example George Eads and Michael Fix, "The Prospects for Regulatory Reform: The Legacy of Reagan's First Term," *Yale Journal on Regulation* 3 (Spring 1985): 302–33; and Gregory Christiansen and Robert Haveman, "The Reagan Administration's Regulatory Relief Effort: A Midterm Assessment," in George Eads and Michael Fix (eds.), *The Reagan Regulatory Strategy: An Assessment* (Washington, D.C.: The Urban Institute, 1984), pp. 49, 69–70, 78–79.

4. See, for example, Portney, "Natural Resources and the Environment," p. 172.

5. National Safety Council, *Accident Facts,* 1986 ed., p. 59.

6. Steven Morrison and Clifford Winston, *The Economic Effects of Airline Deregulation* (Washington, D.C.: Brookings Institution, 1986, p. vii.

7. Elizabeth Dole, "Needless Trucking Rules," *Washington Times,* 2 October 1985, p. 1.

8. Quotations are from Werner Meyer, "Department of Disinformation—Snake Oil Salesmen," *Policy Review* 37 (Summer 1986): 75–77.

9. Kenneth Arrow and Joseph Kalt, "Why Oil Prices Should be Decontrolled," *Regulation* (September/October 1979): 15.

10. Joseph Kalt, "The Creation, Growth, and Entrenchment of Special Interests in Oil Price Policy," in Roger Noll and Bruce Owen (eds.), *The Political Economy of Deregulation: Interest Groups in the Regulatory Process* (Washington, D.C.: American Enterprise Institute, 1983), pp. 97–114.

11. See Christiansen and Haveman, "The Reagan Administration's Regulatory Relief Effort," p. 77.

12. Gregory Christiansen and Robert Haveman, "Public Regulations and the Slowdown in Productivity and Growth," *American Economic Review* 71 (May 1981): 320–25.

13. Wayne B. Gray, "The Impact of OSHA and EPA Regulation on Productivity," Working Paper no. 1405, National Bureau of Economic Research, Inc., July 1984. See also Richard Stewart, "Economics, Environment, and the Limits of Legal Control," Banff Center School of Management, Conference on Environmental Protection and Resource Development: Convergence for Today (Sept. 1984), p. 8.

14. Joseph Kalt, "The Impact of Domestic Environmental Regulatory Policies on U.S. International Competitiveness," Energy and Environmental Policy Center, Harvard University (March 1985).

15. We must caution readers that the authors have participated in some of the Reagan reforms at the Federal Trade Commission.

16. Congress refused to reauthorize the agency in 1979 and 1980 and even shut it down for a day by allowing its funding to lapse. It took the intervention of President Carter to get the agency's funds restored.

17. Public Law No. 96-252.

18. Former Chairman Michael Pertschuk states that only one of the rules he supported passed "substantially intact," *Revolt Against Regulation* (Berkeley: University of California Press, 1982), p. 143.

19. See Economic Analysis and the Pace of Regulatory Reform, this chapter.

20. Joe Sims, "Miller's FTC Chairmanship Merits High Marks," *Legal Times* (18 March 1985): 16.

21. The agency's consumer protection mission is best described as social regulation, since it largely involves the regulation of advertising and product quality. Such matters frequently involve safety and health issues; for example the cigarette labeling rule, the ban on cigarette advertising on television, and the proposed kid-vid rule. The antitrust mission is best described as a form of economic regulation, since it involves mainly issues of pricing and entry.

22. See Timothy J. Muris, "Rules without Reason at the FTC," *Regulation* (September/October 1982): 20–26.

23. Ibid., p. 24.

24. *Federal Register* 49 (1 March 1984): 7740, 7742.

25. *Orkin Extermination Co.,* FTC, D. 9176 (8 May 1984).

26. Bureau Directors of the FTC, "Federal Trade Commission Law Enforcement in the 1980's," Federal Trade Commission (October 1984): 17–18.

27. Phone interview with Howard Beales, Associate Director for Policy and Evaluation, Bureau of Consumer Protection, Federal Trade Commission, 7 November 1986.

28. Gary T. Ford and John E. Clafee, "Recent Developments in FTC Policy on Deception," *Journal of Marketing* 50 (July 1986): 82–103.

29. Federal Trade Commission, "Policy Statement on Deception," followed by dissenting statement of Commissioners Bailey and Pertschuk and concurring statement by Commissioner Douglas, *ATRR* 45 (27 October 1983): 689.

30. Amrep Corp. v. Federal Trade Commission, 768 F.2d. 1171, 1178 (1985). See Ford and Calfee, "Recent Developments in FTC Policy on Deception," p. 83.

31. The commission now follows an explicitly economic approach—one similar to that outlined by now-Judge Posner. See Richard A. Posner, *Antitrust Law* (Chicago: University of Chicago Press, 1976), pp. 55–71.

32. Areas of dubious value included mergers between companies that do not directly compete, so-called predatory practices, such as price cutting below average cost, resale price maintenance that leads to increased information or postsale services, and procompetitive pricing and marketing activities that run afoul of a narrow interpretation of the Robinson-Patman act. For a more detailed discussion, see Sims, "Miller's FTC Chairmanship."

33. See Economic Analysis and the Pace of Regulatory Reform, this chapter.

34. Kellogg Co., 99 FTC 8 (1982) (complaint dismissed).

35. Russell Stover Candies v. FTC, 100 FTC 1 (1982), rev'd. Russell Stover Candies v. FTC, 718 F.2d 256 (8th Cir. 1983).

36. Ethyl Corp., 101 FTC 425 (1983), rev'd, E. I. DuPont de Nemours & Co. v. FTC, 729 F.2d 128 (2d Cir. 1984).

37. Borg-Warner Corp, 101 FTC 863 (1983), rev'd. Borg-Warner Corp. versus FTC, 746 F.2d 18 (2d Cir. 1984).

38. Monsanto Co. v. Spray-Rite Service Corp., 465 U.S. 752 (1984).

39. At one point the Congress even directed the Chairman not to speak in public about his views on this issue.

40. See General Foods Corporation, 102 FTC 812 (1983); ITT Continental Baking Co., 102 FTC 1298 (1983); and Grand Union Co, 103 FTC 204 (1984).

41. Economists tried to identify mergers and horizontal restraints that were likely to increase price and not result in substantial production efficiencies.

42. "FTC Statement Concerning Horizontal Mergers," 2 *CCH Trade Regulation Reporter* (14 June 1982): 516, para. 4; "Justice Department Merger Guidelines," *Federal Register* 47 (1982): 28, 493.

43. See Sims, "Miller's FTC Chairmanship."

44. For example, one study found that physician-controlled insurance boards increased doctors' fees. Paul Pautler and David Kass, "Physician Control of Blue Shield Plans," Bureau of Economics Report to the FTC, November 1979. Other reports include Warren Greenberg, "Competition in the Health Care Sector: Past, Present, and Future," Proceedings of a Conference Sponsored by the Bureau of Economics at the FTC, March 1978; Ronald Bond, John Kwoka, Jack Phelan, and Ira Whitten, "Effects of Restrictions on Advertising and Commercial Practice in the Professions: The Case of Optometry", Bureau of Economics Report to the FTC, April 1980; Judith Gelman, "Competition and Health," Bureau of Economics Report to the FTC, April 1982; Russ Porter, "Improving Consumer Access to Legal Services: The Case for Removing Truthful Restrictions on Consumer Advertising," Report to the FTC, November 1984.

45. State Volunteer Mutual Insurance Co., 102 FTC 1232 (1983).

46. Indiana Federation of Dentists v. FTC, 745, F.2d 1124 (1984), rev'd, dkt. no. 1809 (2 June 1986).

47. See Bureau Directors, "Federal Trade Commission Law Enforcement," p. 60.

48. "The Multiple Listing Service of the Greater Michigan City Area, Inc.," *Federal Register* 49 (1984): 21073.

49. 195 S.Ct. 1713 (1985).

50. See George W. Douglas and James W. Mullenix, "Cities and States as Agents in Restraint of Trade," *Antitrust Bulletin* 31 (Summer 1986): 505–26.

51. These cases were in part brought as a result of a study by the FTC's Bureau of Economics of the effects of the restrictive practices in those cities. See Mark Frankena and Paul Pautler, "An Economic Analysis of Taxicab Regulation," FTC Bureau of Economics Staff Report (May 1984).

52. See Bureau Directors, "Federal Trade Commission Law Enforcment," p. 66.

53. 15 U.S.C. secs. 34–36 (1984 supp.) in response to Community Communications Co. v. City of Boulder, 455 U.S. 40 (1982).

54. "The Local Government Antitrust Act of 1984," Public Law 98-544 (24 October 1984), eliminated treble damages awards against cities, but the FTC and private plaintiffs can still sue for injunctive relief.

55. See Thomas J. Campbell, "The Antitrust Records of the First Reagan Administration," *Texas Law Review* 64 (1985): 353, 364–65.

56. For one legislative accomplishment, see: "National Cooperative Research Act of 1984," Public Law 98-462, (11 October 1984), which detrebled damages for research joint ventures.

57. Of course there may yet be substantive legislative changes to the antitrust laws, given the administration's five-part package for reform. See Joe Sims, "Antitrust Law, 1986: The Old Girl is Still Kicking," *Legal Times* 30 (7 April 1986): 1.

58. See Sims, "Miller's FTC Chairmanship."

59. See Pertschuk, *Revolt Against Regulation,* p. 139.

60. Ann Reilly, "Antitrust Policy after the Steel Veto," *Fortune* (19 March 1984): 98.

61. "Occupational Safety and Health Act of 1970," Public Law 91-596 (29 December 1970) sec. 2b.

62. Although the rate of injury and illnesses rose in 1984, as of 1985 it remained 10 percent below the rate in 1980, when it had declined for the first time since OSHA's inception. See National Safety Council, *Accident Facts.*

63. Under section 6a of the OSHA Act, Congress had mandated that within a two-year period, the agency should "promulgate as an occupational safety or health standard any national consensus standard, and any established Federal standard, unless [it] determines that the promulgation of such a standard would not result in improved safety or health. . . . In the event of conflict among any such standards, the Secretary shall promulgate the standard which assures the greatest protection of the safety or health of the affected employees." Public Law 91-596 (29 December 1970) sec. 2193.

64. Nina Cornell, Roger Noll, and Barry Weingast, "Regulating Safety," in Henry Owen and Charles Schultze (eds.), *Setting National Priorities* (Washington, D.C.: Brookings, 1976), 502.

65. The same kind of correlation exists between injury rates and so-called willful violations and penalties levied as well. It is not possible to assess the effect on occupational health trends, because we cannot assess impacts of exposures to substances with latency periods of up to thirty years.

66. Ann Bartel and Lacy Glenn Thomas, "The Costs and Benefits of OSHA— Induced Investments in Employee Safety and Health," in John D. Worrall and David Appel, (eds.), *Workers' Compensation Benefits: Adequacy, Equity, and Efficiency* (Ithaca, N.Y.: ILR Press, 1985), p. 54.

67. John Morrall, "Workplace Safety and Health," Executive Summary of paper presented to American Enterprise Institute Conference on Health, Safety and Environmental Regulation (18 November 1981), p. 2; see also Gray, "The Impact of OSHA and EPA Regulation," p. 45; William Cooke and Frederick Tautschi, "OSHA, Plant Safety Programs and Injury Reduction," *Industrial Relations* 20 (1981): 245–57; W. Kip Viscusi, "The Impact of Occupational Safety and Health Regulation," *Bell Journal of Economics* 10 (1979): 117–40; David McCaffrey, "An Assessment of OSHA's Recent Effects on Injury Rates," *Journal of Human Resources* 17 (1983): 131–46; John Mendeloff, *Regulating Safety: An Economic and Political Analysis of Occupational Safety and Health Policy* (Cambridge: MIT Press, 1979); Robert Smith, "The Impact of OSHA Inspections on Manufacturing Injury Rates," *Journal of Human Resources* 13 (1979): 145–70; and William P. Currington, "Safety Regulation and Workplace Injuries," *Southern Economic Journal* 53 (July 1986) 51–72.

68. James C. Miller, III, and Thomas F. Walton, "Protecting Workers' Hearing: An Economic Test for OSHA Initiatives," *Regulation* (September/October 1980): 34.

69. Ibid., pp. 34–35. The Miller/Walton article discusses an OSHA requirement that would have increased employees' perceived noise levels by more than 12 dBA at a General Motors component parts stamping plant. An increase of 12 dBA represents more than a doubling in the intensity of the sound reaching the employee's ear. The agency subsequently dropped the proposed requirement for engineering controls. OSHRC Docket no. 78-54-76 (2 April 1984). See also the discussion later in the chapter of implications of three appeals court decisions, Castle and Cooke, RMI, and Turner.

70. Thorne G. Auchter, address to Texas Safety Association, Houston, Texas (25 April 1983), pp. 11–12.

71. *OSHA Instruction* CPL 2-2.35 (9 November 1983), p. 2.

72. See *OSHA Instruction*, CPL 2.25B (1 October 1981).

73. See *OSHA Instruction* 2.12B (1 February 1982).

74. See for example Eads and Fix, *The Reagan Regulatory Strategy*, p. 197.

75. See for example Martin Laurent, Dan Kruger, and Michael Connolly, "OSHA and Collective Bargaining," forthcoming in *Employment Relations Journal*.

76. RMI Company v. Secretary of Labor, 594 F. 2d 566 (6th Cir. 1979). See also Turner Company v. Secretary of Labor, 561 F. 2d 82 (7th Cir. 1977); and Miller and Walton, "Protecting Workers' Hearing," p. 35.

77. Industrial Union Department v. American Petroleum Institute, 448 US 607 (S.Ct. 1980).

78. The Court stated that "if the use of one respirator would achieve the same reduction in health risk as the use of five, the use of five respirators was 'technologically and economically feasible,' and OSHA thus insisted on the use of five, then the 'reasonably necessary or appropriate' limitation [of sec. 3 (8) of the OSHA Act] might come into play as an additional restriction on OSHA to choose the one-respirator standard." American Textile Manufacturers v. Donovan, 452 U.S. 490 (S.Ct. 1981): 513, n. 32.

79. Ibid., pp. 512, 509.

80. Donovan v. Castle & Cooke Foods and OSAHRC, 10 OSJC 2175 (19 November 1982).

81. According to one commentary,

> When the *Benzene* and *Cotton Dust* opinions are read together (and they must be read together in order to understand fully the final analysis in *Cotton Dust*) it can be seen that the concept of cost-benefit analysis remains viable and compatible with the language of the *Cotton Dust* opinion. . . . *Cotton Dust* allows and, perhaps, really even requires the responsible use of cost-benefit analysis as a regulatory tool to ensure that agencies do not force society (through industry) to undertake action that is totally out of proportion to any benefits society can expect to receive. On the other hand, *Cotton Dust* guarantees that a cost-benefit analysis cannot be used as a talisman to destroy the effectiveness of OSHA rulemaking." Joseph Hadley, Jr. and Gerald Richman, "The Impact of *Benzene* and *Cotton Dust:* Restraints on the Regulation of Toxic Substance," *Administrative Law Review* 36 (Spring 1982): 77.

See also Wesley Cann, "Cost-Benefit Analysis vs. Feasibility Analysis: The Controversy Resolved in the Cotton Dust Case," *American Business Law Journal* 19 (Winter 1982): 31. Cann states, "The *American Textile* decision must not be interpreted as the final word on the use of cost-benefit analysis by administrative agencies. For example, the decision does not answer the question of whether a cost-benefit analysis is prohibited or simply not required [for toxic substances]." See also Neil Sullivan, "The Cotton Dust Decision: The Confusion Continues," *Administrative Law Review* 36 (Summer 1982): 492. Says Sullivan, "The question of whether the term 'feasible' requires cost-benefit analysis has been long awaited, but the *Cotton Dust* decision does not settle the issue."

82. See references to productivity studies earlier in the chapter in OSHA—Focused Approach Achieves Results.

83. The Bureau of Economic Analysis of the Department of Commerce estimated that capital expenditures for pollution control in 1978 were almost $8 billion. George C. Eads and Michael Fix, *Relief or Reform: Reagan's Regulatory Dilemma* (Washington, D.C.: Urban Institute Press, 1984), pp. 31–34. As early as 1978, Murray Weidenbaum and Robert Defina estimated the total cost of energy and environment regulations to be over $8 billion in *The Cost of Federal Regulation on Economic Activity* (Washington, D.C.: American Enterprise Institute, May 1978), p. 2. In 1979 a study of 48 companies showed that the EPA accounted for 77 percent of the total cost of regulation and 60 percent of that cost is attributable to air pollution regulations. Arthur Anderson & Co., *Cost of Government Regulation,*

Study for the Business Roundtable, executive summary (March 1979), pp. 22, 24. See also sources cited in n. 11.

84. Congressional Budget Office, *The Clean Air Act, the Electric Utilities and the Coal Market* (Washington, D.C.: G.P.O., April 1982): 62.

85. U.S. General Accounting Office, *A Market Aproach to Air Pollution Control Could Reduce Compliance Costs without Jeopardizing Clean Air Goals* (Washington: D.C.: Government Printing Office, 1982), pp. ii, 32.

86. Palmer and Sawhill, *The Reagan Record,* p. 145.

87. Robert Crandall, "The Environment," *Regulation* (January/February 1982): 29.

88. Thomas G. Moore, "Reagan's Regulatory Record," in John H. Moore (ed.), *To Promote Prosperity* (Stanford, Calif.: Hoover Press, 1984): 245.

89. Eads and Fix, *Relief or Reform,* p. 176.

90. Moore, "Reagan's Regulatory Record," p. 244; Eads and Fix, *Relief or Reform,* p. 152.

91. Palmer and Sawhill, *The Reagan Record,* p. 146.

92. Eads and Fix, *Relief or Reform,* p. 147.

93. Moore, "Reagan's Regulatory Record," p. 246.

94. Edward L. Stohbehn, Jr., "Reasoned Decisionmaking in Regulatory Reform: The Third Circuit Reinstates EPA's Pretreatment Rules," *Environmental Law Reporter News and Analysis* 13 (January 1983): 10011–16.

95. Palmer and Sawhill, *The Reagan Record,* p. 146–47.

96. Eads and Fix, *Relief or Reform,* p. 147.

97. Ibid., pp. 153–54; Bruce Yandle, "The Evolution of Regulatory Activities in the 1970s and 1980s," in Phillip Cagan, (ed.), *Essays in Contemporary Economics Problems, 1986: The Impact of the Reagan Program* (Washington, D.C.: American Enterprise Institute, 1986): 105–45.

98. The four related reforms were "(1) the bubble, which allows managers of one or more existing plants to trade additional control of cheaply controlled stacks or vents for less control of more expensive sources; (2) offsets, which allow new plants or modifications to emit pollutants in non-attainment areas if they secure sufficient reductions from others to improve air quality; (3) netting, which allows use of a bubble to avoid burdensome new source requirements for in-plant modifications, so long as plant-wide emissions do not increase significantly; and (4) banking, which allows sources to store surplus reductions in a legally protected manner for future sale" (Eads and Fix, *Relief or Reform,* p. 306).

99. *Economic Report of the President* (February 1986): 181.

100. Levin, pp. 39–40; Eads and Fix, *Relief or Reform,* pp. 183–84.

101. 467 U.S. 837 (S.Ct. 1984).

102. Eads and Fix, *Relief or Reform,* pp. 306–7.

103. Philip Shabecoff, "E.P.A. Sets Rules on Air Pollution Allowances," *New York Times,* 20 November 1986, p. 19; Robert E. Taylor, "E.P.A. Is Expanding its 'Bubble' Policy for Air Pollution," *Wall Street Journal,* 20 November 1986, 39.

104. For example, Ann Bartel and Lacy Thomas, "Predation through Regulation: The Wage and Profit Effects of OSHA and EPA," *Journal of Law and Economics* 30 (October 1987): 239–64.

105. For example, B. Peter Pashigian, "Environmental Regulation: Whose Self-Interests are Being Protected?" *Economic Inquiry* 28 (October 1985): 551–84; and Robert Crandall, *Controlling Industrial Pollution: The Economics and Politics of Clean Air* (Washington, D.C.: Brookings, 1983).

106. Dominick T. Armentano, "Antitrust Policy: Reform or Repeal?" (Washington, D.C.: Cato Institute, 18 January 1983), p. 3; see also John S. McGee, "Predatory Price Cutting: The Standard Oil (N.J.) Case," *Journal of Law and Economics* 1 (October 1958): 136–69.

107. Posner, *Antitrust Law*, p. 214.

108. U.S. v. Von's Grocery Co., 384 U.S. 270 (S.Ct. 1966).

109. Ibid.; see also Posner, *Antitrust Law*, pp. 105–8.

110. See James Langenfeld and David Scheffman, "Evolution or Revolution—What Is The Future of Antitrust?" *Antitrust Bulletin* 31 (Summer 1986): 287–300.

111. *General Dynamics*, 415 U.S. 486 (S.Ct. 1974).

112. 388 U.S. 365 (S.Ct. 1967).

113. 433 U.S. 36 (S.Ct. 1976).

114. E. I. DuPont de Nemours & Co., 96 FTC 653 (1980).

115. E. I. DuPont de Nemours & Co. v. FTC, 729 F.2d 128 (2d Cir. 1984).

116. *Eichlin*, dkt. no. 9157 (28 June 1985).

117. See the special issue on the future of antitrust in the *Antitrust Bulletin* (Fall 1986); Sims, "Antitrust Law, 1986," p. 30; and the comments of Robert Pitofsky, Phillip Areeda, and William Baxter in "Antitrust: New Directions vs. New Backlash," *Research Bulletin of the Conference Board*, no. 197 (1986): 5–7.

118. See Langenfeld and Scheffman, "Evolution or Revolution."

119. Lucile Keyes, *Federal Control of Entry into Air Transportation* (Cambridge: Harvard University Press, 1951) cited in Morrison and Winston, *Economic Effects of Airline Regulation*, p. 5.

120. Adam Smith, *The Theory of Moral Sentiments* (Indianapolis: Liberty Classics, 1976), p. 74.

4

Consumer Protection at the FTC during the Reagan Administration

William C. MacLeod and Robert A. Rogowsky

Consumer Protection and the Consumer Movement

In Spring 1980 President Carter convened an unusual meeting at the White House. The president invited senators and representatives from a conference committee considering legislation designed to reduce the powers of the Federal Trade Commission (FTC). After listening to the legislators' complaints about the excesses of the commission, the president warned them he would veto any bill that would cripple the agency. The meeting was an ironic crisis in the consumer movement and an ignoble climax in the saga of Michael Pertschuk, the embattled chairman who had inherited the commission at the zenith of its powers and wielded its authority aggressively and with imagination. Congress was contemplating the termination of several controversial rulemakings and cases, the exemption of entire industries from FTC jurisdiction, a legislative veto of future commission rules, and a number of other draconian restrictions of the commission's authority. The commission and its chairman had fallen victim to their own success.

The activity for which the agency was suffering had been inspired by a bipartisan effort early in the 1970s to awaken a quiescent commission. Prior to 1970, the FTC concentrated on trade restraints and deceptive practices, focusing on small firms and narrow points of law. The decade began with consumer groups and a presidential commission criticizing the agency as inept, irrelevant, and even injurious to the interests it was supposed to serve. In 1969 both Ralph Nader and the American Bar Association issued reports declaring the commission a failure and near total disarray.[1]

In 1971, Chairman Caspar Weinberger, a Nixon appointee, conducted a general house cleaning, complete with wholesale personnel changes. Creating the Bureau of Competition and the Bureau of Consumer Protection, he began what was to be a decade-long process of reorganization. Under Weinberger and his successor, Miles Kirkpatrick, consumer protection issues became the most publicized activities in the revitalized agency, led by innovative regulatory initiatives in advertising. More creative interpretation of the unfairness doctrine of Section 5 of the Federal Trade Act led to the initiation of sixteen major trade regulation rules during the 1973 to 1976 chairmanship of Lewis Engman (see Table 4.1). Although this broad reach of the commission's authority was questioned,[2] these rules, designed to transform the practices of entire industries, formed a major regulatory front for the agency. To handle the increased activity, the agency's budget grew from about $21 million in 1970 to nearly $70 million in 1979.

Fueling the surge in consumer protection activity was a rash of new statutory powers heaped on the agency by Congress. The number of statutes under the jurisdiction of the commission grew from eleven in 1970 to twenty-four by 1978, and to twenty-seven by 1986 (see Table 4.2). Two of these significantly increased the FTC's power. The Alaskan Pipeline Act of 1973 (1) doubled penalties for violating FTC orders, (2) empowered U.S. district courts to grant mandatory injunctions and other equitable relief to enforce commission orders, and (3) granted the commission greater powers to appear on its own behalf in federal court.[3] Of even greater impact, the Federal Trade Commission Improvement Act of 1975 (FTCIA)[4] established the authority of the commission to prescribe substantive rules to prevent unfair or deceptive acts or practices. In this way the act erased any question over the commission's power to issue industrywide rules. Thus empowered, the agency was dubbed "the second most powerful legislature in Washington."[5] In addition, the commission received authority to recover civil penalties in federal court for knowing violations of orders and rules issued under the FTC Act or to obtain redress, including restitution for injured consumers.

Special statutes, mostly enacted since the late 1960s, govern much of the commission's activities. For example, the Fair Package and Labeling Act of 1966 requires the commission to issue disclosure regulations on contents and identification of products. The Federal Cigarette Labeling and Advertising Act of 1966, amended in 1969, requires a warning label on cigarette packages. The Truth-in-Lending Act of 1969 requires all consumer creditors to make detailed written disclosures concerning charges and other aspects of loans.

The FTC's power under special statutes increased rapidly in the 1970s.

Table 4.1

Terminated Rule Makings		
	Initial NPRM	Final Termination
Vocational schools[a]	8/74	12/78
Mobile homes	5/75	11/86
Food advertising (I & II)	5/75	12/82
Hearing aids	5/75	9/85
Prescription drugs	6/75	11/78
Cellular plastics	7/75	6/80
Health spas	8/75	12/85
Protein supplements	8/75	12/84
OTC drugs	11/75	5/81
Antacid advertising	4/76	7/84
Children's advertising (kid-vid)	4/78	9/85
Standards and certification	12/78	9/85

Major Rules Pending as of 1 June 1987[b]	
Initial NPRM	
Ophthalmic practices II	12/80
Holder-in-due course II	11/75

Promulgated Magnuson-Moss Rules, Fiscal Years 1978–Present		
	Initial NPRM	Promulgated
Use of negative-option plans[c]		
Cooling-off period for door-to-door sales[c]		
Holder-in-due course I[c]		
Mail order merchandise[c]		
Franchises and business ventures[c]		
Credit practices	4/75	3/84
Funeral rule	8/75	9/82
Used cars	1/76	8/81
Care labeling	1/76	5/83
Ophthalmic practices I	1/76	6/78
Thermal insulation	11/77	8/79

[a] Certain features of the rule were overturned on appeal and remanded. No part of the rule was ever implemented and is, at the time of writing, under reconsideration by the commission.

[b] Does not include proposed amendments to existing rules.

[c] Rules completed prior to passage of Magnuson-Moss but that were grandfathered in and given the authority and penalties attached to Magnusom-Moss because they followed similar procedures for notice and comment before promulgation.

Table 4.2
Statutes Enforced by the Federal Trade Commission

Sherman Antitrust Act	1890
Federal Trade Commission Act	1914
Clayton Act	1914
Export Trade Act	1918
Robinson-Patman Act	1936
Nonprofit Institutions Act	1938
Wool Products Labeling Act	1939
Insurance Act (McCarran-Ferguson Act)	1945
Lanham Trade-Mark Act	1946
Fur Products Labeling Act	1951
Textile Fiber Products Identification Act	1958
Fair Packaging and Labeling Act	1966
Truth in Lending Act	1968
Fair Credit Reporting Act	1970
National Environmental Policy Act of 1969	1970
Postal Reorganization Act (section 3009, Mailing of Unordered Merchandise)	1972
Emergency Petroleum Allocation Act of 1973	1973
Hobby Protection Act	1973
Equal Credit Opportunity Act, as amended	1974
Fair Credit Billing Act	1974
Magnuson-Moss Warranty-FTC Improvement Act	1975
Energy Policy and Conservation Act	1975
Motor Vehicle Information and Cost Savings Act, Title V—Improving Automotive Efficiency (Fuel Economy Labeling): see Title III of Energy Policy and Conservation Act	1975
Consumer Leasing Act of 1976	1976
Railroad Revitalization and Regulatory Reform Act of 1976 (pertinent section affecting FTC from Title II of Public Law No. 94-210)	1976
Energy Conservation and Production Act	1976
Hart-Scott-Rodino Antitrust Improvements Act of 1976 (Title I—Antitrust Civil Process Act Amendments)	1976
Toxic Substances Control Act (pertinent section affecting the Federal Trade Commission)	1976
Fair Debt Collection Practices Act	1977
Electronic Funds Transfer Act	1978
Petroleum Marketing Practices Act	1978
Federal Cigarette Labeling and Advertising Act,	1984
Conservation Services Reform Act	1986
Comprehensive Smokeless Tobacco Health Education Act of 1986	1986

The Fair Credit Reporting Act of 1970 regulated the confidentiality, accuracy, and use of information gathered by consumer-reporting companies, such as credit bureaus. The Equal Credit Opportunity Act (1975) prohibits discrimination against credit applicants on the basis of sex or marital status. The Fair Credit Billing Act of 1975 and the Consumer Leasing Act of 1976 respectively amended the Truth-in-Lending Act to regulate billing practices and require disclosure of relevant costs of certain leases of personal property to consumers. Finally, the Fair Debt Collection Practices Act of 1977 regulates the practices of those who regularly collect debts.

Among the most significant legislative grants was the 1975 Magnuson-Moss Warranty Act, authorizing the FTC to promulgate regulations on the content of warranties. Although forty-nine of the fifty states provided protection under the Uniform Commercial Code, the Warranty Act required extensive disclosure, in simple and intelligible language, of the terms and conditions of warranties prior to purchase.[6] The act delegated authority to the FTC to enforce these prescriptions and promulgate rules and regulations for specific industries. The Energy Policy and Conservation Act required the FTC to establish labeling rules (energy costs and energy efficiency ratings) for such appliances as refrigerators and dishwashers.

The stated premise of the rising statutory standards was that "informed consumers are essential to the fair and efficient functioning of a free market economy."[7] Affirmative disclosure arose as a primary congressional approach to regulating business. The Supreme Court, at the same time, was striking down state laws restricting the dissemination of consumer information.[8] Restrictions on enforcement of "unconscionable" contracts and increasing seller liability for defective products under either common law or federal regulation by agencies like the FTC and the Consumer Product Safety Commission were justified by the claim that consumers lacked adequate information to understand the risks they were taking or to which they were exposed. This imperfect information prevented the market from properly allocating risks among the respective parties.[9] Even with these developments, the principles for determining when the market was unable to respond adequately to consumer information needs and what shape government intervention should take had only begun to evolve.

The Economics of Consumer Protection: Exploring Market Failure and Market Success

It is ironic that although consumer protection is a primary enforcement activity of the FTC, until the early 1970s the commission added minimal economic input into formulating consumer protection policy or case prep-aration. For instance, conventional wisdom judged unfair or deceptive advertising to be an issue that would not benefit from economic input. Predictably, prior to 1974, FTC economists, consistent with the rest of the profession, spent virtually no time on such issues. Not until the mid-1970s did the agency budget time for economic analysis of consumer protection policy. Finally, in 1978 a small division of economists was established to support this activity.

The original failure to supply economic analysis to consumer protection issues is perhaps understandable, since the "economics of information" is less than twenty years old. This line of economic inquiry expanded rapidly beyond advertising into contracts enforcement, liability rules, product quality, retailing organizations, industry structure, vertical integration, and the nature of investment patterns.[10] Investigation into the role of advertising as information in the market process has fundamentally altered conventional negative perceptions that advertising provided little value to consumers. As a consequence, greater understanding of when markets are failing and succeeding permits the scope of regulation to be narrowed. In large part, this new learning provided the intellectual foundation for changes in the FTC's approach to advertising and unfair industry practices during the tenure of Chairman James C. Miller III.

Phillip Nelson's seminal work showed that the kinds of advertising claims made for different goods, and hence the potential for deception, are a function of the characteristics of the good being promoted.[11] "Search goods," such as the style and quality of a dress, are largely verifiable before purchase. "Experience goods," such as the taste of soup, must be evaluated after purchase. Hard product information (versus value-laden claims or "puffery") about search goods is most effective because consumers can evaluate the information directly prior to purchase. Producers receive no pay-off for deception. False claims, on the other hand, may lead some consumers to purchase goods they must experience in order to judge. However, this ploy is self-destructive unless the firm can survive without repeat purchases and without developing a reputation for quality.

Advertising is now more fruitfully analyzed as a signal of quality and reliability. Investment in durable brand name capital (reputation) serves as a guarantee of quality and a constraint on deception.[12] This role for advertising is especially important for "credence goods," goods or, more often, services with characteristics whose quality cannot be easily evalu-ated by the nonexpert even after consumption. Auto repairs and physi-cian's services are examples.[13]

In summary, a more sophisticated understanding of the role of promo-tional information in the market process has tempered the unfavorable view of advertising. Consumer search, augmented by advertising, while not completely eliminating deception, constrains it effectively. In the face of an aggressive interventionist commission in the 1970s, economic analysis supported the need to restrict advertising regulation more closely to issues of fraud and explicit deception, with emphasis on the cost effectiveness of correcting that deception. Ambiguity for policymakers remains, but it is clear that the market mechanism is significantly more complex than was suggested by an earlier, simpler view of advertising, and it works in ways previously ignored.

Consumer Protection Enforcement before Reagan

The commission's consumer protection authority derives principally from section 5 of the Federal Trade Commission Act, which simply prohibits "unfair and deceptive acts and practices." The act defines neither unfairness nor deception; articulation of those concepts was left to the commission. Decades of interpretation, however, provided scarce refinement to the vague statutory terms.

DECEPTION

Over the years the commission settled on the principle that deception lay in any statement that had a "tendency or capacity to deceive."[14] Furthermore, the FTC applied that definition not only "for the protection of experts, but [also for] the public—that vast multitude which includes the ignorant, the unthinking and the credulous."[15] When an act or practice deceived a "significant minority" of these, that is, a significant minority interpreted a claim in a way that could have influenced their decision to purchase and the advertisement, so interpreted, was false, action was in order. The agency, rarely overturned by the courts, seemed to have looked for a "nontrivial minority," holding for example that an ad affecting fewer than 9 percent of consumers was deceptive.[16]

Under this approach, the commission successfully challenged the claim that "Dannon is known as nature's perfect food that science made better"; that a deodorant "kills strongest odors"; and that a certain brand of cigarettes is "always milder."[17] On the other hand the agency or the courts found nonactionable claims that a toothpaste will "beautify the smile"; that a diet plan is "easy"; and that a deodorant is "dry."[18]

The commission's deception authority thrived for decades with little opposition from Congress or the courts. The agency became, for all practical purposes, the Supreme Court of advertising, such was the judicial deference accorded its decisions. During this period, the commission "protected" consumers from ads promoting permanent hair dye bcause they would mislead consumers into believing that the product would dye hair that had not yet grown;[19] from the dime store jewelry department's sale of "turquoise rings" that are not really turquoise;[20] from the toy manufacturer who failed to disclose that its toys did not fire projectiles that actually exploded;[21] and from the maker of "First Prize" bobby pins, lest consumers think that a purchase would make them eligible for a contest.[22]

The ambiguous and occasionally frivolous approach to enforcing the prohibition on deceptive advertising and the latitude of prosecutorial discretion created a dilemma for advertisers, who could not predict with any accuracy which claims were permissible and which were not. Moreover, the agency had only to believe the claim influenced consumer decisions to search, not necessarily to buy, so that even if consumers learned the truth before purchase, the advertisement was actionable. Under this theory, only those who interpreted a claim in the same manner as the agency did in finding deception and relied on this interpretation rather than searching further benefitted from a typical FTC deception complaint.

As became increasingly apparent, this approach to enforcement of section 5 poorly served consumers. An order protecting the credulous could deny valuable information to the majority of those with ordinary intelligence. By prohibiting a grocer from advertising results of informal surveys of comparative prices (because people might mistake the surveys for scientific studies), the commission stifled beneficial price competition.[23] By barring advertisement of a favorable review of a specific automobile in a popular automobile magazine (because consumers might be misled to think that the magazine was recommending the car to the suburban family), the commission helped foster general ignorance about important characteristics of the car.[24] The definition of deception lacked objective specificity distinguishing these claims from misrepresentations that could actually injure consumers as a group.

Establishing the falsity of a claim can be difficult and costly to prove if resisted by the advertiser. After decades of challenging deceptive advertising under the falsity theory, the commission in 1970 broke new ground. The agency issued a complaint against Pfizer's "Un-burn" sunburn painkiller because it claimed to "stop sunburn pain in . . . less time than it takes . . . to slip out of [a] bikini;" it "relieves pain fast"; and "actually anesthetizes nerves."[25] In place of a traditional claim of falsity, the commission alleged that the advertiser did not have evidence before running the ad that proved the truth of each interpretation that could be drawn from the claim by a nontrivial minority of consumers. The complaint alleged that the ad implied its claims were substantiated by scientific evidence; in the absence of such substantiation, the ads were deceptive and unfair. The significance of this new approach was to shift the burden of proof from the commission, which previously had to prove the falsity of the ad, to the advertisers, who now had to establish a reasonable basis for each interpretation of each claim in an ad. The commissioners dismissed the deception claim but established the principle that it was unfair to make a product claim without having a prior "reasonable basis."[26]

After that decision, FTC advertising regulation was increasingly driven by the so-called Pfizer doctrine. By 1979 the prior substantiation doctrine had resulted in more than a dozen litigated matters and more than one hundred negotiated settlements.[27]

UNFAIRNESS

If the doctrine of deception had vague lines, the doctrine of unfairness had no shape at all. Early guidance proscribed practices that cause "substantial injury to consumers"; "offend public policy"; or are "immoral, unethical, oppressive or unscrupulous."[28] The Supreme Court, accepting such language, endorsed the commission's unbridled authority to declare unfair commercial practices that offended public policy.[29] However, defining "public policy" proved elusive.

The enactment of FTCIA in 1975, granting authority to promulgate general rules covering unfair and deceptive practices, greatly increased the importance of the issue. In its first rule, *Advertising of Ophthalmic Goods and Services*, the so-called "Eye-Glass Rule" issued in 1978, the commission developed new unfairness criteria. The "Eye-Glasses" test required two inquiries: (1) whether the acts or practices substantially harm consumers, including the economic and social benefits and losses flowing from the conduct; and (2) whether the challenged conduct offends public policy.[30]

Unfortunately, applying the two-part test did not require the agency consistently to test hypotheses of market failure. Evidence garnered to document the prevalence of alleged substandard practices was the subject of numerous proposed rules often consisting of fragmentary anecdotes that witnesses recounted at rulemaking hearings. Expectations that the regulatory process would improve the market's performance flowed more from naïve faith than objective analysis. As a consequence, proposed remedies not only were tenuously related to the problems they sought to address, but also often spawned a new array of unanticipated burdens for businesses and consumers.

Cut adrift from cost and benefit considerations, the commission's evaluation of frustrated consumer demands slipped into internal debates over what consumers should be demanding. These debates, spilling over into the public arena, alienated nearly every constituent. The commission discovered in its ill-fated escapade seeking to regulate children's commercials (the "Kid-vid" Rule)[31] that its focus on unfairness required even sharper definition. At its nadir, the agency acquired the sobriquet "National Nanny" in a *Washington Post* editorial that labeled kid-vid a "preposterous intervention."[32]

Because rulemaking conducted under the unfairness theory was directed at the practices of specific identifiable industries, affected groups created a vigorous constituency of dissent. The kid-vid debacle finally brought Congressional demand for articulation of the unfairness policy.[33] The commission undertook a review of the case law interpreting unfair acts and practices and synthesized a revised definition of elements constituting a violation. On 17 December 1980 the commission responded with an open letter (the Unfairness Statement) declaring that unfairness would be found if an act or practice caused injury that was (1) substantial, (2) not outweighed by countervailing benefits to consumers or competition, and (3) not reasonably avoidable by the injured consumers.[34] Unfair practices, then, were actions like coercion, intimidation, deception, or withholding material information.

Consumer Protection Policy in the Reagan Administration

James C. Miller III, President Reagan's choice to head the FTC, brought a different perspective on how to remedy the commission's woes. An economist with substantial federal government experience, he viewed his job as one of repairing an economically naïve commission that had overreached its regulatory mandate.[35]

The agenda for the agency's consumer protection mission was already established when the Miller team arrived. The new chairman committed himself to reducing the size of the agency. He also set out to reduce the commission's discretionary power by codifying specific definitions of unfairness and deception. He took aim at the commission's ad substantiation doctrine and at rules that lacked a sound economic basis. He announced his intention to rely more heavily on industry self-regulation. Most importantly, Miller declared his commitment to integrating economic analysis into the development of investigations, the prosecution of cases, and the justification of remedies for alleged market failure.[36]

The chairman met many of his goals and came impressively close to achieving his most ambitious objective—guaranteeing that the progress he made would be codified into new statutory language. He left the agency 30 percent smaller than when he took over. His commission terminated a number of economically indefensible rulemakings. The rules that did emerge from the commission were streamlined, shorn of their most objectionable provisions. The chairman managed to pull together a majority of the commission to issue a policy statement that defined actionable deception under section 5. Miller failed to make one important goal part of his lasting legacy: He could not parlay the commission's new definition into a similar definition in the agency's authorizing statute.

APPLYING THE UNFAIRNESS DOCTRINE TO INDIVIDUAL CASES

By 1981 the commission had progressed toward a consistent approach to defining unfair acts and practices in the context of specific cases. The current criteria—substantial injury not outweighed by benefits and not reasonably avoidable—do not pinpoint unfairness in a generally predictable way, but instead establish economic (cost-benefit) criteria for an act or practice to pass before being considered unlawful. The new standard has proven an effective deterrent to unfounded excursions in social engineering.

Those relatively few recent cases relying on unfairness as a theory of violation tend to resemble class actions for breach of contract. Case selection tends to focus on the systematic failure to meet obligations to consumers where injury on an individual level may be too small to support legal actions, but total injury can be substantial. The commission has successfully used this strategy to seek enforcement of warranties, to prevent the unilateral modification of contracts, and to ensure performance of promised services.[37] The judicial precedents set by recent cases and the fact that the new definition of unfairness and its subsequent enforcement drew no fire from Congress help assure the continued viability of this enforcement theory for the foreseeable future.

The next step toward an economically sound enforcement policy against unfairness practices came in the promulgation of the Credit Practices Rule in 1984. The rule, upheld on appeal,[38] confirmed the substantial injury, cost-benefit, and unavoidability criteria necessary for finding unfairness as set forth in the 1980 Unfairness Statement. In addition it outlined four preconditions for justifying imposition of a rule: (1) the unfair act or practice must be prevalent; (2) the act or practice must cause significant harm; (3) the proposed rule must be effective in reducing the harm; and (4) the benefit of the proposed rule must exceed its cost. Unless each of these conditions is met, an industrywide rule is inappropriate.

Finally, the commission offered guidance on the evidence necessary to justify a rule. Of the three types typically available, quantitative evidence, such as a research survey, expert testimony, and anecdotal evidence, the commission expressed a clear preference for hard data. Anecdotal evidence could provide "evidence that such harm exists [but] is rarely sufficient to provide the substantial evidence which the Commission requires in the rulemaking process."[39]

RULEMAKING: THE THEORY AND ITS RESULTS

The Miller FTC's most significant contribution to rulemaking was to establish this objective test for evaluating the evidentiary record developed during a rulemaking proceeding. The commission required systematic evidence—statistically valid surveys were preferred—before concluding that a practice under scrutiny justified industrywide regulation. A record derived from anecdotes and "horror stories" was insufficient to satisfy this test. Since many of the pending rulemaking decisions had little else, they were canceled.

When the Miller team arrived in 1981, there were nineteen pending trade regulation rules. Of these, only three—the Funeral Rule, the Used Car Rule, and the Credit Practices Rule—have been promulgated in previously unregulated industries. The final rules impose fewer restrictions on the industry than those initially imposed. Several major sectors of the economy targeted for regulatory action escaped the stultifying effect of federal intervention. A rule "federalizing" the vocabulary of food sellers and requiring disclosure of various nutritional details died on the commission's table. The health spa industry's practice of seeking early payments for membership was left to case-by-case enforcement when the commission realized that the perceived abuses were not prevalent and the rule's proposed remedy could devastate legitimate operators. Antacid manufacturers were spared additional labeling requirements when the rulemaking record failed to support allegations that a significant segment of the population was ignorant of the contents of products like Tums. In addition, the commission reduced the burdens or enhanced the benefits for several regulated industries through amendments to existing regulations.

In each of the promulgated rules, congressional involvement raised the level of debate to a relatively high political pitch. Nevertheless, as outlined in the statements of basis and purpose accompanying each rule, the application of the objective evidentiary test for rulemaking allowed the commission to rely on more credible and convincing evidence of abuses. More importantly, it is on this evidentiary basis that federal circuit courts now review challenged rules.[40] Now that the commission has imposed a greater burden on itself to justify issuing rules, a reviewing court will have a more substantial basis on which to challenge the agency's decision.

DEFINING AND APPLYING THE DECEPTION STATEMENT

As stated previously, the most prominent activity of the Bureau of Consumer Protection—policing commercial advertising—has always presented the most difficult challenge. Unlike unfairness, neither significant congressional discontent nor eager coalitions jumped on the bandwagon of deception reform. Victims of overzealous enforcement of deception are likely to be consumers denied access to beneficial information. The beneficiaries (aside from the prosecutors) may paradoxically be the larger companies, because strict enforcement tends to raise costs for smaller entrepreneurs and potential competitors.[41]

The agency's most strident controversy arose from Miller's immediate campaign to have Congress include language in the Federal Trade Commission Act that would more clearly define deception and (presumably) limit the reach of FTC enforcement. Two years into Miller's tenure, a sharply divided commission finally issued a policy statement replacing the "tendency to deceive" language by declaring deceptive an act or practice "that is likely to mislead the consumer acting reasonably in the circumstances, to the consumer's detriment."[42] Although the statement, like the Unfairness Policy Statement, was in part a synthesis of reasoning in past cases, it also incorporated the developing economic theory of information. Like the unfairness statement, the deception statement established a higher, more economically justified standard of proof.

For a finding of deception, the commission first requires a representation, practice, or omission that would mislead the consumer, such as false oral or written claims, misleading price claims, bait-and-switch tactics, or failure to perform promised sales. Second, the commission examines deception from the perspective of consumers acting reasonably in the circumstances. The commission, keeping in mind the specific audience to whom the advertisement is directed, considers deception from the eyes of "the average listener"; the "impression that [an ad] is likely to make on the general populace"; or "in light of the sophistication and understanding of the persons to whom they were directed."[43] Third, the deception must be "material," that is, the consumer would likely choose differently but for the deception.

Neither the House nor Senate was willing to adopt these criteria as the statutory definition of deception. State attorneys general objected to the increased burden of proof such a standard could impose on the enforcement of state consumer protection acts. Despite this opposition, Miller managed to go farther than his critics had hoped, but fell short of his goal of dramatic deregulation. Despite the resistance of dissenting commissioners and constituents, the principles of the Deception Policy Statement have worked their way into commission law. The commission now applies the principles of the statement in adjudications,[44] one of which has been affirmed on appeal.[45] Enforcement energies have turned to stopping such consumer fraud as the misrepresentation of the value of investments, the sale of bogus health services, and the fraudulent theft of homes.[46] The commission avoids pursuing advertisers of inexpensive, frequently purchased products, where the market is as likely as the government to remedy exaggerated claims. Instead the agency has challenged claims relating to health improvement, energy conservation, and safety.[47]

The prior substantiation doctrine has emerged intact, albeit with limitations and a more rational basis than before. A 1984 commission policy statement explains that the amount and the sophistication of information needed to substantiate a claim would depend on the costs and benefits associated with proving the claim.[48] When the veracity of a claim matters little to consumers, or the cost of the proof is exorbitant—for example with cosmetics—less proof is required. When veracity is important—for example, with hazardous products—more substantiation would be appropriate. Postclaim substantiation, while not a defense for the requirement of prior substantiation, will also be considered in determining the veracity of claims.

Conclusions

Robert Tollison, former director of the Bureau of Economics at the FTC, reviewing antitrust enforcement, challenges the theory that people matter: "Change the decision makers and the policy will change. That sounds good but it never seems to work. Government cranks along by an internal logic of its own."[49] Tollison is correct to a degree. Nevertheless, substantial changes in consumer protection enforcement at the FTC were wrought during the last two decades. One set of administrators helped expand radically the FTC's power; then another set moved to cut it back. These were conscious moves by people with a mission. The force of maturing theoretical developments in the economics of information and the efforts of individuals in key posts to integrate economic analysis into policy decisions fundamentally altered the output of a major regulatory agency.

The issue of more abiding interest is the long-run influence of these changes on commission policy. The first term of the Reagan administration was bereft of legislative victories codifying sensible FTC policy. Nevertheless, the legal tally is far from empty. Commission precedent, upheld by the federal courts, now embraces many of the doctrines advanced by Miller. These cannot easily be discarded. While it would be disingenuous to expect that advocates of free markets will ever convert politicians, who do not win elections by expressing devotion to economic theory, it is encouraging that the economic approach has won the respect of at least one dedicated recalcitrant. As Michael Pertschuk, self-confessed "cost-benefit draft resister," stated: "The economists (and presumably their trade) earned my grudging respect . . . for their dogged insistence that we *think through* the reality of what we believed we were achieving with our intervention in the marketplace."[50] After the heady binge of the 1970s, it is unlikely that FTC regulators will soon override the injection of economic rigor into the corpus regulati.

Notes

1. Edward Cox, Robert Fellmeth, and John Schultz, *The Nader Report on the Federal Trade Commission* (New York: Barron Press, 1969); and American Bar Association, *Report of the ABA Commission to Study the Federal Trade Commission* (1969). The latter report concluded, "Notwithstanding the great potential of the FTC in the field of antitrust and consumer protection, if change does not occur, there will be no substantial purpose to be served by its continued existence; the essential work to be done must then be carried on by other governmental institutions" (p. 3).

2. National Petroleum Refiners Association v. FTC, 482 F 2d 672 (D.C. Cir. 1 973), esp. n. 27.

3. 87 Stat. 591 (1973). This act also expanded the commission's information-gathering power and allowed it to seek temporary injunctions and restraining orders when in the public interest.

4. 15 U.S.C. §57a (1976).

5. *Washington Post,* February 1977, p. C-1.

6. The act also attempted to improved consumer access to remedies. For a detailed discussion, see George Priest, "Special Statutes: The Structure and Operation of the Magnuson-Moss Warranty Act," in Kenneth Clarkson and Timothy Muris, eds., *The Federal Trade Commission since 1970* (Cambridge: Cambridge University Press, 1981), pp. 246–76.

7. Fair Packaging and Labeling Act 15 U.S.C. §§1451–1461 (1976).

8. Virginia State Board of Pharmacy v. Virginia Citizens Consumer Council, Inc., 425 U. S. 748 (1976).

9. For a more complete discussion, see Howard Beales, Richard Craswell, and Steven Salop, "The Efficient Regulation of Consumer Information," *Journal of Law and Economics* 24 (December 1981): 491–539.

10. For an excellent review of the literature, from which this section is drawn, see Pauline Ippolito, "Consumer Protection Economics: A Selective Survey," in Pauline Ippolito and David Scheffman (eds.), *Empirical Approaches to Consumer Protection Economics* (Washington D.C.: Federal Trade Commission, 1986), pp. 1–33.

11. Phillip Nelson, "Information and Consumer Behavior," *Journal of Political Economy* 78 (March/April 1970): 311–29; and "Advertising as Information," *Journal of Political Economy* 81 (July/August): 729–54.

12. Benjamin Klein and Keith Leffler, "Market Forces in Assuring Contractual Performance," *Journal of Political Economy* 89 (August 1981): 615–41.

13. Michael Darby and Edi Karni, "Free Competition and the Optimal Amount of Fraud," *Journal of Law and Economics* 16 (April 1973): 67–88. See also Carl

Shapiro, "Premiums for High-Quality Products as Returns to Reputation," *Quarterly Journal of Economics* 98 (November 1983): 659–79; Richard Kihlstrom and Michael Riordan, "Advertising as a Signal," *Journal of Political Economy* 92 (June 1984): 427–50.

14. See generally Charles of the Ritz Distributors Corp. v. FTC, 143 F. 2d 676 (2d Cir. 1944).

15. Id. at 679.

16. Giant Food Inc. v. FTC, 322 F. 2d 981 (D.C. Cir. 1963) and other citations in Mark Grady, "Regulating Information: Advertising Overview," in Clarkson and Muris (eds.), *The Federal Trade Commission*, pp. 234–35.

17. Dannon Milk Products, 61 FTC 840, 842 (1962); Sebrone Co., 135 F. 2d 676, 678 (7th Cir. 1943); Liggett & Myers Tobacco Co., 55 FTC 354, 361 (1958); cited in Mark Grady, "Regulating Information," p. 235.

18. Ibid., p. 235.

19. The circuit court expressed disbelief that any consumer would be gullible but refused to overturn the commission's finding. (Gelb v. FTC 144 F. 2d 580 [2d. Cir. 1944]).

20. FTC v. G & G, 62 FTC 663 (1963).

21. FTC v. Marx, 61 FTC 269 (1962).

22. FTC v. Reiser, 61 FTC 1378 (1962).

23. FTC v. Kroger, 98 FTC 639, modified 100 FTC 573 (1982).

24. FTC v. General Motors, 102 FTC 1741 (1983).

25. FTC v. Pfizer, Inc., 81 FTC 23, 24 (1972).

26. A reasonable basis was not specified, but could range from a scientific study to a literature review. The burden fell on manufacturers because they have the "ability, the know-how, the equipment, the time and the resources to undertake such information by testing or otherwise—the consumer usually does not" (ibid., p. 62). Under pressure from Ralph Nader's petition to promulgate a trade regulation rule requiring national advertisers routinely to submit to the commission documents substantiating advertising claims, the commission adopted in 1971 a resolution requiring advertisers to submit to the commission on demand relevant substantial materials in their possession when they made their claims. The submission, eventually to be released publicly, would inform consumers of unsubstantiated claims and encourage competitors to challenge them. The submissions proved too technical for effective review by nonexperts.

27. See Grady, "Regulating Information," pp. 236–37.

28. The Cigarette Rule, *Federal Register* 29 (1964): 8355.

29. FTC v. Sperry & Hutchinson Co., 405 U.S. 233 (1972).

30. Advertising of Ophthalmic Goods and Services, *Federal Register* 43 (1978): 24000–1.

31. The kid-vid rulemaking investigated whether the government should: (1) ban all television seen by children too young to evaluate the selling purpose of the advertising, (2) ban televised advertising of sugared products directed at older children, and (3) require television advertising of sugared food directed at older children not covered in (2) to be balanced by nutritional and/or health disclosures

funded by advertisers. See *FTC Staff Report on Television Advertising to Children* (February 1978).

32. *Washington Post,* 1 March 1978.

33. Letter of 13 June 1980 to Chairman Pertschuk from the Consumer Subcommittee of the Senate Committee on Commerce, Science, and Transportation, requesting the commission's views on whether the agency's authority should be limited to regulating "false or deceptive" commercial advertising.

34. Commission Statement of Policy on the Scope of the Consumer Unfairness Jurisdiction, letter from Chairman James C. Miller III to Senators Danforth and Ford (17 December 1980).

35. Although he had a head start as leader of Reagan's FTC transition team, Miller suffered the disadvantage of starting about nine months late. It was not until October 1981 that a Republican vacancy opened at the commission.

36. Miller's plans for the commission can be gleaned from a document, claimed to be the Reagan-Bush Transition Report on the FTC, which was inserted in the *Congressional Record* (21 September 1981). Although he never acknowledged the bona fides of the (supposedly nonpublic) document, Miller immediately embraced its recommendations.

37. Ward Corp., D. 9160 (10 March 1982); Orkin Exterminating Co., D. 9176 (8 May 1984); and FTC v. Lady Venus Centers, Inc., Civ. No. 3-84-0158 (M.D. Tenn.; 16 February 1984).

38. American Financial Services Assoc. v. FTC, 767 F. 2d 957 (USCA, D.C. Cir. 1985).

39. Credit Practices Statement of Basis and Purpose, *Federal Register* 49 (1984): 7740, 7742.

40. See American Financial Services Assoc. v. F.T.C., 767 F. 2d 957 (USCA, D.C. Cir. 1985).

41. See e.g. Richard Higgins and Fred McChesney, "An Economic Analysis of the FTC's Ad Substantiation Program," in Pauline Ippolito and Keith Scheffman, (eds.), *Consumer Protection Economics* (1986). Keith Leffler and Raymond Sauer offer alternative explanations in "The Effects of the Advertising Substantiation Program on Advertising Agencies," ibid.

42. Commission Enforcement Policy Statement on Deception, letter from chairman James C. Miller III to Hon. John D. Dingell (14 October 1983). Reported in 45 *Antitrust and Trade Reg. Rep.* (BNA) 689 (27 October 1983) with dissents. The Minority Statement proposed a finding of deception if (1) a practice has the *tendency* or *capacity* to mislead, (2) the practice impacts a *substantial* number of consumers, and (3) the practice misleads with regard to *material* facts (46 *Antitrust and Trade Reg. Rep.* [BNA] 372 [1 March 1984]).

43. Miller letter to Dingell, pp. 8–10.

44. See for example Cliffdale Associates, Inc., 103 FTC 110 (1984); Thompson Medical Co., Inc., 104 FTC 648 (1984) Southwest Sunsites, 105 FTC 7 (1985). In International Harvester, 104 FTC 949 (1984), the commission extended the principles in the statement to a failure to disclose the case involving a risk of fuel geysering in certain farm tractors. The case is important for, among other reasons,

the explicit reliance on cost-benefit analysis to determine whether risk of injury was such that the benefits of disclosure outweighed the burden of disseminating the information (in particular the diminished usefulness of important information by the deluge of information that would be necessary to disclose all possible facts).

45. Southwest Sunsites, 785 F. 2d 1431 (9th Cir. 1986).

46. See, respectively, FTC v. Alaska Land Leasing, Inc., Civ. No. 84-5416, AWT (PX) (C.D. Cal. filed 23 July 1984); FTC v. Furman, 84-0803-A (E.D. Va.; filed 6 August 1984); and FTC v. Rita Walker and Associates, Inc., Civ. No. 83-29-2962 (D.D.C., October 5, 1983).

47. See, respectively, General Nutrition, Inc., D. 9175 (1984); Plaskolite, Inc., 101 F.T.C. 344 (1983); and Amana Refrigeration, Inc., D. 9162 (30 September 1983) and Foote, Cone and Belding, C-3116 (30 September 1983).

48. Policy Statement Regarding Advertising Substantiation, *Federal Register* 49 (2 August 1984): 30999.

49. Robert D. Tollison, "Public Choice and Antitrust," *Cato Journal* 4 (Winter 1985): 905–6.

50. Michael Pertschuk, *Revolt against Regulation* (Berkeley: University of California Press, 1982), p. 139.

5

Antitrust Policy in the Reagan Administration: Pyrrhic Victories?

William F. Shughart II

Introduction

There were two distinct reactions to the November 1980 election returns in the corridors of the building on Pennsylvania Avenue that serves as headquarters of the Federal Trade Commission (FTC). Although one was positive and the other negative, both were based on the feeling that important changes were on the horizon. No one could be quite sure what form these changes might take, but the common perception was that an era of antitrust activism was drawing to a close. Particularly distressed were those who, under the strong leadership of FTC Chairman Michael Pertschuk, had come to regard antitrust policy as a kind of economic engineering project. Over the next few months, ongoing work slowed noticeably. Sales of the book on the FTC edited by Clarkson and Muris (1981) soared. Staff members poured over bootlegged copies of the Reagan Transition Team Reports on the FTC and Department of Justice and waited for the new world of antitrust to take shape. Reactions at the Antitrust Division must have been quite similar.

How did the federal antitrust agencies actually fare during the next six years? Did the radical changes that were expected materialize? What accounts for shifts in antitrust policy, if any, that took place? Without the benefit of much hindsight, answers to such questions may be premature. In a sense, however, the Reagan imprint on antitrust has been fully made. The president's early appointees to antitrust policymaking positions have departed, and noteworthy changes are unlikely to occur in the remaining

I am grateful to Fred McChesney and Robert Tollison for comments on an earlier draft. Remaining errors are my own.

months of his administration. Thus, as President Reagan's second term reaches its midpoint, it is possible to begin marking his antitrust report card.

With this in mind, the next section provides the intellectual background of Reagan antitrust philosophy; the following section contains an overview of selected antitrust policy topics, and the last section offers some concluding remarks, including horizontal and vertical restraints, with an emphasis on public policies toward merger; deregulatory initiatives; and the general drift of antitrust law enforcement activity. The main theme throughout the discussion concerns the transitory nature of the changes that occurred.

Although a firm evaluation must await the judgment of history, it seems fair to say that the character of antitrust policy during the Reagan years has been shaped by the personalities of its administrators rather than by fundamental changes in the law or institutions of antitrust.[1] This simply means that future appointees to the antitrust bureaucracy, bringing with them perhaps an inclination toward more government intervention into the private economy, will face few constraints in remaking the enforcement agencies in their own image. Thus those critical of antitrust policy during the Reagan administration can take solace in the fact that its direction is easily reversible. Those who feel otherwise cannot take much comfort.

Intellectual Background

Antitrust policy in the early days of the Reagan administration was marked by the arrival in Washington of a group of economists and lawyers who brought with them two intellectual traditions that had been underrepresented along the banks of the Potomac River during the 1970s. One was the so-called new learning in industrial organization. This approach challenged the conventional wisdom that a direct link exists between the structure of an industry (measured in terms of the number of competing firms), its conduct (types of business practices adopted), and its performance (quantity of output produced and level of prices charged).[2] The other intellectual capital was familiarity with the interest group theory of regulation, which stresses that models of government behavior must take into account the private interests of those who make public policy.[3] These two traditions were most visibly personified by William F. Baxter, a Stanford University law professor with a strong background in economics who was President Reagan's initial appointee to the post of Assistant Attorney General for Antitrust, and James C. Miller III, the first professional economist to serve as FTC chairman. But economists and lawyers with similar backgrounds also came to populate many of the upper- and middle-management positions in both agencies.

Despite George Stigler's (1982) observation that economists have supplied precious little in the way of tested knowledge to guide antitrust policy, it is nevertheless true that evidence casting doubt on the structure-conduct-performance (S-C-P) paradigm had been accumulating during the 1970s. The S-C-P model held that the empirically observable correlation between high industrial concentration and high profits was a consequence of market power. That is, the power over price available to the small number of large firms operating in highly concentrated industries enabled them to earn above-normal profits at the expense of consumers of their products. Accordingly, such industries were thought to be appropriate targets for antitrust intervention. Such intervention would be aimed at restraining the use of certain business practices that facilitated the exercise of market power. The law stood ready to challenge proposed mergers in an effort to prevent the industry from becoming more concentrated, or at times went so far as to attempt a policy of deconcentration by challenging mergers consummated in the past. Thus began the big headline-grabbing cases against AT&T, IBM, and the major U.S. cereal and gasoline producers.[4]

Although the S-C-P paradigm was still the dominant philosophy of antitrust enforcement, battle lines were being drawn during the 1970s on the basis of evidence supplied by Brozen (1971), Demsetz (1974), Peltzman (1977), and others that suggested that above-normal profit levels observed in highly concentrated industries were due to economic efficiency rather than market power. That is, high levels of industrial concentration could be better explained by the survival over time of a small number of efficient firms whose profitability was traceable to their ability to economize on productive resources. This of course implied that a social policy hostile to high concentration would operate to the detriment of consumer welfare. Such criticisms, while in no way making the S-C-P paradigm a dead letter, did create in the minds of the Reagan appointees a healthy skepticism about one of antitrust's basic theoretical underpinnings.

The second theme of the Reagan administration's antitrust philosophy, the interest group theory of regulation, resulted from the disenchantment with federal enforcement efforts that had been growing from almost the time that the basic legislative framework of U.S. antitrust policy was established at the turn of the century. By 1981 the legal and economic literature was replete with analyses of individual antitrust cases that sharply criticized enforcement agencies and the courts for their failure to apply the laws to better effect. The typical case study found that evidence of anticompetition presented at trial by the government was "weak and at times bordered on fiction"; that "neither the government nor the Courts seemed able to distinguish competition from monopolizing" (Peterman 1975a, p. 143); and that at best "nothing was accomplished by bringing this case" (Peterman 1975b, p. 393). Other critiques suggested procompetitive explanations for the challenged practices (Peterman 1979, Cummings and Ruhter 1979), contended that the economic theory underlying the case was "erroneous" (Flath 1980), or focused on the ineffectiveness of the remedy imposed (Zelenitz 1980).[5] These antitrust policy failures were usually attributed to one or more of a number of correctable errors, leading critics to recommend that enforcement agencies do a better job, that lawyers and judges learn economic principles, or that incumbent policy makers be replaced with people better able to serve the public interest.

This concept of antitrust, which rests on the assumption that policy is formulated by a fallible but basically benign government, stands in stark contrast to the interest-group model. Emphasizing that the ultimate level and pattern of government action results from the interplay between self-interested demanders of wealth transfers and self-interested suppliers of regulation who seek political survival, the interest-group theory poses the question, which "public" and whose "interest" does antitrust serve? The issues raised in answering this question involve such topics as the extent to which Congress influences antitrust case selection, who wins and who loses from enforcement efforts, and the origins of antitrust statutes. In short, the interest-group model provides the basis for a positive theory of antitrust policy.[6]

To summarize, President Reagan's appointees to the antitrust bureaucracy brought with them two intellectual traditions that raised doubts about conventional antitrust wisdom. On the one hand, the new learning in industrial organization suggested that the antitrust attack on big business was based on an incorrect reading of the link between concentration and profits. On the other hand the interest-group model of regulation created suspicions about the process as well as the consequences of antitrust enforcement. There thus existed a strong theoretical and empirical basis for change in antitrust policy. Whether or not these changes materialized is taken up in the following section.

Overview of Antitrust Policy in the Reagan Administration

As it unfolded, the Reagan administration's antitrust policy was marked by a series of events that changed the tenor, if not the substance, of federal law enforcement. These included the promulgation in 1981 of new merger guidelines; the closing or dismissal of several major antitrust cases; the issuing of antitrust complaints against public-sponsored monopolies; and allocation of budgetary resources for interventions before other government agencies for the purpose of stating opinions about the competitive consequences of proposed rules and regulations. All of these changes in direction were guided by the administration's desire to place a stronger emphasis on economic analysis in the conduct of antitrust policy.

This shift in emphasis carried over to consumer protection matters at the FTC. The broad language of the FTC Act, which bans, in part, "unfair or deceptive acts or practices in commerce," gives the commission enforcement authority in the areas of advertising, fraud and deception, credit and billing arrangements, and so on. Indeed, under the Magnuson-Moss Warranty/Federal Trade Commission Improvement Act of 1975 (P.L. 93-637, 15 U.S.C. 2301-2310), the commission has the power to promulgate industrywide rules and regulations. As the Reagan administration took office, the commission had underway a whole series of costly rulemaking proceedings involving, among others, used car dealers, funeral homes, holders of commercial paper, antacid producers, and mobile home sellers. The Reagan effort in this area was to turn away from industrywide regulation and return the FTC's consumer protection mission to traditional fraud and deception cases. This approach dovetailed with the administration's antitrust policy: It was brought about by tightening evidentiary standards applied to proposed rules, and it sought through conventional cost-benefit tests some assurance that consumer injury was widespread enough to justify attacking the problem through rulemaking rather than on a case-by-case basis. The resulting reduction in the number of rulemaking proceedings also freed agency resources that could be employed in the commission's antitrust mission.

As mentioned earlier, however, none of these policy shifts can be viewed as permanent. Because the basic language of the Sherman, Clayton, and FTC acts remains unaltered, there is nothing to prevent future antitrust bureaucracies from returning to business as usual.[7] This point serves as the theme of the following overview.

BREAD-AND-BUTTER ANTITRUST

The return to what Tollison (1983) refers to as bread-and-butter antitrust provides a good illustration of the Reagan administration's law enforcement philosophy. Antitrust complaints based on exotic vertical and "shared monopoly" theories came to a virtual halt—the focus of Reagan policy shifted to more traditional horizontal restraint-of-trade matters.

Dismissal of the protracted, resource-consuming investigations of AT & T, IBM, and the principal gasoline and cereal producers deserves

recognition as one of the major victories of Reagan antitrust policy.[8] Each
of these matters had dragged on for years without producing any coherent
legal or economic theory about what antitrust violations were at issue.
Exxon for example had employed the energies of more than 200 FTC staff
attorneys during a ten-year period, ending up with not much more than
thousands of pages of microfilmed company documents and reams of
internal memoranda. The celebrated cereals case met similar pitfalls, ultimately being beaten by legal procedure in hearings before an administrative law judge. (To the commission's credit, the complaint was
dismissed with prejudice on the staff's appeal of the ALJ's findings.)

Both of these matters, along with the Justice Department's quixotic
pursuit of IBM, had become costly embarrassments to the enforcement
agencies. All may have collapsed of their own weight regardless of the
political philosophy of the administration in office. Given that these investigations had proceeded unchecked through the terms of at least two
previous presidents, however, the timing of their deaths should be counted
in the plus column of Reagan antitrust policy.

If the Reagan administration's shift away from headline-grabbing cases
against large firms in concentrated industries is to be counted as a major
victory, then its policy towards mergers, as contained in the 1982 Department of Justice Merger Guidelines, must be counted as a major failure.[9]

The guidelines issued by the Justice Department in 1982 represented the
agency's first revision to its statement on mergers since such principles had
been promulgated in 1968. On the same day, the FTC released a written
statement on horizontal mergers for the first time in its history. The
antitrust bar had anticipated both events with great interest. Speculation
had run rampant during the time the documents were being prepared
because the new guidelines were to be one of the administration's first
formal statements about its approach to antitrust policy. The denouement
fell far short of its buildup.

Although the new merger guidelines paid much more attention than had
their predecessor to efficiency considerations, technological change, and
other factors mitigating the potential anticompetitive effects of merger,
they retained the numerical concentration measures that are the meat and
potatoes of structural antitrust analysis. More importantly, the structural
numerics were not made very much looser. For all practical purposes, the
main innovation of the 1982 guidelines was to substitute the slightly
mysterious Hirschman-Herfindahl Index (HHI) for the four-firm concentration ratio as a measure for determining whether an industry was
"concentrated" (a change of no consequence to anyone but those laboring
in the antitrust vineyard).

To illustrate the differences between the two sets of merger criteria, consider a merger in a "concentrated" market, assuming that the acquiring firm has a market share of 15 percent. ("Concentrated" markets are defined as those in which the HHI is 1800 or more, which is approximately equivalent to a case where the four largest firms in the industry account for 70 percent of sales.) Under the 1968 guidelines, mergers in which the acquired firm's market share was 1 percent or more would likely be challenged by antitrust authorities. The threshold market share for the acquired firm in similar circumstances was raised to about 5 percent under the 1982 guidelines. Thus the screen was made looser, but not by much.[10]

The failure of the Reagan antitrust bureaucracy to relax substantially, if not eliminate, numerical merger criteria is important not because rules are by themselves undesirable, but because the new guidelines preserved the essentials of the structuralist approach to merger analysis. Given a modicum of creativity on the part of antitrust lawyers and economists, markets can be defined in such a way that any industry becomes "concentrated." (If the neighborhood is found to be the relevant market for antitrust purposes, the corner dry cleaner becomes a monopolist.) Thus even though more mergers presumably pass muster under the new criteria than the old, Reagan antitrust policy had little impact on the *process* of merger analysis. Evidence to this effect is given by the fact that the antitrust bureaucracy took to the new guidelines with remarkable alacrity.

An interesting sidelight on the political economy of antitrust enforcement is given by the FTC's reaction to the Justice Department's new merger guidelines. As mentioned earlier, on the same day that the 1982 guidelines were promulgated, the commission, for the first time in its history, issued a statement of principles concerning horizontal mergers. Although the staffs of the two agencies had coordinated their efforts while the documents were in preparation (and indeed Chairman Miller emphasized the harmony between the separate enforcement philosophies), the FTC statement ultimately differed from the Justice Department guidelines in an important way: It contained no numerical merger criteria.[11] This approach was justified on the ground "that it would be unwise for the two agencies to publish fairly precise standards that might differ in even minor respects."[12]

The consequence of this difference was quite dramatic—the commission's statement was virtually dead on arrival as a matter of public merger policy. The FTC attorneys quickly embraced the Department of Justice (DOJ) guidelines because, in contrast to the approach taken by their own agency, DOJ standards were quite compatible with traditional merger analysis. Quantitative concentration data are much more understandable than the nonnumeric, non-market-share considerations discussed in the commission's statement. Thus although the revised DOJ guidelines required users to learn to calculate a new index of market concentration, the Justice Department approach dominated because it was mechanical. Merger analysis could continue to be based on market definition and market shares.

On the other side of the coin, it is worth noting that a number of large, highly visible horizontal combinations, including several oil industry mergers and the joint venture between General Motors and Toyota, did go through (albeit with some restrictions) during the Reagan years. Such agreements would undoubtedly have met stiffer challenges under previous administrations. Overall, however, structuralism continued to be the economic order of the day in the Reagan approach to analysis of mergers and acquisitions.

Some minor progress was made by the Reagan administration on the other main topic of bread-and-butter antitrust, vertical restraints of trade. By and large this represented a continuation of past trends because there are simply not very many vertical mergers proposed for antitrust scrutiny. Moreover, the current crop of antitrust enforcers is well-schooled in the economic theories of the firm, which view vertical relationships as generally promoting efficiency.

Vertical price restraints are a different story, however. Despite mounting evidence that such practices as retail price maintenance can enhance the competitiveness of markets, little progress was made by enforcement agencies in moving toward a rule-of-reason standard of analysis, that is, treating each case on its merits by weighing possible pro-and anticompetitive effects. To be fair, the potential for change in this area is mightily burdened by judicial precedent, which treats vertical price restrictions as fundamentally different from nonprice restraints, subjecting the former to a per se illegal standard. However, this just highlights the Reagan administration's failure to push for changes in the antitrust law as a means of overcoming the courts' intransigence.

In sum, the Reagan record on traditional antitrust matters is mixed at best. Despite its success in shifting the focus of law enforcement away from "shared monopoly" and other exotic legal theories having little economic foundation, it failed to bring about fundamental change in analysis of mergers or vertical price restraints. Although the dismissal of a number of costly investigations is to be commended, Reagan antitrust policy at this point has left no legacy that assures us that the Antitrust Division and the FTC will not return to business as usual.[13]

DEREGULATORY INITIATIVES

As Demsetz (1974) has argued, there are two systems of belief about monopoly: One sees monopoly in the private sector as the primary threat; the other expresses more concern about government-sponsored monopoly. This distinction ilustrates the Reagan antitrust philosophy better than any other. During the Reagan years, the FTC and to a lesser extent the Antitrust Division allocated budgetary resources for efforts to do something about monopoly in the public sector.

The attack was carried out on two fronts. One was the co-called competition advocacy program initiated by Chairman Miller, which involved intervening before other agencies to put forth the commission's opinions about the competitive consequences of proposed rules and regulations. Targets ran the gamut of the federal regulatory agencies, including the U.S. Postal Service, the International Trade Commission, the Interstate Commerce Commission, and the Federal Aviation Administration, with the commission offering testimony on topics ranging from steel import quotas to the allocation of landing rights at commercial airports. The importance of this effort lies in its potential for stemming the tide of monopolies backed by the force of law. However, because the intervention program is so much a brainchild of Chairman Miller, its fate following his departure from the commission is uncertain.

The second line of attack consisted of a series of antitrust cases initiated by the FTC against the learned professions and other government-sponsored monopolies at state and local levels, as well as suits brought by the Antitrust Division involving bid-rigging in government contracts.

One of the main targets of these attacks was the so-called *Noerr-Pennington* doctrine, which offers antitrust immunity to joint lobbying activities designed to influence public officals even though such efforts are intended to eliminate competition.[14] The Reagan FTC initiated a somewhat controversial series of studies for the purpose of identifying areas where novel antitrust cases might be used to test the limits of the doctrine.

An example of this new direction involved standard-setting activities undertaken by various industry trade associations; such activities are often aided and abetted by government. The Consumer Product Safety commission, for instance, routinely encourages trade associations to adopt uniform, industrywide safety standards for products produced by its members. These standards often specify design, manufacturing, and packaging requirements intended to reduce the risk of injury to consumers using product. Such standards also raise manufacturing costs, however, and this tends to benefit large, profitable firms that are better able to absorb cost increases at the expense of their smaller, less efficient rivals. In addition, potential entrants face higher start-up costs, and consumer welfare is reduced for those who find the added product safety to be worth less than its added cost. This is just another example of the government as part of the antitrust problem. The FTC's interest in such issues during the Reagan years did indeed represent a novel direction in antitrust policy.

It is much too early to evaluate these efforts—the approach is novel, the state-action doctrine protects most state and local government monopoly power, and the receptiveness of the courts to such theories is as yet unclear. But the government's penchant for granting exclusive franchises for such services as taxicabs and cable television, imposing occupational licensing requirements, promulgating building and safety codes that benefit some firms at the expense of others, and so on, represents a major source of anticompetitive behavior in the economy. The Reagan administration's use of antitrust laws to attack monopoly in the public sector therefore represents a potentially important policy change.

THE GENERAL DRIFT IN ANTITRUST POLICY

Given the conservative-libertarian backgrounds of President Reagan's appointees to the antitrust bureaucracy, the lack of substantive change in the areas of antitrust policy just outlined is disappointing. Even though the potential for radical policy shifts was constrained by the language of the law, the weight of judicial precedent, and other factors, it is nevertheless discouraging that more opportunities were not seized, especially those which would have had an impact beyond 1988.

If one looks at only the short run, however, it is clear that the Reagan years deviated significantly from the long-term trend in antitrust policy. Data in Table 5.1 show a substantial reduction in case output during the 1980–84 period, with a more dramatic effect at the FTC. Compared with the previous five-year period, the commission instituted about 20 percent fewer cases; total antitrust output declined on the order of 10 percent. The reduction in enforcement actions during the Reagan antitrust years (1981–84) brought case figures down to levels that, at least at the FTC, had not been seen for twenty years.[15]

Of course, total case output is not the sole criterion for judging the success or failure of antitrust policy in the Reagan administration. Yet the reduction in enforcement actions is more important than it appears on the surface. Bureaucratic incentives run strongly in the direction of producing visible output.[16] The more investigations that are underway, the more opportunities there are for the attorney staff to build the human capital that is valuable in postgovernment employment, and the larger and more secure are the antitrust agencies. Reducing output cuts at the heart of bureaucracies, and case data therefore reflect measurable success by Reagan appointees on the internal agency battlefield.

The shift of Reagan antitrust enforcement toward traditional horizontal restraint of trade matters may also have a positive effect on the general drift of antitrust policy, at least in the short run. This is because the FTC, for one, has been more successful historically in prosecuting horizontal matters, in the sense that the commission's decisions in such cases have been

Table 5.1
Antitrust Cases Instituted by the Federal Enforcement Agencies, 1965–84

Year	Number of DOJ Cases	Number of FTC Cases	Total
1965	29	18	47
1966	36	19	55
1967	34	12	46
1968	47	15	62
1969	43	14	57
1965–69	189	78	267
1970	54	11	65
1971	43	25	68
1972	72	16	88
1973	47	26	73
1974	46	20	66
1970–74	262	98	360
1975	39	20	59
1976	45	24	69
1977	40	16	56
1978	43	14	57
1979	33	30	63
1975–79	200	104	304
1980	50	28	78
1981	18	19	37
1982	30	10	40
1983	52	11	63
1984	40	15	55
1980–84	190	83	273

SOURCE: Gallo and Bush (1985).

overturned less frequently on appeal to the courts.[17] Over the period from 1965 through 1981, for example, a 1-percent increase in FTC complaints charging vertical restraint of trade violations led to about a 0.12-percent decrease in the commission's success rate on appeal, all else equal. This result suggests that the administration's move to devote more resources to horizontal matters may generate a "better" mix of cases, if a good case is one that is subsequently not overturned.

Optimism on this point must be tempered by the fact that no more than 10 percent of FTC complaints ever go beyond the commission level anyway. (About two-thirds of all matters are settled by consent decree, meaning that the commission and respondents reach a mutually agreeable resolution to the complaints that does not involve an admission of guilt by the defendant.) Moreover, vertical restraints have been charged in only seven of the thirty complaints issued by the commission in a typical year since 1965. Thus although Reagan antitrust policy may be more in line with court thinking, there is nothing to prevent future commissions from reversing this change in direction.

Concluding Remarks

Antitrust policy in the Reagan administration was marked by a mixture of successes and failures. Among the former can be counted the dismissal or settlement of protracted cases involving AT & T, IBM, Exxon, and the cereal industry, and the initiation of a competition advocacy program to attack monopoly in the public sector. The latter is best represented by the failure to adopt merger guidelines more compatible with the results of empirical economic research over the past twenty years. As mentioned repeatedly, however, even if changes had been more radical, questions about their permanence would remain. Because the character of antitrust policy during the Reagan years has been shaped by the personalities of its administrators rather than by fundamental changes in law or institutions, it leaves little or no legacy—Reagan antitrust policy could be only a minor lull in the long-term trend.

What is wrong with the process of antitrust law enforcement that so little was changed by the Reagan administration? A good illustration is given by the so-called Hart-Scott-Rodino (H-S-R) premerger notification rules, established by the Antitrust Improvements Act of 1976, which require firms above a given size to announce in advance their intention to merge. Designed to give antitrust enforcement agencies adequate time to assess the competitive effects of proposed takeovers prior to their consummation, H-S-R requirements also penalize firms that have a comparative advantage in discovering undervalued assets in the economy. The penalty is especially heavy when the proposed merger involves two firms in the same industry. In such a case the acquisition is likely to be postponed while enforcement agencies seek information from prospective merger partners, and this delay gives firms outside the industry in question, which have been unaware that assets of the target firm were undervalued, an opportunity to step forward with takeover offers of their own. The H-S-R process essentially allows these other firms to take advantage of the information revealed by the premerger announcement and accordingly reduces the efficiency with which resources are allocated in the economy.

Those who want tougher antimerger law enforcement often complain that the administration's policy permits too many mergers that are too large and do not work. But this is precisely the consequence of combining premerger notification with a narrow set of merger guidelines. It is not by accident that in recent years, steel companies have acquired oil companies, or that tobacco companies have merged with soft drink manufacturers. Rather, such acquisitions have been forced on the economy because the firm that typically steps forward when a previously announced merger falls through due to antitrust considerations is one that represents no overlapping markets. The critics cannot have it both ways.

In early 1986, a Reagan administration proposal for modifying certain provisions of the Clayton Act surfaced (*Washington Post,* 15 January 1986). Without going into detail about the proposal—among other changes, it seeks to exempt import-injured industries from the antimerger section of the law for a period of five years, to relax somewhat restrictions on interlocking directorates, and essentially to codify in the Clayton Act the 1982 merger guidelines—suffice it to say that even if the plan were adopted as now written, its effects on antitrust policy could hardly be described as radical.[18] Although it is encouraging to see that the administration is interested in modifying the language of the antitrust statutes, such proposals might have had a greater impact on the conduct of antitrust policy had they been introduced in 1981 when the Reagan administration took office.

Overall, the conclusions that can be drawn from this survey of antitrust policy in the Reagan administration are not very optimistic in a normative sense. The antitrust policy process does not seem to have been changed in any important way over the past six years. Perhaps the most that can be said is that better people can make better government, but only temporarily.

Notes

1. Discussion of a recent proposal to modify the Clayton Act follows below, p. 101.

2. See Goldschmid, Mann, and Weston (1974).

3. The interest-group theory was formalized by Stigler (1971) and extended by Peltzman (1976).

4. U.S. v. American Telephone and Telegraph Co., 74 Civ. 1968 (2974); U.S. v. International Business Machines Corp., 69 Civ. 100 (1969); In the Matter of Kellogg Co. et al., FTC dkt. no. 8833; and In the Matter of Exxon Corp. et al., FTC dkt. no. 8934.

5. These are just a few examples from what by now is a large literature.

6. For a more complete development of this theme, see Shughart and Tollison

(1985). Most of the research along these lines is collected in Mackay, Miller, and Yandle (1987).

7. In fairness, several proposals by Chairman Miller to clarify the language of the FTC Act were rebuffed by the Congress. On the ability of regulatory agencies to intervene without resorting to formal rulemaking or litigation, see Robert Rogowsky, "Underground Regulation: The Iceberg below the Surface," this volume.

8. See n. 4.

9. "U.S. Department of Justice Merger Guidelines," 14 June 1982. Subsequent but unimportant revisions were made in 1984.

10. Another basic point is whether the guidelines are really guidelines at all. One study has shown that over 20 percent of the mergers challenged under the 1968 guidelines fell *below* the threshold criteria. See Rogowsky (1984).

11. *Prepared Statement of James C. Miller III, Chairman, Federal Trade Commission, on Merger Enforcement Policy, Submitted to the Committee on the Judiciary, United States Senate,* 21 July 1982, p. 2.

12. Ibid. Thus although the commission argued that the weight of accumulated economic evidence justified some "revision of market share benchmarks," it chose not to adopt numeric merger criteria in order to avoid possible confusion between FTC and DOJ standards. See *Statement of Federal Trade Commission Concerning Horizontal Mergers,* 14 July 1982, p. 2.

13. For an even more pessimistic view of antitrust's future, see McChesney (1986).

14. Eastern Railroad Presidents Conference v. Noerr Motor Freight, 365 U.S. 127 (1961) and United Mine Workers v. Pennington, 381 U.S. 657 (1965). In *Noerr,* the court held that a publicity campaign sponsored by a group of twenty-four Eastern railroads supporting legislation putting truckers at a competitive disadvantage did not constitute an antitrust violation.

15. The output effect becomes even more noteworthy when one considers the fact that during the late 1970s, there had been a major shift at the FTC toward rulemaking initiatives.

16. See Lindsay (1976) for more on bureaucratic incentives.

17. The following discussion is based on data contained in memorandum from William F. Shughart II, Bureau of Economics, to Commissioner George Douglas, FTC, 11 March 1983.

18. See Shughart (1987) for a more complete discussion.

References

Brozen, Yale, "Bain's Concentration and Rates of Return Revisited." *Journal of Law and Economics* 14 (October 1971): 351–96.

Clarkson, Kenneth W., and Muris, Timothy J., *The Federal Trade Commission Since 1970: Economic Regulation and Bureaucratic Behavior.* Cambridge: Cambridge University Press, 1981.

Cummings, Francis J., and Ruhter, Wayne E., "The Northern Pacific Case." *Journal of Law and Economics* 22 (October 1979): 329–50.

Demsetz, Harold, "Two Systems of Belief about Monopoly." In Harvey J. Gold-schmid, H. Michael Mann, and J. Fred Weston (eds.), *Industrial Concentration: The New Learning*. Boston: Little Brown, 1974. Pp. 164–84.

Flath, David, "The American Can Case." *Antitrust Bulletin* 25 (Spring 1980): 169–93.

Gallo, Joseph C., and Bush, Steven C., "Guess Who Came to Dinner: An Empirical Study of Federal Antitrust Enforcement for the Period 1963–1984." *Review of Industrial Organization* 2 (1985): 106–30.

Goldschmid, Harvey J., Mann, H. Michael, and Weston, J. Fred, eds. *Industrial Concentration: The New Learning*. Boston: Little Brown, 1974.

Lindsay, Cotton M., "A Theory of Government Enterprise." *Journal of Political Economy* 84 (October 1976): 1061–1107.

Mackay, Robert, Miller, James C., III, and Yandle, T. Bruce, Jr., *The Federal Trade Commission: The Political Economy of Regulation*. Stanford: Hoover Institution Press, 1987).

McChesney, Fred S., "Law's Honor Lost: The Plight of Antitrust." *Antitrust Bulletin* 31 (Summer 1986): 359–82.

Peltzman, Sam, "The Gains and Losses from Industrial Concentration." *Journal of Law and Economics* 20 (October 1977): 229–63.

Peltzman, Sam, "Toward a More General Theory of Regulation." *Journal of Law and Economics* 19 (August 1976): 211–48.

Peterman, John L., "The Brown Shoe Case." *Journal of Law and Economics* 18 (April 1975): 81–146.

Peterman, John L., "The Federal Trade Commission v. Brown Shoe Company." *Journal of Law and Economics* 18 (October 1975): 361–419.

Peterman, John L., "The International Salt Case." *Journal of Law and Economics* 22 (October 1979): 351–64.

Rogowsky, Robert A., "The Justice Department's Merger Guidelines: A Study in the Application of the Rule." In *Research in Law and Economics*, vol. 6, edited by Richard O. Zerbe Jr. Greenwich, Conn.: JAI Press, 1984. Pp. 135–66.

Shughart, William F., II., "Don't Revise the Clayton Act, Scrap It!" *Cato Journal* 6 (Winter 1987): 925–32.

Shughart, William F, II, and Tollison, Robert D., "The Positive Economics of Antitrust Policy: A Survey Article." *International Review of Law and Economics* 5 (1985): 39–57.

Stigler, George J., "The Economists and the Problem of Monopoly." *American Economic Review* 72 (May 1982): 1–11.

Stigler, George J., "The Theory of Economic Regulation." *Bell Journal of Economics* 7 (Spring 1971): 3–21.

Tollison, Robert D., "Antitrust in the Reagan Administration: A Report from the Belly of the Beast." *International Journal of Industrial Organization* 1 (1983): 211–21.

Zelenitz, Arnold, "The Attempted Promotion of Competition in Related Goods Markets." *Antitrust Bulletin* 25 (Spring 1980): 103–24.

6

Deregulating Telecommunications

John T. Wenders

All of the major postwar events in the U.S. telecommunications industry can be explained by the inevitable gnawings of the marketplace on the regulatory cartel that dominated the industry. The cartel was held together by the fact that regulation protected the industry—primarily the Bell System—from competition and antitrust laws; guaranteed its profitability; and in return, regulators obtained a large subsidy flow, primarily from long-distance (toll) users for their largest political constituency, local residence subscribers. Overpricing toll services resulted in the classic barrier to competition, the barrier to entry, and most of the significant political events in this industry developed from struggles between entrants and the entrenched regulatory cartel.

The Reagan years witnessed two cathartic events in this struggle—the breakup of the Bell System (divestiture) and the efforts of the Federal Communications Commission (FCC) to reduce the toll-to-local subsidy by imposing flat end-user charges, the proceeds of which were used to reduce toll prices. Both events were set in motion under preceding administrations. The irony of these events is that both produced results quite unintended at their inception.

The Department of Justice (DOJ) instituted its antitrust suit against AT & T and its Bell Operating Companies (BOCs) in 1974.[1] At that time, the DOJ had a simplistic and superficial view of the case: The Bell System was accused of systematically using the regulatory process to thwart entry to

The author would like to thank Butterworth Scientific, Ltd., for permission to reprint portions of the following articles in *Telecommunications Policy:* "Throttling Competition," 10 (1986): 177–80; "On Modifying the MFJ," 11 (1987): 243–46; and "The Theory of Economic Regulation and the U.S. Telecommunications Industry," 12 (1988) forthcoming.

the toll and terminal equipment markets. The DOJ also said that the Bell System may have used profits from its monopoly services to subsidize its competitive services, even though all of the evidence was, and is, that subsidies flowed in exactly the opposite direction. The DOJ did not realize at the time that the Bell System was not the real defendant in the case: The real defendant was the regulatory cartel held together by a balance struck between the interests of the industry and its regulators. Thus the antitrust suit was not merely an attack on the Bell System, which quite naturally appealed to populistic emotions, but also an attack on the regulators' quid pro quo—the toll-to-local subsidy—which if realized, would have been anathema to these same populist emotions.

The FCC proceeding[2] that produced the end-user charge scheme for reducing the toll-to-residence subsidy started out under the Carter administration as a proceeding to investigate the possibility of broadening the base of the subsidy source by also including a surcharge on private lines, which at the time did not carry the same subsidy load as the rest of toll services. Instead of resulting in an extension of the source of the subsidy to private lines, the proceeding was used by the Reagan FCC to reverse the subsidy flow by imposing a flat, monthly, end-user charge on all subscribers and using the revenues raised to reduce toll prices.

The roots of these events go back long before the Reagan administration and can only be understood in the light of the theory of regulation, the technological change that swept the industry after the Second World War, and other features of this industry. This chapter begins with a review of these. I then discuss the significance of the cathartic events of the early 1980's.

Theories of Regulation

Historically two general theories of regulation have been developed to explain the regulation of markets. The first of these, called the public-interest theory, argues that the reason for regulation is to avoid market failure when an industry is naturally monopolistic.[3] This theory presumes that the goal of regulation is to stimulate competition where it is allegedly impossible because of economies of scale and that this intention will in fact be carried out by the regulatory process. The public-interest approach assumes that the political-regulatory process is a black box into which good intentions are put and the public interest emerges. Except for political scientists, few now believe that the regulatory process works in this way. Simply having good intentions in setting up a regulatory agency with real economic power does not assure that these intentions will be realized in the political marketplace. As Fred S. McChesney has recently observed,

"The notion that government regulates in some disinterested, 'public interest' fashion to repair market failure has crumbled."[4]

The second approach, popularized by Stigler,[5] Peltzman,[6] and Posner,[7] is the *economic* theory of regulation. The essence of this approach is that regulators and politicians, like rational economic man, weigh the costs and benefits of various courses of action in a political framework where the attaining of a voting majority determines success. In its broadest interpretation, this approach emphasizes balancing interest-group strengths and weaknesses at the margin, with the outcome determined by the stake that various groups have in the outcome and the efficiency with which they can influence the regulatory process.

Simply put, resources are allocated according to expected profits in the economic marketplace and according to majority vote-getting in the political marketplace—the currency of the economic market is dollars, and the currency of the political market is votes. There is competition for votes in the political marketplace in exactly the same way there is competition for profit in the economic marketplace. If regulators do not compete for votes, they will be replaced by those who do; the same holds for entrepreneurs and profits.

Thus both the economic and political marketplaces have competitive *mechanisms* by which resources are allocated, one driven by profits and the other by votes. The resource allocation outcome in either market at any point is the result of the balance reached between these two forms of competition. Changes can be effected only by changing the balance of either profit or vote incentives at the margin.

While the outcome in any specific instance depends on the relative interests and forces in question, the presumption is that the dominant group in the regulatory game is likely to be a small one that has a relatively large per capita stake in the outcome, and this leads to the conclusion that "producer interest tends to prevail over the consumer interest."[8] Thus in the scrap between producers and consumers over the gains from available trade, the capture form of the more general theory of regulation presumes that producers are able to capture the regulatory process at the margin to the detriment of consumers.

The capture theory assumes that it will be so costly for a large group, with a small per capita stake, to determine where its interest lies and make its political presence felt, that the payoff will not be worth its while. If it is relatively inexpensive for members of a large group to gauge the impact of regulations on its well-being, and if the threat of the ballot box, either directly or indirectly, easily attracts the attention of regulators, then acording to the general theory of regulation, the largest group may dominate the regulatory process. If a policy clearly and immediately benefits many voters, even if only marginally, all of whom clearly know it, and if the regulatory process is sensitive to the election process, then the minority who will be harmed considerably by the policy will be outvoted by the majority. The fact that tenants greatly outnumber landlords, and rents make up a large and visible portion of tenants' expenditures, clearly explains the political popularity of rent controls.

As Gary Becker has observed, the essence of an economic approach to regulation is a balance at the margin, not capture:

> Although the "capture" theory is something attributed to Stigler, and he has made a few of these studies and encouraged others, he has also argued that rigid adherence to a "capture" theory is not consistent with the spirit of the economic approach. Analytically, economics is a theory of balance, not of all-or-nothing, as implied by the "capture" of legislation. Empirically, even small but vocal minorities have to be appeased: minority opposition is not automatically muted simply because the majority has 51 or 75 percent of the vote. In other words, the concept of a "minimum winning coalition" conflicts with the economist's view of balance at the margin.[9]

Thus a balance at the margin may be struck when the minority with a large per capita stake are the net beneficiaries of regulation. But it may also be struck where they are not.

In most cases the capture theory has been used to explain how regulation has altered the distribution of gains between producers and customers, and the predominant form of the theory predicts that the former will prevail over the latter at the margin. Thus in the telecommunications industry, where the Bell System provided virtually all of the toll service and some 85 percent of local service, the capture theory predicts that regulation will favor producers over telephone subscribers. This explains why telecommunications providers received guaranteed profits and protection from competition and antitrust laws.[10]

Regulation theory does not directly address the cross-subsidy question. However, it is clearly applicable and the capture theory suggests that regulation would underprice services to the few at the expense of the many. In the context of the telecommunications industry, the prediction is that the few very heavy toll users will be favored at the expense of the many local service users. As we shall see, the observed toll-to-local subsidy is clearly inconsistent with this view.

Application to Public Utilities

Public-choice and regulation theory argues that individuals, whether politicians, regulators, or voters, will make political decisions based on their own self-interest, and because votes count in the political process, this often produces an outcome damaging to general economic welfare.

One of the reasons for this perverse condition is that the voter simply finds it expensive to determine relative costs and benefits of alternative courses of political action and to make his political power felt. Thus the cost of obtaining information about alternatives and then acting on this information plays a large role in political behavior.

However, traditional electric and telephone public utilities are unique among our regulated industries in the sense that *all* consumers have very good information about the direct effect of these industries on their well-being. Since they receive an explicit itemized bill for services every month, consumers are very aware of their utility bills.

Further, there is little organizational effort needed for telecommunications consumers to affect the direct election process. Everyone knows that local utility prices are regulated and by whom. In the United States some local regulators are elected, and the rest are appointed by state governors.[11] Thus state regulators are close to the political process. The upshot is that almost no expensive and time-consuming effort is needed to attract state regulators' attention. Consumers are therefore not only relatively well informed about the effect of utilities on their well-being, but they have a known, in-place, and well-defined political mechanism for complaint.

The same is not true of other regulated industries, such as railroads, trucking, or airlines, because the average consumer does not come in frequent direct contact with these industries. If the price of food rose as a result of an increase in trucking rates, the average consumer would have no way of recognizing this, and might not even have known that such rates were regulated.

A second reason why consumers are sensitive to local telephone prices is the predominance of flat-rate pricing for most residence telephone subscribers. The typical consumer pays, say, a flat $12 per month for the right to place and receive unlimited local calls. With local bills invariant under local use, subscribers immediately know when regulatory authorities allow local rates to rise. In addition, there is no way that a subscriber can escape or soften a local rate increase short of disconnecting the phone. In contrast, if the price of almost any other good rises, the consumer can always substitute to some extent and thus avoid some of the price increase. The same is true for toll price increases, but it is not true for local telephone service priced on a flat-rate basis.[12]

The sensitivity of consumers to telecommunications prices, the closeness of state regulators to the electoral process, and the fact that most telecommunications customers are in the residence class, explain why state regulators have been reluctant to raise local residence prices.

Because toll usage is concentrated among relatively few users, and all voters consume local service (access plus usage) more equally, the regulatory process has resulted in toll prices well above cost and local prices well below cost. Thus for the telecommunications industry, and probably other public utilities as well,[13] the capture thoery does not explain the cross-subsidies that prevail. This result is more consistent with the Posner variant of the theory of regulation, which argues that regulation is determined by much the same forces determining taxation and spending by governments.[14]

Features of the Telecommunications Industry

In simplest terms, a regulatory balance was struck at the margin whereby the telecommunications industry was guaranteed profits and regulatory protection from competition and antitrust laws, and regulators received a cross-subsidy from the relatively few toll users to the relatively many local residence subscribers. How this cartel was set up, perpetuated, and challenged can only be understood if two facts are recognized:

- Technological change in this industry has been great, but uneven;
- Toll use is concentrated among a few business and residence telephone users.

The first fact has driven the economics of this industry, and the second has driven the political institutions that implicitly or explicitly have jurisdiction over the industry.

TECHNOLOGICAL CHANGE

The impact of technological change on the telecommunications industry has been relatively uneven, occurring primarily in the traffic-sensitive portions of the business—switching, multiplexing, and trunking. Wherever use can be concentrated, microwave technology, satellites, fiber optics, and the greater multiplexing of channels have combined to reduce greatly the cost of providing long distance and other traffic-sensitive services.[15] For example, the cost of providing long-distance channels decreased about $33 per circuit mile in the late 1950s (using N2 carrier) to less than $4 by the late 1970s (using TD3 radio). AT & T's latest trans-Atlantic cable can carry 38,000 simultaneous voice conversations on four fiber optic hairs. Recently, Rockwell International announced that it had installed some 300 miles of fiber optic cable for Indiana Bell for less than 70 cents per channel mile.[16]

However, where use is not concentrated, technological change has not had nearly the same impact on costs. The non-traffic-sensitive and customer-specific loop that connects *every* subscriber to the telephone company's central office has not experienced anywhere near the degree of technological change that has occurred in the long-distance and other traffic-sensitive portions of the industry. As I shall discuss in more detail shortly, this development has caused switching, trunking, and multiplexing to be substituted for loops in providing local service. But toll costs have still fallen relative to both local costs and revenue requirements.

THE CONCENTRATION OF TOLL USE

Consider the following:

- 10 percent of residence customers account for approximately one-half of all residence interstate messages;
- 10 percent of business locations account for approximately three-fourths of all business interstate message telephone service (MTS) revenues;
- 1 percent of business locations account for approximately 40 percent of all business interstate MTS revenues;
- 10 percent of the interstate WATS locations account for approximately 60 percent of all interstate WATS revenues.[17]

This same concentration of toll usage exists in all intrastate markets as well. Toll use is similarly concentrated in a few locations, a fact that has important implications for toll competition.[18]

The other side of this toll concentration is the fact that many telephone subscribers make only very few or no toll calls each month. Data for a BOC reveal that for March 1984, 46 percent of business customers had intra-LATA[19] toll bills of less than $5. For residence subscribers the comparable figure was 64 percent.

Aside from the already mentioned high concentration of toll usage among a few subscribers that made it politically easy to forgo lowering toll prices, there were some additional features of the industry that contributed to the success of this practice.

IGNORANCE OF FALLING COSTS

Utility prices are like taxes in the sense that from a political standpoint, the best tax is an old one. In a regulatory environment, it is always difficult to raise anyone's rates, and it is even more difficult to raise one set of customers' rates in order to subsidize another set. But in the telecommunications industry, technological change provided regulators with a unique situation: A sizable subsidy to the majority of telephone subscribers could be generated, not by raising toll prices, but by not allowing toll prices to follow costs downward dollar for dollar. This tended to hide the fact that toll users were being greatly overcharged relative to economic costs. This prevented the formation of an effective political coalition of toll users to counteract the regulatory cartel.

LARGE TOLL USER LOOPHOLES

Another factor working against the formation of an effective coalition opposing the overpricing of toll was the fact that some large toll users who, according to the capture theory were most able to form such a coalition, were also at least partly bought off by various other long-distance rulings and prices that favored large toll users. The FCC's Above 890 decision allowed private microwave systems to be set up that completely bypassed the public switched network. Close substitutes for traditional message telephone service, such as private line, TELPAK, and WATS discount tariffs, were economical only for large toll users. Such loopholes clearly reduced the incentive to develop a coalition against toll overpricing.

VERTICAL INTEGRATION

The only national toll carrier during most of this period, AT & T, was tolerant of having local costs built into its toll prices because most of this subsidy flowed to its own subsidiaries, the BOCs. In essence, AT & T agreed with the regulatory process to go along with the politically popular toll-to-local subsidy in return for profits guaranteed by rate-of-return regulation and protection from competition and antitrust laws. The AT & T probably also felt the threat to competition in toll was not very credible, since the regulatory community had a large stake in protecting the source of the popular subsidy. As it turned out, market forces were persuasive, and the FCC, always a lukewarm participant in the toll–to–local subsidy scheme because of its relative political isolation from local subscribers, could not prevent competitive entry in the overpriced toll markets.

Finally, as administered by the separations process, vertical integration meant that it was impossible for AT & T and its toll customers to escape paying the toll-to-local subsidy. Local costs were simply assigned to AT & T's interstate operations, making them unavoidable. The only way toll users could avoid paying the subsidy was to bypass AT & T from end to end by building their own telecommunications networks, which some of them did. In contrast, after divestiture, the subsidy became a tariff on a toll carrier's *local access* minutes of use. Thus paying the subsidy could be avoided by using private-line service or local facilities to bypass the short toll-carrier-to-local-company leg of a switched toll call.

The Outcome

WELFARE LOSSES

Overpricing one service in order to underprice another produces classic welfare losses in both markets. However, due to the relatively high price elasticity of demand in various toll markets and the very low elasticity of demand in local markets, most of the distortions of economic efficiency are in the former. Bruce Egan and I have estimated welfare losses in various toll markets to be about $10.7 billion annually in 1983 as compared to only a $.7 billion loss in local markets.[20]

WINNERS AND LOSERS

The essence of the outcome is that the toll-to-local subsidy has made the *mean* (average) toll user worse off and the *median* toll user better off.[21] Even though the sum of gains and losses to all subscribers is definitely negative, and economic efficiency has been greatly impaired, most subscribers—primarily residence subscribers—were better off, thus providing political leverage for continuing the subsidy arrangement.

Some History

With these features of the regulatory process and the industry in mind, it is useful briefly to outline how these interacted in the regulatory arena over the past few decades.

For almost a century, the telephone industry was dominated by AT & T and the BOCs. They carried almost all of the toll traffic and served some 85 percent of the subscribers. The FCC regulated interstate services, and the state commissions regulated local and intrastate toll services.

A key court decision[22] unintentionally spelled doom for this monopoly structure. This decision, handed down in 1930 but not implemented until 1943, allowed some local costs, primarily customer-specific local loop costs, to be added to toll prices. From 1943 until 1954 a relative-use standard was adopted for allocating these local costs to toll prices. This resulted in the allocation of a modest 3 to 4 percent of local loop costs to interstate toll.

Then technological change and politics combined to increase rapidly the amount of local costs allocated to toll services. Technological change quickly reduced the cost of providing toll service. In an unregulated market, competition forces prices to approach costs; in the telecommunications industry, the opposite ocurred—AT & T's accounting costs were raised, approaching toll prices. Toll prices were allowed to fall somewhat, especially if the customer were large enough to take advantage of some discounted toll offerings, but the decline in toll prices was not nearly so large as the decrease in the economic costs of provision. At every turn state regulators, sensitive to the rates of local residence subscribers, pushed hard for the increased allocation of local costs to toll services. By the early 1980s, about $7 billion of loop costs alone were allocated to interstate toll, amounting to about 14 cents per minute of such toll use. Similar allocations were made, either explicitly or implicitly, to intrastate toll services.

It is important to understand that the separations process that affects the toll-to-local subsidy is largely a creation of state regulators. Unlike the FCC, state regulators directly face the politically potent residence subscriber. Further, Congress is also convinced of the political potency of these subscribers, and has used its influence to intimidate the FCC. Thus in 1970, when the FCC proposed reducing interstate toll prices in response to falling toll costs, state regulators and Congress convinced the FCC instead to add more local costs to toll prices.[23] And when the FCC proposed its plan to return some of these local costs to subscribers via a fixed monthly end-user charge, state regulators and Congress were able to delay seriously, if not permanently cripple, the plan.

Pricing toll services above economic cost distorted economic efficiency. Indeed, as I have already pointed out, almost all of the simple static welfare losses in this industry are in the toll markets. Predictably, the implementation of the politically popular toll-to-residence subsidy was not without competitive response, and thus overpricing toll calls contained the seed of its own destruction. Competition, attracted by wide price–cost margins, performed its classic efficiency-improving function by invading the various toll markets.

As in all cartels, there is an incentive for customers and firms outside the cartel to avoid unnaturally high prices. Likewise, the cartel must deal with competitive attempts either by blocking them, taxing them, or bringing them into the cartel. The FCC's Above 890 Decision, which allowed private telecommunications systems; its various private-line ruling; the appearance of various discount toll offerings, such as Telpak, WATS, and special access tariffs; the appearance of other common (toll) carriers (OCCs); and squabbles over the terms of their connection to the local network (ENFIA); AT & T antitrust cases and the resulting divestiture; the FCC's efforts to implement end-user charges and reduce toll prices in Docket 78-72; freezing the amount of local costs that a local company could allocate to interstate toll—all these can be interpreted as either competitive attempts to deal with high toll prices or as attempts to keep these competitive forces from spreading and further undermining the cartel arrangement.

As the fall-guy for the regulatory cartel, AT & T fought this competition at every juncture, and in the process ran afoul of antitrust laws. How the Reagan administration dealt with this case is probably the most significant event in the industry's history. Before analyzing the administration's handling of this case, let us turn to other promarket developments taking place in the industry.

Developments in Local Telephone Markets

With the breakup of the Bell System and the allowing of free entry into most of the toll market, the last bastion of regulated monopoly is the local network, now presided over by the BOCs and a few other local operating companies. While most activity seemed to be in the various toll markets, technological change and competition were also quietly gnawing away at these markets. The significance of such developments is not yet fully understood, but as I shall argue shortly, the Reagan DOJ has seized on them for leverage to deregulate even the local telephone market.

PROVISIONING LOCAL SERVICE

Understanding local markets requires a brief investigation of the rudiments of provisioning local service. The following is a rather elementary exposition.

There are really three elements of the local network: access lines, switches, and trunks. *Access lines* (or channels) are dedicated solely to calling the end user, and these connect every end user to other portions of the network shared with others. Access lines are often called *local loops*. Generally, access lines are presently connected directly to *switches*. In some instances, where portions of access lines are concentrated along the same route, it is economical to use *subscriber line carrier* (SLC) to channelize many access lines onto fewer pairs of wires to the local switch. This process is called *multiplexing*. In these instances, each end user still has a dedicated channel to the switch, but a portion of this path may be purely electronic in nature and not follow a separate pair of dedicated wires. In other instances, a subscriber line carrier system may be used as a *concentrator,* where several access lines are concentrated into fewer channels for transport to the switch. This becomes possible because all end users seldom want to use their access lines at the same time. In this instance, the concentrator really converts the access lines to a trunklike pathway where users share common physical facilities.[24]

Switches perform two general functions: First, they switch a call from the originating end user to (or toward) the terminating end user; and second, they concentrate traffic for trunking to other switches. They are located in *central offices,* and like all shared facilities, their capacity depends on the busy-hour volume of calling by end users connected to the switch. The earliest switches were the legendary telephone operators who sat at cord boards, manually connecting the access line of the originator to that of the receiver. Operators were first replaced with mechanical switches in the 1920s, but more recently switches have become highly computerized, cheaper, and are capable of performing much more than simple call switching—such as measuring the features of the call for billing, call forwarding and waiting, and other enhancements to local service. Many businesses now own their own switches, called private branch exchanges (PBXs). Where such privately owned switches are shared by different subscribers, they are called shared tenant services (STS). No matter what the ownership, aside from switching calls among all subscribers connected to the switch, switches also concentrate (on trunks) traffic destined for end users connected to other switches.

Interoffice *trunks* connect switches. When someone makes a call to an end user connected to a different switch, the call must be trunked from the originating to the terminating switches. The number of channels between switches depends on the busy-hour volume of calls between switches. Interoffice calling is almost always concentrated into interoffice channels, so that each interoffice path is electronic rather than physical.

There are obvious trade-offs between SLC, switching, and trunking on one hand and access lines on the other. The economic mix of access lines, SLC, switching, and trunking for any given community depends on the relative cost of these elements of the local network. Many small towns and cities have all their switching in a single central office with no interoffice trunking. Larger cities may have a dozen or more central offices with switches, thereby requiring extensive interoffice trunking among them, since each central office must, in one way or other, be connected to every other. When there are several central offices in a city, it is often economical to connect them all via a *tandem switch* to reduce interoffice trunking. Tandems switch calls between trunks, rather than from access line to access line or between access line and trunk. Toll tandems merely switch calls to and from the toll network. Clearly, when switching and trunking are relatively expensive, it is cheapest to provide local service with relatively long access lines and little switching and trunking, and conversely.

With the development of electronic switching, the multiplexing of channels, and microwave, satellite and fiber optic transmission, the cost of switching and trunking has greatly decreased relative to the cost of access lines. Thus it has become more economic to provide local service using relatively shorter access lines and more SLC, switching, and trunking. As we shall see, this is the fundamental point made by Peter Huber in his recent report to the DOJ on competition in the telecommunications industry.

Just as technological change has brought the computer closer to the user, it has brought switching and multiplexing close to the telephone end user. In essence a new class of central offices, really class 6 offices, has appeared, largely in the form of PBXs. There are already more business lines connected to PBXs than class 5 end offices. The competitive significance of these developments is that the minimum efficient size of competitive entry into local telephone markets has been significantly reduced over the past few decades, thus driving another nail in the coffin of the natural monopoly argument for local regulation. From the accountant's standpoint, the technological change that improved switching and trunking also reduced the value of old local plant by making some of it economically obsolete.

THE ROLE OF COMPETITION

We are now in position to see how competition can attack local companies if they are not protected by regulation. We shall also see that even with regulatory protection, local companies are *already* being attacked.

With local service a franchised, exclusive monopoly, and with a rather large subsidy from toll-to-local residence service, local telephone companies were not only able to keep residence prices well below cost, they were also able to charge prices that were averaged over disparate subscribers. This latter practice was called statewide averaging. In addition, local prices were usually a flat rate, with local usage unpriced.

The first casualty due to the loss of regulatory protection was statewide average pricing. Even with the toll-to-local subsidy, some subscribers are overcharged because of averaged, flat-rate pricing. Free entry would give competitors an incentive to try to single out these subscribers even without technological change in the way local service is provided. Under the monopoly provision of local service, averaging has taken place in both the access and usage dimensions. Thus those most likely overcharged by this averaging process are the short-loop, low-usage subscribers, and due to the practice of charging residence subscribers less than business subscribers, the latter would probably be more vulnerable to competitive entry.

Note that such competition would probably force local companies to phase out flat-rate service. By singling out the low-usage, flat-rate subscribers, competitors would force local companies also to offer measured service to such subscribers, and in the process raise flat-rate prices. It is quite possible that this competition would bring an end to flat-rate service.[25]

But the existence of such competition is much more than simply a reaction to averaged pricing. Even though local service is subsidized relative to historic costs, due to technological change, these historic costs are higher than current costs. As we have seen, this is because dramatic shifts in multiplexing, switching, and trunking technology have lowered the cost of providing local service and reduced the value of much of the local plant. The way local services were provided was altered to economize on the use of relatively expensive service—access lines—and to expand the use of relatively inexpensive service—multiplexing, switching, and trunking. This move is access-line-conserving because access lines have become relatively more expensive, making it practical to provide local service with shorter access lines. This was how competitors attacked local companies, and it is certainly how they are presently attacking these companies— witness the accelerating battle over the provision of local services by landlords and developers using their own inside-wire and PBX-type switches.[26] Further, this is exactly the kind of competition that now exists between PBXs and Centrex.

The emergence of access-line-conserving competition indicates the kind of competition that would emerge in the larger local telephone network if it were permitted. Competition has come to the fore first in providing PBXs, local area networks (LANs), STS, and inside wire. This is because relatively little of the toll-to-local subsidy was directed at the business sector where these are most prominent, and common ownership made it cheap for the competition to organize, especially ex ante.

It is difficult for local competitors to attract portions of the local network not under common ownership; yet we now have Centrex resellers doing this profitably. However, with lower regulatory barriers to such competition, and the gradual disappearance of the present toll-to-local subsidy, I expect this form of competition to become much more prevalent. Telecommunications entrepreneurs will obtain a portion of the local network; install a remote multiplexing and switching device, such as a PBX; and connect to the present network via PBX-like trunks. Again, this suggests that the emergence of PBX, LAN, and STS competition is more than a simple response to the statewide averaging of local prices. It goes to the heart of how local service is provided.

These possibilities also indicate drawbacks associated with thinking of competition as an alternative provision of like services. One of the checks on the overpricing of access by local companies is not simply the provision of access by competitors, but the substitution of non-central-office multiplexing, switching, and trunking for access. Given that toll services provided through the typical local company are also priced above cost, such arrangements offer a further advantage in their ability to concentrate toll calling in order to use bypass arrangements with toll carriers. Contrary to the way many local companies and regulators think, PBXs are not simply terminal equipment; they are another switch in the switching hierarchy of the network.

In light of the rapid pace of technological change and gradual disappearance of the toll-to-local subsidy, this analysis suggests that local companies can be completely deregulated if they are *unprotected* and thereby subject to the discipline of actual and potential entry. (I discuss later some of the conditions under which such deregulation would be most effective.)

IMPLICATIONS FOR LOCAL-SERVICE PRICING

It is useful to consider how such competition would alter local-service pricing. Local companies would be forced by competition to price *as if* service were provided in the optimal way, even though new provision methods would be adopted only as obsolete equipment wore out. This, of course, is nothing more than a restatement of the age-old principle that under competition, prices will be determined by the cost of production *at the margin* even if the provider has embedded costs that are higher or lower than marginal costs.

As I have already briefly noted, when economic and regulatory barriers to entry were higher under old methods of local service provision, it was possible to engage in a great deal of price averaging. Competition will change this as well and force much more unbundling of local service prices. The pressure for measured service is one kind of deaveraging that is already being felt.

In the extreme, new methods of providing local service may mean that relatively few loops will be directly connected to switches in present central offices. Employing attendant concentrators and switches remote from present central offices means that present switching machines will begin to assume the characteristics of local tandem offices, which are entirely traffic sensitive. The upshot is that local measured service will be an even more desirable way of pricing the network of the future, and its implementation will be hastened by the spread of local competition. And conversely the spread of measured service will aid the spread of competition and the beneficial discipline it will bring to local telephone markets.

DEALING WITH TECHNOLOGICAL CHANGE

Aside from its effects on competition, technological change has raised some nasty regulatory issues. In a market environment an unexpected fall in the economic value of existing assets due to new technology is not uncommon. Technological change occurs at the margin, prices fall, and the present value of cash flow from old technology is reduced below book value. Eventually, the accountants wake up and reduce the book value of existing assets.

As long as price is greater than variable costs, old assets still yield some positive cash flow and therefore have some value, albeit reduced. Of course, when old methods of production wear out, they will be replaced by new ones. In the meantime, depending on how production has been financed, the firm in question may simply write off some of the value of old assets or go into bankruptcy and be sold, reorganized, and so on. But such financial machinations have little economic consequence for supply: As long as any method of production yields a positive cash flow above operating costs, it will have value and be kept by someone.

There is no question that the financial recognition of the reduced value of assets, be it a simple write-down of asset value or formal bankruptcy, is painful and likely to capture headlines and pleas for rescue. But it is important to understand that such things are a symptom of changes that have already occurred in the underlying technology.

The pain of having to write down assets, or undergo reorganization, will certainly affect the behavior of managers. They will become more attuned to the pace of technological change, exercise caution before investing in even current technology, and in general be more alert for ways to minimize costs. Pricing below the long-run marginal cost of even obsolete equipment is always painful even if it does not directly affect supply.

If the telecommunications industry had been operating in an unregulated market environment, unexpected improvements in technology, such as those just described, would have been greeted by some combination of write-offs and early increased prices to reflect the shortened economic life of assets. As improved technological change was realized, prices would have decreased more rapidly because competitors using new methods of production would drive prices to approach the long-run marginal cost of the new technology.

But this did not happen in the regulated monopoly environment that existed. Regulation produced at least two general effects. First, given the rate-base-regulated environment, local operating companies were probably not so quick as they might have been to include for technological changes in provisioning decisions. The toll-to-local subsidy and exclusive local franchises insulated them from the discipline of competition. Second, even where the increased pace of technological change was realized, the response of local companies was to increase depreciation charges for both in-place and new equipment. The market, of course, would sustain such charges for new equipment but not old, which would have been written off against assets in a competitive market environment. Given the nature of political competition discussed earlier, regulators wanted to protect their largest political constituency, the residence subscriber. They refused to allow such write-offs against rate payers and continued to stick to old, uneconomic, depreciation schedules for the purpose of determining revenue requirements. The BOCs alone now find themselves with an estimated $25 to $30 billion in unfunded depreciation charges. This probably amounts to around $200 to $250 per access line. Few states seem willing to deal with this financial problem with a short and well-defined plan to amortize the shortfall.[27]

While this unfunded depreciation is certainly a financial problem, whether or not it becomes an economic problem depends on how it is handled by the regulators. If local companies believe that local competition, operating with new technology, would prevent them from collecting the unfunded depreciation from local rate payers, then they are likely to oppose deregulation of the local market. Let me note here that failure to deal with the problem of unfunded depreciation may pose a considerable barrier to local telephone deregulation.

Assessing the Record

On entering office in 1981, the Reagan administration inherited two hot potatoes that had to be reckoned with. The first was the AT & T antitrust suit that went to trial on 15 January 1981. The second was how to deal with the overpricing of toll services that had for decades brought toll competitors pounding on the door of the FCC.

THE AT & T ANTITRUST CASE

What was amazing about the inherited antitrust case was that it never directly addressed the primary monopoly distortion in the industry— overpriced toll services caused by the separations arrangement that affected the toll-to-local subsidy. In fact, the DOJ presented testimony at trial that there was no toll-to-local subsidy, and Judge Harold Greene, displaying his ignorance of the fundamental issues of the case, commented that he found no evidence that toll was supporting local service.[28] Neither the DOJ nor Judge Greene understood that the real defendant in the DOJ's antitrust case was not AT & T but the separations process that added a large, efficiency-distorting sum to toll prices. It is a clear condemnation of the antitrust process when the two parties charged with protecting the public from monopoly abuses cannot figure out the primary source of monopoly distortion in an industry.

The administration clearly brought with it a mandate to get the government off the backs of both business and taxpayers. The conservative knee-jerk reaction was to reduce the DOJ's level of antitrust activity, especially with respect to its two high-profile cases, IBM and AT & T. However, William F. Baxter, the new assistant attorney general for antitrust, carefully distinguished between these two cases. IBM had clearly become the leader of the computer industry by outcompeting its rivals in the marketplace. Further, by the time the administration came into office, it was clear that classic market forces were afoot in this industry and IBM was faced with strong competitors and losing market shares. After reviewing the status of the IBM case, Baxter correctly asked that the suit be dismissed because it was "without merit."

We shall never know if Baxter fully understood the nature of the regulatory cartel in the telecommunications industry, but he clearly behaved as if he did. Whatever the motives, the upshot was the use of antitrust laws to attack the regulatory cartel by breaking up the Bell System.[29]

From all accounts, however, it was a close call. Many, including AT & T, believed that the administration would take a probusiness stance in the antitrust arena, and AT & T was like God, motherhood, and apple pie in the business world. From such a perspective the AT & T antitrust suit was an attack on business rather than an attack on the regulatory cartel, which the Bell System represented. Fortunately, Baxter understood the distinction, lost on most businessmen, between being probusiness and being pro-market. Given the way the industry was organized and regulated, Baxter instinctively understood that a market outcome could be brought much closer if the structure of the industry were dramatically changed.

It is easy to criticize the resulting Modification of Final Judgement (MFJ).[30] The intention of the initial agreement between AT & T and DOJ was to leave competitive services with AT & T and the monopolistic local service with the BOCs. Line-of-business restrictions on the BOCs kept them out of the inter-LATA toll and manufacturing markets, and virtually no restrictions were put on AT & T. However, as Gerald Faulhaber has commented, while the intention of AT & T and DOJ was to separate the competitive yolk from the monopoly white, Judge Greene ended up making an omelette.[31] As a result, in addition to all local service, which was alleged to be naturally monopolistic, the BOCs ended up with such clearly competitive services as Yellow Pages, terminal equipment retail sales, and 25 percent of the toll traffic. Nine of the BOCs' local service areas were defined as whole states, and there were only 164 Local Access and Transport Areas (LATAs) for the United States as a whole. Clearly, the BOCs ended up with much more than local service, and as I have already argued, even that can no longer be characterized as a natural monopoly.

The MFJ addressed the primary monopoly distortion—overpricing toll services—only to the extent that it removed the new AT & T's incentive to support the separations plan that effected the toll-to-local subsidy. By no longer owning the BOCs that were major recipients of the subsidy flow from toll, AT & T could, like its competitors, bypass the BOCs and thereby avoid at least in the short run, toll carrier access charges by which the subsidy was administered after divestiture. The importance of this crack in the cartel arrangement is yet to be determined. On the other hand, both AT & T's and its competitors' economic incentive to bypass were blunted by the tentative nature of the MFJ's line-of-business restrictions on the BOCs. By explicitly subjecting these restrictions to triennial review, the Court actually suppressed competition by giving AT & T and other toll carriers the incentive to go easy on bypassing, stay off the BOCs' local turf, and avoid giving Judge Greene an excuse to allow the BOCs into the inter-LATA toll market, which is exactly what they have done.

It is one thing to criticize the MFJ because it was not perfect, but I do not think anyone can argue that it was not an improvement over the existing arrangement. It would clearly have been better had Judge Greene not read the political winds and served up an omelette and, as I shall argue shortly, if some of the line-of-business restrictions on the BOCs had been pro-grammed to be lifted rather than subjecting them to endless gamesmanship and litigation as things now stand. And it would have been better if the separations process that supports the wasteful toll-to-local subsidy had been attacked more directly. But given legal and political realities, it is difficult to see how the Baxter DOJ could have done better.

But there is no question that the MFJ in its present form contains the seed of its own destruction. It wrongly perceived local service to be a natural monopoly, and even if it were, the competitive yolk was never separated from the monopoly white. The only question is when, and under what circumstances, it will collapse.

THE FIRST TRIENNIAL REVIEW

Under the terms of the MFJ, the DOJ is required to review and report to the court every three years on the continuing need for the BOCs' line-of-business restrictions. For its first review, the DOJ retained Peter W. Huber to provide a factual basis for its report on BOCs' restrictions. Both the DOJ[32] and the Huber[33] reports were filed 2 February 1987 with the U.S. District Court in Washington. Even though both reports were largely ignored by Judge Greene, their provocative central theme revealed that for the first time, the DOJ realized that the real defendant in the case was a regulatory cartel, not AT & T.

The key conclusion of the Huber report is that technological change has reduced switching and trunking costs relative to loop costs and caused an economic substitution of the former for the latter. As I have argued previously, this results in a proliferation of switching below the traditional end offices, decentralizes processing and control functions of the network, and erodes the BOCs' local market power. This has transformed the network model from a pyramid to a geodesic dome, hence the title of the report, *The Geodesic Network*. Hueber concluded that the primary barriers to effective BOC local competition are no longer economic but lie in the many restrictive state regulations that protect the BOCs' local markets.

Based on the Huber report, the DOJ recommended waiving most of the BOCs' line-of-business restrictions. The key exception was not to allow the BOCs to provide toll services that terminate and/or originate in their local service territories, something the BOCs want very badly. This ban would be lifted only when state regulation no longer impedes entry and resale in local telecommunications service.

While the DOJ eventually developed cold feet on this issue, and ended up recommending that the BOCs be excluded from inter-LATA toll markets, its analysis was remarkable because for the first time, the DOJ addressed the real source of monopoly power and distortion in the tele-communications industry—the panoply of regulations that have been the dominant feature of the industry for decades. Further, the recommendation to ban the BOCs from much of the toll market until local regulatory restrictions have been removed would have placed useful corrective pressure on state regulators presiding over these restrictions. What is unfortunate is that neither Dr. Huber nor the DOJ spelled out how removing local restrictions would attack these distortions. Thus we are largely left to infer the benefits of the reports' recommendations and how they would be achieved.

There is probably no simple and feasible solution to the problem. But it is important to recognize that any solution is going to have to be brought about and implemented via the same political and regulatory institutions that brought about the problem to begin with. Under what circumstances would the industry and its regulators choose to implement local deregulation in return for lifting the BOCs' line-of-business restrictions?

The key recommendation by the DOJ was to relieve the BOCs of all line-of-business restrictions if restrictive local regulations presided over by state regulators were lifted. I think it is important to analyse how this latter recommendation addresses the monopoly distortion in the toll markets and the feasibility of its implementation in the context of today's local telecommunications markets.

Since monopoly distortions in the toll markets are caused by the separations process that effects the toll-to-local subsidy, merely allowing the BOCs into now-forbidden parts of this market would have no *direct* effect on either the subsidy or the distortion it causes. And completely removing the regulatory restrictions in the local service markets will affect the monopoly distortion only to the extent that it encourages bypass competition. Further, not only will the welfare-distorting, toll-to-local subsidy not be affected unless bypass competition is enhanced, the mere existence of the subsidy seriously handicaps the local competition that both Dr. Huber and the DOJ relied on to discipline the BOCs.

On the one hand, Dr. Huber's analysis of how technological change has reduced the minimum efficient size of entry into the local service market was correct. He was also correct in arguing that competition can be a viable substitute for much local regulation. On the other hand, as long as the price of much local service is still held below both accounting and economic costs, such local competition is not likely to provide much discipline at existing rate levels. Further, as long as this situation prevails, neither the BOCs nor state regulators will have much incentive to lift restrictions on local competition in return for the BOCs' full entry into the toll markets.

As I have already pointed out, the same technological change that in a more receptive environment makes effective local competition possible also made a good deal of the BOCs' local plant economically obsolete. In turn, by sticking to obsolete depreciation schedules, state regulators have refused to allow this plant to be written off against residence subscribers. This capital recovery problem remains a real financial concern for most BOCs.

Thus looking at only the local market, the political feasibility of local competition made possible by technological change depends on the relationship among (1) the current cost of provisioning local residence service, (2) its embedded book cost, and (3) existing local residence prices. Because of the toll-to-local subsidy and the overvaluation of local plant, present book costs are above current costs, which in turn are probably above existing prices. As long as this situation exists, deregulating local service in a competitive environment will result in an increase in local residence prices (to current cost). Regulators will not find this attractive because it will result in higher local rates for residence subscribers. Even local companies may not be in favor of such an outcome, since it could require them to write down some assets.

If existing residence prices rise above current costs and state regulators understand the situation, they should be in favor of deregulation because it will result in lower residence prices. If local companies have already recovered their unfunded depreciation, they might be willing to trade the resulting lower residence prices for pricing flexibility. If considerable unfunded depreciation remains, local companies will probably oppose such a move because it would again require them to write down some assets.

Thus an environment most conducive to implementing the local deregulation envisioned by the DOJ is one where the local companies' capital recovery problem has been resolved and local residence prices are at or above current costs. These are not imminent, and piecemeal efforts should be studied carefully, since they run the risk that those who benefit might try to stall the process at a point that gives them an advantage and handicaps their competitors.

In sum, the DOJ was correct that there is a reasonable set of future circumstances under which local competition can be substituted for local regulation. How we go from here to there is more problematic because neither the BOCs nor state regulators are likely to comply as long as local residence service is subsidized and the BOCs' capital recovery problem remains. The DOJ did not address these issues. Further, simply deregulating the BOCs in today's institutional environment does not reach the largest source of monopoly distortion in the telecommunications industry—overpricing toll services.

This does not mean that no steps can be taken to lessen the grip of local regulation. Substituting pricecaps for rate-of-return regulation and developing deregulation plans that soften rising residence rates would be steps in the right direction. However, the welfare effects of such steps are likely to be small until the continued overpricing of toll is dealt with.

THE FCC'S END-RUN

While the DOJ was trying to use the market to attack regulation-caused distortions in the telecommunications industry, the FCC was working on the same problem through more traditional regulatory channels.

Recall that the major economic distortion in the industry was caused by overpricing toll services. This was accomplished by either explicitly or implicitly forcing an increase in toll prices to cover a portion of customer-specific local loop costs. At the interstate level a formal mechanism was set up, called separations, by which these local costs were, before divestiture, assigned to AT & T's interstate rate base; they were covered by toll prices and revenues returned to the local companies. After divestiture, the same local costs were assigned to the interstate jurisdiction, but, as required by MFJ, collected from interstate toll carriers, like AT & T, MCI, U.S. Sprint, and so on, via carrier access charges. Thus toll carriers paid for the toll-to-local subsidy via inflated access charges to originate and complete toll calls through the local network. As I have already noted, this method of implementing the toll-to-local subsidy on the federal level gave toll carriers an incentive to bypass local companies in order to avoid the carrier access charges, a threat that has not yet been realized.

Unable to change the assignment of local costs to interstate jurisdiction, the FCC tried to improve the efficiency with which these costs were collected from end users.[34]

There are three ways of collecting local costs from customers.

The first and by far the most preferable, is to leave these costs where they are incurred—at the local level—and treat the local transport leg of a toll call in exactly the same way as a local call. In the past, this would certainly have caused local residence prices to be higher, especially in rural areas where customer-specific loop costs are much higher. At the present time, with improved technology for providing local service, these prices would be falling to a level not too much higher than at present, depending on how the unfunded depreciation was treated at the local level. Because of the political sensitivity of local residence prices, this alternative is probably not feasible in today's political environment.

The second way of collecting these local costs is to assign them in one way or another to toll prices, where they are collected on a minutes-of-use basis. In essence, costs that are incurred primarily on a non–usage sensitive basis are then collected from end-users on a usage sensitive basis. The point is that this method raises toll prices well above toll costs, causing a classic, welfare-reducing, price-cost wedge. And as I have already indicated, due to the skewed distribution of toll usage, this causes a few toll users to pay most of the local costs—certainly far more than they incurred, making most local subscribers better off and explaining the political popularity of the scheme.

Finally, there is the alternative of taking local costs assigned to the interstate toll jurisdiction and simply charging them to the end-user *as a fixed monthly toll access charge*. If all of the assigned local costs were collected in this way, the end-user charge at the federal level would be about $7 to $8 per month per line; if intrastate toll prices were similarly reduced to economic costs, local prices would have risen on the average by a similar amount. This method takes the efficiency-reducing sting out of toll usage prices, but it is politically unpopular because it makes most local end users, who are below average toll users, worse off. In essence, this scheme causes most local end-users' toll bills to decrease by less than their fixed monthly bills rise.

The first method of collecting local costs was in effect through the mid-1950s. The second method thereafter until 1985, when the FCC tried to phase in its so-called end-user charge. As expected, the FCC's end-user charge plan met strong political resistance and has been scaled back well below original plans. Initially, the residence end-user charge was to begin at $2 per month per line in 1984 and eventually rise until all of the loop costs assigned to interstate toll were covered by 1990. By that time, it would have been in the $7 to $8 per month per line range. In reality, political pressure forced the end-user charge to be scaled back so that it is now programmed to rise to only $3.50 per month per line in 1989. Beyond that further increases are uncertain.

Concluding Comments

There are two complementary ways of improving the economic performance of the U.S. telecommunications industry. The first is by introducing market forces into a system long ossified by protection and regulation. The second is by instituting regulatory procedures that approximate a market outcome. Given the panoply of regulation of this industry and the politically popular cross-subsidies that necessarily emerged from this regulation, it is not surprising that efforts to improve the industry's economic performance have met with strong political resistance. Yet the Reagan administration made considerable progress on both fronts. It is obvious that there is a long way to go, but powerful market forces have strengthened and the regulatory cartel is now on the defensive. Further painfully slow progress will occur as these market forces continue to gnaw on wasteful regulation.

Given political realities, it is difficult to see how more could have been done. However, the following improvements would probably have been feasible even in the politically charged context of the early 1980s.

First, the line-of-business restrictions on the BOCs, with the exception of the restriction on their entry into the inter-LATA toll markets, should have been programmed to be removed by a certain date. As things now stand, all existing competitors in these markets can set up a four-corner offense to erect a sizable legal barrier to entry to these markets.

While there is no question that the BOCs should eventually be allowed to enter the inter-LATA toll markets, holding this restriction hostage to a triennial review puts considerable pressure on the BOCs and state regulators to deal with the local bottleneck. Given the historically lucrative nature of this market, and the fact that for years local regulators have viewed it as a cow to be milked, both the BOCs and state regulators strongly desire that the BOCs be allowed to return to this market. The only way the BOCs can eliminate this restriction is to demonstrate conclusively that restrictions on local competition have been significantly reduced in most states. The other side of this coin is that the triennial review process opens the question to endless legal and regulatory gamesmanship, a process at which AT & T and the other OCCs are master players. Any lifting of this restriction will undoubtedly be appealed as part of their four-corner offense. There is also the risk that the BOCs will become frustrated by the triennial review process and take the issue to Congress, where, driven by the same conditions that held the regulatory cartel together for so long, a whole set of blatantly political forces will be unleashed. Any telecommunications bill that emerges from Congress will likely have a variety of anticompetitive and cross-subsidy ornaments attached to it that would only make matters much worse.

Second, the administration could have taken a more deregulatory posture toward AT & T. President Charles Brown of AT & T clearly believed that by agreeing to the MFJ he had also bought deregulation. This seems to have been Baxter's understanding as well.[35] Nothing was further from the truth. Instead, AT & T gained dozens of regulators by virtue of its new intrastate operations, plus Judge Greene to boot. The only solace AT & T now has is that Judge Greene has assumed the burden of keeping the BOCs out of most telecommunications markets, something that caused AT & T and the regulatory cartel to be involved in an antitrust suit to begin with! Perhaps the DOJ will somehow find a way to sue Judge Greene for violating the antitrust laws.

The problem with deregulating AT & T is that it is largely beyond the control of both the DOJ and the court; only the FCC or Congress can proceed on this front. In the case of the former, due to strong political pressures against its end-user charge, the mind was willing, but the body was weak. In order to further its end-user charge attack on the toll-to-local subsidy, the FCC had to be able to announce a cut in toll prices every time there was an additional increment to the end-user charge. Subscribers, especially residence subscribers, had to see some payoff for higher end-user charges. Leaving the payoff to the uncertainties of the toll marketplace was simply politically unacceptable. AT & T simply had to be regulated to connect events in subscribers' minds and thus short-circuit the opposition of state regulators.

In the case of Congress the body was willing, but the mind was weak. While it was quite clear that Congress wanted to head off the threat presented by the MFJ and the FCC to the politically popular toll-to-local subsidy, this issue became so entangled with various other self-interested protectionist pressures that Congress was fortunately unable to produce any telecommunications legislation.

Again, it is difficult to specify exactly what deregulatory measures would have developed in this environment. But planning to lift at least some of the line-of-business restrictions on the BOCs, taking a more deregulatory stance in the MFJ, and possibly having the FCC jurisdictionally preempt intrastate inter-LATA toll traffic might have been feasible.

Notes

1. United States v. Western Electric Company, Inc., et al., U.S. District Court for the District of Columbia, Civil Action 82-0192.

2. Federal Communications Commission, *Third Report and Order,* CC Docket 78-72, Phase I; adopted 22 December 1982; released 28 February 1983.

3. James C. Bonbright, *Principles of Public Utility Rates* (New York: Columbia University Press, 1961), chap. 8.

4. Fred S. McChesney, "Rent Extraction and Rent Creation in the Economic Theory of Regulation," *Journal of Legal Studies* 16 (1987): 101–18.

5. George J. Stigler, "The Theory of Economic Regulation," *Bell Journal of Economics and Management Science* 2 (1971): 3–21.

6. Sam Peltzman, "Toward a More General Theory of Regulation," *Journal of Law and Economics* 19 (1976): 211–40.

7. Richard A. Posner, "Taxation by Regulation," *Bell Journal of Economics and Management Science* 2 (1986): 22–50.

8. Peltzman, "Toward a More General Theory," p. 212.

9. Gary Becker, "Comment," *Journal of Law and Economics* 19 (1976): 245.

10. For discussions of how Theodore Vail traded regulation for protection from competition and immunity from the antitrust laws, see Gerald W. Brock, *The Telecommunications Industry* (Cambridge: Harvard University Press, 1981), chaps. 4, 6; Robert Bornholtz and David S. Evans, "The Early History of Competition in the Telephone Industry," in David S. Evans (ed.), *Breaking up Bell* (New York: Elsevier, 1983), pp. 7–40.

11. In eleven states, commissioners are elected; in the remainder and the District of Columbia, they are appointed. William T. Gormley, Jr., *The Politics of Public Utility Regulation* (Pittsburgh: University of Pittsburgh Press, 1983), p. 26.

12. In the jargon of the economist, an increase in flat rate local tariffs has only a pure, utility-reducing, income effect, which, dollar for dollar, has a greater effect on the consumer's welfare than increases in the prices of other goods and services for which there is also a possible substitution effect. The significance of the flat rate nature of local telephone prices for subscriber resistance to such price increases was first pointed out to me by Lester D. Taylor. The FCC has now made several increases in its end-user charge without a whimper from subscribers, thus providing some evidence that subscribers are not so sensitive to such charges as previously thought.

13. John T. Wenders, "Economic Efficiency and Income Distribution in the Electric Utility Industry," *Southern Economic Journal* 52 (1986): 1056–67.

14. Posner, "Taxation by Regulation."

15. See Leland L. Johnson, *Competition and Cross-Subsidization in the Telephone Industry* (Santa Monica, Calif.: RAND Corp., publication R-2976-RC/NSF, 1982); and Paul W. MacAvoy and Kenneth Robinson, "Winning by Losing: The AT & T Settlement and Its Impact on Telecommunications," *Yale Journal on Regulation* 1 (1983): 1–42, for discussion of this technological change and its impact on costs in the telecommunications industry.

16. *Wall Street Journal,* 25 June 1984.

17. *Comments of the Bell System Operating Companies and the American Telephone and Telegraph Company in Response to the Fourth Supplement Notice of Inquiry and Proposed Rulemaking,* Federal Communications Commission CC Docket No. 78-72, 6 August 1982, p. 92. For some evidence of similar concentrations at the

state level, see John T. Wenders and Bruce L. Egan, "The Implications of Economic Efficiency for U.S. Telecommunications Policy," *Telecommunications Policy* 10 (1986): 33–40.

18. Wenders and Egan, "The Implications of Economic Efficiency," p. 38–40.

19. LATA is an acronym for local access and transport area and defines areas among which only AT & T and the OCCs can carry toll traffic. The local Bell Operating Companies are forbidden, for the present, by provisions of the Modification of Final Judgment from carrying toll traffic between such areas. Most states have several LATAs.

20. Wenders and Egan, "The Implications of Economic Efficiency."

21. For a discussion of the political effect of the difference between the mean and the median, see Allan H. Meltzer and Scott F. Richard, "A Rational Theory of the Size of Government," *Journal of Political Economy* 89 (1981): 914–27.

22. Smith v. Illinois Bell, 282 U.S. 133. See also Johnson, *Competition and Cross-Subsidization,* for a good summary of the succeeding events described below.

23. MacAvoy and Robinson, "Winning by Losing," p. 5.

24. For a discussion of some of the techniques of loop provision, see Norwood G. Long, "Local Access Technology in the Bell Operating Companies," in Alan Baughcum and Gerald Faulhaber (eds.), *Telecommunications Access and Public Policy* (Norwood, N.J.: Ablex, 1984), pp. 15–22.

25. For a discussion of the flat rate versus local measured service question in the context of a competitive local telephone market, see John T. Wenders, "On the Sustainability of Flat-Rate Telephone Pricing," Dept. of Economics, University of Idaho, draft, 28 August 1987.

26. For useful surveys of the status of STS service, see *State Telephone Regulation Report,* 7 November 1985, pp. 1–6; 17 November 1986, pp. 1–8.

27. Harold Gold, "$26 Billion Write off," *Telephone Engineer and Management* 89 (1 October 1985): 104.

28. See United States v. Western Electric Company, Inc., et al., U.S. District Court for the District of Columbia, Civil Action No. 82-0192, Opinion, filed 20 April 1983, p. 16.

29. Gerald W. Faulhaber, *Telecommunications in Turmoil* (Cambridge, Mass.: Ballinger, 1987), chapter 6 has a useful and entertaining discussion of events surrounding the negotiation of the MFJ.

30. United States v. Western Electric Company, Inc., et al., 552 F. Supp. 131, 194-5 (D.D.C. 1982); 592 F. Supp. 846, 852-53 (D.D.C. 1984).

31. Faulhaber, "Telecommunications in Turmoil," p. 98.

32. United States v. Western Electric Company, Inc., et al., United States District Court for the District of Columbia, Civil Action 82-0192, *Report and Recommendation of the United States Concerning Line of Business Restrictions Imposed on the Bell Operating Companies by the Modification of Final Judgment,* filed 2 February 1987.

33. Peter W. Huber, *The Geodesic Network, 1987 Report on Competition in the Telephone Industry* (Washington, D.C.: Antitrust Division U.S. Department of Justice, 1987).

34. In the industry, this proceeding was known simply as "docket 78-72." For a summary of the FCC's original access charge plan, see *Telecommunications Reports* (Washington, D.C.: Business Research Publications), vol. 48, no. 51 (20 December 1982); no. 52 (27 December 1982); vol. 49, no. 9 (7 March 1983).

35. Faulhaber, *Telecommunications in Turmoil,* pp. 83–87.

7

Privatization of Federal Lands: What Did Not Happen

Robert H. Nelson

Introduction

The ownership by the federal government of vast areas of land in the West is an anomaly in the American system, violating basic principles of reliance on private enterprise and the decentralization of government authority. Indeed, these were among the most important principles on which candidate Ronald Reagan compaigned for the presidency in 1980. Once elected, they became central themes for his administration. Given the conflict between the huge federal land holdings—some have labeled these holdings an American element of socialism—and Reagan principles, a challenge to federal land ownership was to be expected during the Reagan years.

Such a challenge had in fact been posed even before the election of President Reagan. Known popularly as the Sagebrush Rebellion, several western state legislatures had voted in 1979 and 1980 to request that much of the federal lands be transferred to state ownership. Although this effort would have served to advance the Reagan principle of decentralizing government authority, the new administration announced that its goal would instead be to defuse and thus end the Sagebrush Rebellion. The administration offered its own plan for reducing federal land ownership, selling off—or "privatizing"—much of the federal lands.

As matters turned out neither the proposal to transfer federal lands to state ownership nor the proposal to sell federal lands made any headway.

The author is an economist in the Office of Policy Analysis, U.S. Department of the Interior. The department does not necessarily agree with his analysis or conclusions.

By mid-1983 both proposals were effectively defunct; no significant effort has since been made to revive either one.

Chapter 7 reviews this history, focusing on privatization efforts by the Reagan administration. If future plans for privatization of federal lands are to make greater headway, they will have to be based on a sound understanding of powerful opposing forces.

In the end, it was not only political opponents of the Reagan administration, but equally the administration's normal supporters who combined to squelch the idea of selling federal lands.

A Changing Federal-Western Relationship

Historians and other writers on the West have often commented on a central paradox: The West sees itself as the land of rugged individualism; politically, westerners have voted more conservatively than the rest of the country. Yet the West is also the region of the country most dependent on the federal government, which owns around 50 percent of its land. In Nevada 86 percent is owned by the federal government, while in urban and industrial California, 47 percent of the land is federally owned. Federal funds have built dams and other projects to supply the West with critical water supplies and, more recently, to link its cities with high-speed highways. The growth of western economies has been fueled by federal expenditures for defense and space exploration.

For many years an informal compact existed betwen the federal government and western states containing the following implicit terms: (1) Western states accepted federal ownership of large land areas, water projects, and other infrastructure, and the resulting federal control over much that happens in western states; (2) the federal government paid most of the cost of managing the lands and building the infrastructure, as well as providing other needed financial support; and (3) through its congressional representatives, the West retained substantial, if less than complete, control over federal actions in the West.

This compact was acceptable to both sides. Throughout the nineteenth century and well into the twentieth century, the federal government pursued a regional policy to promote the development of the West.[1] Its growth was considered beneficial to the whole country, providing markets for eastern goods and raw materials for eastern industry. The West for its part accepted the resulting federal control because it needed financial and other development assistance that the federal government was willing to provide.

Although the informal federal-western understandings worked to the satisfaction of most in the past, there has been rising discontent in recent years. Citizens outside the West have begun to question their traditional support of government efforts to promote western economic development for two reasons. First, eastern and midwestern economic interests have come to see the growth of the West as perhaps as much of a threat as a complement to their own economies. Concerns about the "deindustrialization" of the midwest and Great Lakes region bring into question the desirability of federal subsidies to stimulate western growth. A second and equally important factor is changed national attitudes toward economic growth itself. With the rise of the environmental movement, a second highly influential national constituency has also come to see economic development in the West as a threat.

Protection of eastern industry is often an important element in attitudes toward the federal role in the West, but it typically remains unspoken in public debate. Environmental organizations have been the public spearhead for challenges to the traditional federal-western relationship. Environmentalists saw in the traditional federal role in the West an obstacle to their objectives. Public land activities, such as livestock grazing, timber harvesting, and coal mining, often conflicted with creating wilderness areas, protecting endangered species, establishing wild and scenic rivers, setting aside archeological and historic sites, and other newly important concerns. The environmental movement had its greatest impact through the federal judiciary. Environmental groups often sought to move key cases to federal courtrooms outside the West, where judges with few western ties made decisions with critical consequences for western interests. Perhaps the single most important event in precipitating the Sagebrush Rebellion was the *Natural Resources Defense Council (NRDC)v. Morton* case, decided in late 1974 by Judge Thomas Flannery of the federal district court in Washington, D.C.[2] The environmental groups that brought the suit hoped to achieve significant reductions in livestock grazing on public lands. After seeing an erosion of western dominance in the legislative and judicial arenas, the arrival of the Carter administration posed a further threat to western influence over federal actions in the West. The Carter administration appointed staff members from environmental organizations to key policy-making positions in the White House and Department of the Interior. The 1977 Carter "hit list," recommending cancellation of a number of western water projects already under construction, came to symbolize the antagonistic relationship between the Carter administration and the West.

New economic gains experienced by the West in the 1970s, combined with environmental and other challenges to traditional western influence over federal actions, led some westerners to conclude that the federal role in the West should be reconsidered. Perhaps financial and other gains for the West were no longer worth the trouble of having to deal with the federal government. As three professors at Utah State University put it,

> Historians and commentators on the western scene have often described the persistent colonial status of the West's most arid states. Lacking viable economies, these states have existed on federal subsidies for many years. Now, with prices for extractive resources (including the renewable ones) soaring, the natural response is to consider transfers of lands and rights.

They conclude that "perhaps the [Sagebrush] Rebellion marks a time for the intermountain West to stand on its own feet, cut the federal apron stings, and take the bad with the good."[3]

Western unhappiness with federal policies did not receive wide visibility until 1979, when the Sagebrush Rebellion erupted into national headlines. In June 1979, the Nevada legislature enacted Assembly Bill 413 (the Sagebrush Rebellion Act). This bill declared public domain lands in Nevada to be the property of the state, specified steps for management of the lands by the state of Nevada, and provided support for litigation to achieve the purposes of the bill. Following the Nevada Sagebrush bill, similar legislation was enacted in 1980 in Utah, Arizona, New Mexico, and Wyoming.[4] The California legislature passed a Sagebrush bill, but it was vetoed by Governor Jerry Brown. The Sagebrush Rebellion also received strong support from many western political leaders, including then–candidate Ronald Reagan. In the summer of 1980 he stated, "I happen to be one who cheers and supports the Sagebrush Rebellion. Count me in as a rebel."[5]

Contradictions of the Sagebrush Rebellion

Despite all the activity, and the many supporters, the Sagebrush Rebellion made almost no headway, never receiving serious congressional or judicial consideration. The lack of greater success had several explanations. From the beginning, there were many critics who did not take seriously the land transfer demands of the Sagebrush Rebels.[6] Instead, they regarded these demands as a tactic for pressuring the federal government to make policy and management concessions to livestock and other traditional western interests. Whatever the actual original intentions, the results in many ways support this interpretation. Once the federal government moved to conciliate western interests—especially following the selection of James Watt to be secretary of the interior—the momentum of the Sagebrush Rebellion was rapidly dissipated.

Moreover, while the Sagebrush Rebels may have genuinely sought to obtain federal lands for the states, any real progress toward this goal was bound to run up against contradictions in the ideas of the rebellion. The rhetoric of the Sagebrush Rebellion suggested that federal land ownership was imposed by a domineering federal government on the western states. Yet in reality western states have historically chosen to maintain federal ownership; until now at least, the rewards have been worth the aggravations. This was realized when specific details of transfer proposals were examined. Western livestock operators, for example, benefit from the federal presence in various ways. Most important, informal understandings have evolved over fifty years or more that effectively give ranchers the right to graze certain areas of public lands. If the lands were transferred to the states, these arrangements—which convey de facto property rights—would be up for renegotiation. What assurances would ranchers have that new state land administrators would be bound by past federal practices? More fundamentally, what assurances would ranchers have that they could wield the same political clout in state legislative arenas that they have possessed at the federal level? With the rapid population growth of the West, livestock interests will probably continue to diminish in importance and political power in western legislatures.

Many westerners also realized that the Sagebrush Rebellion's suggestion of federal "exploitation" of the West did not correspond to the reality of substantial federal subsidies for public land management—a public land version of the subsidies long provided by the federal government for western water projects. Thus before proceeding further, Governors Matheson of Utah and Lamm of Colorado, along with other western leaders, sought financial analysis of the impacts of state assumption of ownership responsibilities for existing federal lands. As expected, these analyses tended to show that fiscal impacts on the states would be negative.[7]

Strong recreationist opposition to the Sagebrush Rebellion received fundamentally the same explanation as that of other western interests. Hunters, hikers, fishermen, and other recreational users had free entry to public lands under the existing system. Who could say what would happen under state ownership? State ownership might also simply prove a transitional stage on the way to private ownership, which could sharply reduce recreational access.

The responses of ranchers, miners, recreationists, and other public land users to the Sagebrush Rebellion all had a common thread. Over many years, sometimes involving bitter controversy, and much political effort, these groups had established recognized entitlements to use of public lands in certain areas and certain ways. In some sense, they had established property rights—individual rights for ranchers to specific public land allotments, collective rights for other private groups to use of wider areas of public land. State ownership of public lands might in fact preserve these property rights, but it would create uncertainty, and there might be a long transition period. Politics at the state level would be different from politics at the national level. The risks involved would be worth it to various user groups only if clear benefits to them from state land ownership could be demonstrated. The Sagebrush Rebels were never successful in showing—indeed hardly tried to show—that these benefits in fact existed.

Social change in America requires a marriage of ideology with interest group pressures. While the Sagebrush Rebellion at least had the surface support of strong interest groups, it lacked a well-developed ideology. Leaders of the Sagebrush Rebellion could effectively express their anger with the federal government and rouse the troops, but they could not present a consistent theory or concept in support of their cause. As a result, they could not effectively argue that their cause served a broader national interest, nor could they rebut charges that the rebellion mainly served narrow interests in the West. There was also no ready answer to western concerns that the Sagebrush Rebellion might in fact be harmful to the West itself.

These circumstances reflected an absence of intellectual or academic enlistees in the Sagebrush Rebellion. To many people the Sagebrush Rebellion appeared to be an emotional or populist movement that could not attract the support of "serious" thinkers.

The Privatization Movement

The second major challenge to federal land ownership, the movement to sell federal lands to private ownership, had the opposite elements. The privatization movement was supported by a small group of intellectuals who had respectable credentials. Their arguments were carefully developed in both scholarly and popular outlets. However, although the movement gained the support of the Reagan administration, privatization never attracted a broad interest group nor other popular support. Its impact proved in the end to be significantly less than that of the Sagebrush Rebellion.

The privatization movement combined several key themes, which were mixed together in the thinking of most privatization proponents—often with different emphases; these included criticism of poor public land management, the concept of public ownership of large land areas, and fragmented and therefore unmanageable patterns of federal land ownership.

The failures of public land management have largely been analyzed by researchers who would not go so far as to propose privatization of the lands as the remedy. However, the magnitude and persistence of the failures described by these analysts suggest that a cure may require major institutional changes. Many of the leading critics are economists who apply a standard of national economic efficiency.[8]

Economic researchers have found that efficient use of resources is seldom a decisive factor in decisions made by public land managers. As a result, public land management exhibits pervasive inefficiencies, including allocation of public land to lower rather than higher value uses; investments for which costs substantially exceed benefits; investments made in one place when other places offer much higher returns; conservation of public resources when their immediate production would be appropriate; or conversely the current production of public resources when reserving them for future use would be appropriate.[9]

Marion Clawson is widely regarded as the leading student in the field of public land management—and has a career spanning fifty years. Stimulated by service on the president's Advisory Panel on Timber and Environment in the early 1970s, Clawson by the mid-1970s was coming to the conclusion that major inefficiencies in public timber management were not isolated incidents, but were in fact pervasive. In a widely noted 1976 article in *Science* magazine, Clawson labeled Forest Service management "disastrous."[10] In a further 1976 study he stated that "a resource management record of this kind is unacceptable for either privately or publicly owned natural resources. More serious than the record of the recent past is the danger that the future performance will be equally bad unless positive measures are taken to change it."[11] The political orientation of the Forest Service had led it to promote various popular-sounding but economically irrational objectives. As Clawson put it,

> Foresters as a professional group and the Forest Service as the agency managing the national forests have emphasized "silvicultural considerations," "multiple use," "sustained yield," "community stability," and other relatively undefined (at least to an economist) terms, while at the same time rejecting economic considerations or economic analysis as applied to the national forests.[12]

Other students of timber harvesting confirmed that the Forest Service tended to hold excessive inventories of timber; to delay the harvest age for timber too long; and to misallocate investment funds.[13] Particularly disturbing, these analysts also found that the Forest Service was harvesting large amounts of uneconomic timber in prime recreational areas, a timber-harvesting policy that was both economically inefficient and environmentally damaging. In some regions, these below-cost timber sales were the norm rather than the exception.

John Baden and Richard Stroup have argued that this is in fact a common tendency in government programs—the greatest danger to the environment may lie in government subsidy of otherwise uneconomic activities.[14] As Baden states, "Government intervention in resource markets is the major cause of both the environmental and economic problems that surround resource policies."[15]

Criticisms of the Bureau of Land Management (BLM) have tended to focus on the expansion of the BLM administrative staff and the high costs involved, far in excess of rangeland values at stake or revenues collected by the government. As the BLM has asserted greater authority over grazing use, this has diminished the security of rancher tenure, making rancher investments on public range lands less likely and increasing the need for public investment. One student who is close to the problem identifies "fundamental flaws of the current institutional arrangement for managing federal rangelands. That arrangement relies on bureaucratically assigned use rights, which encourage inefficient land use for a number of reasons."[16]

Like the management of BLM surface lands, Forest Service land management has for many years operated at a large deficit. In 1983, the total costs of Forest Service management were $1.7 billion, compared with total revenues of $813 million. This deficit was particularly striking because the Forest Service obtained much of its resources from natural processes, not involving an expense to the Forest Service. For example, most timber currently harvested comes from "old-growth" forests in which little money has been invested. Reviewing the BLM and Forest Service deficits, Sterling Brubaker of Resources for the Future was led to comment:

> Both the forest and grazing lands operate at large deficits even though no capital charge is made for the land. Most national forests outside the Pacific northwest are not commercially viable for sustained timber production. Analysts have figured that managing the surface estate of grazing lands costs about 4 to 5 times the revenues generated by that use. Are these discrepancies matched by the value of nonmarketed goods produced on the land? No one has ever established that to be the case. In fact, it seems implausible for much of the land, which is without any special distinction.[17]

In 1983 Clawson reexamined his earlier views on public land in *The Federal Lands Revisited*, reaffirming his conclusion of the mid-1970s that public land management exhibits major and pervasive inefficiencies. Clawson stated:

> Anyone who has been a member of the federal land managing bureaucracy, as I have, or one who has observed rather closely the operations of the federal land-

managing agencies, as I have, can agree with much of the criticism regarding inefficiency in the federal agencies. There are indeed many pressures that result in inefficiency, and few rewards for efficiency.[18]

The Anomaly of Public Land Ownership

For many years the federal government's retention of public lands was almost never questioned by land management professionals. As a result, there was little commentary on the anomalous nature of such extensive ownership of land in an economy based on free enterprise principles. It is only in the past decade that economists and others have begun to ask the obvious question: Why should the federal government own so much land?

Presumably the burden of proof should lie on the defenders of public land ownership. Across a wide spectrum of American opinion, there is agreement that as a general proposition, the market mechanism is preferable to government allocation of productive resources. For example, Charles Schultze of the Brookings Institution wrote:

> The public has become disenchanted with the ability of government, especially the federal government, to function effectively. . . . The rash of new regulatory mechanisms established in recent years—for pollution control, energy conservation, industrial health and safety, consumer-product quality and safety, and the like—have generated a backlash of resentment against excessive red tape and bureaucratic control.[19]

Rather than centralized government control of resource allocation decisions, Schultze recommended relying on the decentralized incentives of a market system. Although addressing reform of regulatory practices, similar principles would apply to issues of public land management. According to Schultze,

> There is a growing need for collective influence over individual and business behavior that was once the domain of purely private decisions. But as a society we are going about the job in a systematically bad way that will not be mended simply by electing and appointing more competent public officials or doing better analysis of public programs. . . . We usually tend to see only one way of intervening—namely, removing a set of decisions from the decentralized and incentive-oriented private market and transferring them to the command-and-control techniques of government bureaucracy. With some exceptions, modifying the incentives of the private market is not considered a relevant alternative. For a society that traditionally has boasted about the economic and social advantages of Adam Smith's invisible hand, ours has been strangely loath to employ the same techniques for collective intervention. Instead of creating incentives so that public goals become private interests, private interests are left unchanged and obedience to the public goals is commanded.[20]

Defenders of the current public land system have not provided any systematic or well-developed theoretical justification for such a conspic-uous departure from market methods. One argument may simply be that as long as the system works well, why make drastic changes. But as already noted, the quality of public land management has been severely criticized. Indeed, many of the criticisms are similar to broader criticisms made of government-owned enterprises in other countries, and in the American economy in other cases where government ownerhip is found.[21]

Various arguments are also made that public land ownership is required to protect environmental and other public values in the lands;[22] yet public values are affected by many private activities as well. In the American system, regulation is the standard procedure for controlling impacts exter-nal to the market. No convincing argument or empirical evidence has been presented to date to show that external impacts from public land activities differ significantly from similar impacts from a number of activities now conducted privately. Indeed, current arguments that defend the public land system also lead to the conclusion that much of the existing private lands throughout the United States should be in public ownership. Yet few would make such a proposal.[23] A satisfactory theoretical justification for public land ownership must also be able to explain the overall predomi-nance of private land ownership in the United States.

The most effective defense of the current public land system has thus far been made by attacking weaknesses in arguments by privatization propo-nents.[24] Proponents of privatization of public lands sometimes seem to suggest that the U.S. private sector actually achieves results in practice as well as theory that are close to socially optimal. Such obvious overstate-ment creates skepticism about the whole privatization argument; more realistically, a reasonable case for the market must be that its substantial failings are simply fewer than the failings of alternatives, including public ownership.

To be sure, there are some good arguments for public land ownership, although they are not usually the ones made by defenders of the current public land system. These arguments are primarily related to public lands for which recreation is the primary and most valuable use.[25] For example, wilderness areas may provide a true "public good." If the private sector will not provide appropriate amounts of wilderness, public provision may be necessary (although subsequent management could be private). Or on lands used for dispersed recreation activities, the cost of collecting private access fees may be so high that it precludes private provision of recreational access. Private owners might therefore post "no-trespassing" signs and seek to exclude recreational use. However, such arguments are best made for a limited class of public lands, certainly not for all public lands.

Achieving More Rational Patterns of Land Ownership

The least controversial case of privatization advocates public land sales as a house-cleaning operation to achieve more rational patterns of land ownership. The federal government owns many small parcels of land in the midst of urban areas and small isolated parcels of grazing lands surrounded by private range lands. There is little if any prospect that these parcels can be managed effectively by the federal government. Indeed, surrounding private owners typically regard and treat isolated parcels of range land as their own private property.

Land ownership patterns in the West generally reflect numerous historical accidents;[26] thus they often make little sense in terms of achieving efficient management. Federal and nonfederal lands in many areas are closely intermingled, requiring consolidation to achieve a unit large enough to be properly managed. For example, there are still large areas of public land in a checkerboard ownership pattern that is a legacy of railroad land grants of the nineteenth century. In checkerboard areas the government and private owners each own alternate sections (one square mile), yet livestock grazing, coal mining, and some other important uses of public lands require consolidated blocks of land larger than a single section.

Former director of the BLM during the Carter administration, Frank Gregg, proposed in 1982 a major effort to achieve more manageable land ownership patterns in the West. As Gregg stated,

> The Federal Land Policy and Management Act should be the basis of an aggressive program to address currently heated issues of public land retention, disposal, and management policy in the West. What is missing from FLPMA— or more precisely what is missing in carrying out FLPMA—is a deliberate effort to assess and act on land tenure adjustments in ways that anticipate changing needs in a growing West. This could be provided either by Congress or the Secretary of the Interior in the form of a deliberate program, operating within the policies and processes set forth in FLPMA, to identify those lands that should remain in federal multiple-use management, to evaluate and facilitate large-scale exchanges where ownership patterns suggest the need, and to identify those public lands that might best be offered for disposal, either as trading stock for consolidation of existing federal areas or through outright disposal.[27]

Gregg would include as a chief objective of his proposed programs

> to identify those public lands suitable for disposal, with priority given to (1) meeting community expansion needs, and State and community needs under the Recreation and Public Purposes Act; (2) using such lands as trading stock for consolidation of ownership in existing federal areas (including exchanges to

block up ownerships in public land retention areas); (3) assisting in needed acquisition in national parks and wildlife refuges; (4) offering such lands to private parties at fair market value.[28]

While Gregg no doubt would not describe his proposal as a plan for privatization, and would take pains to emphasize that it does not involve a wholesale disposal of public lands, nevertheless it might well result in substantial sales of public land, probably at least several million acres, possibly 20 or 30 million acres.

From Idea to Action

In 1981 the idea of privatizing public lands had a well-developed theoretical rationale but hardly any political constituency. Its support base consisted of a few intellectuals—Steve Hanke of Johns Hopkins University (on leave to the Council of Economic Advisors (CEA) from 1981 to 1982), John Baden and Richard Stroup of Montana State University (Stroup was on leave to be director of the Interior Department Office of Policy Analysis during 1982–1984) and Barney Dowdle of the University of Washington College of Forest Resources.

In 1981 first Dowdle and then Hanke as well undertook to transform the Sagebrush Rebellion by converting it from a movement to transfer federal lands to the states into a movement to sell public lands to private owners. One sign of progress in this regard was a September 1981 letter from Sagebrush Rebellion leader Dean Rhoads to the *Washington Post*. Unlike previous statements emphasizing federal to state land transfers, Rhoads now considered that "a primary goal of the Sagebrush Rebellion is to strengthen our free enterprise system, the circumscription of which in the management of federally owned resources creates so much waste and inefficiency."[29]

Also in September 1981, Steve Hanke, at the time on the staff of the CEA, addressed the Public Lands Council, a chief supporting group in the West for the Sagebrush Rebellion. Hanke stated to the CEA that "private property is always more productive than public property"; moreover "It is . . . false, contrary to the belief of most sagebrush [rebellion] supporters, that a transfer of public lands from federal to State ownership would improve productivity. The *only* way to improve the productivity and efficiency of public lands is to privatize them."[30]

In October 1981, William Niskanen, one of three members of the CEA, gave a speech criticizing the sizable financial losses and major inefficiencies of public land management; according to him, "We can privatize, selling much of our federal lands."[31] Prompted by this spadework, the Reagan administration reportedly decided to pursue the privatization concept further as a result of a meeting between presidential assistant Edwin Meese and President Reagan on 7 January 1982.[32]

By this point key leaders of the Sagebrush Rebellion were also advocating privatization of public lands. Dean Rhoads stated that "we've shifted positions drastically," partly because "we've had to face the hard fact that the federal government was not going to give one-third of America to the states for nothing." Rhoads also stated that "if lands are sold, traditional rights and uses should be retained, such as recreation and hunting and fishing, to be managed by states."[33] In short, by January 1982 prominent western spokesmen and leading Reagan administration officials favored selling substantial areas of public lands. This would be included as part of a broader plan to sell surplus and otherwise unneeded federal properties.

The Property Review Board

In early February 1982, President Reagan formally approved a proposal from the CEA for "promptly developing a program to dispose of unneeded public lands." A prime purpose of the program would be to obtain revenue to hold down the national debt. The program would also have to be tentative because "most likely sweeping revisions in existing federal laws and regulations" would be required. The CEA also informed President Reagan of the difficulties such a program would face.

Altering present policies, either selling the lands or raising user fees, would likely generate considerable controversy. Several groups would probably oppose major sales of public lands, including

- Western ranchers unless they could purchase the land at below market value;
- environmental groups fearing a shift in environmental protection values and large scale development;
- local communities that have in the past received lands for "public purposes" at less than fair market value;
- private landowners who might fear that a large sale of federal lands would diminish the value of their own properties;
- citizens whose use of these lands for hunting, fishing, and recreational purposes would be restricted if they passed into private hands.[34]

Despite these recognized obstacles, President Reagan decided to proceed with the effort. On 25 February 1982 he signed an Executive Order establishing the Property Review Board.[35] The board, which reported directly to the president, was assigned the function of identifying disposable federal properties and establishing procedures for their sale. Such properties were to include surplus lands, buildings, and other facilities throughout the government, as well as unneeded public lands. On the same day Office of Management and Budget (OMB) Director David Stockman testified to Congress on the purposes of this program:

> In addition to the practice of maintaining unneeded property assets, the federal government has a dismal record of evaluating land holdings against the criterion of highest and best use. Some federal holdings that were initially acquired at low cost have substantially appreciated in value because of changing land use patterns. The government has not responded to changing market demands for alternative uses of land and structures as have private sector owners of real property. Government agencies continue to maintain operations on high value sites even though these operations could be relocated to lower cost areas without any negative effects on the program.[36]

Stockman tentatively proposed a target of $1 billion from sales of surplus federal property in 1983 and then $2 billion per year in following years. He also indicated an intent to obtain an additional $2 billion per year from public land sales, beginning in fiscal 1984. Thus over the next five years, the proposed program had an approximate target of $17 billion in sales, about half from public lands. The administration later used the figure of $17 billion in sales, about half from public lands, as a five-year target. This was widely quoted in press reports.

Stockman made it clear that he excluded national parks and other special areas from the public land sale program, saying it would focus on "residual BLM land and limited Forest Service lands." He gave as an example the possible sale of 8,900 acres of BLM land five miles from downtown Palm Springs, California. In addition, he indicated that the Forest Service possessed at least 150,000 acres in "isolated ownerships, road right-of-way, and unintentional trespass situations" to be sold.[37]

The Stockman testimony already exhibited the conflicting objectives that would beset the privatization effort. On the one hand, the objective was to raise large amounts of revenue. On the other, in order to gain political acceptance, it was necessary to exclude numerous categories of land, and to minimize likely disruptions resulting from land sales.

Although not explicitly mentioned in the presidential Executive Order or in the Stockman statement, the sale of lands and property was described by the administration as part of its effort to reduce the national debt (or limit its increase). Reducing the debt seemed to give added importance to the land sale effort at a time of large federal deficits. Proponents of land sales argued that it was only logical to sell some unneeded federal assets at

a time of national fiscal crisis. For example, in April 1982, Senator Paul
Laxalt of Nevada stated:

> The national debt of the United States is now more than a trillion dollars. The
> total debt is 36 percent of our Gross National Product. The interest we will pay
> to finance this massive debt in fiscal year 1983 will be approximately 13 percent
> of our total budget. Given a similar economic mess, any rational businessman
> would begin selling off excess capital assets. Some of the federal lands are quite
> liquid, very desirable, and not essential to the government's operation. There-
> fore, after reserving land with scenic, wilderness, or historic resource values for
> parks, recreation and other uses, I believe we ought to examine whether some of
> the federally held public land should be sold to private purchasers. The proceeds
> should be applied to the national debt, and the land added to the local tax rolls.
> Let me emphasize the point that I have no intention of touching scenic and
> recreational areas, such as parks, wilderness areas, recreation areas, and the
> like.[38]

One critical issue was the effect of land sales on existing public land
users, such as ranchers and recreationists. If lands were sold by competitive
bid, ranchers who had used the land for years might be displaced. In many
cases ranchers had already effectively paid for grazing rights, which were
attached to particular parcels of private land (and water) property. Because
of the grazing rights attached, these properties sold at a substantial premium, in some cases constituting half or more of the total private ranch
value.

As previously noted, plans for the Property Review Board and public
land sales had been developed with the assistance of Steve Hanke, then a
staff member at the CEA. In order to deal with the problem of rancher and
other user rights, Hanke in effect proposed to grandfather existing rancher
rights.[39] Public access for hunting and other recreational use could also be
maintained through protective easements. Under the Hanke plan ranchers
would be given the opportunity to purchase outright grazing rights to
public land at a highly preferential price. This price would equal the
expected future value of government grazing fees—calculated according to
a formula proposed by Hanke. In April 1982 Senator Laxalt endorsed the
Hanke approach, stating:

> I believe a need does exist to sell *some* of our *excess* public lands. However, I
> intend to do all in my power to protect existing public land users from being
> 'locked out.' To this end, I endorse a proposal developed by Dr. Steve Hanke, a
> senior economist on the President's Council of Economic Advisors, that deals
> with the protection of existing grazing rights which, I believe, can serve as a
> model for protecting miners as well. In many instances, this would give each
> rancher the security of private property ownership for approximately $20 per

acre. A similar proposal is currently in the works to assist small miners. A creative land use policy will also allow continued access to sportsmen and recreation enthusiasts who view the public lands in terms of the recreational or aesthetic uses.[40]

The creation of the Property Review Board gave the effort to sell public lands high visibility. It made privatization the central issue for a year or more in public land debates, which were widely covered in the western press. This had advantages and disadvantages: It exposed the public to new information and concepts, and the involvement of the White House assured prompt bureaucratic responses. However, the issue soon became highly politicized, leading to the polarization of opinion and the over-simplification characteristic of much political debate. As far as achieving any real short-term results, the disadvantages would soon overwhelm the advantages. For the long term, there may have been some benefits, since the agenda for policy debate had been considerably widened.

Asset Management in the Interior Department

Interior Secretary James Watt was not one of the proponents of the privatization effort. Instead, Watt's preferences were embodied in his "good neighbor" policy, which proposed to transfer limited amounts of land to state and local governments for special purposes they had identified. Moreover, because privatization was intended to raise large revenues in order to reduce the national debt, its objectives were incompatible with the free or highly preferential transfer of federal lands, as proposed by Watt. As a consequence, the adoption of the privatization program effectively displaced the Watt "good neighbor" program, although earlier state applications for lands were grandfathered.

Following the creation of the Property Review Board in February 1982, the Department of the Interior was asked to submit plans for future land sales. In response the department chose to characterize its efforts as an "asset management" program, distinct from privatization.[41] The desire to make this distinction reflected Watt's discomfort with the privatization effort, both because it infringed on his own areas of responsibility and because he sensed the political liabilities it might entail. The term asset management had a less radical tone, suggesting a campaign simply to improve the efficiency of public land management.

On 30 April 1982 the Department of the Interior formally submitted its asset management plans to the Property Review Board. The plans were based on a classification system that put public lands in one of three categories: (1) "national system lands and mineral resources," (2) "lands and mineral resources designated for transfer," and (3) "lands and mineral resources requiring further study."[42] Lands in the first category, such as wilderness areas and national conservation areas, would be reserved for permanent federal retention. Lands in the second category would be sold or transferred to new owners. And land in the third category would be studied further, including an examination of such alternatives as long-term leasing of grazing lands rather than outright sale.

Public lands designated for immediate sale under the asset management plan were limited in extent and not likely to provoke much controversy. They included public lands within urban areas, potentially needed for residential or commercial development; small rangeland parcels in non-federal rangeland, difficult if not impossible to manage by themselves; lands with potential for farming use; and other lands with significant commercial or industrial potential. In March and April 1972 the Department of the Interior had rapidly canvassed its field offices to assess the total amount of land in these and other categories. Existing land use plans—mostly completed prior to the Reagan administration—already contained designations of lands for sale that could be matched with the asset management categories.

Table 7.1 shows the acreages and estimated sale values developed in the field. The BLM found that there were 2.7 million acres with an estimated value of $2.0 billion already identified for sale in previously prepared land use plans. A further 1.7 million acres were found with an estimated value of $439 million that were suitable for sale, but the sale would require amending an existing land use plan. The 4.5 million acres in these two categories constituted in total less than 3 percent of the 175 million acres of BLM land in the lower forty-eight states.

In Table 7.2 acreages identified for sale are shown by individual state. Nevada contained 20 percent of the land identified for sale; Wyoming, 15 percent; and Arizona, 14 percent. Much of the BLM land in the West is intermingled with private lands; thus BLM land often contains only part of a land unit large enough to be managed efficiently. In addition to the categories of lands previously identified, the inventory prepared by the BLM also identified 7.5 million acres of BLM land in a railroad checkerboard pattern of ownership. A further 9.6 billion acres of BLM land was located in townships (6-mile-by-6-mile squares) where BLM owned less than 20 percent of the total land in the township. Finally, another 9.8 million acres was contained in townships where BLM owned 20 to 40 percent of the township land. Because of fragmented ownership patterns, these lands might not be suitable for efficient public management and were to be included in category 3 lands for further study.

Following review of the Interior plans, the Property Review Board in

Table 1
Lands Identified by the Interior Department for Sale[a]

Type of Land	Sale Would Be in Conformance with Existing Land use Plan or No Land Use Plan Existed		Sale Would Require Amendment of Existing Plan	
	Acres	Estimated Value (Surface Only) (millions/dollars)	Acres	Estimated Value (Surface Only) (millions/dollars)
1. Lands in urbanizing areas or with residential, commercial, or industrial value	485,989	$1,626.1	103,834	$100.9
2. Lands with potential for cultivated agriculture				
a. Encumbered by an agricultural application (DLE, Carey Act) or lease	200,908	50.1	56,084	19.4
b. Not encumbered	250,294	80.4	238,258	65.1
3. Lands meeting #1 disposal criterion of section 203, FLPMA	1,525,642	253.4	1,255,598	242.8
4. Lands meeting #2 or #3 disposal criteria of section 203, FLPMA	244,180	67.7	92,769	10.5
Total	2,707,013	2,007.7	1,746,543	438.8

SOURCES: Attachment to memorandum from Frank A. Dubois and R. W. Piasecki (Interior Department Asset Management Coordinators) to Bruce Selfon (Acting Executive Director, Property Review Board), 30 April 1982.

[a] These lands were identified by the Bureau of Land Management for potential sale in a field review conducted in March and April 1982.

Table 7.2
Lands Identified in 1982 by the Interior Department for Sale by State
(thousands of acres)[a]

State	Urban Lands	Cultivated Agricultural Lands	FLPMA #1 Disposal Criterion	FLPMA #2, 3 Disposal Criteria	State Total
Arizona	57.8	75.6	475.9	2.9	612.2
California	111.4	47.8	133.7	27.2	320.1
Eastern states	12.5	0.9	42.4	0	404.4
Idaho	8.9	170.7	114.9	0.5	295.0
Montana	1.6	27.3	375.5	0	404.4
Nevada	275.5	241.4	154.0	214.1	885.0
New Mexico	30.8	5.2	409.0	3.5	448.5
Oregon	9.7	58.2	185.9	0.5	254.3
Utah	18.1	20.1	91.0	4.1	133.3
Wyoming	42.7	79.1	450.5	82.0	654.3
Total	589.8	745.5	2,781.2	337.0	4,452.6

SOURCES: Attachment to memorandum from Frank A. Dubois and R. W. Piasecki (interior department asset management coordinators) to Bruce Selfon (Acting Executive Director, Property Review Board), 30 April, 1982.

[a]These lands were identified by the Bureau of Land Management for potential sale in a field review conducted in March and April 1982.

May 1982 approved the proposed framework for public land sales. At a White House press briefing, Secretary of the Interior Watt emphasized that "the National Parks, the wilderness areas, the refuge areas, the conservation areas will not be for sale." Watt also sought to calm fears in the West of massive land sales:

At this time, we have no parcels of any real size that we are singling out. There will not be massive land transfers under this program.

For example, the Department of the Interior owns eight thousand acres in the State of Oklahoma, eight thousand acres. All of those should be sold. The largest tract is 160 acres. And that happens to be in downtown Oklahoma City. And we would hope to sell every one of those acres.

And so we are looking for isolated, small tracts of land. And that will total up to millions of acres. And we have already identified a possibility of sales in excess of . . . four million acres of land. And those are urban oriented, values like that.

We do not foresee massive transfers of this land. And I keep saying that, because there have been misunderstandings that we are going to dump out 340 million acres of land on the market-place. This is not the case. We will protect hunting and fishing rights. The mineral rights are within federal ownership. And we expect this program to go along smoothly and effectively. There will be sales of land. And we expect to generate several billions dollars in the years ahead as we allow the private sector to take these lands and put them to more constructive use.[43]

In subsequent reports Watt elaborated on these themes by stating that land sales would be no more than 5 percent of public lands. Since there are about 700 million acres of public lands in total, the cap on sales was widely reported in the press to be 35 million acres. This was, of course, substantially more than the 4.4 million acres of prime prospects for sale that the Department of the Interior had actually identified at that point.

Belated Reagan administration efforts to minimize the scope of proposed public land sales conflicted with the obvious large magnitude of sales required to achieve the stated revenue target of $17 billion over five years (which included sales other than public lands). Also, thirty-five million acres seemed a very large amount of land to many people, even if it represented only 5 percent of the public lands. The press, moreover, was inclined to maximize the magnitude of likely land sales, finding a good story in suggestions of a massive disposal program.

Thus the *New York Times* ran a front-page story in July 1982, headlined "U.S. plans biggest land shift since frontier times." The story opened by stating that "the Reagan administration has begun what could be the most extensive transfer of public property and resources to private control in recent American history."[44] In August 1982 a *Time* magazine cover story was devoted to "the land sale of the century." *Time* reported that "the scope of the proposed sales is enormous. . . . Both President Reagan and his Interior Secretary James Watt are convinced that the U.S. owns far more land than it needs or can manage. And both believe that unneeded land should be turned over to private owners."[45]

As a result of such press coverage, the idea became firmly implanted in the public mind that much of the existing system of public lands was subject to privatization. Few people were in fact prepared to see public land sales carried out on such a large scale, certainly not without much more public discussion, planning, and other preparations than had occurred to date.

In August 1982, Secretary of the Interior Watt formally established an Asset Management Program Coordination Office in the Department of the Interior, stating, "I firmly believe that our coordinated efforts to carry out the President's initiative can be one of our greatest achievements."[46] The actual plans thus far developed by the Department of the Interior's asset management program were fairly modest in scope; indeed, they were not much different from Frank Gregg's proposal for rationalizing western land patterns already described. Nevertheless, scarcely a year later, to his great relief, Watt would abolish his asset management office and sever the ties of public land management with the Property Review Board. In part because public fears of a massive land sale program could not be dispelled, the privatization initiative for public lands proved a political liability in the West too great to bear further.

The Contradictions of Privatization

Obviously, sale of some federal lands makes sense; indeed, even the strongest critics of privatization will concede this point. For example, there is little if any reason for the federal government to hold lot-sized parcels in Las Vegas, Palm Springs, and other urban areas in the West. In fact the Department of the Interior's plan submitted to the Property Review Board focused precisely on these opportunities for immediate sales.

Why then, did privatization fail? As is often the case, the problem was a mixture of ideology, interest group resistance, management miscalculations, and individual personalities.

The privatization effort was beset from the beginning by contradictory objectives. On the one hand its principal objective was supposedly to raise revenue to reduce the national debt. With such an objective, two things had to be the case: First, large acreages of public land would have to be sold; and second, the land would have to be sold for high prices. If current land users in the West had to pay these prices, privatization would generate large financial outflows from western states to the federal government. Or if new buyers purchased the land, existing users would be displaced. Neither of these results would be acceptable to traditional public land users.

Privatization had the avowed purpose of using public lands for a national purpose—to pay off the national debt. While this may have conformed to popular myth that public lands are really "public" in a national sense, such a plan was out of touch with the political realities of public land management. In fact, public lands have primarily benefitted the West, and frequently particular land users in the West, in terms both of financial support and of western control over land management activity.

Indeed, to the extent the privatization effort was linked to the national debt, it most closely resembled the water project "hit list" of the Carter administration. Both initiatives sought to impose a policy that was probably rational from a national perspective but would upset long-standing land management practices. Both privatization and the hit list arose from similar circumstances—policy development based on strong convictions but not much practical experience in public land and resource management. Again, in both cases, the respective secretaries of the interior, Cecil Andrus and James Watt, were more the victims than the sponsors of these activities, forced to carry the load for policies they had not initiated and well understood to be politically flawed.

The staff of the Property Review Board and other privatization proponents recognized the need for political acceptability. In fact, as indicated previously, a proposal was developed whereby ranchers could purchase grazing rights for the expected future value of government grazing fees—thereby conceding that in practice, the rancher had already paid for most of the value of the grazing rights. Similarly, a general strategy for other users involved conceding rights to public lands that these users already hold de facto but selling other unappropriated rights. For example, privatization proponents have proposed transferring wilderness areas to wilderness organizations, thereby formally recognizing that these organizations now in effect already hold many of the property rights to wilderness areas.[47]

Nevertheless, there were several major problems with this strategy. First, it involved dividing use rights to public lands into various categories—grazing rights, hunting rights, mineral rights, water rights, and so on. This approach could well create an administrative nightmare just as the separation long ago of surface and subsurface rights in federal coal areas has created major administrative headaches for current federal coal managers.[48] Creating perhaps even more difficulty, however, is the fact that a separation of user rights would require explicit agreement on the boundaries of these rights. While it seems clear that various user rights have evolved de facto, the lack of explicit definition may prove to be a drawback: In many cases, different users may presently believe that they possess the same rights, thereby avoiding conflict. What are the actual bounds, for example, between grazing rights and the rights of hunters to have forage allocated for wildlife? These bounds have never been precisely delineated.

Because people still believe that public lands are a national benefit, it is questionable whether informal grazing rights acquired long ago could be formalized by transferring those rights to ranchers at a highly preferential price. However erroneously, the public would probably perceive such formal recognition as giving away public lands; the head of the Property Review Board, Joshua Muss, took precisely this position. In short the defense of rancher rights may depend on maintaining the status quo and avoiding a highly visible national controversy. As long as the public land issue does not attract undue attention nationally, ranchers may even be able to expect further evolution of grazing rights in an incremental fashion.

From a strictly national viewpoint, it would be economically and managerially efficient to give away significant portions of public land. These lands produce few national benefits and are a significant drain on the federal treasury. Yet it is also obvious that at present, large segments of the American public would find this policy unacceptable.

Privatization proponents also seemed unsure of their own objectives. On the one hand, privatization could be viewed as a pragmatic undertaking to increase national benefits from range and forest lands now held by the federal government. This goal might involve a limited number of land sales, focusing on specific parcels of public land where benefits of private ownership would be greatest and political resistance to land sales would be least.

On the other hand, the privatization effort also offered an opportunity to campaign against the intellectual foundations of the modern welfare state. Public lands offered a good example of the tendency of government powers to be captured for private purposes—much as regulatory agencies have often been captured. The public bureaucracy responsible for managing public lands has often been heavy-handed, slow to respond to change, and highly ineffective. In short, the public lands provide some good case material for developing antigovernment or libertarian themes.

Privatization proponents found it difficult to decide whether the real purpose of their efforts was long-run education or short-run pragmatic change. Both could not be achieved, because the educational campaign would be sure to inflame public opinion, polarize debate, and create insuperable obstacles to achieving actual change.

These tensions were illustrated in the efforts of Steve Hanke, who, as noted previously, helped develop the privatization effort while a CEA staff member. In some of his activities, Hanke sought to promote pragmatic measures to make privatization a practical and politically feasible undertaking. Yet Hanke also chose to present these measures in a broader framework of radical social change in the relationship between the private sector and government.

In a 1982 magazine article focusing on Hanke's land sale efforts, the author observed:

> Hanke says, although in moderate and reasonable tones, some of the most radical things ever spoken by 20th-century employees of the U.S. government. For instance: "I'm very much opposed to virtually all the public sector activities except for some police functions and national defense, and even those could be contracted out."[49]

As already noted, public land ownership is in fact an anomaly in the American system, one that conflicts with basic American beliefs about the role of private enterprise. However, it typically alienates rather than conciliates the many defenders of public lands to have this pointed out. Hanke was not willing to compromise on this matter as well, for example, stating that "the real issue in the privatization debate is coming to the forefront: the choice between capitalism and socialism, or between private property and individual freedom versus public ownership and serfdom."[50]

The exercise of governmental powers inevitably requires elements of discretion. If laws and other rules are too rigid, the results prove arbitrary and ineffective. Thus it is important for citizens to have confidence in government administrators to exercise good judgment. Such confidence is primarily achieved through the perception that administrators are acting in the interests of those affected and generally share similar goals and objectives. Thus the West has always sought to ensure that the secretary of the interior was a fellow westerner, someone who understands western needs and shares western goals and values. Westerners looking at the privatization effort did not have this feeling. As a result they proved unwilling to entrust federal administrators with the ample powers and discretion necessary to carry out a privatization effort. Privatization on any large scale would have required a delicate hand in dealing with matters of utmost concern in, and impact on, the West.

While limited sales of urban lands and scattered grazing parcels would have entailed few risks to the West, such sales might also have set a precedent that would have made it more likely for much larger land sales to take place in the future. Rather than open the way to such a possibility, ranchers and other traditional western land users joined with environmentalists and other national interest groups to seek to eliminate the entire privatization effort.

The Demise of Privatization

As already noted, by the end of 1981, Dean Rhoads, one of the founders of the Sagebrush Rebellion, was endorsing the concept of privatization. For a time, some other leading western politicians similarly supported privatization. As indicated earlier, in April 1982, Senator Paul Laxalt of Nevada endorsed the goal of privatizing large areas of public lands, as long as existing users could be protected.

However, as the contradictions described above and other problems in the privatization effort became more apparent, this western support rapidly disappeared. By May 1982 Rhoads asked, "What does 'privatization' mean, anyway? If it means selling all the public lands for private ownership, I'm sure everyone in this room would be against it."[51] According to the *Nevada State Journal* on 5 May 1982,

Leading sagebrush rebels in Nevada, where the rebellion was born and where 87 percent of the land is under federal control, sought Tuesday to put as much distance as possible between their cause and privatization.

Mining and livestock industry spokesmen sought to dispel what they said is a myth: that ranchers and miners want to buy up federal lands. Actually, said Ned Eyre of the Nevada Cattlemen's Association, their members can't afford to buy the lands they use.

Assemblyman Paul Prengaman, R-Washoe, also raised the specter of foreign interests buying Nevada lands if privatization took hold.[52]

Thus by the summer of 1982 traditional ranching users of western public land had concluded that privatization was a threat. There was too much risk of privatization resulting in their displacement with less than full compensation for lost rancher rights. Hunters and other recreationists similarly feared that they would lose their traditional open access to public lands, while miners feared losing free access to lands for exploration. The privatization effort gradually developed into a major political headache for the Reagan adminsitration. For a time Secretary of the Interior Watt got along well with the predominantly Democratic governors from the public land states. Those governors shared many of the western grievances with the Carter administration, and recognized that Secretary Watt had moved efficiently to eliminate at least some of them. The privatization effort, however, proved a watershed (along with disagreements over the federal coal-leasing program, which was itself perceived by some in the West as an effort to privatize federal coal holdings). The changing political climate was aptly captured in a September 1982 editorial from the *Daily Sentinel* in Grand Junction, Colorado:

> When Interior Secretary James Watt first proposed a public sale of unspecified tracts of federal property, we cautiously endorsed the plan and said the administration's proposal at least deserved a fair hearing before anyone gets too flustered about it.
>
> Unfortunately, as details of the administration's proposal have been made known, it's becoming increasingly clear that some of the early misgivings expressed about the proposed federal land sale were well warranted.
>
> Although supporters of the administration's proposal deny it, it's not unlikely that huge expanses of federal land will have to be sold if the administration's goal of generating $17 billion worth of sales over five years is to be reached.
>
> That worry was uppermost in the minds of Colorado Governor Richard Lamm and Utah Governor Scott Matheson when the two men testified against the administration's land sale proposal before the House public lands subcommittee this week.
>
> The opposition of the two western governors is significant. Matheson is a conservative Democrat who has been generally supportive of the Interior De-

partment's policies under Watt. Lamm's criticism of the administration's plan, if anything, is even more surprising than Matheson's. As a relatively liberal governor in a relatively conservative western state, Lamm has been extremely reluctant to publicly, as well as privately, criticize Watt and the administration's federal land policies. Lamm has observed on more than one occasion that it makes little sense to him to carp about one's landlord—i.e., Watt. Well, this week in Washington, Lamm gave up playing the good soldier role.

"When a public land disposal program of undefined dimension is viewed in the context of this administration's resource development policies, I must conclude that the long-term future of the public domain is in serious jeopardy," said Lamm.

Matheson was equally blunt. Matheson reportedly called the plan a "fraud."[53]

In other states similar reactions began to occur. In October 1982, the *Idaho Statesman* reported that Idaho Governor Evans "denounces U.S. land sale plan" and that the governor had

sent a telegram Wednesday morning to President Reagan asking him to cancel the Asset Management Program, which aims to sell $17 billion worth of federal property and lands over the next five years to help reduce the national debt.

"If this continues, it could put a lot of ranchers out of business. People don't realize just how serious this is to stockmen," said rancher Louis Cenarrusa, a brother of Idaho Secretary of State Pete Cenarrusa.

Ranchers could not compete with "tourists and out-of-state interests," who pay high prices for land in Blaine County, rancher Bud Simpson said.

Asked what he could do to stop the Reagan administration's program, Evans said, "We'll call out the National Guard if necessary. We're not going to be bullied on this."[54]

The privatization effort thus stirred resentments in the West reminiscent of those generated by the "hit list" and various other Carter administration policies. However, unlike the Carter administration, much of President Reagan's support in 1980 was derived from western states. Indeed, the Reagan administration entered office pledging to eliminate causes of western resentment. Hence the days of privatization were almost certain to be short. But in government momentum is important, and it was not until summer 1983 that the privatization effort was officially abolished with respect to public lands.

On 15 July 1983, Secretary Watt announced that he had reached an agreement with Edwin Harper, chairman of the Property Review Board. As a result of the agreement, public land sales would no longer be included within the scope of the Property Review Board. The Department of the Interior issued a press release stating that "Watt and his land managers are free to make all the decisions where land is offered for sale at fair market value."[55]

Watt also sought to mend some of his political fences in the West. Writing to all the western governors, he acknowledged that

> one of the areas that continues to draw criticism deals with the disposal of lands no longer needed by the federal government. I am satisfied that the mistakes of 1982 are not being, and will not be, repeated. Each Governor has been briefed, or his staff has been briefed, on our plans for disposing of the few isolated tracts in the respective states. I am satisfied, based on the private conversations and the public dialogue, that there is no room for criticism of this program as it relates to future activities. Criticism of the past is for the most part justified.[56]

As shown in Table 7.3, public land sales have been minimal for many years. A small increase has occurred since 1983, but land sales nevertheless remained well below levels in the fifties and sixties. Thus while the privatization effort provoked wide debate and fierce controversy, it had little substantive impact. If anything, the impact was to ensure that the Department of the Interior would not step up land sales through a low-profile reordering of administrative priorities: Without much fanfare, the Interior Department could have increased substantially its sales of urban and scattered rangeland parcels—potentially amounting to several million acres over a few years.

Conclusion

Since the abandonment of the privatization effort in mid-1983, there have been no indications of new government interest in major sales of federal land. Interior Department successors to Secretary Watt, who re-signed in October 1983, appear to have concluded from his experiences that whatever its intrinsic merits may be, it would in fact be difficult to design a political plan for privatization that could be implemented without adversely affecting in a significant way some important political group. As long as the possibility of damaging any group effectively precludes further political movement, large-scale and direct privatization of federal lands would seem to be ruled out.

If privatization of federal lands is to occur, it may have to take place incrementally and to a considerable extent out of public view. Historically, major changes in land tenure have seldom occurred rapidly. Typically these changes have evolved slowly, masked by myths and fictions, and may not even have been recognized until well after the fact. Indeed, such a process appears to be at work on the public lands, slowly and gradually bringing about increasing privatization. However, the process is still well short of

Table 7.3
Sales of Public Lands by the Bureau of Land Management[a]

Fiscal Year	Parcels	Acres	Receipts
1946	133	10,725	$ 126,492
1947	99	10,124	148,409
1948	72	7,303	252,099
1949	387	37,436	476,148
1950	563	65,054	456,259
1951	748	99,099	518,979
1952	565	74,540	690,491
1953	654	91,494	1,024,829
1954	855	98,695	1,218,239
1955	963	168,013	1,925,975
1956	1,359	202,705	2,288,456
1957	1,312	190,698	3,427,299
1958	908	132,251	3,029,294
1959	776	120,096	4,239,230
1960	701	99,225	5,101,297
1961	345	63,842	4,250,000
1962	563	91,910	3,581,482
1963	447	71,582	3,382,561
1964	392	66,636	3,169,208
1965	592	87,061	3,061,158
1966	549	84,426	2,583,863
1967	438	61,387	2,583,863
1968	346	66,632	2,521,132
1969	274	37,877	1,802,126
1970	258	35,150	2,099,849
1971	219	30,113	2,013,823
1972	170	22,005	1,941,520
1973	148	13,669	1,797,933
1974	79	8,691	2,055,637
1975	69	5,105	233,438
1976	84	3,641	584,751
1977	24	1,295	284,964
1978	16	709	82,585
1979	86	1,760	6,480,499
1980	159	4,115	7,326,599
1981	111	7,120	2,868,087
1982	55	1,312	1,466,022
1983	103	5,369	7,471,609
1984	309	17,667	4,387,097
1985	308	17,283	3,340,376

SOURCE: Data supplied by the Bureau of Land Management to the author.
[a] Excludes land sales in Alaska.

complete; many private rights to public lands have been created and recognized, but the lands are obviously still in public ownership.

In an indirect way, considerable additional informal privatization of public lands has occurred in the past five years. For example, ranchers withstood the onslaught of environmentalists in the 1970s and have shown that their exercise of grazing rights on public lands was still secure. In recent years the BLM has sought in various ways to enlist rancher cooperation in grazing mangement, and to avoid actions that are harmful to rancher interests. Reversing a decade-old policy, ranchers are now encouraged to finance range investments themselves, and have been assigned a much enhanced responsibility for maintaining range investments.

Even more impressively than ranchers, wilderness organizations in the past five years have demonstrated their ability to control use of wilderness areas. They emerged victorious in the widely publicized battle over oil and gas drilling in wilderness areas. In the process, further de facto privatization of wilderness occurred, although the private rights created in this case are collective rather than individual. Wilderness user groups have established a claim to controlling the use of wilderness areas that is at least as strong as ranchers have asserted over use of grazing land allotments.

One special form of de facto privatization is a throwback to the squatter takeovers of public land in the nineteenth century. According to congressional testimony by the Forest Service, marijuana growers are using as many as 1.5 million acres of the national forests for their activities. Just as their nineteenth-century counterparts, law enforcement agencies have sought with minimal success to remove these activities from public lands. In one recent case, Congress enacted a privatization measure, although it went by another name. Because approximately half of the federal coal is covered by private surface, development of underlying federal coal would be difficult given opposition from the private surface owner. Much as ranchers have obtained de facto grazing rights, many surface owners have de facto rights to control mining federal coal. In 1977, Congress formalized surface owner rights by including a surface owner consent requirement in the Surface Mining Control and Reclamation Act. Ironically, this privatization measure was actively supported by many environmental and other groups that are in other contexts strongly opposed to privatization.

Access rights to public lands for hunters, hikers, fishermen, and other recreationists have also been bolstered by events of recent years. These groups have shown formidable and still-growing political strength in defending their interests, both in western state governments and at the federal level. The informal evolution of private rights to public lands provides security to users, and encourages their interest in properly maintaining and managing the land. However, the absence of full property rights, which would require outright privatization, also entails some major liabilities. Because user tenure is not formally guaranteed, the resulting uncertainty may discourage investments. Ranchers, for example, are less likely to invest in rangeland improvements when they face the prospect of the BLM allocating some or all of the resulting increased forage to wildlife.

Perhaps more important, the system of de facto privatization that has developed on public lands discourages new users of the lands. Under a regime of ordinary property rights, new users obtain land and other property rights by purchasing it from the existing user. However, holders of de facto rights to public land either cannot legally sell their rights to new users, or face numerous restrictions on such sale (as in the case of ranchers). For example, if wilderness groups actually owned wilderness areas, they might be willing to sell some oil- and gas-drilling rights when resulting revenues could be used to purchase additional wilderness areas. Under the existing system, these groups can defend their rights and successfully exclude oil- and gas-drilling from wilderness areas, but they cannot waive these rights for a direct cash payment.

In the long run the prospects are good for a continuing gradual and informal process of privatization of public lands. Prospects that this evolutionary process can be speeded up in the short run, and privatization accomplished by a direct sale of land, are poor. There may be substantial resulting efficiency losses to the nation, as some high-value users are denied access to public lands. However, these costs may simply be unavoidable in the American system. The greatest hope for reducing them is greater public education about the benefits of private ownership, which might then translate into greater public and political support for privatization measures.

Notes

1. For this history see Paul W. Gates, *History of Public Land Law Development* (Washington, D.C.: Government Printing Office, 1968); Benjamin H. Hibbard, *A History of Public Land Policies* (1924; Madison: University of Wisconsin Press, 1965); and Roy M. Robbins, *Our Landed Heritage: The Public Domain 1776–1970* (1942; Lincoln: University of Nebraska Press, 1976).

2. Natural Resources Defense Council v. Morton, 388 F Supp. 829 (1974).

3. Allen D. Lebaron, E. Bruce Godfrey, and Darwin B. Nielsen, "Sagebrush Rebellion: An Economic Analysis," *Utah Science* 12 (Fall 1980): 90.

4. See Richard M. Mollison, "The Sagebrush Rebellion: Its Causes and Effects," *Environmental Comment* (Washington, D.C.: Urban Land Institute, June 1981).

5. Quoted in Richard M. Mollison and Richard W. Eddy, Jr., "The Sagebrush Rebellion: A Simplistic Response to the Complex Problem of Federal Land Management," *Harvard Journal on Legislation* 19, no. 1, (Winter 1982): 105.

6. See Lawrence Mosher, "Reagan and the GOP are Riding the Sagebrush Rebellion—But for How Long?" *National Journal* (21 March 1981): 480; also Richard Mollison, "The Sagebrush Rebellion: Its Causes and Effects."

7. Allen D. Lebaron, Darwin B. Nielsen, John P. Workman, and E. Bruce Godfrey, *An Economic Evaluation of the Transfer of Federal Lands in Utah to State Ownership,* a report submitted to the Four-Corners Regional Commission by the Utah Agricultural Experiment Station Personnel (Logan, Utah, May 1980), pp. 23–24.

8. See Marion Clawson, *The Economics of National Forest Management* (Washington, D.C.: Resources for the Future, 1976); Marion Clawson, *The Federal Lands Revisited* (Washington, D.C.: Resources for the Future, 1983); Thomas Lenard, "Wasting Our National Forests," *Regulation* (July/August 1981): 29–36. Robert T. Deacon and M. Bruce Johnson, (eds.), *Forestlands: Public and Private* (San Francisco: Pacific Institute for Public Policy Research, 1984); Sterling Brubaker, (ed.), *Rethinking the Federal Lands* (Washington, D.C.: Resources for the Future, 1984); John Baden and Richard L. Stroup, (eds.), *Bureaucracy vs. Environments: The Environmental Costs of Bureaucratic Governance* (Ann Arbor: University of Michigan Press, 1981); and William F Hyde, *Timber Supply, Land Allocation, and Economic Efficiency* (Baltimore: Johns Hopkins University Press for Resources for the Future, 1980).

9. See Clawson, *The Economics of National Forest Management;* Lenard, "Wasting the National Forests;" Robert Deacon and Bruce Johnson, (eds.), *Forestlands; Report of the President's Advisory Panel on Timber and the Environment* (Washington, D.C.: Government Printing Office, 1973); Jack Hirshleifer, "Sustained Yield versus Capital Theory," paper presented at a symposium on the Economics of Sustained Yield Forestry, sponsored by the University of Washington, Seattle, November 1974; and Thomas J. Barlow, Gloria E. Helford, Trent W. Orr, and Thomas B. Stoel, Jr. *Giving away the National Forests: An Analysis of U.S. Forest Service Timber Sales below Costs* (Washington, D.C., Natural Resources Defense Council, June 1980).

10. Marion Clawson, "The National Forests," *Science* 7 (20 February 1976): 763.

11. Clawson, *The Economics of National Forest Management,* pp. 99–100.

12.. Ibid., p. 144.

13. See Hyde, *Timber Supply, Land Allocation and Economic Efficiency;* and Lenard, "Wasting the National Forests."

14. See Richard L. Stroup and John Baden, *Natural Resources: Bureaucratic Myths and Environmental Management* (San Francisco: Pacific Institute for Public Policy Research, 1983); also Baden and Stroup, (eds), *Bureaucracy vs. Environments.*

15. John Baden, "Clark's Opening to a New Environmentalism," *Wall Street Journal,* 5 January 1984.

16. Gary D. Libecap, *Locking up The Range: Federal Land Controls and Grazing* (San Francisco: Pacific Institute for Public Policy Research, 1981), p. 100.

17. Sterling Brubaker, "Land, Lots of Land," *Resources* 3 (February 1983): 5.

18. Marion Clawson, *The Federal Lands Revisited* (Washington, D.C.: Resources for the Future, 1976), p. 163.

19. Charles L. Schultz, *The Public Use of Private Interest* (Washington, D.C.: Brookings, 1977), p. 2

20. Ibid., pp. 5–6.

21. See, for example, Michael Ellman, *Socialist Planning* (Cambridge: Cambridge University Press, 1979).

22. See Daniel W. Bromley, "Public and Private Interests in the Federal Lands: Toward Conciliation," in George Johnston and Peter Emerson, (eds.), *Public Lands and the U.S. Economy* (Boulder, Colo.: Westview Press, 1984); Joseph L. Sax, "Why We Will Not (Should Not) sell the Public lands: Changing Conceptions of Private Property," *Utah Law Review* no. 2 (1983); and John V. Krutilla, Anthony C. Fisher, William F. Hyde, and V. Kerry Smith, "Public versus Private Ownership: The Federal Lands Case," *Journal of Policy Analysis and Management* 2, no. 4 (Summer 1983).

23. At least a partial exception is Sax, "Why We Will Not (Should Not) Sell the Public Lands." See also Joseph L. Sax, "The Claim for Retention of the Public Lands," in Sterling Brubaker, (ed.), *Rethinking the Federal Lands* (Washington, D.C.: Resources for the Future, 1984).

24. See Krutilla, "Public versus Private Ownership: The Federal Lands Case"; Bromley, "Public and Private Interests in the Federal Lands"; Carlisle Ford Runge, "The Fallacy of 'Privatization,'" *Journal of Contemporary Studies* 22 (Winter 1984); and Christopher K. Leman, "The Revolution of the Saints: The Ideology of Privatization and Its Consequences for the Public Lands," paper prepared for a panel on The Political Economy of Privatization: Two Points of View, at a National Symposium on Selling the Federal Forests, University of Washington, Seattle, 22–23 April 1983.

25. See Robert H. Nelson, "The Public Lands" in Paul R. Portney, (ed.), *Current Issues in Natural Resource Policy* (Washington, D.C.: Resources from the Future, 1982); Robert H. Nelson, "A Long-Term Strategy for the Public Lands," in Richard Ganzel, (ed.), *Resource Conflicts in the West* (Reno: Nevada Public Affairs Institute—University of Nevada, March 1983); and Robert H. Nelson, "Making Sense of the Sagebrush Rebellion: A Long-Term Strategy for the Public Lands," paper prepared for presentation at the Third Annual Conference of the Association for Public Policy Analysis and Management, Washington, D.C., 23–25 October 1981.

26. See Paul Gates, *History of Public Land Law Development* (Washington, D.C.: GPO, 1968).

27. Frank Gregg, *Federal Land Transfers: The Case for a Westwide Program Based on the Federal Land Policy and Management Act* (Washington, D.C.: The Conservation Foundation, 1982), pp. 17–18.

28. Ibid., pp. 18–19.

29. Letter to *Washington Post,* from Dean A. Rhoads (assemblyman, Nevada legislature), 21 September 1981.

30. Quoted in Gordon T. Lee, "What if the Government Held a Land Sale and Hardly Anyone Showed up?" *National Journal,* 25 September 1982, p. 1630.

31. Quoted in *Public Land News,* 29 October 1981.

32. Reported ibid., 21 January 1982.

33. Quoted ibid., 4 February 1982.

34. Memorandum for the president from the Cabinet Council on Economic Affairs, on "Federal Property Review Program," 9 February 1982.

35. Executive Order 12348 of 25 February 1982, printed in *Federal Register* 47, no. 50 (1 March 1982).

36. Statement of David A Stockman, director, Office of Management and Budget, before the Senate Committee on Governmental Affairs, 25 February 1982.

37. Ibid.

38. Press release of Senator Paul Laxalt, 16 April 1982.

39. See remarks of Steven Hanke in "Privatizing Public Lands: The Ecological and Economic Case for Private Ownership of Federal Lands," *Manhattan Report,* May 1982; Steve Hanke, "The Privatization Debate: An Insider's View," *Cato Journal* 2 (Winter 1982); Steve Hanke, "Privatize Those Lands," *Reason* (March 1982); Steve Hanke, "On Privatizing the Public Domain," in Phillip Truluck, (ed.), *Private Rights and Public Lands* (Washington, D.C.: Heritage Foundation 1982.); and Steve Hanke, "Department of the Interior Land Policy," in Richard Holwill, (ed.), *Mandate for Leadership* (Washington, D.C.: Heritage Foundation, 1983).

40. Press release of Senator Paul Laxalt, 16 April 1982.

41. Attachment to memorandum from Frank A. Dubois and R. W. Piasecki (Interior Department asset management coordinators) to Bruce Selfon (acting executive director, Property Review Board), 30 April 1982.

42. Ibid.

43. Transcript of White House briefing for reporters by Secretary of the Interior James Watt and Edwin Harper, chairman of the Property Review Board, 21 May 1982.

44. Philip Shabecoff, "U.S. Plans Biggest Land Shift Since Frontier Times," *New York Times,* 3 July 1982, p. 1.

45. Peter Stoler, "Land Sale of the Century," *Time,* 23 August 1982, p. 16.

46. Memorandum from the secretary of the interior to the interior solicitor and all assistant secretaries, "Establishment of Asset Management Program Coordination Office," 9 August 1982.

47. John Baden and Richard Stroup, "Saving the Wilderness," *Reason* (July 1981).

48. See Robert H. Nelson, *The Making of Federal Coal Policy* (Durham, N.C.: Duke University Press, 1983).

49. Patrick Cox, "Land Sales Man," *Reason* (November 1982): 49.

50. Hanke, "The Privatization Debate: An Insider's View," *Cato Journal* 2 (Winter 1982) p. 662.

51. Quoted in Patrick O'Driscoll, "Legislators Blast Federal Land Sale to Pay U.S. Debt," *Nevada State Journal* (5 May 1982).

52. Ibid.

53, Editorial in the *Daily Sentinel* (Grand Junction, Colo.), 23 September 1982.

54. Larry Swisher, "Evans Denounces U.S. Land Sale Plan," *Idaho Statesman* (7 October 1982), p. 1.

55. Interior Department news release, "Interior Reaffirms That Asset Manage-

ment Land Disposals Will Be Only Small Isolated Tracts, Not Large Amounts of Acreage," 25 July 1983.

56. Memorandum from Secretary of the Interior James Watt to all Western governors, "Good Neighbor Policy," 18 July 1983.

8

Deregulation at the U.S. International Trade Commission

Lloyd R. Cohen

Introduction

Deregulation refers to the process of diminishing and reforming the scope, mandate, and role of various government agencies. The title of this paper is an oxymoron. Whatever application deregulation may have had at other government agencies, it has precious little application to the U.S. International Trade Commission (ITC).

During the course of the Reagan administration, there has been no deregulation at the ITC. This has not been the fault of President Reagan or any of his appointees. However, it is not the case that they have struggled valiantly but unsuccessfully against the "forces of darkness." The explanation for the absence of deregulation at what is arguably the most socially costly government institution is more prosaic. The legislative mandate of the ITC permits scant scope for deregulation. The ITC is fundamentally a quasi-judicial fact-finding agency, with no authority to formulate policy, and only limited discretion in carrying it out.

Although this story is bleak, it is not hopeless. There is limited scope for personal intitiative and the exercise of discretion by commissioners committed to deregulation. There are several areas where clever legal and economic analyses can ameliorate the effect of otherwise invidious laws. However, since trade regulations generally provide benefits to discrete groups that can, and do, form politically active coalitions, the possibility of reform is limited and conditioned by the political strength of those whose oxen are about to be gored. The primary focus of this paper is the tension between the fundamental and necessary social-wealth-dimishing character of the commission and the limited scope for deregulation by commisssioners who are so inclined.

Perhaps the most important role that can be played by ITC commissioners is in changing the rhetoric of regulation. Many social-wealth-diminishing policies, trade regulation included, exist because of widespread ignorance of their net cost. Were a commissioner who believes in the efficacy of markets to use his office as a pulpit and criticize the trade laws he is required to administer, those criticisms would carry great authority and like a "man bites dog" story, receive media attention. By undercutting the intellectual foundations of social-wealth-diminishing trade regulation, the deregulator can change the political debate and thereby ultimately affect the substantive law. To date, not even free trade partisans on the commission have seen that as their most significant function and raised the standard of free trade in the battle for the hearts and minds of the American people, and their congressional representatives.

Trade Laws

International trade was important enough in the late eighteenth and early nineteenth centuries to form the centerpiece of the works of Adam Smith and David Ricardo. Yet compared to today's economy, trade at the time of Ricardo was negligible. With the relative fall in transportation and communication costs, the gains from trade have multiplied. These factors, combined with some degree of international political stability and liberal tariff policies, have resulted in markets awash with products from all over the world.

Considering the importance of foreign trade, we would think there would be a high-level office of government specializing in the formation of trade policy. There are a number of government agencies whose names might imply that they had that authority. The ITC, the International Trade Administration, and the Special Trade Representative all nominally have some authority over trade policy. However, with the limited exception of the Special Trade Representative, none of these institutions creates policy; rather, they carry it out. The policy they carry out is determined by the Congress and the president.

The absence of a specialized branch of government with authority to determine trade policy might be eminently reasonable. With a few arcane exceptions, such as the optimal tariff or protection for infant industries that are of academic interest, but probably of no practical significance, economics is unequivocal in arguing that free trade is Hicks-Kaldor wealth maximizing.[1] Therefore it is reasonable for an enlightened nation to adopt a policy of free trade and be done with it. That is not the explanation for the failure of the federal government to designate an agency to formulate the nation's trade policy. We do not have a policy of free trade. Any government body made up of honest and knowledgeable individuals would have to point out that the corpus of American trade laws is not in the aggregate interest of the American people. It may be precisely to avoid such a result, while perpetuating the illusion that trade policy is being determined by independent and specialized government agencies, that the impressive and deceptive title of the ITC was chosen.[2]

Some agencies are regulatory in nature, while others, such as the ITC, are administrative. Regulatory agencies usually have a broad legislative mandate, while administrative agencies, as the name implies, administer a set of laws that are often very specific in their instructions. For example, the Justice Department has jurisdiction over certain business activity under the Sherman Act, which, in its vagueness, permits wide administrative discretion. The ITC, in contrast, administers a set of laws that give clear instructions to the commission about inquiries it must make, values it may consider, and remedies it may impose or recommend. While there is a plethora of laws that grant some jurisdiction to the ITC, well over 95 percent of the complaints that come before the commission fall into three statutory categories, known colloquially as Fair Trade, Unfair Trade, and Unfair Practices.[3] The laws applicable to each category of cases differ greatly in the procedures they require, the wrongs they seek to address, and the remedies they permit or compel.

The trade laws differ fundamentally from much of the rest of American jurisprudence. Unlike the vast body of common law and much statutory law, dealing with torts, contracts, and property, the trade laws do not reflect either an efficiency or moral standard. Rather, they are the product of political forces and reflect and embody political standards. I note this not merely to criticize the trade laws but to aid in understanding them. Criticism of the trade laws is obvious: Their net effect is to reduce the wealth and liberty of the American people. As true as that may be, the trade laws are not simply an unrestrained evil; they are not the Nuremberg race laws. The trade laws reflect political compromises and direct the commission to embody those compromises in the standards and conditions for import relief that it imposes.

FAIR TRADE LAWS

The Fair Trade Laws, as the name implies, place no burden on the domestic industry seeking import relief to allege any wrongdoing by a foreign firm or nation against which it seeks to raise an import barrier. The purported purpose of these laws is to "facilitat[e] an orderly adjustment to import competition." The commission's mandate requires it to "make an investigation to determine whether an article is being imported into the United States in such increased quantities as to be a substantial cause of serious injury, or the threat thereof, to the domestic industry producing an article like or directly competitive with the imported article."[4] The statute then goes on to define what is meant by substantial cause and to describe the variety of evidence that would lead to a conclusion of serious injury. When a finding of serious injury caused primarily by rising imports is found, the commission is required to recommend to the president to impose a tariff or quota that will remedy the injury. In lieu of such action, the commission may recommend adjustment assistance to workers, cities, and firms of the affected industry.

If the commission makes an affirmative determination, the president then has the authority to impose a trade barrier no greater than the one that the commission has recommended. The president is directed to provide import relief to the domestic industry "unless he determines that provision of such relief is not in the national economic interest of the United States."[5] This grant of authority permits the president, even if he is the most scrupulous strict constructionist, to follow a policy of free trade. Yet President Reagan, who is widely viewed as an advocate of free trade, followed a policy that cannot be sharply, or even favorably, distinguished from his predecessors.

In 1986 he adopted a commission majority recommendation and imposed a tariff on Canadian shakes and shingles in a Fair Trade case. The Canadians retaliated and imposed new restrictions on the importation of American books, computers, and semiconductors. Perhaps such examples of retaliation will have a salutary effect on protectionist sentiments in Congress.[6] All of this has something of a tempest in a teapot character. Shakes and shingles represent approximately 0.23 percent of total imports from Canada. Furthermore, after extended negotiations, the government signed a treaty to create a U.S.-Canada free trade area. It must also be said on the president's behalf that Canadian shakes and shingles compete with the same product produced in Senator Bob Packwood's state. The case was decided at the same time that the Senate Finance Committee, of which Packwood is chairman, was wrestling with the tax reform bill.

As much sympathy as one may have for the president, one must remember that there will always be political toes stepped on in following a policy of free trade. If the president's decision on shakes and shingles stood as a lonely pimple on an otherwise umblemished record, sympathy for the president's predicament might develop into understanding and approval, but it does not. In a number of other fair trade cases, he has sided with the commission majority and imposed import barriers, for example, on motorcycles and steel. In addition, early in the administration, the president continued the Voluntary Restraint Agreements (VRAs) on the importation of Japanese automobiles. On the other hand, he did remove the VRAs in 1985, and rejected the commission majority recommendations for import barriers in cases involving copper and shoes. However, even in those cases, the president failed to use the occasion as an opportunity to make the case for free trade to the American people.[7]

UNFAIR TRADE LAWS

The Unfair Trade Laws are directed at subsidies by foreign governments to their export industries, and "dumping"[8] by foreign firms. These antidumping and countervailing duty laws require the commission to determine whether a domestic "industry . . . is materially injured . . . by reason of" certain imports, and if it finds in the affirmative, a duty is automatically imposed.[9]

The various justifications for these laws range in sophistication from the naïve to the Machiavellian. Sometimes the forces of protection, recognizing that they have lost the intellectual battle on the question of the benefits of free trade, hoist the banner of fair trade. They note correctly that the world does not follow a free trade policy, governments subsidize exports and erect tariff and nontariff barriers to imports. They assert that this changes the nature of the game; in a world in which other nations do not have a free trade policy, it is not in the interest of the United States to do so.

This argument is easily countered by a return to the principles of economics. The gains to the United States from trade require only that foreigners are willing to sell goods to us more cheaply than are Americans. The source of that differential in price is of no consequence. Whether it rests on one nation: floating on an ocean of oil, having an abundance of cheap labor, or a government policy of subsidization makes no difference. Government subsidization of foreign export industries is simply a tax placed on foreign citizens for the benefit of American consumers.

Those who defend the Unfair Trade Laws assert that foreign governments could be engaged in a plan of predatory pricing. Their strategy is to price low now in order to drive out the American firms and then charge a monopoly price once they capture the market. Although intentional predatory pricing is not a logical impossibility, I know of no empirical example that supports this argument. There are few markets that could support such a possibility. For the argument to have credibility, the product in question must be broad enough so that the demand curve is relatively inelastic, and the costs of entering the industry must be so high that, having been driven from the market, American firms would require a long time to reenter, during which foreign firms could recoup earlier losses by charging monopoly prices. Consider the steel industry, a broad product category with few good substitutes requiring enormous capital.

Steel is one of the most heavily subsidized European industries. In spite of the difficulties of U.S. producers over the last quarter-century, we still hold 75 percent of the American market. It would probably take several more decades before a concerted policy of underpricing could eliminate the American steel industry as a player in the market. After that time it would require the collusion of all steel producers in all nations to maintain a monopoly price in this market. That price could last only until either the cartel broke down or American or new foreign producers entered the market. Such a scenario is more than far fetched, it is fantastic.

Others argue that we should enforce and maintain the Unfair Trade Laws and other import barriers because other nations have such barriers to our exports. In its simple formulation, this argument can be countered by a mother's response to her child, "If all your friends jumped off the Brooklyn Bridge would you want to join them?" The reason we permit imports to enter our nation is not to have markets for our exports, but rather because imports are valuable.

However, there is a form of this fair trade versus free trade argument that has some merit. There may be a game theory reason for exluding some imports. If other governments are attempting to set an optimal tariff or are captives of protectionist special interests, we need a stick and carrot to make them eliminate their barriers. When used in the *limited* roles of a bargaining chip and a deterrent, such barriers may be useful. Although this provides a justification of the Unfair Trade Laws, like arguments about infant industries or the optimal tariff, this game theory justification of barriers to imports is misused and abused by protectionist interests that have no interest in eliminating foreign barriers to our exports, but use those foreign barriers as an excuse for erecting and maintaining American barriers.

UNFAIR PRACTICES LAWS

The Unfair Practices law states that

(a) Unfair methods of competition and unfair acts in the importation of articles into the United States, or in their sale by the owner, importer, consignee, or agent of either, the effect or tendency of which is to destroy or substantially injure an industry, efficiently and economically operated, in the United States, or to prevent the establishment of such an industry, or to monopolize trade and commerce in the United States, or to restrain or monopolize trade and commerce in the United States, are declared unlawful, and when found by the Commission to exist shall be dealt with, in addition to any other provisions of law, as provided in this section.

(d) If the Commission determines as a result of an investigation under this
section, that there is violation of this section, it shall direct that the articles
concerned, imported by any person violating the provision of this section, be
excluded from entry into the United States . . . .[10]

The Unfair Practices Laws are something of a conundrum. They are part
and parcel of the Smoot-Hawley Tariff Act of 1930 and were described by
one of the supporters as "an anti-dumping law with teeth." With such a
pedigree, one would be prepared for the most pernicious of trade laws.
However, with a few bizarre twists and turns to the contrary, this statute
has proven to be the only socially beneficial trade law administered by the
commission. Section 337 has been interpreted as a remedy statute for the
protection of common law and statutory property rights. Violations of
trademarks, patents, contracts, and other tortious acts have been attacked
and remedied using section 337. This law is often the sole source of
effective relief because the wrongdoer is frequently beyond the reach of
other American laws.

The objectionable parentage of section 337, the Draconian relief it
provides, and some curious statutory language has, at times, resulted in
failures to grant relief to wronged parties. Perhaps because the commission
is in essence a protectionist institution, even these aspects of its jurisdiction
that are not socially harmful have been mistakenly viewed as being so.
Some commissioners, apparently viewing section 337 as extremely protectionist, have at times made 337 complainants jump through more hoops to
obtain relief than they require of ordinary domestic industries that only
complain of not making enough money because the Japanese are tough
competitors.

For example, during my stay at the commission, Smuckers attempted to
bring a case against a French jam manufacturer that was using gingham jar
tops virtually identical to those for which Smuckers had a common law
and registered trademark. No only did Smuckers fail to win the case, the
ITC failed even to permit institution of the case. The apparent reason was
that the imported product was sold at a higher price than Smuckers and
was marketed as a specialty item. Therefore Smuckers would not be
"destroyed or substantially injured." Section 337 has thus evolved through
commission interpretation and the deference of the Court of Appeals for
the Federal Circuit to be a nonprotectionist remedy statute, the scope and
applicability of which have been narrowed as one would hope would
happen to socially wealth-diminishing protectionist statutes.

With the limited exception of section 337, the tight legislative leash does
not permit the ITC either to make policy or carry it out in a social-wealth-
maximizing fashion. Nevertheless, it would be incorrect to assume that

the "intent" of Congress was merely to create the commission as an unrestrained force for protection. The language of each of the statutes places constraints on when the commission may recommend and impose trade barriers. The fact that those standards reflect neither an efficiency nor an ethical standard should not lead one to believe that the constraints are meant to be merely illusory. On the contrary, implicit in the injury and causation standards of each of the laws is a political judgment. The ITC is intended to be a "political body." I use that term not to imply that the commissioners are subject to the entreaties of lobbyists and government officials. To the contrary, the ITC is intended to be the forum that explicitly measures at least some dimensions of the political strength of those forces without being subject to their pressure. The trade laws are intended to give relief to domestic industries when they are suffering sufficiently and can justifiably blame that suffering on imports.

Rationales for Commissioners

The scope for discretion permitted by the statutes is limited, and the factual determination the commission is called on to make does not allow for consideration of economic factors like efficiency and consumer welfare. A commissioner who believes in free trade may be tempted to ignore the oath of office and the wishes of Congress as expressed in the statutes and instead carry out the policy he *knows* to be right. On the other hand the commissioner's scrupulous side urges respect for, and faithful execution of, the law. These are hardly a pleasant set of choices: Enforce laws that reduce the wealth and freedom of American citizens or further erode the constitutional support on which our liberty rests. Commissioners have charted different courses between this Scylla and Charybdis in their efforts efficaciously and honorably to perform the duties of their office. In addition to philosophical concerns about the nature of constitutional government, and adherence to one's oath of office, some commissioners have chosen scrupulously to enforce the trade laws out of fatalistic public-choice considerations.

The public-choice argument runs as follows. From a distance the federal government can appear to the ordinary citizen as a monolith, exercising power with single-minded direction. Up close, it is apparent that power is exercised and rents are generated through a variety of often competing institutions. Perhaps there is something like an equilibrium in the political marketplace. Were that balance to be upset at the ITC by a group gaining more influence over policy than its power would warrant, countervailing groups will redress the imbalance, perhaps by exercising power in other forums. If the alternative forum is a less efficient conduit of political power, social wealth may be further diminished, and although rent gatherers at the new forum will be wealthier, society as a whole will probably be worse off than it was before the balance was upset.

In the international trade area, domestic industries that compete with imports have significant political power. One way or another they will obtain some protection from import competition. The ITC is one avenue to this relief. Some sophisticated observers suggest that the ITC is an efficient institution for channeling protectionist sentiment and minimizing its impact. They argue that, given the political power of protectionist forces, if the ITC does not provide "sufficient" protection from imports, import-competing industries will exercise their power in a different forum. That alternative path to protection may result in a greater diminution in social wealth for a given level of benefit to the domestic industry.

Is the ITC, as an institution, a neutral buffer, designed to provide the optimal level of protection?[11] If the commission, out of a new free trade zeal, were to turn down pleas for relief by interpreting the statutes in a more restrictive way, would protectionist forces exercise their influence in a different forum, for example Congress? Would Congress, being a more clumsy institution than the commission, grant relief that is more costly to the American people?

It is not clear whether protectionist forces can succeed in Congress, and if they can, whether Congress will provide a more costly form of relief than the ITC. It is clear that the current body of ITC-administered laws is not economically efficient, and it is doubtful that the laws are "optimal" even given our political system.

The relief that the commission is empowered to provide imposes substantial deadweight costs in addition to those inherent in any form of import barrier. First, the process for obtaining relief involves high transaction costs. Depending on the case there will often be a small army of industry witnesses, economists, and, of course, attorneys appearing for both sides.[12] Second, under some of the statutes that the commission administers, the class of imports for which relief may be granted is arbitrary and bears no relation to the cost imposed on the American people and the benefit conferred on the domestic industry. For example, in the antidumping and countervailing duty cases, relief is only granted upon a finding of dumping by a foreign firm or subsidization by a foreign government. There is little reason to suspect that dumping and subsidization bear any relation to the domestic industry's desire to exclude the imports or the American public's loss by that exclusion. Third, the commission is empowered to recommend quotas in cases brought under the fair trade laws. Quotas are generally held to be the least economically efficient form of import barrier. It is not credible that the ITC, nor any other government agency, is the product of some sort of infallible invisible hand of political economy. Therefore the public-choice argument for a scrupulous enforcement of the trade laws by the ITC is far from proven.

Economically Beneficial Statutory Construction

Regardless of whether the ITC's erection of import barriers is in some public-choice sense optimal, there remains the problem that the laws that the ITC must administer have a nefarious purpose and effect. They diminish the aggregate wealth of the United States in order to create and protect economic rents in import-competing industries. The statutes were written to perform that role. If the statutes the ITC administers are so specifically drafted that they do not permit a straightforward attack on the evils of rent seeking by a consideration of factors relevant to the national interest, how can a free trade commissioner administer the law in a socially productive manner?

The ITC commissioners have represented a variety of ideological perspectives on trade issues. In defending their positions in various cases, each has found it possible and necessary to engage in statutory construction. Statutory language and legislative history are open to reasonable interpretations that ameliorate the costs of social-wealth-diminishing laws.[13] Although there are numerous laws whose intent is to raise economic rents received by paticular groups at the expense of the rest of society, no statute *explicitly* states that intent. Congress has the good sense not to state its nefarious purpose. Instead, it couches its social-wealth-diminishing legislation in language that obfuscates its true purpose. Federal agencies are commissioned by Congress to carry out the law as written in the United States Code. They are not obliged, in fact, they are not permitted, to inquire into the "intent" of Congress unless the language of the statute is unclear. And that intent, when they must inquire into it, is to be discerned from a limited set of legislative pronouncements.

The Fair Trade Laws are arguably the most egregious statute the ITC is called on to administer. Although enforcement of these laws protects or creates rents for various domestic industries at a cost to the rest of the nation, Congress did not state that as the laws' purpose. Nor does it state that they are a political compromise intended to give proper weight to the political strength of those who suffer because of imports. Instead, the statute's stated goal and purpose is to "facilitat[e an] orderly adjustment to import competiton." It probably was not the intent of the sponsors of this legislation that its nominal purpose be taken seriously. Nevertheless, there is no reason why its stated purpose should not be employed in the public interest. The relief that the commission is empowered to recommend may not exceed five years' duration. What temporary import relief could help the domestic industry adjust to import competition better than the market? In the major Escape Clause cases that came before the ITC in 1984, involving tuna, steel, and copper, then-Vice-Chairman Liebeler found that there was no relief that could be granted that was superior to the market in serving the stated goal of the law. Creative, and in these cases literal, interpretation of statutory language can sometimes undermine the most socially damaging aspects of the law.

To engage in creative statutory construction, an interesting hybrid of skills proves necessary. The preceding example of the statutory construction of the Escape Clause illustrates why a commissioner will benefit from both a like-minded economist and a like-minded lawyer on his staff. Both skills are required to grapple effectively with the issues and chart a path through statutory and procedural minefields. Many nonlawyers, economists in particular, have a justifiable suspicion of lawyers. Nevertheless, when attempting to enter the legal structure substantively to change the administration of the law, it is a necessity to come armed with your lawyer. The knowledgeable economist comes to Washington well equipped for substantive analysis. He is often unprepared for, and indeed, unaware of the procedural roadblocks to instituting desired reforms.

Consider the following example. In unfair practices cases, the ITC has in the past determined that a petitioner must engage in some sort of "manufacturing" before it is willing to grant relief. Thus an American distributor, installer, and servicer of an imported product who is suffering an infringement of some property right (patent, trademark, and so on) by another import will frequently be denied relief by the commission because the complainant does not engage in sufficient on-shore activity to constitute a "domestic industry." The ITC, like virtually all federal agencies, is subject to some sort of judicial review. Some egregious past agency practice may have been affirmed by a reviewing court. In the case of the domestic industry standard, *Shaper Mfg. Co. v. ITC,* 717 F. 2d 1368 (CAFC 1983) is such an affirmance. A commissioner who is not a lawyer may be thwarted in efforts to change administration of the law by a general counsel who argues that such affirmance is controlling and that agency practice may not be altered. Out of respect for our constitutional structure, and fear of doing something outrageous, the commissioner may decline to act aggressively.

Legal arguments can be made to support a more aggressive attempt to reform past practice. In this case there are two substantial legal reasons that suggest it is legitimate for the commission to change its stance on the domestic industry standard. First, it might be argued that the reviewing court was tacitly deferring to the discretion of the commission and likely to assent to any change in policy that could plausibly be found within the intention of the statute. Second, a good lawyer would point out that the commission was not in the posture of an inferior court, controlled by its reviewing court, and need not acquiesce to an adverse ruling. Instead, it might seek to appeal an anticipated adverse ruling by the Court of Appeals to the Supreme Court. In ferreting out areas where clever statutory construction can deflect otherwise onerous laws, commissioners have been well served by their market-oriented staff trained in economics and law.

Collecting Rents

Although the single most significant factor affecting the establishment and continuance of rent-creating and rent-maintaining institutions, such as the ITC, is the strength of political coalitions on each side, the potential marginal effect of committed deregulators is large. These principles can be illustrated by comparing the recent evolution of international trade policy and antitrust policy. The economic theory of international trade and the policy lessons to be learned from those teachings are largely unchanged since the time of Ricardo. With the exception of a few qualifications and addendums from Scitovsky and others, which have played no discernible role in forming American trade policy, economic theory unambiguously teaches that restraints on imports are social wealth dimishing. Nations and eras characterized by free trade have been prosperous compared to those characterized by protectionism.

On the other hand, in the area of merger theory and other aspects of antitrust law, the policy implications of economic theory are ambiguous, and the empirical evidence, though persuasive, is not overwhelming. A merger could be intended to result in economics of scale and scope and may do so. Alternatively, its purpose and effect may be to monopolize the industry. The "new learning" has persuaded more and more economists that on balance mergers are procompetitive and the better policy is to allow them. Nonetheless, the certainty attached to this view is far less than that of the efficacy of free trade.

What has been the history of deregulation in these two areas during the last several years? In the field of international trade, there has been no progress. In fact, in some respects, protectionist interests have grown in power. There have been VRAs for autos, and similar "voluntary" restraints are being negotiated for steel. This is in sharp contrast to recent antitrust policy, where deregulation has proceeded apace. The FTC and Justice Department have substantially liberalized their regulatory policies; mergers are no longer viewed with the same suspicion.

What explains the anomaly that in international trade, an area where economists should be most persuasive, no progress in deregulation has been made, while in antitrust, an area where economic analysis is more problematic, substantial progress has been made? The answer lies in the strength of political coalitions on each side.

The primary beneficiaries of import barriers are a number of well organized import-competing industries; the primary losers are consumers. In the antitrust field, the primary beneficiaries of a system of government restrictions on mergers and other "monopolistic" behavior are lawyers and others with expertise in this area. The losers are the firms planning such activity, and if mergers are efficient, the public at large. Although lawyers are a politically powerful group, their interest in maintaining a body of inefficient antitrust laws is not on the same scale as the interest of assorted industries in protection from imports.[14]

The lesson in all this is that the possibility and scope of deregulation is conditioned and limited by special interests[15] that must be overcome. The growth of the misguided body of antitrust law appears to have rested more on misunderstanding than organized special interests. Therefore it was relatively easy for a new broom to sweep clean. One should not be overly hopeful about the prospects of dismantling those areas of federal government regulation that generate large rents for special interests.

However, when political forces are nearly in equipoise, and public ignorance or inadequate analysis supports the promulgation and continuation of social-wealth-diminishing regulation, there is an opportunity for administrators to play a positive role. The single most intellectually challenging case that came before the ITC during my tenure illustrates this point. It involved gray market goods.[16] In the gray market there are large organized coalitions on each side, so that neither side has the political power to affect the law critically. I believe that in dealing with this case, none of the relevant government bodies based its position on the political power of the contending parties. Aside from deciding the issue on the merits, the only other discernible concern was turf. While in this case the position I favored was rejected, in the next case free market/property rights analysis could carry the day with minimal political consequences.

Why Do They Call It "Dumping"?

Public-choice economists have demonstrated the importance of coalitions as a major force in generating government policy. Nevertheless, public discussion and debates about policies do take place. For example, in the 1984 election campaign, the AFL-CIO used television advertising to promote protectionist legislation. The expression of ideas matters. How else do we explain the desire to classify imports as "unfairly" traded or "dumped"? If there were no one to fool, and if fooling someone did not serve a purpose, such deceptive language would not be employed. By using the authority of public office to buttress the logic of arguments, the free trade commissioner can educate the public about the evils of protectionism.

Those steeped in the teachings of the efficacy of markets are prone to forget that those teachings, and the policy implication of deregulation, are not obvious, and in fact may be counterintuitive. Policy makers, legislators, and their constituencies have a tendency in the absence of knowledge and understanding to regress to populist positions. Undercutting the intellectual legitimacy of special interest, social-wealth-diminishing government activity will help destroy its popular support. For better or worse, we are governed through a representative democracy with universal suffrage. Therefore we must educate the public and rely on the strength of ideas to help protect our liberty and our wealth.

The logic and science that support the argument for free trade are not esoteric. They have been presented in academic journals and, to a lesser extent, in the popular press for decades. Nevertheless, the variety of myths that surround the area of international trade are no mean obstacle to eliminating trade barriers. The median citizen probably believes that imports destroy jobs, that jobs must be protected, that subsidies by foreign governments to their export industries are harmful to the United States, and a host of other flawed propositions that support a body of invidious laws and policies.

How is it that convincing scholarly analysis fails to erase public ignorance and misunderstanding? Logic and science are frequently either ambiguous in their policy implications, or as a practical matter inaccessible to a general audience. To some extent we are persuaded not only by the logic that supports a proposition but by the authority of its source as well. This highlights a most important role for the free market commissioner. When academics or importers argue that trade barriers are a net cost to the nation, it does not carry the same weight as when these views are presented by individuals or agencies whose legislative mandate is to erect and enforce those barriers. The promarket commissioner is in a position to use the authority of office to buttress sound analysis and thereby change the rhetoric of regulation.

In presenting arguments to the public, the economist/administrator must use language persuasively. I attended a Senate hearing on takeovers at which a prominent economist was testifying against more regulation, and a prominent securities lawyer was testifying in favor. This debate is not new. Both theory and empirical evidence support the economist's position. Arguments based on such evidence should be convincing. However, the lawyer's presentation was more persuasive than the economist's, because he employed metaphor and analogy to great advantage in arguing his case.

Metaphor is a formidable rhetorical tool; however, when used inappropriately, it leaves the speaker open to being hoisted by his own petard. The securities lawyer constantly referred pejoratively to "bust-up" mergers, attempting to convey the image of a successful corporation being dismantled and its assets sucked into the vortex of a black hole. The economist could have played on the metaphor, explaining that the image it conveyed was precisely the opposite of the reason for, and result of, mergers. Following the merger assets remain in existence, and in fact move into hands that value them more highly. He would have been more persuasive if, besides presenting empirical evidence of the wealth-increasing effect of tender offers, he had illustrated the theory of tender offers by metaphor, that is, the market for corporate control that disciplines managers and benefits consumers and shareholders.

Economists are trained to argue in a way that convinces other economists. They tend to rely on the tools of their profession: "scientific" models and empirical evidence that never prove anything. Because the premises and assumptions employed by economists are not treated as holy writ by a wider audience, the arguments presented often fail to persuade the layman. Lawyers are less constrained in the form of argument they employ, and often are better equipped to persuade the public and policymakers of the correctness of their views. Whatever his professional training, the free trade commissioner must craft arguments and use language that will convince an audience.

Ideas Can Have Consequences

One reason for believing that ideas matter is that many of the other things that determine how decisions are made are trivial. There are various models of public decision making that purport to explain government activity. The public-interest model, resting on notions of government as the efficient provider of collective goods, may describe the necessary minimum characteristics of government expenditure, but it clearly does not explain its discretionary activities. On the other hand, the public-choice paradigm is based on the self-interest of decision makers to explain government activity. However, because the preferences of decisonmakers are so varied, this model has not fully explained agency decision making.

Commissioners will indeed probably decide issues in a manner that reflects their interests. Those interests are never merely financial in a narrow sense because laws restricting unethical behavior by government officials constrain and discourage self-serving behavior in a grossly financial sense. With the exception of those decisions that may affect future employment opportunities, the benefits are too small and the costs too great for a commissioner to act in an obviously self-serving manner.

Nevertheless, there are many ways in which decisionmakers may serve their own interests. Some are apparently as petty as scheduling official activities out of town in order to take free trips. More common, and less visible, are commissioners simply deciding issues in the manner that requires the least effort. When a decision is difficult to make, the very effort of weighing various considerations on each side entails mental and time costs. In addition, there is fear of making the "wrong" decision, and appearing stupid and ill-informed. Therefore when a commissioner lacks sufficient expertise to understand arcane issues, he may simply follow the lead of other commissioners. Alternatively, out of laziness, inertia, or fear, a commissioner may adopt a particular narrow technique for analyzing issues and apply it ad nauseam.

Finally, some commissioners get psychic satisfaction from administering laws as they perceive Congress intended. I point out these different types of self-serving behavior, first, to illustrate that utility maximization encompasses a wide variety of behavior and that models based on that assumption do little to narrow the predicted character of government activity; and second, to reemphasize that ideas can make a difference because the interests they must battle against are often not that strong.

Conclusion

Government is a varied place, filled with a congeries of institutions designed to serve multiple political roles. Even in this varied group, the ITC is a singularly curious agency. Its pernicious purpose and clear mandate from a vigilant Congress give scant room for socially productive administration by truly public-spirited commissioners. Nevertheless in tailoring an agenda to the mandate of Congress, an ITC commissioner need not behave as a passive functionary, but can exercise some personal discretion. Some ITC commissioners, aware of the pernicious effect of protectionism, have managed to be active warriors in the battle against an overactive government, while at the same time adhering to their constitutional duty to administer the law. Thus far they have usually found themselves in the minority on commission votes. Should they at some point form a majority and effectively dam the flow of successful import relief petitions, it will set the stage for the next act in the drama. The possibility of thwarting social-wealth-reducing policies is limited and conditioned by the political strength of the special interests whose rents are at stake. The triumph of a free trade philosophy at the commission will lead lobbyists for import-competing industries to seek relief elsewhere.

Nevertheless, protectionist policies exist and flourish in part because of widespread ignorance of their net cost. Therefore the most useful role that the commissioner who believes in the efficacy of markets can perform is to use public office as a pulpit. Were an ITC commissioner to criticize the trade laws that the commission is required to administer, it would carry greater authority, and be more newsworthy, than when the same views are uttered by academics. By undercutting the intellectual, moral, and political legitimacy of the rent-creating and rent-gathering institutions of the state, trade regulation in particular, the deregulator can perform a most useful role. The ITC has been around a long time and unless there is a greater awareness on the part of the American people of the evils of protectionism, it will be here for a long time to come. More importantly, whether or not the ITC exists, as long as the forces of protectionism can drape themselves in the cloak of national interest without the public recognizing the sham, import-competing industries will seek and receive comfort from some branch of the federal government.

Notes

1. The truth of this assertion may not be apparent to some readers. Scitovsky was the first to note that the goal of increasing social wealth is not necessarily achieved by a policy of free trade. Each nation has it within its power to impose an optimal set of import tariffs and export duties in order to improve terms of trade. As a practical matter any attempt to create such a policy is doomed to failure for three substantial reasons.

First, such a policy would be part of a negative-sum game. A nation can only gain from such a policy if other nations do not respond in kind. The gain to the United States in engaging in such a policy can come only at the greater expense of the rest of the world and vice versa. Some might object on those grounds alone, arguing that the U.S. government should be as concerned about those in other nations as about Americans. However, even those who still cling to the traditional notion that the first duty of a government is to secure the welfare of its own citizens should see the fallacy of such a policy. The policy prerogatives of the United States are available to the rest of the world as well. Every country can seek to impose the optimal tariff; however, because it is a negative-sum game, if all nations engage in it, *all* are likely to be worse off. Our world trading system is based on a quid pro quo that no nation will try to enrich itself through such a beggar-thy-neighbor policy.

Second, discovering the optimal tariff is a substantial, costly, and possibly insoluble problem, and is certainly subject to error. Further, the optimal tariff is not like the rate of acceleration of a free-falling object on Earth; it is not a fixed number. The optimal tariff on each item of commerce will change continually, and adjusting tariff schedules would be an impossible task. On the other side it might be argued that we need not achieve perfection in order to improve national wealth, only a movement in the right direction is required. However we must recognize that we can diminish national wealth if we overshoot the mark.

Third, there is the public-choice problem: It is inconceivable that any attempt to discover and adopt an optimal tariff structure will take place without substantial interference from special-interest groups. Knowing that all calculations and estimates of appropriate tariffs are tenuous and subject to error, it would be easy for special interests to argue for higher tariffs and persuade the appropriate authorities. It is naïve to imagine that a group of experienced, professional, neutral economists will be commissioned to perform the calculations and that our legislative bodies will simply acquiesce and adopt their prescriptions. The theoretical musings of academic theoreticians are the food on which lobbyists feed.

2. The previous name of the commision was the Tariff Commission, a title that more accurately captured the flavor of the commission's mandate.

3. Respectively, sections 201–203 of the Tariff or Trade Act of 1974, 19 U.S.C. sections 2251–2253 (1982); the countervailing and antidumping duty (unfair trade) laws are contained in Title VII of the Tariff Act of 1930 (Smoot-Hawley), 19 U.S.C sections 1671–1677 (1982); and section 337 of the Tariff Act of 1930 (Smoot-Hawley), 19 U.S.C. section 1337 (1982).

4. 19 U.S.C. section 2251.

5. 19 U.S.C. section 2252.

6. See "Canada's Quick Retaliation for Shingles Tariff Prompts Some on the Hill to Rethink Protectionism," *Wall Street Journal*, 19 June 1986, p. 60.

7. President Reagan's record in appointing commissioners is perhaps somewhat better. Susan Liebeler, whom he was forced by Senate rejection to renominate several times, was quickly named vice chairman after her ultimate confirmation as commissioner. In 1986 she began a two-year stint as chairman. Mrs. Liebeler, along with the president's most recent appointees, Anne Brunsdale and Ronald Cass, are almost certainly the most antiprotectionist commissioners to sit on the ITC in memory. The president's nominations have not been universally antiprotectionist, however. Two other appointees, Seeley Lodwick and Dave Rohr, are cast from the standard quasi-protectionist mold. Rohr, a Democrat, it is rumored, was renominated in 1985 as part of some sort of package deal involving approval of Brunsdale. Lodwick's nomination to the commisison is at first blush inscrutable. Commissioner Lodwick, a Republican, has no discernible trade philosphy. This makes him an ideal candidate from the Senate's perspective but it is difficult to see why a president with the freedom to address more catholic concerns, and an alleged appreciation of the virtues of free trade, would choose such a man. However, once one recognizes that the Senate views the ITC as its own creation and is more inclined to reject nominees for this commission than for any other governmental body, it is easier to understand why the president must compromise in the personnel choices he makes.

8. It is the International Trade Administration (ITA) of the Department of Commerce, rather than the ITC, that determines whether or not imports are being

dumped. Those not familiar with the art of government linguistics should note that dumping as understood by economists bears only a passing resemblance to the concept employed by the Department of Commerce in its calculations. For example, the ITA's definition allows it to calculate dumping margins for firms that do not even have a home market for their product! Several years ago an American sporting goods company suggested to the Polish government that it produce golf carts for sale in the American market. Since there were no golf courses in Poland, it is difficult to see how dumping could take place. Nonetheless when an American competitor brought suit, the ITA was not deterred and attempted to determine whether the golf carts were being sold in the United States at less than cost. One major difficulty in this case was that cost data is even more unreliable in nonmarket economies than in our own. The ITA's procedure in such cases is to find a market economy at a similar level of development as the nonmarket economy and assume that costs are the same. The ITA chose Spain as the appropriate country of comparison. Unfortunately Spain did not produce golfcarts, nevertheless the ITA "proved" that had the Spaniards produced golfcarts, they would have cost them more than the Poles were selling them for. Case closed. If this case were merely apocryphal it would be humorous. Considering the level of Polish external debt, it is at best tragicomic.

9. A countervailing duty is designed to offset subsidies placed on American imports by the government of the exporting country. The Countervailing and Antidumping Duties laws are part of the Tariff Act of 1930, 19 U.S.C. sections 1671–1677 (1982).

10. Section 337 of the Tariff Act of 1930, 19 U.S.C. section 1337 (1982).

11. The optimal level of protection is the minimum level consistent with the political power of protectionist forces, provided at the lowest social cost.

12. On another level of analysis, these transaction costs benefit the nation. By raising the costs to those who seek import relief they decrease the supply of import relief petitions.

13. Administrators do not have the discretion of the Supreme Court, which is wont to construe statutes to mean the opposite of their language and intent. See, for example, United Steelworkers of America v. Weber, 443 U.S. 193 (1979), in which the Court interpreted Title VII of the Civil Rights Act of 1964, which declared it unlawful "to discriminate [in hiring] . . . because of . . . race," to condone such discrimination when blacks are being favored. Justice Rehnquist in his dissent compares the majority's statutory construction to the "newspeak" of Orwell's *Nineteen Eighty-Four,* ibid. p. 219. Nevertheless the Supreme Court has set a precedent that has been followed, albeit not so shamelessly, by other government bodies, of construing the law as they believe it should be, rather than as it is.

14. Another difference between protectionism and antitrust law is the longevity of the interest group. The steel industry's gains from protection are true economic rents, while those of lawyers from the antitrust laws are quasi rents. Even if we did away with import barriers tomorrow, in fifty years there would still be a steel industry and its labor union wanting protection. On the other hand, if we did away with antitrust laws tomorrow, in fifty years lawyers with human capital in antitrust

would all be out of the market. The new crop of lawyers learning a new set of antitrust laws would earn only their opportunity cost.

15. I am using the term "special interest" to refer to a group seeking a policy that subsidizes a segment of society at a greater cost to the rest of the nation, that is, a social-wealth-diminishing policy.

16. Gray market goods are unauthorized but otherwise authentic imports. They enter the domestic market against the wishes of authorized importers and depress the price. The issue before the ITC was whether holders of the trademark in this country had the right to use Customs to exclude gray market imports. Our office argued that there was substantial and legitimate trademark justification for such a vertical restraint and that its enforcement by Customs was appropriate.

9

Civil Aeronautics Board Sunset: Sunrise at the Department of Transportation?

George W. Douglas and Peter Metrinko

Introduction

It is the thesis of this paper that Congress may have made a grave mistake in turning over the remaining economic regulatory controls over the airline industry possessed by the late, but not lamented, Civil Aeronautics Board (CAB) to an unwilling recipient, the Department of Transportation (DOT). The DOT's overall mission is to develop and support transportation modes. Questions remain: Can a free market regulatory approach survive in such an atmosphere, and will the stated intentions of DOT leadership to prevent regeneration of the CAB be successful?[1]

Students of regulation and government policy who analyze the economic activities of governments from a rent-seeking perspective should not be at all surprised that such a question is raised so soon after the CAB's wake. Nor should they be surprised at details of the funeral preparations during the preceding eighteen months. We have occupied the first pew observing the process, and believe a recounting of preburial ministrations and DOT's handling of its executor duties is worth reflecting on.

The Need for Regulatory Reform

First, consider the events that led to the CAB's demise. The pre-1978 regulatory system governing airlines was established in 1938.[2] It had not changed substantially since that date. During the ninety-fourth and ninety-fifth Congresses, the Aviation Subcommittees held extensive hearings on the need to reform airline regulation, and scores of witnesses expressed dissatisfaction with the existing regulatory system.[3]

Under the existing regulatory system, airlines were subject to extensive economic regulation that created an imperfect cartel producing supracompetitive rents for employees and managers and no better than compensatory returns for airline stockholders.[4] The traveling public was adversely affected as well: CAB regulation severely limited price-service alternatives available to consumers, preventing low-fare service, so that consumers had to use high-service interstate airlines or not use interstate airlines at all.[5]

Airline management did not have the same control over its basic operational decisions as did management in other industries.[6] For example if an airline wanted to change the routes it served or the rates it charged, it had to obtain permission from the CAB.[7] Even if the board ultimately granted an airline's request, it would do so only after lengthy administrative proceedings.[8] Hearings frequently took years to complete and often required the parties to spend hundreds of thousands of dollars for lawyers and economists.[9]

During the congressional hearings there was little support for these anticompetitive regulatory policies. From the industry's standpoint, financial conditions under restrictive CAB regulation were worsening. The CAB's target rate of return on investment for airlines was about 12 percent. Between 1968 and 1975, CAB-regulated airlines' rate of return was less than 7 percent for all but one year.[10]

At first blush, it is difficult to understand why airlines were doing so poorly, since the CAB was providing the industry with more secure restrictions on entry and fare competition than the strongest private cartel. However, with entry restricted and fares fixed, airlines sought to compete the only way they could: through service-quality rivalry.[11] The most costly form of service-quality rivalry commonly engaged in by the airlines was increased flight frequency to accommodate scheduling preferences of prospective passengers. This nonprice competition also contributed to cost and ate away at profit.[12] It was only after the CAB loosened its regulatory grip that the industry started to prosper.[13]

Airline employees were perhaps the major beneficiaries from CAB regulation. A wage increase under rate regulation is simply passed on to customers as a fare increase. Employees knew they could demand higher wages without fear of the airline's failure because the CAB would seek to prevent the failure of firms in the industry.[14]

Results of Deregulation

ENTRY AND ROUTE RESTRUCTURE

Commentators have disagreed about the extent of the success of airline deregulation, but there is a general consensus among neutral commentators that it has been mostly successful:[15] There has been substantial new entry by air carriers;[16] existing carriers have expanded route systems so that a larger number of carriers serve most major city pairs;[17] and route structures have substantially improved. Many airlines have adopted efficient hub-spoke systems marked by a large number of flights arriving at a hub during a short period of time, followed by an equally large number of turnaround departures.[18]

FARES AND SERVICE

Reduced fares have received a great deal of postderegulation discussion. When adjusted for inflation, the vast majority of airline fares have decreased.[19] The greatest decline in fares paid has taken place in long-haul and major-city markets. The average fare paid in the long-haul market has fallen about 9 percent, while it has fallen nearly 15 percent in the short-haul, large-city market.[20] On the other hand, even though the average fare paid in short-haul and medium-haul small-city markets is up, this fact must be contrasted with what would have occurred had pervasive economic regulation continued. For example, in Australia, which has two major airlines subject to regulation, an index of coach airfares shows substantially greater increases in real terms than U.S. increases.[21]

While many airline travelers are now flying in long-haul and medium-distance markets for less, their comfort has apparently suffered. Load factors have increased from around 55 percent in 1976 to 59 percent in 1982, and the number of passengers per plane is up 25 percent.[22] But that is not all bad news—it also means that airlines are operating more efficiently and passengers have a greater number of alternative price-service options.[23]

EFFECT ON CAPITAL AND LABOR

Stockholders have generally benefitted from deregulation. For example, despite the bankruptcy of Braniff and the poor economic performance of some other major airlines, the real value of the ten trunk airlines, including Pan Am, was virtually unchanged from 1976 through 1983, and regional carriers substantially outperformed the overall market.[24]

Although labor captured most of the economic rents under regulation, it has not fared well under deregulation.[25] Competitive forces have dissipated rents with startling efficiency. Fourteen nonunion airlines have entered the industry, and some established airlines have set up nonunion subsidiaries. These airlines are paying their employees considerably less and expanding their duties. People Express, for example, requires its employees to be willing to fill any job as needed. In 1984 a People Express pilot was paid about $30,000 per year; the counterpart at TWA received about $104,000.[26] The growth of this nonunion sector has caused organized labor to agree to wage reductions.[27] In 1982, for the first time, railroad wage-fringe levels outstripped those of the airline industry.[28]

Legal Problems with the ADA

While economists were analyzing the economic effects of deregulation, lawyers were noticing something else—the Airline Deregulation Act of 1978 (ADA) had not been a statutory draftsman's masterpiece. Many loose ends needed to be gathered up.

The ADA provided, among other things, for the sunset of the CAB on 1 January 1985. The functions of the CAB not terminated by the ADA were to be transferred to various federal agencies.[29] For example, the authority to grant antitrust immunity to the industry was to go to the Department of Justice. Most other functions (foreign air transportation jurisdiction, small-community essential air service program) were to be transferred to DOT. No provisions were included in the ADA concerning the CAB's consumer protection activities. It now appears this was simply an oversight.

The most recent legislation, the Civil Aeronautics Board Sunset Act of 1984,[30] was motivated by several concerns, including what would happen to consumer protection rules enforced by the CAB at sunset. These rules dealt with smoking, denied-boarding compensation, public charters, baggage liability, and rules on airline-owned computer reservation systems.

In the absence of any specific provisions dealing with the consumer protection issues, the current administration—whose voice on transportation matters is DOT—believed the Federal Trade Commission (FTC) could use its general powers to police airline consumer protection matters.[31] Essentially, DOT believed that an exception in the FTC Act for "air carriers. . . . subject to the Federal Act of 1958"[32] should be ignored because the exception was placed in the FTC Act when the CAB was created in order to avoid overlapping jurisdiction. The DOT's legal analysis concluded that the bar would dissolve at the sunset of the CAB. This was, however, widely viewed as an open invitation to litigation.

The DOT's position was part of an overall plan to forestall perceived attempts to reregulate legislatively. Although wishing away the consumer protection legal problem was a noble idea, it failed. The FTC itself testified that it doubted it had the statutory authority to assume the function because of section 5.[33] The FTC noted existing CAB rules would not be transferred to the FTC under the ADA and it would be difficult for the FTC to formulate new rules quickly. Under the so-called Magnuson-Moss rulemaking procedures, enacted by Congress to put reins on the runaway FTC of the 1970s, rulemakings take several years at a minimum to complete.[34] Essentially, the Magnuson-Moss rules require a hybrid between informal rulemaking and rulemaking on the record.

Another perceived problem, at least by Representative Mineta who initiated the hearing process for the 1984 sunset legislation, was the fact that the ADA provided for international and essential air service consumer functions to be performed by DOT. Thus two separate federal entities could be formulating aviation consumer protection rules beginning in 1985. The DOT and FTC spokesmen testified that measures could be worked on cooperatively, with the FTC taking the lead on most consumer protection matters. Mineta believed, however, that only one agency should enforce consumer protection laws. The FTC seemed the logical choice to the administration, and DOT did not want the authority. In addition the FTC enforces similar consumer protection laws involving many other industries. Expertise was not a problem—a small FTC consumer protection staff would be transferred to the FTC. Why, then, did DOT receive the authority?

For one, transferring functions to the FTC would have stripped Representative Mineta's committee of authority to deal with airline consumer protection matters. This is not meant pejoratively—Representative Mineta has an avid interest in airline matters and is frequently a leading voice on important airline issues. Second, airlines were lobbying for antitrust authority over airlines to be placed with DOT rather than the Antitrust Division of the Justice Department. They believed DOT would be more compliant on antitrust issues and might be more willing to grant exemptions from the antitrust law for intercarrier agreements.[35]

In additon, some air carriers feared that the FTC would advocate competition, and ignore individual pleas for protectionism that might seem warranted. They knew that two FTC commissioners, Chairman James C. Miller III and George W. Douglas, had collaborated on a book that championed an efficiency approach to the airline industry.[36] They also misperceived FTC staff comments in the CAB's computer reservation systems rulemaking as indicating insensitivity to the competitive implications of computer reservation system ownership controlled by two major carriers.[37] Rather than simply assuming that consumers and air carriers were being harmed by so-called bias in operating computer reservations systems owned by American and United Airlines, these comments instead suggested that the CAB should try to measure consumer harm and assess the net effects of imposing a regulatory "solution" to this perceived market failure.

The FTC staff position was sound. It is bad policy to *assume* a major premise like consumer harm. It is also bad policy to consider a regulatory solution to a perceived market failure without considering all the pros and cons of such action. The FTC had been roundly criticized for years for much the same thing in its own rulemakings.

In any event, the final, *final* deregulaiton bill passed with little fuss— Representative Mineta was one of the few members of Congress showing any interest in this "clean-up" legislation, and his decisions carried the day. The administration, for its part, realized it could not threaten a veto over such an isolated issue as which agency would receive antitrust and consumer protection authority. The administration's only persuasive argument was that the bill not be a "Christmas tree" of special interest legislation, to which Representative Mineta readily agreed. While it may not have been a Christmas tree, the legislation did contain several special-interest ornaments.

The new legislation's major effects were to give DOT several new responsibilities, including:[38]

- review and approval authority over the consolidation, merger, and acquisition of control of air carriers;

- authority over interlocking relationships among air carriers;

- authority to approve cooperative agreements among air carriers; and

- authority to grant antitrust immunity to the already-mentioned agreements.

The legislation also preserved the CAB's rulemaking authority under section 204, which would otherwise sunset. It transferred the authority to prevent unfair or deceptive practices and the authority to assure "safe and adequate service" to DOT. This is the core of the so-called consumer authority that the ADA did not address. It also sunset all merger and antitrust exemption authority effective 1 January 1989.

The Opportunity and Demand for Reregulation

What the legislation does from a political standpoint is perhaps more important. It is the thesis of this paper that by placing all residual airline regulatory functions in DOT, it creates an opportunity for reregulation of the airline industry. Surely, attempts at regulation are constantly made by those seeking special favors or advantages over rivals.[39] Why should DOT be a more fertile ground for airline reregulation than, for example antitrust agencies that were deliberately bypassed in the final sunset legislation?

The thesis we advance is that because DOT's overall goals of supporting and developing transportation through subsidies and the like stand in marked contrast with the competition-oriented goals of antitrust agencies, reregulation stands a better chance at DOT than it would if antitrust agencies had been given a direct role over airlines.[40] We also advance the thesis that the human response to problems is different at DOT than it is at antitrust agencies because bureaucrats' goals at the two types of agencies differ.

The DOT's function is largely to be supportive of the transportation network and the operating modes. Under the DOT umbrella stand nine administrations whose jurisdictions include highway, urban mass transit, railroad, and maritime development, construction, and subsidization. For the most part these administrations openly view their constituency to be transport providers. For example, in order to support the airline network, the Federal Aviation Administration (FAA) is responsible for airspace and air traffic management, and construction and development of air navigation facilities.[41]

In marked contrast, the antitrust agencies seek to promote consumer welfare by ensuring a level playing field on which businesses of all sizes can compete fairly. This is done by intervening in the market only in those rare cases when there is a market imperfection. How does this difference in missions translate into real differences in policy execution? We must focus on the human factor. Our first focus is on the desire of bureaucrats to minimize risk and seek rewards.

Many government agencies and their personnel (from the cabinet secretary to the lowliest clerk who has any policy contribution) minimize *risks* by trying to avoid public error. This is especially true when the agency's mission is sensitive and prone to newsworthy disasters.[42] At an agency like DOT, which has responsibility for transportation safety, this may include, for example, avoiding public perception that the airline traffic control system is unsafe. An air crash attended by stories of an overworked traffic controller must be avoided at all costs. One must also avoid perceptions that air traffic delays have been caused by bureaucratic mismanagement—indeed, some portion of the general public may believe the two problems are one and the same.[43] Recognizing the need to avoid these public perceptions, DOT staff are probably inclined to emphasize short-run solutions to problems involving airport congestion—the public must be reassured at all times that the air traffic system works, even if one must use high cost, short-run solutions. Thus DOT staff are likely to dismiss "invisible" economic inefficiencies as long as the system runs smoothly. We discuss the congestion example in more detail later, for it shows how bureaucrats react to problems with high public awareness.

Because of the nature of their mission, DOT staff are also prone to seek *rewards* by identifying solutions that involve active government supervision. Indeed paradoxically many bureaucrats with an affirmative mandate to regulate in the "public interest" seek to ensure future rewards by eagerly identifying even the smallest problem. This enables them to do two complementary things: avoid the chance that the problem will become highly public, and seize an opportunity to prove their necessity. For example, a bureaucrat may try a series of piecemeal regulatory approaches that attempt to correct small-scale public errors, avoiding a full-scale free market approach that invites scrutiny because of newsworthy short-run dislocations.

In contrast, bureaucrats at agencies where free market solutions are the norm have different risk and reward incentives. For example, the antitrust mission of the FTC and Antitrust Division are anathema to an intrusive regulatory approach. Antitrust agency staff see the world in terms of market systems that generally solve "problems" over time. Even minimal restraints (and regulations are viewed as particularly potent restraints) on competition are viewed with suspicion. Thus the antitrust viewpoint on airport congestion would be that it would not infinitely worsen and the problem would probably be self-correcting: At some point air carriers with less highly valued flights would be forced by the high costs attendant to congestion to move flights to less congested times.

Antitrust personnel seek to avoid *risk* in a different way than the typical bureaucrat. Imminent disaster is usually not a realistic fear. If a merger is unwisely allowed to proceed, for example, the deleterious results will not be known for some time and may be publicly invisible (the "truth" will appear only in obscure economics journals). Staff attorneys know they cannot propose antitrust enforcement without a solid empirical basis for the proposal. Staff supervisors are acutely aware of the antitrust movement away from the structuralist school, where, briefly put, "big was bad," and toward a more analytical approach.[44] The agencies also seek to avoid the displeasure of the courts for cases that are empirically unsound—the FTC suffered in the courts for its wildly experimental antitrust cases brought in the late 1970s.[45] Indeed both agencies have extensive "intervention" programs where the staff participates in regulatory and judicial proceedings on all levels of government advocating free market approaches to perceived "problems."[46]

Antitrust agency personnel receive *rewards* by policing the free market, on the lookout for those who would impose restraints to disrupt the market. Thus it is not surprising that the FTC's Bureau of Competition has gone as far as suing local governments for allegedly establishing local taxicab cartels, recognizing that the most pernicious cartels are those that have power to enforce their anticompetitive rules.

Differences can also be found in the training and education of antitrust personnel and most other government personnel. The FTC and Antitrust Division, for example, are predominantly staffed by lawyers trained in economics, and by economists. On the other hand, DOT has, of necessity, a highly trained, technical staff to oversee such matters as construction projects and engineering defects that cause safety problems.

Economists and engineers have distinctly different approaches and perceptions. Economists view the world and describe its characteristics in terms of equilibrium systems. A positivist economist seldom characterizes an observed characteristic as a problem. And not all problems require solutions—the equilibrium system takes care of most problems.

The engineer, by contrast, perceives the world pragmatically. By instinct and training, he seeks to solve problems by adjusting mechanisms; an engineer is a tinkerer by nature. We would suggest that the engineer's instinct to identify and solve probvlems is shared by most noneconomist public servants.

Simply put, there is a legitimate fear that DOT may eventually respond to its role as economic regulator (perhaps in a more regulatorily activist administration) by allowing the (vastly superior in number) industry-supportive and engineering side of the agency to dominate. A recent example involving delays in takeoffs and landings at busy airports, discussed below in the section on airline competition and the slot market, demonstrates the possibility that even under highly procompetitive leadership, DOT has a tendency to respond with "engineered" approaches to problems.

From where are demands for reregulation likely to come? Obviously, groups that see themselves suffering long-term disadvantages from deregulation may demand protection. Thus it was not surprising that the head of the wage-embattled Air Line Pilots Association proposed minimum fare legislation.[47] It is difficult to tell what other long-term losers might exist since the industry is still in its postderegulation shakeout period (albeit with much less volatility). Interestingly, industry executives have largely been quiet on the subject of the need for regulation. They may remember that airlines did not do very well under strict regulation.

Demands for reregulation may persist among other groups, however. Bureaucrats have job security incentives that may lead them to entertain questionable regulatory solutions. Members of Congress may seek to make political capital out of perceived problems; they can use the potential of regulation to attract hopeful campaign contributors. Congressional committee staffs have much the same set of bureaucratic incentives as their executive branch counterparts. Indeed, one can imagine that a perceived yet nonexistent "problem" might develop into a newsworthy debate if enough of these groups simply reinforced one another's incentives to have regulation-worthy problems debated. Simply put, if enough people talk about a problem, the problem has a tendency to seem "real." Thus the incentives of these groups are complementary. In the following section, we evaluate DOT's performance on one early problem under deregulation— airport congestion.

Airline Competition and the Slot Market

The initial culprit was probably the PATCO strike in August 1981, in which a majority of the nation's air traffic controllers left their jobs.[48] Faced with reduced air traffic capacity, the FAA cut back landings at twenty-two of the nation's busiest airports. Previously landings had been restricted only at O'Hare, LaGuardia, Kennedy, and Washington National.

The DOT, now the guardian of airline economic regulation as well as guardian of technical control of that industry, has had mixed success handling the so-called "slots" issue. Faced with a simple competitive alternative, buying and selling slots, DOT has instead tried a variety of regulatory approaches in rapid fire order, with more twists than an Agatha Christie novel. When DOT has tried a free market approach, it has been half-hearted, laced with regulatory trappings that seem to try to reach "fair" results.

The FAA's first response to the overcapacity problem was to cancel carriers' landing rights on a proportional basis, ignoring the probability that it might not be canceling the least important or least productive slots. Next, the FAA announced that with new slots becoming available because the air traffic system was getting up to speed, it would grant a certain percentage of all new slots, in a random drawing, to carriers new to the industry. Perhaps the FAA believed this would inject competition into the industry. This solution ignored the possibility that incumbents might have the highest valued uses for the slots and created another issue: Should airlines be allowed to transfer slots to each other?

Seven months after the strike, the FAA overcame its free market fears and allowed slot trading. But once again, the agency could not take the final step to allow the market to work freely. It was permitted to work under only regulated conditions: The agency permitted only one-for-one bartering of slots, not buying and selling. In addition, the identity of the transacting firms was kept anonymous. Apparently, the FAA thought it wise to discourage strategic trading behavior, although it is unclear why this would be anticompetitive. What the FAA overlooked was that barter, unlike money trading, requires a "double coincidence of wants." This means not all efficient trades will be made.

The FAA followed its barter experiment with perhaps the only idea that approached a real solution—it agreed to permit slot sales, although only on a short-term, six-week experimental basis. The market responded: In a short time, the FAA had taken applications for the transfer of 314 slots[49]—obviously, there were gains to be had from trading.

Then the FAA announced that slot trading could continue, but cash payments would be prohibited; the FAA cited strong opposition from the aviation community. But later in a strange twist the FAA asserted that the policy had been so successful at providing scheduling flexibility that it was unnecessary to continue.[50]

Outside events conspired against the FAA, however. In 1984, a combination of bad weather, increased summer travel, and a still understrength air traffic control system led to delays at several airports at certain times of the day. Affected airports included three—Atlanta, Denver, and Newark—that heretofore had not been slot constrained. These joined the previously slot-constrained airports of LaGuardia, Kennedy, and O'Hare. In other words, at the prevailing zero price for the use of air traffic control services, demand exceeded supply.

The problem centered around "bunching" flights at popular times. For example, in Atlanta there were ninety-nine commercial operations between 9:00 A.M. and 9:30 A.M., and just twenty-six at the equivalent time slot an hour later.[51] Obviously, business travelers like early morning flights in order to reach business appointments. As we shall see shortly, the problem was "solved" by CAB-immunized scheduling agreements, which moved flights to less popular times—9:00 A.M. flights were reduced from ninety-nine to fifty-seven, whereas 10:00 A.M. flights increased from twenty-six to sixty-eight.[52]

At the request of Eastern Airlines, and perhaps inspired by a direct request to airlines from the FAA,[53] the CAB began a proceeding in August of that year—about the time the summer travel season was peaking—proposing that airlines be granted antitrust immunity to engage in multilateral discussions for the purpose of integrating schedules in an effort to reduce the number of flights.

The DOT supported the petition, promising to provide enforcement of the agreements. The DOT filed comments with the CAB and through the FAA issued its own notice of proposed rulemaking.[54] The FAA proposed to enforce any agreements the carriers reached and announced that if the CAB failed to grant Eastern's request, it would impose tight slot restrictions at congested airports. It is noteworthy that the FAA grounded its proposal on efficiency losses—congestion, not safety, was said to be the problem.

Airport congestion is an example of a common property resource problem, which has the essential element that no one controls access to a resource, in this case the air traffic control system, that is available in fixed supply. As a result, competing users overuse the resource. This causes congestion. The end result is that each airline imposes costs on other airlines—each carrier with an aircraft in a queue waiting to take off imposes congestion costs on carriers with aircraft further back in line.

An efficient solution to such a problem includes setting a limit on the use of the resource and allocating use rights to those who value the resource most highly.[55] One cannot argue with the FAA for limiting the number of takeoff and landing rights during certain periods. To ensure efficient usage, however, the slots must end up in the hands of carriers with the most valuable flights. To ensure that travelers obtain the flights they value the most, carriers must be able to buy and sell slots continually.

What the CAB and FAA advocated and obtained was a series of immunized meetings where carriers could trade off different value slots with one another. The CAB decision required the FAA to determine the number of takeoffs and landings during congested periods. In such a situation, carriers have an incentive to agree to less than the socially optimal number of flights. If coordination is perfect, then the number of flights will be reduced to the monopoly level and each carrier will share in the monopoly level of profits. It is highly possible that consumers will suffer a loss due to higher fares and fewer flights that is greater than the loss they would have suffered because of congestion problems.

While we have not analyzed whether the absolute number of flights was less than optimal, we can state with a fair degree of certainty that the scheduling committees reached inefficient outcomes because carriers could not buy and sell slots at the busiest flight times. For example early morning flights are preferred by business travelers anxious to reach meetings. Business use of these times tends to be more highly valued than use by pleasure travelers, who are less concerned about departure time. If slots at these times were bought and sold, they would tend to their highest valued uses, business-oriented flights.

Unfortunately, the CAB lacked the authority to permit slot buying and selling. The FTC staff recommended that the CAB deny antitrust authority and that at the same time the FAA permit slot buying and selling. Regrettably, that did not happen.

It appears there are opposing views within DOT on the slots issue. The FAA proposed permitting slot sales in a rulemaking proceeding begun 7 June 1984.[56] There is no indication of any imminent decision in this case, however.[57]

On the other side, there is the continued threat that the engineering and industry support side of DOT will play a dominant role in scheduling. In a recent letter to the Air Transport Association, FAA administator Engen

has pronounced the scheduling committees a success[58]—although decreased winter travel, better weather, and more experienced controllers
may have played a part. Moreover Mr. Engen has decided that there is no
need to continue the September 1984 scheduling agreements beyond 1
April 1985. Thus carriers are free to make adjustments in their schedules at
the six schedule-constrained airports. However, Mr. Engen goes on to say,

> I hope that all carriers will recognize the importance of considering the
> scheduling problems identified and addressed 1st September as they make
> adjustments to existing schedules. To this end, I would hope that any carrier
> making a significant adjustment or addition to their existing schedules at one of
> these six airports will discuss such moves with agency officials in order to ensure
> that the least possible impact on the system occurs.
>
> Certainly, it is my hope that neither the agency nor the carriers will have to
> again become involved in these types of restrictions. We will, however, consis-
> tent with the public interest, monitor closely the system and will react quickly
> to address any major problems which might result if current conditions change.

Does this mean that government bureaucrats displeased with congestion
around choice takeoff and landing times (and sensitive to public error) will
be permitted to force airlines to relinquish some of these lucrative spots? It
would seem that if airlines start gravitating to the most valuable takeoff
times, a DOT bureaucrat will eventually have to decide which airline
should receive the better time. We cannot envision that such a process will
include a selection based on value-related criteria—one that requires buying and selling.

We also fear the trend toward even more intrusive regulation will grow.
First, assume that after a preliminary selection, other airlines complain.
Might not a continual trading process take place with the DOT staff
member as the broker?

There is also the risk of political pressure on the agency to resolve
problems in the favor of certain constituencies once the bureaucratic allocation process becomes known. A prominent member of Congress who
can no longer book a convenient flight to his home district is a potential
intrusion. Once this happens, pressure will build from other members,
especially if it is perceived that some smaller cities cannot support the most
highly valued slots.

There are, of course, a number of general political factors that we have
not touched on. For example, it is doubtless true that someone seeking
special favors from Congress will have an easier time negotiating those
lengthy marble hallways simply because DOT houses all airline regulatory
authority and congressional oversight is similarly compact. This can be
seen in the recent spate of activity involving the alleged problem of bias in
airline-owned computer reservation systems. Recently, airlines complain-

ing about being unfairly disadvantaged because of system bias (some translate this as their attempt to recover from their lack of foresight in developing their own systems)[59] were able to air their grievances effectively at a single set of congressional hearings.[60] However, that issue has consumer protection and antitrust overtones. If the 1984 legislation had not been passed, there is a possibility that airlines would have had to deal with the Antitrust Division because the issue has antitrust overtones, and with the FTC because of consumer protection overtones. Those agencies are overseen by different committees in the two houses. And doubtless, the various transportation subcommittees would have wanted a say in the matter. Admittedly, it is more convenient to deal with one agency and one congressional committee about a problem. However, in a situation involving an industry with a history of asking for protection, one wonders whether convenience is such a blessing.

Another concern is the potential for misuse of DOT's antitrust immunity powers. That is, of course, precisely the legal vehicle that enabled airline schedules to be rearranged. It takes little imagination to foresee that the process will be instituted again if airlines do not accede to the FAA's wishes not to realign schedules significantly. The fact that DOT's power to grant antitrust immunity runs out in 1989 is of little solace—if the power is used with any frequency it will be "proof" that continuation of the power is needed. And asking for antitrust exemptions is almost an annual rite of spring in Washington, D.C.

Conclusion

There are many economic problems that DOT will have to deal with in the coming months and years. Airline ownership of computer reservation systems is an unresolved issue. Contentions of exclusionary behavior might conceivably arise in the context of agreements between airlines and travel agent associations involving the marketing of airline transportation.[61] Obviously, in our dynamic economy, other issues will arise over time.

The study of economic regulation and public choice may find the next decade a revealing laboratory for testing theories of the demand for, and supply of, regulatory constraints. We have suggested that the regulatory processes thought to be terminated by the 1978 ADA may be dormant but alive within the walls of DOT.

Notes

1. The secretary of transportation, Elizabeth Hanford Dole, made a conscious management decision not to consolidate airline functions in a separate operating

administration within DOT to avoid the notion that the airline industry requires a "special, one-stop oversight agency." See U.S. Department of Transportation, DOT Guide to CAB Sunset 1 (1 January 1985). And indeed, the department strenuously tried to avoid receiving this additional regulatory authority. See below, pp. 189–91.

2. Civil Aeronautics Act of 1938, P.L. no. 75-706, 52 Stat. 111 (1938). The board was then named the Civil Aeronautics Authority.

3. See legislative history of the Airline Deregulation Act of 1978, P.L. no. 95-504, 92 Stat. 1705 (1978). 1978 U.S. Code. *Congress & Administration News* 3737-3821 (hereinafter cited as *News*).

4. A number of books summarize the practices and ill effects of airline regulation. See, e.g., George W. Douglas and James C. Miller, *Economic Regulation of Domestic Air Transport: Theory and Policy* (1974); Daryl P. Wyckoff and David H. Maister, *The Domestic Airline Industry* (1977); Robert Burkhardt, *CAB—The Civil Aeronautics Board* (1974), William A. Jordan, *Airline Regulation in America* (1970); Richard E. Caves, *Air Transport and Its Regulators* (1962); and Paul W. MacAvoy and John W. Snow (eds.), *Regulation of Air Fares and Competition among the Airlines* (1977).

5. In the intrastate markets airline customers were better off. Most students of regulation are familiar with the example of intrastate carriers, whose regulatory systems enabled them to offer a greater variety of price-service alternatives. Jordan, *Airline Regulation in America*, pp. 73–114; Subcommittee on Administrative Practice and Procedure of the Committee on the Judiciary of the United States Senate, Civil Aeronautics Board Practices and Procedures, 94th Congress, 1st Sess. 48–51 (1975) (hereinafter cited as Senate Report); Michael E. Levine, "Is Regulation Necessary? California Air Transportation and National Regulatory Policy," 74 *Yale Law Journal* 74 (1965): 1416–47. Intrastate carriers were offering service at about one-half the fares of CAB-regulated interstate carriers. This low-fare service permitted intrastate airlines to attract traffic from alternative means of transportation, enabling intrastate airline traffic to increase dramatically. This effect, coupled with the intrastate airlines' liberty to offer lower price-service alternatives, enabled intrastate carriers to schedule more flights and have higher capacity factors. Senate Report, 45–46. For example a twelve-year weighted average load factor for California intrastate carriers was 71.2 percent, as against only 59.1 percent for interstate regulated carriers during the same period. Jordan, *Airline Regulation in America*, p. 33.

6. Senate Report, pp. 5–21. See also Report of the CAB Special Staff, Regulatory Reform (1975). One of the board's most unfortunate experiments was to grant antitrust immunity to permit capacity control agreements that allowed airlines to collude on the amount of service they would provide. Since fare competition was not permitted, these capacity agreements eliminated one of the few areas of competition the board had permitted. *News*, p. 3738; Senate Report, pp. 142–48.

7. Before 1975, the board systematically restrained airline management by denying or dismissing most applications for new routes. Senate Report, p. 84. It also discouraged experiments with discount fares. Ibid., p. 120.

8. Ibid., p. 101.

9. For example, during the board's route moratorium, it denied or dismissed all seventy-nine new route applications filed by trunkline carriers. Some of these applicants intended to provide competitive rates. A leading example is World Airways. In 1967, it submitted an application to the CAB in which it proposed low-fare transcontinental service. The board took no action on the application for seven years, then dismissed the application as stale. *News,* pp. 3738–39.

10. Ibid., p. 3738.

11. Douglas and Miller, *Economic Regulation of Domestic Air Transport,* p. 43.

12. If price is prevented from falling to marginal cost, to the extent that the industry is competitive, marginal cost will tend to rise to the level of price. This is precisely what happened in the interstate airline market. With prices fixed, airlines competed through service-quality rivalry, thus hoping to increase demand for their product, their revenue, and profit.

13. Just prior to the Airline Deregulation Act of 1978 (ADA), the board, under the chairmanships of John Robson and Alfred Kahn, moved toward less restrictive policies. With the CAB's encouragement, the industry started many discount fares. The board gave carriers virtually automatic authority to experiment with fare reductions of up to 50 percent. The board also liberalized new route policies to introduce much more actual and potential competition. It granted "permissive authority," under which carrier management was permitted to use its discretion to decide whether to serve a market immediately if an incumbent carrier provided poor service or left the market entirely. The board also initiated rulemakings to allow some route applications to be decided without full evidentiary hearings. *News,* p. 3739.

These new policies were followed by improved financial conditions. During 1976 and 1977, the rate of return on investment for trunk carriers was 8.51 and 9.55 percent, while local service carriers realized returns of 10.71 and 13.56 percent. Of course, these results are attributable partly to general economic trends as well as the board's policies. The point is, however, that lower fares and better service for consumers were not necessarily incompatible with industry profits.

14. That there may be multiple beneficiaries in the regulatory game is one of the principles espoused by Sam Peltzman in his formalization of George Stigler's Economic Theory of Regulation. See Sam Peltzman, "Toward a More General Theory of Regulation," *Journal of Law and Economics* (1976): 211–40, and George J. Stigler, "The Theory of Economic Regulation," *Bell Journal of Economics and Management Science* (1971): 3–21. See also Thomas G. Moore, *The Beneficiaries of Trucking Regulation* (Palo Alto: Hoover Institution, 1977), for a discussion of the effect Peltzman suggests in the trucking industry. Moore's study found that three-quarters or more of the increased cost due to ICC regulation of trucking took the form of income transfers to labor and capital. Ibid., p. 27. Note the conclusion of the Senate Report, p. 46, that less regulated intrtastate airlines paying union wages had lower costs because of more productive use of labor.

15. The most recent comprehensive study is Thomas G. Moore, *U.S. Airline Deregulation: Its Effects on Passengers, Capital, and Labor* (Palo Alto: Hoover Institution, 1985).

Early examinations of the effects of airline deregulation include *Deregulating the*

Airlines (Washington: Civil Aeronautics Board, 1983); John R. Meyer, Clinton V. Oster, *Airline Deregulation: The Early Experience* (1981); Douglas W. Caves, Laurits R. Christensen, and Michael W. Tretheway, "Airline Productivity under Deregulation," *Regulation* (November/December 1982): 25–28; George Dorman, *Air Service to Small Communities after Airline Deregulation* (National Economic Research Associates, 1982); Report of the House Republican Research Committee, Task Force on Congressional and Regulatory Reform, "Are the Skies Really Falling? A Look at Airline Deregulation," 10 November 1983 (hereafter cited as House Report); Hearings before the Subcommittee on Aviation of the Committee on Public Works and Transportation, 98th. Cong., 1st sess., 33 (1983) (statement of Hon. Dan McKinnon, Chairman, Civil Aeronautics Board).

16. The number of new certificated carriers, both passenger and freight, approximately tripled between 1976 and 1983, from thirty-three to ninety-eight. The number of passenger carriers more than doubled, from twenty-eight to sixty-one. Moore, *U.S. Airline Deregulation*, p. 6.

17. For instance, in a sample of thirty-seven long-haul city-pair markets, four lost one or more carriers, eleven had the same number of carriers, and twenty-two gained from one to four carriers. Even in short-haul, small-city markets, for which most fears were expressed, thirteen of the thirty city pairs gained carriers. Only three had fewer carriers at the end of the sample period. Ibid., p. 7.

18. Better known examples are TWA's hub at St. Louis, United's at Chicago and Denver, People's at Newark, and Eastern's at Miami.

19. Moore finds that for the industry as a whole, the average per-mile rate fell 8.5 percent from 1976 to 1982. (Ibid., p.11). He finds this especially impressive, since average costs have risen in real terms nearly 15 percent over the same period, mainly as a result of a 73-percent increase in fuel cost.

20. Ibid.

21. In Australia's long-haul markets, coach fares, which are what almost all passengers pay, went up 17 percent, compared to an 11-percent rise in similar U.S. markets. Ibid., p. 14.

22. Ibid., p. 15.

23. Deregulated airlines are making significant efforts to be more efficient. For example, on some routes, airlines are dealing with increases in the number of passengers by using larger aircraft and putting more seats in existing planes. The average number of seats per departure on long-haul flights has increased by 12 percent. (Ibid., p. 16). On the other hand, the number of travelers on each short-haul flight is decreasing. There has been a corresponding sharp drop in the size of aircraft being used on these routes. In the small-city, short-haul market, the number of seats per departure is down almost 50 percent. The number of passengers is down even more sharply, resulting in a drop in load factors even with smaller planes. Ibid., p. 17.

24. Over the same period, the real value of all stocks on the New York Stock Exchange fell 3 percent. (Ibid., p. 29). Airlines that benefited most from deregulation were the thirteen regional carriers—in real terms the value of their companies has increased almost sixfold from 1976 through 1983. (Ibid., p. 30.)

25. For example, membership in the International Association of Machinists

and Aerospace Workers (IAM) declined from 84,000 to 70,000 in the first five years after airline regulatory reform; the Transport Workers Union went from 33,000 to 28,000 members. Hearings before the Subcommittee on Aviation of the Committee on Public Works and Transportation, 98th Congress, 1st Sess., 230 (1983) (statement of William G. Mahoney on behalf of the Brotherhood of Railway and Airline Clerks). Frank Waldner, a negotiator for the IAM, stated, "Deregulation is a total disaster. We have been pretty well devastated" ("Retailers in the Air," *Economist* [survey] 292 [25 August, 1984]: 3–4 [hereinafter cited as "Retailers"].

26. "Retailers," p. 5.

27. House Report, p. 1.

28. "Rails Replace Airlines in Top Spot in Employe Earnings-Fringe Levels," *Traffic World* 199, no. 78 (24 September 1984). The *Economist* notes, "In retrospect, the surprise is that the established carriers waited so long before they cut their labour costs. Between 1979 and 1983 TWA actually increased its pilots' pay and benefits by 48.6%; Republic, flying deeper and deeper into debt, nevertheless paid its pilots another 44.4%; and Eastern, skating on thin ice it pretends can never break, gave its pilots an increase of 69.7 % over the four years" ("Retailers," p. 5).

29. 49 U.S.C. § 1551 (b).

30. P.L. no. 98-443, 98 Stat. 1704 (1984).

31. U.S. Department of Transportation, Civil Aeronautics Board Sunset 42–53 (February 1984).

32. 15 U.S.C. § 45.

33. Statement of George W. Douglas, commissioner, on behalf of the Federal Trade Commission, before the Subcommittee on Aviation, Committee on Public Works and Transportation, U.S. House of Representatives (13 March 1984).

34. A good description of the convoluted process is Kanwit, Federal Trade Commission § 6 (1984).

35. The chief of the Antitrust Division's transportation section, Elliot Seiden, is viewed by many as a strict enforcer of the antitrust laws. The pro-antitrust, free market positions typically advocated by that section can be examined in the Antitrust Division's filings in CAB Dkt. No. 36595, Investigation into the Competitive Marketing of Air Transportation Agreements Phases.

36. Douglas and Miller, *Economic Regulation of Domestic Air Transport*.

37. FTC staff comments, CAB Dkt. No. 4186—Airline Computer Reservation Systems (filed 17 November 1983).

38. 49 U.S.C. § 1553 (1985).

39. See George J. Stigler, "The Theory of Economic Regulation," p. 3; Richard A. Posner, "Theories of Economic Regulation," *Bell Journal of Economics and Management Science* 5 (1974): 335–58.

40. One might also argue that any regulatory agency with no or only minimal support and development functions, not just an antitrust agency, would inherently be a better choice as an economic regulator. The modern regulatory agencies have been transformed by statute in recent years into competition-oriented agencies and have performed admirably. Since the late 1970s, regulatory agencies, such as the FCC, CAB and ICC, have been largely in step with the new learning about the merits of the competitive process. Thus, for example, the CAB, under Alfred

Kahn, and the ICC, under A. Daniel O'Neal and Darius Gaskins, were making many of the market-oriented changes later mandated by Congress in a variety of deregulatory pieces of legislation. Space does not permit full amplification of these views, however.

41. The *United States Government Manual 355* (1984–85) provides a more complete description of the agency's overall mission.

42. This point is made in Ryan C. Amacher, Robert D. Tollison, and Thomas D. Willett, "Risk Avoidance and Political Advertising: Neglected Issues in the Literature on Budget Size in a Democracy," in *The Economic Approach to Public Policy* (Ithaca: Cornell University Press, 1976), pp. 405–33.

43. The FAA correctly sees that takeoff and landing delays are an efficiency problem. It has not compromised safety to lessen transitory inconvenience.

44. "Federal Trade Commission Law Enforcement in the 1980s" (Federal Trade Commission, October 1984), pp. 52–54.

45. Ibid., p. 41. Between 1977 and 1983, the commission won just thirteen of thirty-five substantive antitrust cases in federal court, most of these emanating from the prior administration. In contrast, the commission won twenty-one of twenty-three between 1970 and 1976.

46. Winston S. Moore, Assistant Director for Planning, Federal Trade Commission, suggested this view may be overly optimistic. He pointed to prior years when the Commission was severely criticized for being too experimental and that under certain administrations, this result could reoccur. While such a short-term aberration might occur, long-term trends in antitrust seem to point away from experimentalism and toward a more analytical approach. See Peter M. Gerhart, "The Supreme Court and Antitrust Analysis: The (Near) Triumph of the Chicago School," in *Supreme Court Review* (1982): 319–349.

47. Henry Duffy, president of the Air Line Pilots Association, "A Plan to Set a Minimum Fare," *New York Times,* (10 October 1983), F2. His plan envisioned carriers being free to charge prices up to a fixed percentage over cost, but not below cost, enabling airlines "to compete on price and quality of service."

48. An excellent summary of the "slots" story is "Airline Competition and the Slot Market," *Regulation* 6 (September/October 1982): 8–10.

49. Ibid., p. 9.

50. Ibid., p. 10

51. Letter from Donald D. Engen, Administrator, Federal Aviation Administration, to Norman J. Philion, President, Air Transport Association (12 March 1985) (hereinafter cited as Engen letter).

52. Ibid.

53. It appears that the airlines and DOT worked closely on filing the petition. The Eastern petition and the DOT petition were filed on the same date, 10 August 1984. (CAB dkt. no. 42410, Application for Discussion Authority and Prior Board Approval of Carrier Agreements to Integrate Schedules).

54. Elimination of Airport Delays, 49 Fed. Reg. 33082 (proposed 20 August 1984).

55. This position is articulated most fully in Donald Koran and Jon Ogur,

Airport Access Problems: Lessons Learned from Slot Regulation by the FAA (Washington: Bureau of Economics, Federal Trade Commission, 1983).

56. Slot Transfer Methods, 49 Fed. Reg. 23788 (proposed 7 June 1984).

57. The decision is up to the secretary of transportation. It may be that other burning issues—selling Conrail and defederalizing National and Dulles airports—have been given priority.

58. Engen letter, p. 20.

59. "Airline Reservation Systems: Curse of the Mummy's Tomb," *Regulation* 9 (January/February 1985): 8.

60. Hearings before the Subcommittee on Aviation, Committee on Commerce, Science, and Transportation, U.S. Senate (19 March 1984).

61. "Competitive Marketing of Air Transportation in the Post-CAB Era," remarks by Elliott Seiden, Chief, Transportation Section, Antitrust Division, before the Association of the Bar of the City of New York (15 November 1984), describes the history of these agreements and remaining antitrust issues.

References

"Airline Competition and the Slot Market," *Regulation* (Sept./Oct. 1982: 8–10.

"Airline Reservation Systems: Curse of the Mummy's Tomb." *Regulation* (Jan./Feb. 1985): 8.

Amacher, Ryan C., Tollison, Robert D., and Thomas D. Willett. "Risk Avoidance and Political Advertising: Neglected Issues in the Literature on Budget Size in a Democracy." In *The Economic Approach to Public Policy,* Ithaca: Cornell University Press, 1976, pp. 405–433.

Burkhardt, Robert. *CAB—The Civil Aeronautics Board.* New York: F. A. Praeger Company, 1974.

Caves, Douglas W., Christensen, Laurits R., and Michael W. Tretheway, "Airline Productivity Under Deregulation." *Regulation* (Nov./Dec. 1982): 25–28.

Caves, Richard E. *Air Transport and Its Regulators.* Cambridge: Harvard University Press, 1962.

Civil Aeronautics Board. *Deregulating the Airlines.* Washington: Civil Aeronautics Board, 1983.

Dorman, George. "Air Service to Small Communities after Airline Deregulation." Washington: National Economic Research Associates, 1982.

Douglas, George W., and James C. Miller III. *Economic Regulation of Domestic Air Transport: Theory and Policy.* Washington: Brookings Institution, 1974.

Duffy, Henry, "A Plan to Set a Minimum Fare." *New York Times,* 10 Oct. 1983, p. F-2.

Gerhart, Peter M. "The Supreme Court and Antitrust Analysis: The (Near) Triumph of the Chicago School." *Supreme Court Review* (1982): 319–349.

Jordan, William A. *Airline Regulation in America.* Baltimore: Johns Hopkins Press, 1970.

Koran, Donald, and Jon Ogur, "Airport Access Problems: Lessons Learned from

Slot Regulation of the FAA." Washington: Bureau of Economics, Federal Trade Commission, 1983.

Levine, Michael B., "Is Regulation Necessary? California Air Transportation and National Regulatory Policy." *Yale Law Journal* 74 (1965): 1416–47.

MacAvoy, Paul W., and John W. Snow, eds. *Regulation of Passenger Fares and Competition Among Airlines.* Washington: American Enterprise Institute, 1977.

Meyer, John, and Clinton Oster, *Airline Deregulation: The Early Experience.* Boston: Auburn House Publishing, 1981.

Moore, Thomas G. *The Beneficiaries of Trucking Regulation.* Palo Alto: Hoover Institution, 1977.

———. *U.S. Airline Deregulation: Its Effects on Passengers, Capital, and Labor.* Palo Alto: Hoover Institution, 1985.

Peltzman, Sam. "Toward a More General Theory of Regulation," *Journal of Law and Economics* 19 (1976): 211–40.

Posner, Richard A. "Theories of Economic Regulation." *Bell Journal of Economics and Management Science* 2 (1974): 335–58.

"Rails Replace Airlines in Top Spot in Employe Earnings-Fringe Levels." *Traffic World* (24 September 1984): 199.

"Retailers in the Air." *Economist* (25 August 1984): 3–4.

Stigler, George J. "The Theory of Economic Regulation." *Bell Journal of Economics and Management Science* 3 (1971): 3–21.

Wyckoff, Daryl D., and David H. Maister. *The Domestic Airline Industry.* Lexington, Mass.: Lexington Books, 1977.

Part III

POLITICS, REGULATION, AND BUREAUCRACY

10

Sub Rosa Regulation: The Iceberg beneath the Surface

Robert A. Rogowsky

Recently President Reagan revived the regulatory reform initiative begun in his first administration. The Presidential Task Force on Regulatory Relief has been reestablished to develop legislative and other proposals to further reduce unnecessary regulatory burdens. In the wake of changes during the first term to over one hundred existing burdensome rules, the perception from many quarters that the regulatory burden has not diminished correspondingly is curious. Regulatory reform is, however, a complex task. The nature of regulatory bureaucracies and the numerous ways in which they achieve their goals must be understood fully in order to control federal intervention into the economy.

In 1981 Antonin Scalia, now a U.S. Supreme Court justice, warned that the successes of deregulation would have unexpected and unwelcome consequences. As Congress and the White House increased their efforts to control rulemaking by regulatory agencies, he predicted that they simply may be "squeezing the balloon of bureaucratic arbitrariness at one end, only to have it pop out somewhere else."[1] Regulatory bureaucracies are able to accomplish their goals outside the realm of formal rulemaking. Encumbering rulemaking with extra procedural safeguards would "produce a renaissance of the previously favored mode of making law and policy—a movement back to basics, to adjudication."[2]

In the years since, the balloon has popped out visibly.[3] But the balloon of bureaucratic arbitrariness is not limited to adjudication. A regulatory agency can typically accomplish most of its agenda informally, even sub rosa. Will Rogers once expressed gratitude that we do not get all the government we pay for. In fact, in the regulatory area, we seem to get all we pay for, and more than we can keep track of.

An impressive underground regulatory infrastructure thrives on investigations, inquiries, threatened legal actions, and negotiated settlements. Without having to "break cover," as one career regulator termed it, savvy bureaucrats can fulfill an agenda of intervention without resorting to rulemaking or other formal mechanisms. Threats of regulation or litigation and the skilful use of public opprobrium can be very effective instruments of a command and control economy. Many of the most questionable regulatory actions are imposed in this way, most of which escape scrutiny of the public, Congress, and even the regulatory watchdogs in the executive branch.

At the outset it must be pointed out that the results are not always undesirable. Avoiding costly litigation or rulemaking procedures can be efficient. Nevertheless, outcomes that circumscribe due process are potentially quite undesirable. When formal procedures are not at work, some other monitoring mechanism must be put into place to keep excessive power from the hands of individuals well placed in the bureaucracy, no matter how well-intentioned they may be.

This paper examines underground regulation in two independent commissions, the Consumer Product Safety Commission (CPSC) and the Federal Trade Commission. They have been chosen because of the author's experience with them, and because they also characterize the problem well. Both are relatively small agencies in terms of budget and personnel. Both have, however, broad mandates resting on enabling legislation that lends itself to substantial regulatory independence. Both, finally, have caused fearful reactions in the business community beyond what seems appropriate for their size and level of formal regulatory activity. Thus for pedagogical purposes, they are useful specimens to dissect.

The Consumer Product Safety Commission

The Consumer Product Safety Commission has a short but controversial history. The heat generated around the agency is surprising in light of the amount of substantive formal regulatory activity. Only about a dozen substantive product safety standards have actually been imposed.

The Consumer Product Safety Act of 1973 (CPSA) originally envisioned rulemaking as the agency's primary regulatory tool. The first chairman of the CPSC predicted twenty substantive safety rules each year for the first ten years. Forty standards were promised by the commission in 1975, with a hundred to be in place by 1982. By 1985 only six safety rules had been promulgated under the CPSA, along with two labeling requirements and six product bans (one of which has been overturned in the courts). Five rules have been imposed under the Federal Hazardous

Substances Act (FHSA) and some requirements for child-resistant caps imposed under the Poison Prevention Packaging Act (PPPA).[4] Although not trivial, the visible output of the agency does not seem to justify the alarm within the industry that the agency has caused.

Over the years, Congress has played with ways of making the agency more productive, specifically by easing procedural requirements on rulemaking. In 1981, a more conservative Congress amended the CPSA, placing restrictions on rulemaking that required the agency (in line with amendments to regulatory statutes in other agencies) to be more responsive to economic criteria. The agency must file an Advanced Notice of Proposed Rulemaking (ANPR) to begin the process. A cost-benefit analysis must be done at that stage. Passing that hurdle, a formal rulemaking procedure can be initiated. A second cost-benefit analysis is required at the final stage before a rule can be imposed. For chemicals alleged to be carcinogenic, outside peer review of the evidence is required before the commission can file an ANPR. Moreover, voluntary standards have to be adopted when these adequately address the safety concern and the probability of compliance is high.

As appropriate measures for regulatory control, these restrictions work too well. The added procedural burden seriously impaired rulemaking as a regulatory tool.[5] The costs of rulemaking to the commission and staff are substantively greater than the benefits.

The agency does not lie dormant, however. Other available means of producing its output have been made more attractive. Litigation is a first choice. The powerful adjudicatory authority of the CPSA, originally intended as a recall authority for specific products presenting a hazardous defect, has in many instances replaced rulemaking by attacking generic hazards associated with products not originally under authority of that act.

RULEMAKING VERSUS ADJUDICATION: WHY FIRMS CARE

Standard setting by adjudication can be sharply distinguished from traditional rulemaking. Technical differences in the process are clear. The more important distinction is in the substantially different effect the two procedures have on firms, especially manufacturers of consumer products. Both rulemaking and adjudication provide procedural safeguards for affected parties. Both processes potentially consider all relevant information. In practice, however, the effects can be quite different.

A rulemaking procedure is designed, as the Supreme Court pointed out, "to assure fairness and mature consideration of rules of general application."[6] The agency notifies the public of its interest in a particular safety hazard and then gathers evidence to enable it to assess the hazard and prospectively determine an appropriate remedy. Cost-benefit analyses are often required. The impact on small business and the environment must be weighed. Interested parties are advised of the action and participate through written and oral comments. A body of evidence is created on which to base the need for, and extent of, a rule.

The target of an adjudicatory complaint does get a day in court, but it is not quite the same as rulemaking. While the rulemaking process involves all parties in the cooperative development of a safety standard for a perceived hazard, litigation is an adversarial response to a charge that a product in commerce is "defective" and presents a "substantial product hazard." Litigating to impose safety standards focuses retrospectively on actions that at the time were legal. Moreover, the courtroom offers less scope than a rulemaking procedure for complicated technical comment on economic questions or scientific or engineering issues. Input from interested parties is limited.

Generally, the competitive disadvantage of having the federal government publicly label your product "defective" and a "substantial product hazard" combines with the financial strain of the pending lawsuit to bring quick settlement. (The government's lawsuit is only the tip of the iceberg, of course. Corollary product liability suits quickly begin to surface. It is not surprising that the bulk of Freedom of Information Act requests to the commission originate with private law firms.)

More importantly, adjudication can leverage the regulatory authority of the agency. By targeting a single firm, the CPSC can impose a "standard" that applies to the entire industry. Once a single firm's product is found to constitute a substantial product hazard, any similar product not complying with the remedy chosen for that good violates the "standard" and is liable to prosecution as "defective". Like goods cannot be imported. Unless all members of the industry act in concert (which poses an interesting antitrust problem), the victim is left to its own resources to ward off the challenge.

Regulation of children's products, which fall under the FHSA, nicely illustrates this leverage. Prior to 1984, the FHSA required administrative rulemaking to ban a product and order a recall remedy. The CPSA, on the other hand, has always had a powerful provision, section 15(d), which enables the agency to charge a product as a substantial hazard and under section 15(g) to proceed directly to district court for a preliminary injunction against the manufacturer. As rulemaking became more onerous, the commission used a special provision of the CPSA to transfer regulatory authority from the FHSA to the CPSA each time injuries associated with children's products were felt to require retroactive remedial action. Between 1982 and 1984, the commission transferred five separate children's products from the FHSA to the CPSA for litigation action.[7] In two of the cases, the commission named as defendants every manufacturer of the product in question, thus using adjudication in a way most closely imitating rulemaking.

The purpose of each transfer was to avoid rulemaking and have access to adjudicatory authority without the burden of first promulgating a rule. The Federal Register notice announcing the transfer of squeeze toys stated that corrective action would be available under the FHSA "only if the commission had first issued a rule under the provisions of [that Act]." Under the CPSA, "no requirement for rulemaking would exist in order to invoke the [recall] provisions of that Act."[8] In 1984 Congress made it easier for the CPSC by adding the adjudicatory power of the CPSA to the FHSA, eliminating the need to transfer authority.[9]

"VOLUNTARY" SETTLEMENTS

In other ways the targeted firm is worse off facing litigation. If it can afford to contest the charge of substantial product hazard, the defendant may still find its corporate reputation badly damaged. A toy manufacturer is especially susceptible to charges of "child killer." An entire reputable brand name can be tarnished by a dispute involving one minor product line. Is it any wonder that virtually all of the CPSC staff's 3,500 preliminary allegations of substantial product hazard have been settled "voluntarily" before a complaint was issued, a record typically held up as a monument to cooperative effort?

The implications of this last fact are profound. Regulation by the threat of litigation has proven a powerful tool in consumer product safety regulation. More problematic is the absence of administrative constraint. Many allegations are settled prior to formal agreement that would come from the commission. Political appointees running the agency face at least a modicum of political constraint; staff does not. The threat of litigation is usually sufficient to produce a de facto industry-wide standard. If a dispute does proceed to a formal agreement, the staff can present as fait accompli a negotiated consent. Overworked (or at least preoccupied) commissioners are likely to go along.[10]

One example is found in the ban on accordion style baby gates. For quite some time the CPSC was interested in the pattern of injuries sustained with accordion style baby gates. A standard product in the home for many decades, approximately ten deaths and injuries had been associated with these gates. As a preliminary to rulemaking, the agency began working with the industry to devise a voluntary standard. When subsequently another death was reported, the entire calculus changed; the agency adopted the adjudication mode. The litigation staff wrote to all remaining producers to "urge [them] to stop manufacture of accordion gates immediately."[11] The majority of commissioners, though dismayed, were made aware after the fact. Production ceased within two months. A product ban effectively was imposed without a single page being added to the code of federal regulations or even a complaint filed.

Negotiated regulation gives regulators greater flexibility than rulemaking. For instance, amendments made to the CPSA in 1981 call for "performance" rather than "engineering" standards. Performance standards are superior because they create an incentive for firms to seek the most efficient and effective way of accomplishing the desired result. Engineering standards impose a set technology or physical structure to be added or built into the product, which can be changed only by revising the standard. However, a negotiated settlement can easily and legally take the form of an engineering standard.

In a recent example, CPSC staff negotiated an engineering solution for a group of cabinet heater manufacturers to settle a product defect allegation. As the manufacturers report, the staff made it very clear that if manufacturers produced heaters with a certain structural addition, there would be no reaction from the agency. If, on the other hand, a manufacturer offered a heater that did not conform, proceedings would begin at once. The product, in the staff's estimation, would constitute a substantial product hazard.[12] In other words, that product would not comply with the "standard' established by the litigation staff.

Regulation by threat is illustrated nicely by the CPSC's handling of plasticizers, which keep rubber and plastic products pliable, in baby pacifiers. In 1981, nitrosamines were found as a by-product of amine precursors used to plasticize rubber. While nitrosamines had been found to cause cancer in animals, available data did not permit a way of estimating risk at any given dose. Moreover, actual exposure of humans to nitrosamines from consumer products was not known. The amount of nitrosamines released from pacifiers varies, since these chemicals are not added directly to the rubber, but rather are formed as by-products.

With no clear evidence of the degree of hazard or the appropriate remedy (but faced with the unexpected news that FDA "was going to do something" about nitrosamines in baby nipples), the commission on 27 December 1983 issued an enforcement policy under the FHSA, effective 1 January 1984.[13] The policy set an action level of 60 parts per billion,[14] so that any pacifier tested after January that released more than 60 parts per billion of nitrosamine into a saliva-type solution used in the CPSC's testing method would be considered defective. The manufacturer would be charged with producing a cancer-causing baby pacifier. Not surprisingly, all producers fell into line. The staff subsequently turned toward 10 parts per billion as a standard.

The CPSC has been criticized as much by public interest activists for inaction as by industry for over-zealous regulation. The two-sided attack is confusing unless you understand that the one side measures bureaucratic output by what can be read in the Code of Federal Regulations, while the other measures it by the intervention actually felt in the normal conduct of business. If regulatory zeal is to be calmed at the CPSC, simply adding requirements to rulemaking or other formal regulatory mechanisms will not suffice.

Antitrust Division and the Federal Trade Commission

A charge of unfair competition or violation of some antitrust law does not carry the same opprobrium as producing a cancer-causing pacifier, but the Federal Trade Commission (FTC) and the Antitrust Division of the Department of Justice can get a great deal of mileage from the threat of litigation. For the last decade and a half, the intellectual underpinnings of antitrust enforcement have been challenged and as a result significantly revised.[15] Nevertheless, the antitrust bureaucracies have been able to pursue aggressive enforcement against the tide of scholarly guidance and in antimerger enforcement, beyond the Antitrust Division's own guidelines.

The antitrust laws, unlike the CPSA, were set up to be enforced through litigation, not rulemaking. The laws, in general, specify that the government shall challenge unfair competition, a substantial lessening of competition, or a tendency to monopolize. A great deal of prerogative is deliberately given to the agencies by these vague guidelines. Constraints are imposed by congressional oversight, political constraints on agency directors, and judicial interpretation of competitive harm.

The courts, ideally responsive to both congressional intent and current scholarly thought underlying antitrust enforcement, establish the boundaries for antitrust regulation. Appointed directors and commissioners guide the agencies within those boundaries. Enforcement should follow the benchmarks established by the courts fairly closely; the agencies, however, can exceed and have far exceeded those guidelines. In the period from 1968 through 1981, antitrust regulation reached far beyond visible limits in ways that nicely illustrate the notion of underground regulation.

MERGER GUIDELINES

In 1968 the Department of Justice offered formal Merger Guidelines to "acquaint the business community, the legal profession, and other interested groups and individuals with the standards currently being applied by the Department of Justice in determining whether to challenge corporate acquisitions and mergers under Section 7 of the Clayton Act."[16] The guidelines were established to decrease uncertainty for business decision-makers by setting specific numerical combinations of market share that the Antitrust Division considered anticompetitive. For instance in industries with four-firm concentration ratios of less than 75 percent, challenges would be directed toward horizontal mergers involving the following market shares:

Acquiring Firm	Acquired Firm
5%	5%
10%	4%
15%	3%
20%	2%
25% or more	1%

Standards for industries with higher concentration ratios were even more stringent. Corresponding numerical standards were imposed for vertical and conglomerate mergers.

Antimerger enforcement was not constrained effectively by the guidelines. Between 1968 and 1982, the period the 1968 guidelines were in force, 21 percent of the horizontal and vertical cases filed by the Antitrust Division and the FTC fell below the guidelines' structural standards.[17] These cases, it was found, could not be explained by exceptions to the guidelines that would trigger a below-guideline case, nor by any other traditional criteria of economic performance.[18]

Rather than responding to more stringent judicial standards, the agencies were aggressively enforcing harsh antitrust standards in spite of them. During that time the courts relied to some extent on the guidelines, but in general tended to assess more rigorously than the agencies the "competitive realities" in weighing the probable effect of a merger. Attempts by federal prosecutors to expand jurisdiction were not successful. The government racked up an 84-percent loss rate between 1968 and 1982 for merger cases brought to trial. The broader framework of analysis relied on by the courts set the Justice Department's Merger Guidelines as the most stringent standard.[19]

The large number of cases that fall below the market share standards suggests that the guidelines did not effectively constrain attorneys in the agencies who enforce antitrust laws. Careful examination of the caseload reveals that there were no reliable quantitative benchmarks guiding enforcement. Even mergers of small firms with low market shares in deconcentrating industries that contain no significant impediments to entry have been attacked rather consistently.[20]

To regulate extensively beyond judicial boundaries, and even its own guidelines, the FTC and Antitrust Division, like the CPSC, rely on informal means. Like consumer product safety regulation, underground regulation in antitrust takes the form of investigations, inquiries, threatened litigation, and negotiated settlements. It is not clear how many mergers were aborted simply because the agency threatened to investigate nor how many were deterred simply because they would have to be reported to the federal government.[21] It is recorded, however, that more than 75 percent of the merger cases in which some form of remedy was imposed were negotiated settlements. Moreover, of the seventy-eight FTC cases, thirty-three were submitted to the commission as simultaneous complaint-consents. These are cases where a remedial order was negotiated by the staff before the matter was formally raised to the commission.[22] It is easy for the commission to accept a decree to which both sides agree (an extensive file search uncovered only two instances where the commission overturned the recommendation of the staff). In this way agency staffs can regulate merger activity extensively, adjusting the standards for mergers in a way that does not formally enter the regulatory or judicial system set up to deliberate those laws.

Driven by a reward system that requires output, good or bad,[23] antitrust bureaucrats have effectively bypassed standards established by the courts. In the midst of the intellectual and judicial trend during the 1970s moving toward less antitrust intervention—a move that ultimately led to a revision of the Justice Department's Merger Guidelines in 1982—the number of below-guideline cases as a percentage of federal enforcement increased.[24] The cases involved such obvious "problem" industries as band uniforms, paint brushes, frozen pizza pies, motion pictures, and suntan lotion.[25]

RESALE PRICE MAINTENANCE AND CONSUMER PROTECTION

The pattern of informal regulation is not limited to merger enforcement. A study published by the FTC shows that the agency resolved sixty-eight resale price maintenance (RPM) cases between July 1965 and the end of 1982.[26] Fifty-six of these cases, more than 82 percent, were brought to the commission as simultaneous complaint-consents.[27] Several others were subsequently settled. But the vast majority were faits accomplis by the time they reached the commission.[28]

Consumer protection regulation poses a similar concern.[29] Data available for 1977 through 1983 show that twenty-eight administrative complaints were filed. 205 consent decrees were recorded; 164 of these, 80 percent, were simultaneous complaint-consents.[30] The threat of charges of fraud, deception, and discrimination, no matter how poorly substantiated, can be a strong inducement to minimize damage by acquiescing to the government's remedial demands.

No Way Out

The point of the examples drawn from the CPSC and antitrust enforcement is not the specific merits of any given policy of or case involving the two agencies. The point rather is to clarify and emphasize the lesson learned by anyone who interns in Washington, that the real regulatory authority of the federal government and most of the regulatory burden are not to be measured by the number of pages in the Code of Federal Regulations. The bulk of economic control exercised by Washington is underground control.

Three avenues to relieve the regulatory burden are often proffered. First, establish a system of control that will make the agencies responsive to the political management of the White House. Second, change legislative mandates to make more specific congressional intent and reduce the leeway of the bureaucracies. Finally, tighten bureaucratic management, that is, change the people in the bureaucracies. Unfortunately none of these work as well in practice as they do in theory, largely because of the power of the regulatory underground.

The Reagan administration's attempt to control regulation through the Office of Management and Budget (OMB) left the underground regulatory structure largely untouched. OMB control, of course, is one of the major "squeezes" on the bureaucratic balloon, causing it to pop out in the form of more creative command and control measures. More recently, OMB has considered becoming involved in regulatory ventures at an earlier stage, deeper down in the bureaucracies. Such an effort could be partially effective, but requires a considerable amount of professional resources.

Making legislation more specific, the second proposal, is not as useful as it would seem at first glance; the Delaney clauses of the Food, Drug, and Cosmetic Act are good examples.[31] Those provisions prohibit the marketing of any food additive, color additive, or animal drug that contains any substance found to cause cancer in man or animal—period. The provision leaves no room for reasonableness in using suspected substances.[32] It is not at all clear that we want Congress to decide a priori what precisely constitutes a substantial product defect or unfair competition. The costly consequences of the Delaney clauses make it clear that we would have been better off if it had been left to the courts to fill the interstices of the law in specific cases. On the other hand, experience with the Merger Guidelines suggests that laws of great specificity are unlikely to constrain bureaucracies determined to regulate.

Selecting the proper managers, the third suggested solution, is critically important because of their direct influence on day-to-day activities. Public-choice theory suggests that people do not matter much because an organization has a reward structure that determines its direction. Robert Tollison, former chief economist of the FTC, reviewing antitrust enforcement, challenges the theory that people matter: "Change the decision makers and the policy will change. That sounds good but it never seems to work. Government cranks along by an internal logic of its own."[33] Tollison is, of course, correct to a large degree, for reasons outlined in this paper. And yet, James C. Miller at the FTC, William Baxter in the Antitrust Division, and Alfred Kahn at the Civil Aeronautics Board clearly made a difference, at least in the short term.

Conclusion

Like controlling the federal budget deficit, regulatory reform is less a problem of weakness of will than one of implementation. Effectively controlling the regulatory bureaucracy requires a two-pronged solution. First, whenever a regulatory activity is not absolutely required, eliminate it; terminate the legislative mandate. Efforts to control the activity are extremely costly and generally short-term. Second, when the function and the structure cannot be eliminated, entrust people who understand the field, how public bureaucracies work, and how that particular bureaucracy works, and with enough energy to fight the entire incentive system driving the bureaucracy toward more aggressive and creative regulatory output.

Notes

1. Antonin Scalia, "Back to Basics: Making Law without Rules," *Regulation,* (July/August 1981): 28.
2. Ibid., p. 27.
3. For an example see Terrence Scanlon and Robert Rogowsky, "Back-Door Rulemaking: A View from the CPSC," *Regulation,* (July/August 1984): 27–30.
4. The CPSC enforces five statutes: the CPSA, which covers all consumer products not covered in the following acts; the Federal Hazardous Substances Act, which focuses on chemicals in consumer products and on children's products; the Poison Prevention Packaging Act, which basically imposes child-resistant caps on containers with harmful ingredients; the Refrigerator Safety Act, which prohibits latches on refrigerator doors that prevent egress from inside a refrigerator; and the Flammable Fabrics Act, which permits rulemaking to control fire retardancy in clothing and rugs. These statutes give the CPSC authority over all consumer

goods used in homes and schools, excluding firearms, automobiles, and food, drugs, and cosmetics.

5. Two rulemaking procedures have been undertaken since 1981; one ended with a voluntary standard and one is ongoing at the time of this writing.

6. National Labor Relations Board v. Wyman–Gordon Co., 394 U.S. (1969).

7. The five alleged hazards were: (1) stuffed toys with looped string that posed a strangulation hazard; (2) squeeze toys that could become impacted in the throat; (3) mesh-sided cribs that present a suffocation hazard; (5) crib hardware that, if missing or not functioning properly, could allow cribs to collapse.

8. *Federal Register* 49 (15 March 1984): 9722.

9. Toy Safety Act of 1984, P.L. 98-491, 98 Stat. 2269, 17 October 1984.

10. The problem of bureaucratic control is not a new one. Writing of Winston Churchill, biographer William Manchester notes that even that most tenacious of leaders could not prevail over the bureaucrats running the British Treasury. Paul Craig Roberts described how President Reagan succumbed to the tax reform agenda of the bureaucrats in the U.S. Treasury. See *Business Week,* 20 January 1986, p. 14. See also Robert A. Rogowsky, "The Pyrrhic Victories of Section 7: A Political Economy Approach," Robert Mackay et al. (eds.) *The Federal Trade Commission: The Political Economy of Regulation,* (California: Hoover Press, 1987).

11. Letter to manufacturers from director of litigation, CPSC, 9 November 1984.

12. Letter to Commissioner Terry Scanlon, CPSC from National L-P Gas Association, 15 November 1984.

13. *Federal Register* 48 (27 December 1986): 56988.

14. The level sixty parts per billion rested on a technological rather than a scientific base. The CPSC staff believed it was a level that could be reached and still allow nipples to be pliable; that is, just short of destroying the nature of the product.

15. Some examples include Richard Posner, *Antitrust Law: An Economic Perspective* (Chicago: University of Chicago Press, 1976), Robert Bork, *The Antitrust Paradox* (New York: Basic Books, 1978), and a rather substantial literature surrounding recent revisions to the Antitrust Division's Merger Guidelines.

16. U.S. Department of Justice Merger Guidelines (30 May 1968). Reprinted in 2 Trade Reg. Rep. (CCH) para. 4510 (9 August 1982).

17. Robert A. Rogowsky, "The Justice Department's Merger Guidelines: A Study in the Application of the Rule," *Research in Law and Economics* 6 (1984): 136.

18. Exceptions that would trigger a below-guideline case, as enumerated in the Merger Guidelines, included (1) a significant trend toward concentration in the relevant market or (2) the acquisition of a "disruptive" rival that "possesses an unusual competitive potential." Other economic criteria tested include (1) high concentration, (2) unusually large firms, (3) high entry barriers, (4) industries with a history of price fixing, and (5) mergers involving leading (that is, top-four) firms. Rogowsky, "Merger Guidelines," pp. 144–48.

19. Ibid., pp. 148–54, esp. table 4.

20. See for example F.T.C v. Bohack, 74 F.T.C. 640 (1968), in which the FTC challenged the merger of two grocery retailers in New York City. One held 2.9

percent of the market and the other 0.9 percent. The complaint acknowledged that market concentration declined for the preceding decade, but the attorneys feared the merger might slow this process. More recently a 1981 consent decree filed by the commission imposed a remedy for the merger of two firms holding 3.6 percent and 4.9 percent of grocery retailing in Los Angeles and Orange County, California. (F.T.C v. Albertson's, Inc., dkt. no. C-3064) The Antitrust Division recently challenged the merger of two moviemakers holding 2.2 percent and 9.7 percent of a movie production market in which the top-four firms controlled only 31 percent. U.S. v. Tracinda Investments, 1979-2 Trade Cases 62,6889. It is noteworthy that the court on dismissing the government's case, awarded court costs to the defendant.

21. It is generally believed that deterrence has been substantial. See for example David B. Audretsch, *The Effectiveness of Antitrust Policy toward Horizontal Mergers* (Ann Arbor: University of Michigan Press, 1983). The dilemma is what is being deterred—mergers that should be deterred or mergers that should not. For an argument that antimerger activity has likely deterred many desirable mergers, see Robert Rogowsky, "Effectiveness of Section 7 Relief," *Antitrust Bulletin* 31 (Spring 1986): 187–233.

22. Commissioner George Douglas, testifying before Congress after sitting on the commission for a year, remarked, "In appraising the commission's direct law enforcement activities, it is instructive to consider that fully two-thirds of the orders by the Commission are consent orders. Of these consent orders, about 80 percent are Part II Orders—negotiated by the staff without any prior evaluation by the Commission. Clearly the agency can elicit a large number of consents through its coercive power—particularly in relation to smaller enterprises, which always seem to account for a disproportionate share of the government's antitrust cases. . . . *I am particularly struck by the fact that many of these consent orders had scant evidentiary support when they were initially entered. Even more troubling, there were some cases where the orders proved not just burdensome, but anticompetitive as well*" (emphasis added). Prepared statement of George Douglas, commissioner, FTC, before the Subcommittee on Commerce, Consumer and Monetary Affairs, U.S. House of Representatives, 9 November 1983.

23. Win or lose, litigation experience is prized by government attorneys because it is highly marketable in the private sector. See Rogowsky, "Pyrrhic Victories"; Susan Weaver, *Decision to Prosecute: Organization and Public Policy in the Antitrust Division* (Cambridge: MIT Press, 1977); and Robert Katzman, *Regulatory Bureaucracy: The Federal Trade Commission and Antitrust Policy* (Cambridge: MIT Press, 1980).

24. Rogowsky, "Merger Guidelines," table 1, p. 142.

25. The government's above-guidelines enforcement is largely suspect as well. A small sample of negotiated settlements imposing relief orders "preserved competition" in such markets as janitorial services in Southern California; dry-mix concrete in bags in Baltimore/Washington, D.C. area; independent book stores in Cleveland; artificial Christmas trees over two feet tall; bedsprings east of the Rockies; purchase of soybeans in Kansas; beer production in three separate "markets": (1) Minnesota, (2) Kentucky, and (3) Indiana.

26. Thomas Overstreet, *Resale Price Maintenance: Economic Theories and Empirical Evidence* (Washington, D.C.: Federal Trade Commission, 1983), p. 63. Resale price maintenance agreements require retailers to maintain a certain price level for specified products in order to retain the right to sell that product. Until 1975 these arrangements were protected by so-called Fair Trade laws, although they have had a history of statutory enforcement, per se illegality, and rule-of-reason legality. See Overstreet, *Resale Price Maintenance,* pp. 3–7.

27. Ibid.

28. The impact is more striking when we understand the nature of the enforcement. Only 12 percent of the cases touched firms that could have made the Fortune 500 directory in 1978; only 22 percent would have been in the Fortune 1000. Fifty-one percent of the cases in the sample were in five-digit S.I.C product classes with four-firm concentration ratios of 40 percent or less. Only 24.4 percent of these narrowly defined product markets has four-firm concentration ratios in excess of 50 percent. The study concludes, rather generously, one might think, that "the substantial percentage of FTC RPM cases involving relatively small firms does suggest that, unless the relevant economic markets are also very small, the market power in the supplier side necessary to sustain economic hypotheses of competitive harm from RPM might not have been present in many of these cases." Ibid., p. 71.

29. Consumer protection is broken down into sixteen classifications of enforcement activities, covering advertising, credit information; equal credit opportunity enforcement; fair credit reporting; deceptive sales practices; warranties, standards, and certifications; rulemaking; and statute enforcement.

30. Prepared statement of James C. Miller III, chairman of the FTC, before the Subcommittee on Commerce, Consumer, and Monetary Affairs, U.S. House of Representatives, 9 November 1983, attachment B.

31. The Food, Drug, and Cosmetic Act contains three Delaney clauses—one for food additives, one for color additives, and one for drugs administered to food animals.

32. Attempts to loosen the rigid regulation prescribed by the Delaney clauses have been problematical and are likely to induce a harsh backlash. See Richard Cooper, "Stretching Delaney till it Breaks," *Regulation* (November/December 1985): 11–17.

33. Robert D. Tollison, "Public Choice and Antitrust," *Cato Journal* 4 (Winter 1985): 905–6.

11

Regulation, Taxes, and Political Extortion

Fred S. McChesney

Introduction

In the past decade or two, our understanding of government regulation has progressed markedly. Belief that government regulates in some disinterested, "public-interest" fashion to repair market failure has crumbled. Too much regulation is demonstrably at odds with the general welfare for any such public-interest explanation now to be taken seriously. Noting "the paradigm shift that has clearly occurred over the past decade," one analyst writes that no one "would today advance the simplistic notions of disinterested public servants carefully weighing the pros and cons of the public interest to derive the optimal social policy, notions that were still common in text books just a few years ago."[1]

The traditional public-interest model has been found wanting especially when contrasted with an emerging "economic" theory of regulation. The economic model seems to explain much better the reasons for, and effects of, government regulation. "The economic theory of regulation," another source observes, has "put public interest theories of politics to rest."[2]

The essential insight of the economic model is that, like any other good or service, regulation will be provided to the highest bidder.[3] Private producers will bid for regulation because it will generate higher prices and increased returns. Airlines benefited, for example, when the Civil Aeronautics Board awarded them certificates of convenience and necessity and then gave them exclusive routes, but refused to grant certificates to their potential competitors.

Producers' demands are thus now accepted as a principal determinant of the amount and forms of regulation supplied,[4] although politicians responding to private regulatory demands will also reckon the cost to them in consumer-voter dissatisfaction with the higher prices and restricted outputs that accompany regulation.[5] Recognition of the returns ("rents," in economic parlance) available from regulation has also focused attention on rent seeking, that is, the costs that producers incur to obtain the benefits regulation can offer.[6] These dead-weight social losses apparently dwarf any losses attributable to private monopoly.[7]

Despite its superior explanatory power, the economic theory of regulation has not proven capable of explaining all aspects of government regulation. Posner notes, for example, that much consumer protection legislation seems inexplicable in terms of the economic theory:

> The "consumerist" measures of the last few years—truth in lending and in packaging, automobile safety and emission controls, other pollution and safety regulations, the aggressiveness recently displayed by the previously lethargic Federal Trade Commission—are not an obvious product of interest group pressures, and the proponents of the economic theory of regulation have thus far largely ignored such measures.[8]

Studies of specific consumer protection statutes bear out Posner's assertion. Priest studied principal portions of the Magnuson-Moss–Federal Trade Commission (FTC) Improvement Act of 1975 but found no reason to believe they had been of benefit to any identifiable group.[9] Other consumer rules and regulations, such as the FTC's Cooling-Off Rule, seem merely to duplicate contractual remedies already being provided in private markets—again, with no apparent gain for any private group.[10] More generally, the newer "social regulation" seems to entail imposing costs on regulated industries more often than creating regulatory benefits.[11]

While analysts have tried but been unable to fit much of consumer protection into the economic theory of regulation, they have not even attempted to integrate into the economic model perhaps the most obvious sort of government regulation: taxation. This must be counted a major omission. Unlike most regulation, which focuses on specific industries or transactions, taxation affects virtually every aspect of production and exchange. A model of regulation that does not encompass taxation thus misses a significant part of what government is about.

Aside from its inability to explain some of the most visible activities of government, the current version of the economic model of regulation fails to integrate the role of the politician satisfactorily into the model. While much attention is paid to private demands for regulation, little thought has been given to the determinants of the supply of regulation provided by politicians. And almost no consideration has been given to the various ways the politician benefits by acting as supplier. The politician has remained a "mystery actor,"[12] a passive broker among competing private demanders.[13] The nature of politicians' compensation for brokerage services is never fully specified: often, it is treated simplistically as consisting just of votes.

This chapter focuses more specifically on politicians than do most other studies of regulation.[14] It views politicians, not as mere brokers redistributing wealth in response to competing private demands, but as independent public actors making their own demands to which private actors respond. With the roles of buyer and seller conceptually reversed, one is led to consider how politicians gain from private groups other than by creating rents. The economic theory of regulation is extended to show how politicians reap returns by first threatening to extract returns from private producers' capital already in existence, and then being paid to forebear from doing so. These private returns, as opposed to regulation-created rents, represent returns to their owners' entrepreneurial ability and private capital investments. The consideration that private capital owners will pay to keep politicians from expropriating the returns to their capital is measured not so much in votes as in cash.

Political office confers a right, not just to legislate regulatory rents, but to impose costs. A politician can thus gain by forebearing from exercising his right to impose costly restrictions on private actors. Taxes and certain other regulations do not ordinarily create rents, but reduce returns that private capital owners will receive from their skills and investments. In order to protect these returns, private owners have an incentive to contract with individual legislators not to have costs imposed. In compensation, private parties can offer votes, campaign contributions, in-kind donations of service and property, and even direct (and quite legal) payments to politicians. The strategy of threatening regulation and then forebearing— for a price—from regulating has not been recognized heretofore. But in fact one observes private producers being compelled to pay legislators to prevent returns to private capital from being extracted via threatened regulation.

This chapter spells out the theory of regulatory extraction of private capital value and the gains such extraction represent to politicians. The following section outlines briefly the current state of development of the economic theory of regulation. The next section then shows how demanding payments to avoid rent extraction—political extortion—represents an attractive strategy to legislators. The final section presents several instances of private payments to avoid adverse regulatory action; these include

recent episodes from consumer protection regulation (particularly the rise
and fall of the FTC's Used-Car Rule) and from taxation legislation (including the Tax Reform Act of 1986).

Rent Creation in the Economic Theory of Regulation

The first and simplest version of the economic theory of regulation is
that formalized by Stigler.[15] In this model regulation "substitutes" for
private cartelization, permitting private producers acting cooperatively to
restrict outputs and fix prices legally. The Interstate Commerce Commission (ICC), for example, has traditionally allowed truckers to collude in
rate bureaus to fix shipping tariffs. Not only were such agreements
shielded from antitrust attack, but the government solved the two biggest
problems any private cartel faces: enforcing the agreement and defeating
new entry. The government made it illegal for any carrier to deviate from
the rates agreed on. In addition, because entry into the industry was not
free—carriers needed a certificate from the ICC to carry interstate ship-
ments—new entrants could not compete away cartel profits. The result
was significant rents (supracompetitive earnings) for certificated carriers.[16]

Once sensitized by this earliest economic model, analysts began to
realize that cartelizaton-by-regulation was not the only way that government creates rents. Several recent contributions have noted that regulation
can create rents for some firms by increasing the costs of their rivals.[17] An
especially useful strategy is to have government increase the costs of
certain inputs. Firms do not use all inputs in the same way and amounts:
Some firms may be labor-intensive, others capital-intensive, for example.
Thus a regulation that raises the cost of an input can actually benefit a firm
that must pay the higher cost, if the input is used even more intensively by
that firm's competitors.

Minimum-wage legislation has in fact been shown to penalize labor-
intensive firms while enhancing the competitive position of their capital-
intensive rivals.[18] Several instances of environmental[19] and occupational
safety[20] regulations have been shown to have differential impacts on firms
that use different amounts of the inputs affected. These "social" regulations therefore actually permit some firms to profit because their competitors are disproportionately affected. The gains available to producers
have created unusual lobbying coalitions to press for regulation: Private
producers link arms with environmentalists, populists, muckrakers, and
other groups with whom they otherwise have little in common.[21] Comparing the process to the coalitions fighting the legal sale of liquor in the
South, Yandle labels this the "bootleggers and Baptists" phenomenon.[22]

The ability of regulation to raise the costs of certain inputs and thereby benefit firms that use less of them is not limited to productive inputs like labor or capital. Marketing or promotional inputs can also be regulated, to the detriment of firms that use more of them and to the advantage of those firms' competitors. The ban on "payola" in broadcasting was at least partly due to pressures from record firms that did not use it but saw firms that did increasing their market shares.[23] Traditional restraints against advertising and other forms of promotion that professional associations impose on their members, and which the law allows them to enforce through licensing statutes, work the same way.[24] In law, for example, the bar has maintained restraints against advertising, solicitation, and referral fees. These are all forms of promotion that less-established attorneys use most. Not surprisingly, then, the organized bar, dominated by more established lawyers, has outlawed these types of promotion. Promotional means favored by larger firms, such as hiring public-relations firms, are not constrained.

Political Extraction of Returns to Private Capital

The strategy of using government to raise competitors' costs differs from that of cartelization by government, in that only some firms in the industry gain while others lose. Industry cooperation to obtain rents for all firms is replaced by rivalry among industry subgroups to benefit some firms at others' expense. The cooperation and rivalry models of regulation are the same, though, in their focus on the private purchase of rents. In both models, politicians respond to private demands for rent creation with a supply of regulation, but do not actively enter the market for rents with their own demands. To quote one description of the regulatory contract, "[private] groups supply votes and campaign contributions to politicians who in turn supply regulation."[25]

In this sense, the economic model of regulation is a powerful yet highly stylized model of political market behavior. Clearly, a politician actively seeks votes, campaign contributions, and other forms of recompense, contracting to receive certain goods or services from private parties in response to his own demands. Politicians are not just suppliers, but also demanders.

Moreover, insufficient attention has been paid to other ways a politician can demand and obtain benefits from private individuals besides rent creation. He may demand votes or money as consideration for rents, as in variants of the economic theory of regulation previously explained.

A politician may also make demands on private parties by threatening to impose costs—political extortion—instead of by promising benefits. If expected costs exceed the value of the consideration that private groups must give up to avoid legislative action, they will surrender the tribute demanded. With a constant marginal utility of money, a private citizen will be just as willing to pay legislators to have rents of $1 million created as to avoid an imposition of $1 million in losses.

In other words, once a politician is viewed as an independent actor, it is clear that he has several sources of gain. A politician maximizes total returns to himself by equating at the margin the gain from votes, contributions, bribes, power, and other sources. All these, in turn, are positive functions not only of private benefits the politician confers but also of private costs he agrees to forebear from imposing.

The political strategy of cost forebearance can assume several forms. Perhaps most obvious is the threat to deregulate an industry previously regulated, thereby destroying future regulatory rents. Expected political rents created by earlier regulation are quickly capitalized into firm share prices. If politicians later breach contracts and vote unexpectedly to deregulate, firm shareholders suffer a wealth loss. Rather than suffer the costs of deregulation, shareholders would pay politicians a sum up to the amount of wealth they would lose in order to avoid deregulation. In fact, one routinely observes payments to politicians to protect regulatory rents.[26]

The problem of guaranteeing the durability of politically created rents has received extensive discussion in the literature on regulation, and will not be discussed further here.[27] But recognition of the rent extraction value that capitalized cartel rents represent to politicians suggests that similar political strategies may offer similar gains. In particular, it leads one to focus on the value of returns to *privately* created capital, and predictable political responses to the existence of private capital.

There are various forms of private capital. The most obvious sort is the plant, machinery, and other fixed-cost investments that firms make. But capital also includes reputational investments, commonly known as brand-name capital or simply "goodwill." Capital likewise includes human capital, that bundle of acquired skills and experience owned by productive labor. All these—physical, reputation, and human capital—are analytically similar, however. Each requires an investment at one time that will yield returns over subsequent periods. The investment may be building a plant, creating brand-name recognition, or learning a skill, but in each case the investment is made now in anticipation of earning a stream of returns in the future.

Because returns are not simultaneous with the investment itself, there are risks associated with owning any capital. Circumstances may change by the time returns are due, and the returns anticipated at the time of investment may not be paid. Some risks naturally and inevitably accompany a market economy. Consumer preferences change and new technologies evolve, reducing or ending the stream of returns expected at the time of the earlier investment. For example, the development of the automobile greatly reduced the value of horse-shoe manufacturing plants and the investments in human capital made by blacksmiths.

But not all risks arise naturally in the market. The presence of government creates artificial risks that returns to private capital will later be expropriated. Taxes on firms with high fixed-cost tangible investments (for example, the "windfall profits" tax on oil companies) are the most obvious illustration. But intangible capital is exposed to similar risks. Federal Trade Commission suits for false advertising against firms with significant reputational-capital investments have been shown to have devastating effects on the value of that capital.[28]

Rather than suffer the costs that taxes and other sorts of regulation can impose, private victims predictably would offer to compensate legislators *not* to impose (or to reduce) the costs. A legislator can thus profit by threatening to expropriate private capital returns, then allowing himself to be bought off. (Several examples of private parties buying off legislators follow later.) As with threatened deregulation of government-created rents, private individuals and firms must pay politicians to protect a stream of future payments. But unlike regulation, where rents are first created by the government itself, a legislator threatening to expropriate private investment returns will be paid to let firms earn interest on capital they have created or invested for themselves.

This political extortion is facilitated by the many ways the law allows legislators to be compensated. There is no limit to the amount of campaign contributions politicians can accept, and it is not difficult to use some of these funds for personal expenses.[29] More lucrative is legislators' ability to take their campaign war chests into retirement for personal use. Thus they have been able to use unspent campaign money to create de facto "individual retirement accounts." (The law has now been changed to outlaw these political IRAs, but Congress exempted all members in office as of January 1980.)

Campaign contributions are not the only way politicians obtain money personally. Potential beneficiaries of legislation have increasingly paid legislators directly through honoraria for personal appearances and speeches.[30] While there are disclosure requirements and fee limits these do not apply to politicians' spouses, who often pick up fees of their own from private groups.[31]

What are private groups paying for? Many payments are made to ward off harmful regulation. "Milker bills" and "juice bills" are terms used by politicians to describe legislative proposals intended only to milk or squeeze producers for payments not to pass costly legislation.

> Early on in my association with the California legislature, I came across the concept of "milker bills"—proposed legislation which had nothing to do with milk to drink and much to do with money, the "mother's milk of politics". . . . Representative Sam, in need of campaign contributions, has a bill introduced which excites some constituency to urge Sam to work hard for its defeat (easily achieved), pouring funds into his campaign coffers and "forever" endearing Sam to his constituency for his effectiveness.[32]

To milked or squeezed victims, the process is just blackmail or extortion to avoid future losses. One political action committee (PAC) director complains that invitations to purchase tickets to congressional receptions "are nothing but blackmail."[33] Likewise, "[T]he 1972 reelection effort for President Nixon included practices bordering on extortion, in which corporations and their executives were, in essence, 'shaken down' for cash donations."[34] Threats are made quite openly; one newspaper reported not long ago, for example, that "House Republican leaders are sending a vaguely threatening message to business political action committees: Give us more, or we may do something rash."[35]

The political strategy of milking the value of private investments can succeed to only the extent that threats to expropriate returns to capital are credible. Credibility depends partly on the strength of constitutional rules protecting private property and contract rights from the government. Legislative threats to expropriate returns to private capital will elicit fewer payments to politicians the more likely it is that capital owners can later have that legislation voided judicially on constitutional grounds. Constitutional scrutiny of legislative expropriations involving private contract and property rights has diminished throughout the late nineteenth and twentieth centuries.[36] The scope for credible legislative threats against private capital has expanded apace. In effect, as courts have retreated from affording constitutional protection against legislative takings, potential private victims are forced to employ more self-help remedies by buying off politicians.

It is important to understand the economic implications of regulation that is threatened but ultimately not imposed: The fact that no regulation is passed does not mean no losses are suffered. The possibility that regulation may later reduce returns to private capital unless politicians are paid off reduces firms' incentives to invest in the first place. The minatory presence of government also induces an inefficient shift of capital to more mobile or salvageable investments, including those made in the underground economy, to avoid future expropriation.[37]

In either event, the allocative losses from politicians' ability to extract returns from private capital are measured by investments never made. An important similarity between capital expropriations in less-developed countries and regulation in developed nations thus has been overlooked. In both cases the very existence of a threatening government reduces private investment.[38] The consequences of political extortion are no different, then, from those of ordinary theft: "One way of minimizing loss by theft is to have little or nothing to steal. In a world in which theft was legal we could expect this fact to lead to a reduction in productive activities."[39]

Political Extortion in Practice

The principal conclusion from the extortion model is that the costs of government regulation are greater than heretofore realized. The costs must be measured not only in markets the government regulates, but also where politicians are paid not to devalue capital investments by regulation. The magnitude of the capital stock reduction resulting from the need to pay protection money would obviously be difficult to measure in any given situation. The purpose of this section, therefore, is to present cases in which costs have demonstrably been imposed on private firms, even when legislators ultimately did not regulate. It follows a fortiori from the demonstration of losses that rational individuals reduce their stock of investments potentially subject to costly political expropriation.

CONSUMER PROTECTION

The history of the FTC's "Used Car Rule" provides a detailed case study of the opportunity for congressional profit from ensuring that regulation is not imposed. In 1975, Congress passed the Magnuson-Moss Warranty—Federal Trade Commission Improvement Act. In the act, Congress took the unusual step of ordering the FTC to initiate within one year "a rulemaking proceeding dealing with warranties and warranty practices in connection with the sale of used motor vehicles." The commission instituted the rulemaking as ordered, and eventually promulgated a rule imposing on used-car dealers costly warranty and auto defect disclosure requirements.[40]

In the meantime, however, Congress legislated for itself a veto over FTC actions.[41] On promulgation of the rule, used-car dealers and their trade association descended on Congress to seek veto of the rule, spending large sums of money for relief from the proposed rule's costs. One study found that

[o]f the 251 legislators who supported the veto resolution and ran again in 1982, 89 percent received contributions from NADA [the National Auto Dealers Association], which averaged over $2,300. This total included 66 legislators who had not been backed by NADA at all in 1980, before the veto resolution vote. Just 22 percent of the 125 congressmen who voted against NADA received 1982 money, and they averaged only $1,000 apiece.[42]

Congress then vetoed the rule.

The used-car episode exemplifies the sort of relief from costly regulatory action that Congress can provide—even when Congress itself initially threatened to impose the costs. By ordering the FTC to promulgate a rule, Congress created an opportunity to extract concessions from dealers to void the costly measures. When those concessions were forthcoming, Congress vetoed the rule.

Why were used car dealers willing to pay for regulatory relief? The FTC's rules do not provide standing for private litigants to enforce the rule. Only the commission can enforce its rules, and typically the FTC obtains only a consent order against an alleged rule violator, not monetary penalties.

But suits brought by the FTC, as already noted, have a demonstrated ability to destroy a firm's reputational capital. This type of capital is especially important in the used car industry, where quality uncertainty (the risk of getting a "lemon") is high.[43] Dealers have responded by investing heavily in brand name capital,[44] the sort the FTC's actions could destroy.

The possibility of suit, though, is only part of the threat to auto dealers' reputational capital that the Used Car Rule posed. Having invested earlier in creating reputation capital, a firm incurs a lower cost of guaranteeing the quality of goods or services that it sells today. Rival firms without significant brand name capital must incur higher costs in the current period to make their names and product quality as well known and trustworthy to consumers. All firms charge higher prices to provide the greater reliability that consumers demand, but the function of the higher market price is different from firm to firm. For no-reputation firms, higher prices cover their higher current costs of guaranteeing quality. For firms with significant reputation captial, the price includes a premium over current cost that represents the return on prior brand-name capital invested.

But that premium, and thus returns to the earlier investment in reputation, can be reduced or destroyed later by government intervention. Politicians can pass legislation to have administrative agencies guarantee quality or truthful information by imposing minimum quality standards or mandatory information disclosure regulations. Government agents would then police the market for quality and truth, substituting both for the brand name capital invested earlier by reputational firms and for the current testing that no-reputation firms would have to commission to guarantee equivalent quality.

Thus to the extent it substitutes for private reputation capital, government regulation like the Used-Car Rule destroys the premium value of the capital, while relieving nonreputational firms of the need to incur new costs to warrant their quality. Even if regulation "only" substitutes for activities currently provided privately, it reduces the expected returns to private reputation investments. And so, over time, it reduces the amount of investment.

The threatened Used-Car Rule is just one example of this phenomenon. Regulation of consumer loans over the past two decades is likewise most explicable as an attempt to impose on lenders costs that could later be relieved. By requiring detailed disclosure of information to borrowers, the Truth-in-Lending Act apparently operates like the Used-Car Rule in substituting government for brand-name capital investments in the consumer loan industry. As with the Used-Car Rule, the precise configuration of costs was left to a specified agency. Indeed, the detailed lender disclosures required by the Federal Reserve Board's regulation Z, promulgated to enforce the Truth-in-Lending Act, went well beyond what the act itself required. This induced lenders to appeal to Congress for relief from the act and the Fed's Regulation Z, which in turn led Congress to mitigate the costs by the Truth-in-Lending Simplification and Reform Act. But the cost relief was not provided free to lenders.

Another form of consumer regulation apparently best explained as a way of expropriating firms' reputational capital is government attempts to require sale of generic drugs. In the late 1970s, the FTC proposed a model state act to facilitate substituting generic for brand-name drugs.[45] The potential effect on major pharmaceutical firms' stocks of brand-name capital is obvious, and the proposal led large research firms to spend heavily on lobbying against the act. Many states have, in fact, refused to adopt the statute. But even with no regulation ultimately being imposed, the episode has not been costless to capital owners.

TAXES

Perhaps the most blatant forms of politicial extortion have occurred in the area of taxation. Politicians are routinely observed to accept money in order not to impose taxes on firms and individuals. It is hardly even news to read, for example, that in 1981, "twelve major oil companies gave $1,000 or more to a U.S. Senator's 1982 campaign fund; two weeks later the senator introduced a bill to repeal certain aspects of the windfall profits tax."[46]

Almost all forms of taxation are useful to politicians in evoking payments to lower or at least not to increase taxes. The system of excise taxes yields substantial revenues to politicians in return for their inaction; of late, the excise tax on beer has proven quite lucrative. A recent report notes that "there hasn't been an increase in the 65-cent-a-case federal tax on beer since the Korean War, and nobody is seriously proposing one right now." Yet the industry has organized a coalition of brewers and wholesalers to compensate key members of Congress anyway: "Members of House and Senate tax-writing committees regularly drop by the coalition's monthly meetings to talk about budget and tax trends, [and] pick up $2,000 appearance fees." Though new beer taxes "haven't generated much interest in Congress," the president of the brewers' trade association says they "want to be prepared."[47]

As remunerative to politicians as not increasing excises has been, the real political action in the 1985–86 Congressional session came from proposals to overhaul the income tax system. Considering the amount of money at stake, it is not surpirising that the payments to politicians to avoid detrimental tax action have been substantial. Much of the evidence comes from the public record of spending by political action committees (PACs), which shows legislators being paid not to tax:

> [M]embers of the tax-writing committees nearly tripled their take from political action committees during the first six months of this year. . . . [The] money is pouring in from . . . insurance companies that want to preserve tax-free appreciation of life insurance policy earnings, from horse breeders, who want to keep rapid depreciation of thoroughbreds, from drug companies seeking to keep a tax haven in Puerto Rico, and from military contractors seeking to retain favorable tax treatment of earnings from multiyear contracts.[48]

Nontaxation does not come cheap: Common Cause reports that in 1985 alone, a year before the real tax action began, PACs gave House Ways and Means and Senate Finance Committee members more than two times as much ($6.7 million) as they did ($2.7 million) in 1983, a comparable non–election year period.[49] Total campaign receipts of the fifty-six tax-writing committee members were $19.8 million, an average of over $350,000 per politician. As another report concluded, "It is clear that a seat on a tax committee gives a legislator a fund-raising advantage over members of other congressional panels."[50]

The goodies are not spread evenly among all committee members, though; Predictably, it is the most influential members of the tax-writing committees that garner the greatest contributions. Finance Committee

Chairman Packwood (perhaps that should be PACwood) led Finance Committee members in PAC receipts (just under $1 million) and total receipts ($5.1 million).[51] On the Ways and Means Committee, Chairman Rostenkowski was the big winner,[52] though he professes to be "nauseated" by the amount of giving to tax committee members.[53]

The money is of course given to purchase tax favors: As Rostenkowski admits, "It's not my personality" that induces the contributions.[54] The tax bills are loaded with special interest breaks, with nicknames like "the Marriott amendment" or "the Gallo amendment" identifying the benefici-aries. The milking process is straightforward. "How do people or groups win such breaks?" one report asks. A former Treasury Department tax specialist responds, "It helps if you've been a big supporter of [a] senator. I'm afraid that's democracy."[55] The Gallo family, for example, has contrib-uted hundreds of thousands of dollars to candidates in recent federal elections to avoid heavy taxes on intergenerational wealth transfers.[56]

It is tempting to blame the entire process of procuring tax breaks on the private beneficiaries who pay. This is the standard populist perspective: Fat cat lobbyists corrupt basically upright but weak legislators. But politicians themselves are principal beneficiaries of the tax process, profiting politi-cally and personally through campaign contributions, speech and ap-pearance fees, and payments to their spouses. Given the benefits to politi-cians themselves, one should anticipate that they would actively seek contributions, rather than wait for lobbyists to come to them.

The 1985–86 tax season was in fact noteworthy for the initiatives politi-cians took in generating funds. Legislators "began tapping contributors for dollars almost immediately after the 1984 campaign."[57] As the round of proposed tax changes began in 1985, tax lobbyists said that they had not seen "such ravenous appetites for contributions in a nonelection year before."[58] It takes two to tango, and the 1985–86 tax bills were just politicians' invitations to the dance.

AVOIDING OTHER COSTLY REGULATION

In addition to payments for nontaxation, one observes legislators being compensated not to impose other costs on firms. Some recent threats include legislative proposals to require financial institutions to start costly reporting and tax withholding from depositors' interest and dividend checks, and proposals to impose "unisex" premiums and benefit payments on insurance firms. Both episodes are difficult to square with the rent creation model of regulation, as they consumed considerable political time and energy but resulted in no regulation at all.

But even if never actually imposed, these measures would be politically attractive if they could elicit private payments to legislators *not* to impose the threatened costs—which in fact they did. The banking industry contributed millions of dollars to politicians in 1982 in a successful effort to obtain repeal of the statutory provision requiring banks to withhold interest and dividend taxes. There are no precise figures on contributions to politicians to stop legislation banning gender-based insurance rate and benefit schedules, but their magnitude may be inferred from the American Council of Life Insurance's media budget of nearly $2 million in 1983 and 1984 to defeat the legislation.[59]

Finally, even antitrust is coming to be seen as a useful system for generating income for politicians. Easterbrook and Stigler have both noted that it is difficult to locate any significant rents attributable to the antitrust laws.[60] Yet the FTC is recognized by many as a creature of politics,[61] and the FTC's antitrust enforcement jurisdiction gives a politician "a great deal of power to advance the interests of businesses located in his district."[62]

One way legislators can benefit themselves and their constituents is through a cost-relief strategy by allowing the FTC to sue any firm but then frequently having the Commission dismiss cases against constituents. And in fact, among firms investigated and sued by the FTC there is a significantly higher dismissal rate for those located in the jurisdictions of important congressional committee and subcommittee chairmen than for firms outside those jurisdictions.[63] One must assume that antitrust favors do not go to constituents without charge.

Conclusion

This chapter has extended the economic theory of regulation. It presents the theory and some examples of an apparently large subset of government activities, those designed to extract payments from private capital owners in exchange for politicians' forebearance from imposing burdensome (costly) regulations. Many regulations—consumer protection, taxation, and other costly interventions in the marketplace—are threatened but not imposed once potential private victims compensate politicians. While these episodes do not fit the current version of the economic theory of regulation, which concerns creating regulatory rents, they are cognizable as political attempts to extract the value of returns from physical, reputational, and human capital.

It is important to emphasize that, however deplorable, there is nothing necessarily illegal in extracting the returns to private capital. On the contrary, the process is constitutionally protected. Article I of the Constitution specifically grants Congress the power to tax, but does not require any particular form or amount of tax, leaving that to congressional discretion. Thus the power is allocated to one party, the politician, to decide whether and whom to tax, setting the stage for contracts with potential victims who wish to pay not to have costs imposed. Would-be victims' ability to make payments like campaign contributions is likewise constitutionally protected as a matter of first amendment freedom of speech. In short, politicians can at their discretion impose costs or not, and a private party can just as legally compensate politicians for not imposing those costs on him. Under those circumstances, is it any wonder that political extortion occurs?

Notes

1. Robert Poole, "The Iron Law of Public Policy," *Wall Street Journal*, 4 August 1986, p. 15.

2. Joseph Kalt and Mark Zupan, "Capture and Ideology in the Economic Theory of Politics," *American Economic Review* 74 (June 1984): 279–300.

3. See generally Richard Posner, "Theories of Economic Regulation," *Bell Journal of Economics* 5 (1974): 335–58.

4. George Stigler, "Theory of Economic Regulation," ibid. 2 (1971): 3–21.

5. Sam Peltzman, "Toward a More General Theory of Regulation," *Journal of Law and Economics* 19 (1976): 211–40.

6. Gordon Tullock, "The Welfare Costs of Tariffs, Monopolies, and Theft," *Western Economic Journal* 5 (June 1967): 224–32.

7. Richard Posner, "The Social Costs of Monopoly and Regulation," *Journal of Political Economy* 83 (1975): 807–28. For reviews of the theoretical and empirical literature on rent seeking, see Robert Tollison, "Rent Seeking: A Survey," *Kyklos* 35 (1982): 575–602, and Robert McCormick, "A Review of the Economics of Regulation: The Political Process," chapter 2 of this volume.

8. Posner, "Theories of Economic Regulation," p. 353. Migue also discusses consumer and other regulations that "do not appear at first sight to be designed for the sole benefit of producers' pressure groups. This evidence seems difficult to reconcile with the economic theory of regulation." Jean-Luc Migue, "Controls versus Subsidies in the Economic Theory of Regulation," *Journal of Law and Economics* 20 (1977): 213–14.

9. George Priest, "The Structure and Operation of the Magnuson-Moss Warranty Act," in Kenneth Clarkson and Timothy Muris (eds.) *The Federal Trade Commission since 1970* (Cambridge: Cambridge University Press, 1981), pp. 246–76.

10. Fred McChesney, "Regulation without Evidence: The FTC's 'Cooling-off' Rule," *Journal of Contemporary Studies* 7 (Winter 1984): 57–70.

11. For example, James C. Miller, III and Bruce Yandle (eds.), *Benefit-Cost Analysis of Social Regulation* (Washington, D.C.: American Enterprise Institute, 1979); see also Eugene Bardach and Robert Kagan (eds.), *Social Regulation: Strategies for Reform* (San Francisco: Institute for Contemporary Studies, 1982).

238   *Fred S. McChesney*

12. Tollison, "The Social Costs of Monopoly and Regulation," p. 592.

13. Robert McCormick and Robert Tollison, *Politicians, Legislation, and the Economy* (Boston: Nijhoff, 1981).

14. Fuller and more technical treatment of the issues discussed in this article may be found in Fred McChesney, "Rent Extraction and Rent Creation in the Economic Theory of Regulation," *Journal of Legal Studies* 16 (January 1987): 101–18.

15. Stigler, "Theory of Economic Regulation." Suggestions that regulation was actually government cartelization antedate Stigler's article. See for example papers published through the 1960s collected in Paul MacAvoy (ed.), *The Crisis of the Regulatory Commissions* (New York: Norton, 1970).

16. James Frew, "The Existence of Monopoly Profits in the Motor Carrier Industry," *Journal of Law and Economics* 24 (October 1981): 289–316; Denis Breen, "The Monopoly Value of Household-Goods Carrier Operating Certificates," ibid. 20 (April 1977): 153–86.

17. Steven Salop and David Scheffman, "Raising Rivals' Costs," *American Economic Review* 73 (May 1983): 267–71; Sharon Oster, "The Strategic Use of Regulatory Investment by Industry Sub-Groups," *Economic Inquiry* 20 (October 1982): 604–18.

18. David Kaun, "Minimum Wages, Factor Substitution, and the Marginal Producer," *Quarterly Journal of Economics* 79 (1965): 478–94.

19. Peter Pashigian, "The Effect of Environmental Regulation on Optimal Plant Size and Factor Shares," *Journal of Law and Economics* 27 (April 1984): 1–28; Michael Maloney and Robert McCormick, "A Positive Theory of Environmental Quality Regulation," ibid. 25 (April 1982): 99–124.

20. Ann Bartel and Lacy Thomas, "Direct and Indirect Effects of Regulation: A New Look at OSHA's Impact," ibid. 28 (April 1985): 1–26.

21. This point is discussed by McCormick in chapter 2 of this volume.

22. Bruce Yandle, "Bootleggers and Baptists," *Regulation* (May/June 1983): 12–16.

23. Ronald Coase, "Payola in Radio and Television Broadcasting," *Journal of Law and Economics* 22 (October 1979): 269–328.

24. Fred McChesney, "Commercial Speech in the Professions," *University of Pennsylvania Law Review* 134 (1985): 45–119.

25. See McCormick, chapter 2 of this volume.

26. Dairy interests pay well for continuing congressional milk-price supports. Physician and dentist political action committees (PACs) contribute large sums for continuing cartel-like self-regulation. See Larry Sabato, *PAC Power: Inside the World of Political Action Committees* (New York: Norton, 1984), pp. 133–37.

27. Because more durable rent contracts are in the interest of both private parties and politicians, the intervention of third-party institutions would predictably be sought to hold legislators to their deals. The judiciary for example may help guarantee congressional rent-creation contracts, since courts can overrule legislators' attempted revisions of earlier contracts by holding them unconstitutional. William Landes and Richard Posner, "The Independent Judiciary in an Interest-Group Perspective," *Journal of Law and Economics* 18 (December 1975): 865–907;

Robert Tollison and Mark Crain, "Constitutional Change in an Interest-Group Perspective," ibid. 8 (January 1979): 165–76. Executive veto of attempted changes in legislative deals is another way of increasing the amounts private parties would spend for rent creation. Mark Crain and Robert Tollison, "The Executive Branch in an Interest-Group Theory of Government," ibid. 8 (June 1979): 555–68. Finally rents achieved by constitutional change will be more durable than those obtained by legislative action. Gary Anderson, et al, "Behind the Veil: The Political Economy of Constitutional Change," (manuscript, 1986).

28. Sam Peltzman, "The Effects of FTC Advertising Regulation," *Journal of Law and Economics* 24 (December 1981): 403–48.

29. Brooks Jackson, "Congressmen Charge All Kinds of Things to Campaign Chests," *Wall Street Journal,* 3 December 1985, p. 1.

30. Brooks Jackson, "Interest Groups Pay Millions in Appearance Fees to Get Legislators to Listen as Well as to Speak," ibid., 4 June 1985, p. 62; Brooks Jackson, "Lawmakers Got Record Fees in '83," ibid., 25 May 1984, p. 58.

31. Ronald Shafer, "Pay My Wife—Please!," ibid., 24 May 1985, p. 1.

32. Craig Stubblebine, "On the Political Economy of Tax Reform," paper presented at the 1985 Western Economic Association annual meeting. See also "California's Political Gold Rush," *Time,* 3 February 1986, p. 42, for a discussion of "juice bills."

33. Sabato, *PAC Power,* p. 86.

34. Ibid., p. 5.

35. Brooks Jackson, "House Republicans Are Pressing PACs for Contributions," *Wall Street Journal,* 27 June 1985, p. 30.

36. Richard Epstein, *Takings: Private Property and the Power of Eminent Domain* (Cambridge: Harvard University Press, 1985); Terry Anderson and Peter Hill, *The Birth of a Transfer Society* (Stanford: Hoover Institution Press, 1980).

37. James Alm, "The Welfare Cost of the Underground Economy," *Economic Inquiry* 24 (April 1985): 243–63.

38. The effects of third-world government expropriations of private capital in diminishing the amount of investment made are analyzed and measured in Jonathan Eaton and Mark Gersovitz, "A Theory of Expropriations and Deviations from Perfect Capital Mobility," *Economic Journal* 94 (March 1984): 16–40.

39. Tullock, "The Welfare Costs of Tariffs, Monopolies, and Theft," p. 229, n. 11.

40. *Code of Federal Regulations* 16 (1982) part 455.

41. Since Congress has always been able to annul any agency rule or regulation statutorily, the question arises why it would want a veto. The legislative veto can be explained in terms of the model of capital-value extraction presented in this article. Statutes to change agency action require the president's signature. The president is therefore able to exact payment for participating in cost-mitigating legislation, lowering payments offered to legislators. Thus, the legislative veto is hardly a check on agency action as claimed. It is a congressional attempt to avoid splitting fees with the executive. If Congress has a veto, it then has an incentive to fund even more cost-imposing activities by bureaucratic agencies.

42. Sabato, *PAC Power,* p. 134, citing Kirk Brown, "Campaign Contributions

and Congressional Voting," paper prepared for the American Political Science Association annual meeting, 1983. The Supreme Court of course later invalidated the legislative veto, but the commission nevertheless recalled the proposed Used-Car Rule and essentially gutted it. See *Code of Federal Regulations* 16 (1982) part 455.

43. George Akerlof, "The Market for 'Lemons': Quality Uncertainty and Market Mechanism," *Quarterly Journal of Economics* 84 (August 1970): 488–500.

44.

> Both intuition and empirical data suggest that the used-car market attracts lemons. . . . A number of market mechanisms serve to alleviate these problems. The most visible solutions take the form of dealer guarantees and warranties, which recently have been beefed up with extended coverage backed by national insurers. Indirectly, dealers invest in brand-name maintenance (local television ads, for instance), which makes it more costly for them to renege on a reputation for quality. The reputation of the parent automakers is also laid on the line. All four domestic car manufacturers have certified the quality of the better used cars sold by their dealers. Two generations of Chevrolet dealers, for example, have designated better used cars with an "OK" stamp of the dealer's confidence in the car's marketability. ("Can Regulation Sweeten the Automotive Lemon?" *Regulation,* 8 [September/December 1984] : 7–8.)

45. Oster, "The Strategic Use of Regulatory Investment," pp. 612–16.

46. Sabato *PAC Power,* pp. 130–31.

47. Brooks Jackson, "Brewing Industry Organizes Lobbying Coalition to Head off Any Increase in U.S. Tax on Beer," *Wall Street Journal,* 11 July 1985, p. 52.

48. Brooks Jackson, "Tax-Revision Proposals Bring Big Contributions from PACs to Congressional Campaign Coffers," ibid., 9 August 1985, p. 36.

49. "Gimme a Break," *Common Cause News,* 11 February 1986 (hereinafter cited as *Common Cause*).

50. Steven Pressman, "PAC Money, Honoraria Flow to Tax Writers," *Congressional Quarterly* 43 (14 September 1985): 1806.

51. *Common Cause.*

52. Ibid.

53. Brooks Jackson, "Even the Beneficiaries Are Deploring System of Financing Elections," *Wall Street Journal,* 18 July 1986, p. 1.

54. Ibid.

55. Alan Murray, "Lobbyists and Chums from College Leave Imprint on Tax Bill," ibid., 16 May 1986, p. 1.

56. Brooks Jackson and Jeffrey Birnbaum, " 'Gallo Amendment' Backed by Wine Family Opens Multimillion Dollar Estate Tax Loophole," ibid., October 1985, p. 64.

57. Pressman, "PAC Money, Honoraria Flow to Tax Writers," p. 1807.

58. Jackson, "Tax Revision Proposals."

59. Sabato, *PAC Power,* p. 125.

60. Frank Easterbrook, "The Limits of Antitrust," (*Texas Law Review* 63 [1984]: 1–40), p. 33, n. 70 ("efforts to verify the interest group hypothesis have not been

successful"); George Stigler, "The Origin of the Sherman Act," *Journal of Legal Studies* 14 (January 1985): 1–12.

61. Richard Hofstadter, "What Happened to the Antitrust Movement?" in Richard Hofstadter, *The Paranoid Style in American Politics, and Other Essays* (New York: Knopf, 1965), p. 200 (antitrust "essentially a political rather than an economic exercise"); Wesley Liebeler, "Bureau of Competition: Antitrust Enforcement Activities," in Clarkson and Muris (eds.) *The Federal Trade Comission Since 1970*, p. 97 ("the FTC can be understood only in political terms").

62. Richard Posner, "The Federal Trade Commission," *University of Chicago Law Review* 37 (1969): 47–89, p. 83.

63. Roger Faith, Donald Leavens, and Robert Tollison, "Antitrust Pork Barrel," *Journal of Law and Economics* 25 (October 1982): 329–42.

12

The Unpredictable Politics behind Regulation: The Institutional Basis

Richard L. Stroup

People value stability in any system under which they must live and make decisions. The comparative systems literature emphasizes the fact that instability is the enemy of progress and productivity. Investors are less willing to invest when property rights are uncertain, and the rules cannot be anticipated with some degree of confidence.

On the micro level, in developed countries, the profitability of brand names and franchising arrangements reflects the premium people are willing to pay for a predictable product with low search and information costs. As the Holiday Inn advertisement says, "The best surprise is no surprise!"

One characteristic of economic regulation, cited by those supporting it, is the added stability it might in principle give to the economic environment. The "chaos of the market," it is said, can be calmed by the presence and actions of regulatory agencies. Both buyers and producers gain from increased certainty. Regulators may be viewed as agents of consumers (and the firms that serve consumers best), representing them by formulating and administering "long-term contracts."[1] At the federal level citizens elect politicians, who appoint the heads of regulatory agencies. These politically chosen regulators are presumed to represent the electorate in controlling the economic environment in which firms and consumers operate, providing stability, predictability, and other characteristics preferred by the electorate.

Can citizens actually obtain the same sort of stability, or predictability, in the political arena, they seek and find in the private sector? Does real world

Work on this paper was supported by the Political Economy Research Center, Bozeman, Mont. I want to thank Randy Simmons and Jane S. Shaw for helpful comments. The usual disclaimer applies.

regulation, via the political process, provide added certainty? The democratic process in the United States is strongly competitive, with many candidates currying the favor of voters. Yet there is good reason to expect that in order to compete, politicians might *not* act to give voters the predictability they want, especially in a world of rationally ignorant voters. An additional factor working against the provision of certainty is that one legislature or Congress, or one administration in the executive branch, cannot legally bind its successor to provide regulatory rules. Each of these problems is analyzed in this chapter.

Rational Ignorance

The fact that voters are ignorant about even the most important issues is one of the more consistent findings in political science.[2] It is rational for an individual to remain ignorant about most issues, even those most critical to society—nuclear disarmament, the budget, and so on—simply because the individual voter's decision is almost never decisive. That is, his or her vote will probably never influence the outcome of an election, so that a mistaken vote is virtually irrelevant, and so is a more informed vote. Yet to become well informed is costly. Consider this classic quote from the *Chicago Tribune*, describing how to become an informed voter:

> First, get a list of the four or five hundred primary candidates, and memorize their names. Attend all of the political meetings. Study the pictures and posters of all office seekers. Tune in on every political address. Discuss the various candidates with your friends. Save and study carefully every political pamphlet. Weigh the qualifications of each aspirant, during office hours. By this time you have lost your friends, your wife and your job, but you have the satisfaction of knowing you can vote intelligently, and you're a good citizen.[3]

The upshot is that while the individual voter would have to pay the entire cost of efforts to become well informed on political issues, there is little incentive to do so. Only the easiest to-obtain information is typically utilized. Few, therefore, cast an informed vote;[4] instead most are easily swayed by image, style, and surface appearances—the kind of characteristics that public relations experts and advertising people can manipulate—as opposed to careful consideration of substantive issues.[5] Effective public relations and political campaigns are expensive, of course; thus advertising budgets are a critical element in determining the winner when election campaigns are competitive.

Competition

Elections in the United States are highly contestable (and frequently contested) "markets." Competition for elective office can be fierce, and since voters have little incentive to seek information about candidates and their positions, expensive advertising campaigns can provide an important competitive edge. How expensive are these campaigns? In 1982 the average U.S. Senate candidate spent $1,782,000, and the average candidate for the House of Representatives spent $228,000.[6] Since the early 1970s, however, the real cost of both House and Senate campaigns has more than doubled every six years.[7] The 1986 Senate campaign in California cost each candidate more than $10 million.

Unlike bidders in a market auction, both winners and losers pay the full cost of an election bid. It is common for lobbying groups—which provide the bulk of campaign funds used by political candidates—to support both candidates in a general election race. This may seem odd to an observer, until the major purpose of the campaign donations is recognized.

Access for Lobbyists

During and after the election, lobbying groups are to a large extent competing for access—for the ear—of elected officials and their key staffers.[8] It is easy to get a courteous hearing from the staff of a senator or representative, but to reach the decisionmakers—senior staffers and the principal—is another matter. Their time is extremely valuable, but it can be purchased.[9]

The majority of campaign funds raised by incumbents are in fact not raised at election time, but over their entire term of office. A large portion of the cost of many races is actually paid for after the fact, since many campaigns finish far in the red. Campaign contributions are not intended by their donors to influence election outcomes so much as to purchase access to the incumbent.

A large campaign contributions may not "buy" a vote, but it certainly enhances a lobbyist's chance of being able to sit down with the elected official and the key member of his staff on a specific issue, to explain the client's position on that issue. Without access to the politician, the lobbyist would operate at a serious disadvantage; of course the arrangement also benefits the elected official. Without extra campaign contributions from lobbyists, the politician, too, operates at a disadvantage in a very competitive political marketplace.

Allocating Funds for Lobbying

How do lobbyists allocate their limited funds as they attempt to purchase the access needed to influence congressional outcomes? When this sort of access is their goal, they attempt to maximize the impact of what they buy, subject to their budget constraint—that is, they will try to get the biggest bang for their lobbying buck. To do so, they target their giving for this purpose, ignoring those on whose votes they can already count and those whose votes are already committed against the lobby's interest. Instead, recipients of these optimally allocated dollars for campaign aid will be those who are "reasonable" on the issue: the uncommitted, or "fence sitters."

The decision process just described resembles the triage process practiced by medical teams on the battlefield. The wounded who are judged to be so badly injured that medical attention is unlikely to ensure survival do not receive the highest priority, nor do those who will apparently survive even without immediate attention. Instead, scarce medical attention goes to those for whom it will do the most good—the wounded for whom the probability of survival will be increased the most.

Both triage and allocating political lobbying funds are a simple application of the marginal principle: Allocate each increment of scarce resources where it will make the greatest desired change in the outcome. Just as in a private market, efficient "buyers" of political services allocate their scarce resources in accord with the marginal principle. Donations intended to purchase access go to politicians who might listen to the lobbyist's arguments and be persuaded.

Here the political marketplace diverges dramatically from the operation of the commercial market: Unlike private suppliers, political suppliers find it costly to be dependable and predictable. For a lobbyist access to the politician whose vote is already announced has no value. While Holiday Inn can provide a perfectly predictable product, to those who pay for it, the politician cannot. In contrast with the private business owner, it is illegal and immoral for a politician to say to a voter or lobbyist, "You know how I want to vote on this issue, but if I do not receive enough money from you, I will not vote that way." A vote cannot legitimately be sold. But the politician who is not committed to a position on the issue, and has not made his or her principles so clear as to imply a position, implicitly has the ability to "sell" access to lobbyists on the issue. Only the uncommitted politician has anything of value to offer to those seeking access.

At this point we should recognize another "commodity" that a politician can offer a lobbyist or special interest group on an issue: leadership. A dependable, predictable stand can be (and often is) taken by a politician on a few select issues, yet those issues can still be big money-makers for the campaign. The politician can, in effect say to the lobbyist, "I will certainly vote your way, but if you want me to spend time and political capital on this issue, can I count on you for campaign contributions? I simply must spent a large amount of time and effort gaining campaign support, and if I get a lot of support from you, that will free me to campaign for this issue that we both feel so strongly about." However, the politician can gain from this time-intensive strategy on only a handful of issues,[10] while "access" donations will be available on the vast majority of issues.

A strong commitment to clear positions at the outset may also help a politician during a close election campaign. Friends of a position want to see the politician elected who favors it, and may well contribute at election time if the other candidate takes the opposing position *and* if they think that their donation may affect election results. Of course a clear position in this situation also makes enemies who may be willing to donate to the opposition in a close campaign. Remember, too, that only about a third of all campaign funds typically will be received during the course of an election. The rest have been raised (or will be raised) by the incumbent and the winner, explaining in part why incumbents tend to be heavy favorites. About three out of every four candidates at the national level end the campaign in debt. The loser, of course, often has a very difficult time paying campaign debts, having little of value to offer those who finance campaigns.

The Value of Being a Fence Sitter

It is easy now see one important reason why politicians are reluctant to commit themselves in advance to positions, or clearly stated principles that imply such positions. To do so reduces a candidate's eligibility for lobbying funds disbursed to those whose might be swayed on an issue. Only potential swing voters are reasonable targets for carefully allocated funds intended to buy access for lobbyists in the legislative process. For the politician looking ahead, it is difficult to forecast which issues will be significant and how announced principles will reduce flexibility on issues in the future.

Obviously then, clearly stated positions and principles can be expensive for a politician, in fact survival in the highly competitive political arena may be hindered by just such statements of positions and principle. In addition to alienating interest groups opposing those positions, firm positions and principles are costly because they make the politician predictable and reduce his or her ability to trade political votes.

The Postelection Penalty: The Ron Paul Problem

For the politician already elected, there is another penalty associated with being predictable on an issue, even a minor one: an inability to trade votes or participate in logrolling. The politician who strongly desires to accomplish some specific ends finds that such trading can be critical to success. Elected representatives are well known for trading votes—"You vote for my key issue, and I'll help you when yours comes up." This is especially important for expenditure and other programs to help local constituents, since rational ignorance means that the rest of the nation is unlikely to know, or individually to care much, about the program. Specifically, the politician who votes for the expenditure as a favor to a politician in another state will not be held accountable by taxpayer-voters back home. Of course in total such programs may be very expensive and inefficient, but no individual politician is responsible for the bottom line, so "pork barrel" and other such programs thrive on the basis of vote trading.

To reiterate, any issue on which the politician's position is clear has no trading value (unless of course the politician makes known a willingness, for exchange purposes, to change that position). In general, announcing a position on an issue makes one valueless *on the margin* to others on that issue. An announcement of a position on the issue had better come, one might say, *after* the tradeoffs involving that issue have already been made. I have dubbed this the "Ron Paul problem" after the former Texas congressman who was in fact principled and predictable. He openly admitted to being powerless and thoroughly frustrated in Congress as a result.[11]

Note that the preceding principle holds in the executive branch: A president's arm twisting and wooing to gain support for the administration's programs's is naturally concentrated on the fence-sitters. They are the ones quietly promised good things for themselves and their constituencies, in exchange for supporting the president's key issues. A corollary, of course, is that the president and the administration cannot afford to be committed on many issues in advance either. They must also be "flexible," in order to make trades to gain support for their own program. A cabinet secretary, for example, unwilling to make "political" decisions on water projects, military bases, or federal office locations will hinder an administration in the arm-twisting process. The coin of the realm in these exchanges is a new commitment or a *change* in one's stance (perhaps from neutrality), not simply the existence of support.

The high cost to a politician of being predictable is a particular form of the principal-agent problem. A politician is the voters' agent, but has different goals (typically reelection and a personal agenda), and it is expensive for voters to monitor results of a politician's individual actions. To some degree a politician is also the agent of those who provide campaign support. Those special interests find it easier to monitor the narrow band of a politician's activities with which they are concerned, however, so for them the principal-agent problem is smaller in comparison to their gains on the issue. We can thus expect their influence over a politician to be correspondingly greater on their specific issues, as compared to voters' influence. This of course, is the well-known "special-interest effect." But even, here the consistency and dependable support that special interests seek from a politician can usually be obtained only from the few who are leaders on that issue; others find it too costly to be predictable.

Good Politics versus Principled Behavior

In order to be elected, it is important for a politician to appear principled. Each candidate must have the voter's confidence. However, to state clearly the principles on which decisions will be based increases one's predictability, simultaneously reducing one's ability to trade votes without violating principles, and one's value to lobbyists making campaign contributions when seeking swing votes.

To actually *be* principled in a serious and systematic way is to be predictable, thereby sacrificing important potential campaign support. Being principled also causes one to become less effective in vote trading once elected. The optimal strategy for many politicians, then, is to take a strong and popular stand on those few issues frequently in the headlines (or for other reasons well known to voters) back home, but to be flexible—uncommitted—on thousands of other issues that arise during the term of office.

The truly principled politician, then, is in a terrible bind: wishing to take a stand on many issues, but also wanting campaign funds with which to be elected, and wanting to be effective in office after the election. Thus a politician must somehow strike a compromise between competing objectives: strongly principled stands, a well-funded and successful election campaign, and effectively attaining goals (principled or otherwise) once in office. At any moment in time, then, most political stands are potentially reversible, for when the political wind changes direction, the flags of most politicians follow it.

Another Barrier to Institutional Stability

Are there institutional ways of protecting market participants from the vagaries of political winds? In the case of regulation, for example, can stability be attained through "long-term contracts"? Can regulations be set for a finite period of time, as in a long-term lease? Unfortunately for those who must do business in a politically controlled environment, the rules cannot be set beyond the term of the current legislative body. Whatever privilege, funding, or regulation that Congress (for example) grants, under any terms whatsoever, it can also legally take away.[12]

Consider the case of treaties with American Indian tribes. Time and again, Congress has found it expedient to abrogate such treaties.[13] In regard to these and other cases, the Supreme Court has ruled that one Congress cannot bind another, so that a congressional decision to abrogate is constitutional and cannot be prevented.

The Unstable Nature of a Regulatory Regime

Because politicians find that taking dependable (predictable) stands on most issues puts them at a competitive disadvantage and because democratic political institutions themselves are incapable of providing stability legislatively, a regulatory regime in a democracy is inherently unstable. Of course with sufficient and continuous investments in political muscle, an interest group can potentially (and frequently does) control a regulatory environment for its purpose for long periods of time. Even for powerful special interests, however, the regulatory environment can prove to be a fickle one.

A good example of this type of instability can be seen in the history of freight transportation in the United States. Railroads were originally brought under Interstate Commerce Commission (ICC) regulation in the 1880s to keep rail rates above competitive levels. By the 1930s, deregulated truck carriers were threatening rail markets. To protect the railroads, the 1935 Motor Carriers Act brought truck freight under ICC regulation. Unfortunately for the railroads by the late 1940s, truck interests had gained control of the ICC, and regulation began to tilt against the railroads. A counterattack by the railroads was fought off in the 1950s by truckers.[14] Railroads continued to decline until nearly the entire industry went bankrupt. A coalition of most of the surviving railroads was able to defeat the truckers in 1980 and push large-scale deregulation of railroads through Congress.[15]

The general public, of course can never realistically be expected to sustain the political pressure needed to use regulation to its advantage consistently. Its interest in any given regulation or regulatory body is simply too diffuse and the free rider problem too great to permit regulators or politicians to gain from upholding the interests of the general public, or even the interests of consumers as a group, under normal circumstances.

Political outcomes are very different from private transactions. One difference is that losers in the political process need not be compensated, unless they are politically powerful. Another difference is that a political outcome cannot be bought, nor can it even be leased for a finite term: It can only be rented. Its duration will coincide closely with the relative political clout of its supporters. Thus, only those who pay sufficient political dues, and pay them constantly, can expect their interests to be represented well, in the political arena.

Conclusions

When a particular behavior is more costly, we expect to see less of it. In politics being predictable is costly, so we therefore expect less predictability than in the private sector, where a firm's ability to deliver predictability commands a premium. Presumably voters want predictability but are not willing to monitor the election process and Congress sufficiently well to obtain it. Long-term institutional "contracts" on regulation are, as we have seen, not possible in our democracy.

It is natural, in our world of imperfect and costly information, for each of us to be somewhat doubtful of his ability to deal individually with many suppliers, some of them quite large. This is especially true in an environment with rapid technological change. It is natural to hope that governmental regulation of suppliers and of buyer-seller relationships will improve our chances of avoiding serious errors and unsatisfactory outcomes. After all, bad food and bad drugs, for example, will be sold in private markets despite the protection of brand names and other entrepreneurial devices intended to provide the security and certainty sought by individuals. But what will be the outcome if we turn over control of the market to regulators?

The principal-agent problem alone guarantees that regulation, too, will fall short of perfection. Rational voter ignorance and the special interest effect ensure that politically organized groups, typically suppliers, will be a powerful force in regulation.

The forces discussed in this paper also imply that the regulatory environment is likely to be rather unstable. Broken campaign promises are hardly news these days, and regulation-deregulation-reregulation turnabouts that surprise even the pundits also occur with some frequency. The notion that the political process simply provides voters with agents to help them deal efficiently with firms and other economic entities is naïve. The high cost to politicians of being predictable helps explain why the performance of regulation—as well as tax regimes and other components of government—can be expected to provide less than a stable environment in which investment and other decisions can be made, and business conducted.

Notes

1. See for example Goldberg (1976). Recently, in the more general context of economic interests, Peltzman (1985) inferred from several decades of data that politicians do indeed have some tendency, though not always a decisive one, to represent their constituents' economic interests.

2. For a more complete treatment of "rational ignorance," see Gwartney and Stroup (1982), pp. 632–33.

3. *Chicago Tribune,* 5 April 1932, as cited in Lentz (1976).

4. In fact, poll after poll, decade after decade, reflects this fact. For example a Louis Harris poll conducted for the U.S. Senate (Harris 1973, pp. 215–16) found that fewer than half of all citizens of voting age could even name their congressman.

5. See Joe McGinnis, *The Selling of the President, 1968,* on the importance of these factors in the presidential campaign.

6. Data are from Ornstein et al. (1984).

7. See Gary C. Jacobson, "The Republican Advantage in Campaign Finance," in Chubb and Peterson (1985).

8. Lobbyists use funds for other purposes also, of course, Two of these are (1) at election time, to influence close elections in favor of candidates likely to be friendly on future votes, and (2) to buy, or at least encourage leadership on their issues on the part of their friends in Congress. We should not expect that access is the only political good purchased by lobbyists, or sold by politicians.

9. See Jackson Brooks, "Lobbyists Who Pay Lawmakers $1,000 an Hour Have Found an Effective Way to Communicate," *Wall Street Journal,* 25 June 1986, p. 58, for additional nuances and data on this point. Personal income, as well as campaign funds, plays a role.

10. An additional cost of taking a clear and consistent stand is that the stand may attract strong and consistent enemies when the issue is controversial. Voters are frequently known to be motivated to vote against one candidate almost as often as they are motivated to vote for that candidate's opponent. A low profile on most issues, together with sympathetic concern expressed to each side on an issue, is thus the politician's usual stand on most issues.

11. See Paul (1984) for an explanation in some detail of this problem.

12. A contract with an individual or a firm, for delivery of a good or service, however, becomes private property. Unlike regulations or grants of aid, private property cannot (in principle) be taken away even by Congress without due process.

13. See the classic history of the United States, Morison (1980), pp. 441, 586, for some examples of this issue.

14. See Kahn (1971), pp 14–28.

15. See Derthick and Quirk (1985), pp. 15–16.

References

Chubb, John E, and Paul E. Peterson (eds). *The New Direction in American Politics.* Washington, D.C.: Brookings 1985.

Derthick, Martha, and Paul S. Quirk. *The Politics of Deregulation.* Washington, D.C.: Brookings, 1985.

Goldberg, Victor. "Regulation and Administered Contracts." *Bell Journal* (Autumn 1976): 426–48.

Gwartney, James D, and Richard L. Stroup. *Economics: Private and Public Choice.* New York: Academic Press, 1982.

Harris, Louis. *Confidence and Concern: Citizens View American Government* (part 2). Washington, D.C.: U.S. Government Printing Office, 1973.

Kahn, Alfred E. *The Economics of Regulation,* vol. 2. New York: Wiley, 1971.

Lentz, Bernard F. "Public Sector Wage Determination: A Democratic Theory of Economics." Yale Ph.D. thesis, 1976.

McGinnis, Joe. *The Selling of the President 1968* (New York: Trident Press, 1969).

Morison, Samuel Eliot, Henry Steele Commager, and William E. Leuchtenburg. *The Growth of the American Republic,* vol. 1. New York: Oxford University Press, 1980.

Ornstein, Norman, et al. *Vital Statistics on Congress, 1984–85 Edition.* Washington, D.C.: American Enterprise Institute for Public Policy Research, 1984.

Paul, Ron. Speech to Congress 19 September 1984. *Congressional Record* 130, no. 118.

Peltzman, Sam. "An Economic Interpretation of the History of Congressional Voting in the Twentieth Century." *American Economic Review* 75, no. 4 (1985): 656–75.

13

A User's Guide to the Regulatory Bureaucracy
Daniel K. Benjamin

To the outside observer, the federal bureaucracy seems paradoxical if not bizarre. Some observations are commonplace, even mundane: The federal bureaucracy is slow to change its structure in response to external stimuli; it is lackadaisical in dealing with routine matters; and it virtually refuses to respond to out-of-the-ordinary requests from the clients it is presumed to serve. Moreover, despite the absence of any obvious increase in social product on its part, the bureaucracy shows an insatiable appetite for consuming an increasing share of resources over time.

In addition to these obvious anomalies, there are others, albeit of a smaller order of magnitude, that are just as puzzling:

- At any given level of the bureaucracy, the more powerful the staff members serving that level, the smaller their offices.
- Despite the preceding observation, office space is one of the most hotly contested commodities within the federal bureaucracy.
- Although the production of paper is the most commonly used standard of productivity ("I want that memo *now*"), the people who produce the least paper generally have the most influence.
- Human resources are frequently unemployed (or at least under-employed) in the bureaucracy, while nonhuman resources (such as office space) are almost never unemployed.

Roger Meiners and Bruce Yandle provided helpful comments on an earlier draft. As fellow former bureaucrats they are probably just as responsible as I for remaining errors, ambiguities, and grammatical mistakes, but professional courtesy dictates that I absolve them of all blame.

• Despite the existence of paper chains of command that are sufficiently formal and precise as to have been set into law by Congress, internecine struggles for power are rife, and once settled, often leave the actors in positions in the paper chain that are seemingly unchanged.

This list could be extended, but I think its present length is sufficient to demonstrate the salient point. The federal bureaucracy exhibits the characteristics of a vignette from *Through the Looking Glass*—nothing is as it seems to be, but everything is as it should be, given the constraints faced by the actors. In what follows, I hope to elaborate on this point and tie together the common threads that bind these apparent anomalies into a coherent whole.[1]

Bureaucratic Structure and Control: This Is a Chain of Command?

Every agency of the executive branch has a formal, structured chain of command established legislatively by Congress. In principle, all directives from above are supposed to follow this chain, as are all reports from below. A typical example of the upper echelons of such a chain of command within a cabinet-level agency is shown in Figure 13.1.In principle, the secretary makes the department's broad policy decisions and interacts with other Cabinet members and the president in setting and coordinating policy goals of the administration. The under secretary serves as a surrogate for the secretary and, in the idealized model, acts as the day-to-day manager of the department, implementing the policy decisions made by his immediate superior. In this model, the assistant secretaries interact on a regular basis chiefly with the under secretary, receiving managerial directives from him and reporting managerial progress to him. Their direct contact with the secretary comes at the direction of the under secretary and involves briefing the secretary or providing other staff support functions for him in response to requests funneled through the under secretary. In addition, the assistant secretaries are responsible for the day-to-day management of the operational programs they oversee. Within this textbook chain of command, the role of the chief of staff is exactly what the title suggests: He supervises the operations of the secretary's immediate staff, which includes various special and staff assistants responsible for preparing the secretary's schedule, handling his press relations, and preparing background briefing material to serve as a counterpoint for material provided by the assistant secretaries or submitted by congressional interests or outside lobbyists.

This stylized picture of the chain of command is in fact followed (by and large) in some Cabinet departments, for example, the Defense and Agriculture departments during the first Reagan administration. However, the

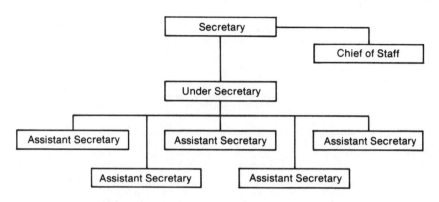

model portrayed above is more often violated than observed. Although the real chain of command is not always what it appears to be on paper in the private sector, discrepancies between appearances and reality are much greater in the federal bureaucracy. The reason for this is quite simply, the federal bureaucracy's missing profit motive. In the private sector, when the wrong person is hired for a job, he is fired. In the federal bureaucracy, even among political appointees, unsatisfactory employees are much more likely to be retained, since the appropriable benefits from replacing them are lower than in the private sector. The other actors simply work around the weak links, cutting them out of the real chain of command.

Although there are many ways in which the real chain of command deviates from the paper chain, the two most frequently observed variations on the legislatively mandated chain of command are links *A* and *B,* shown in Figure 13.2. The existence of Link *A* simply means that the chief of staff takes an active role in the day-to-day management of (portions of) the department in conjunction with the under secretary. Typically, this arrangement arises because of the existence of a close relationship between the Cabinet member and his chief of staff and the lack thereof between the Cabinet member and his under secretary. Such an arrangement can result because the choice of chief of staff is almost wholly the prerogative of the Cabinet member, while the choice of the under secretary is importantly influenced by the wishes of the White House. If, for reasons noted below, the White House imposes on a Cabinet member an under secretary whose political instincts are not totally consonant with those of his principal, the under secretary must be extremely adept at mind reading to avoid the Cabinet member manage the department through his hand-picked chief of staff—if for no other reason than to avoid having to remind the under secretary what it is that *he* wishes to accomplish.[2]

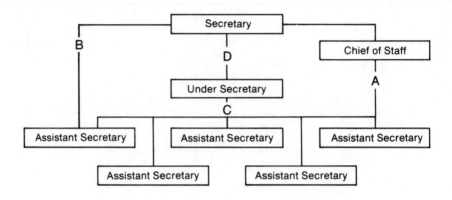

Link *A* generally emerges from the aftermath of a (largely silent) power struggle between the chief of staff and the under secretary, which yields an unspoken but clearly understood division of responsibilities (and hence power). The struggle often leaves a residue of underlying tension between the parties involved. The outcome of both the power struggle and its aftermath depends on the personalities of the actors as does so much in a bureaucracy. This is a tautological statement, but I shall later attempt to give it more operational meaning.

Link *B* generally occurs when the assistant secretary in question not only passes muster with the White House (a necessary condition for his appointment) but also has close ties to the Cabinet member, either because of prior association or because he has proved to be particularly loyal or useful to the Cabinet member while in his present position. Although the development of link *B*, in which an assistant secretary bypasses the formal chain of command, is typically much less fractious than the development of *A*, it may be accompanied by considerable disruption.

One of the purposes of a formal chain of command is to ensure that (when it is adhered to) the relevant parties know *what* they should know, *when* they should know it. Few situations are more embarrassing to the bureaucrat than to know less than his boss does. If the assistant secretary reporting directly to the secretary through link *B* is not careful to keep the under secretary or the chief of staff "in the loop," embarrassment may be the least of the problems the parties will face.

Two additional frequently observed mutations in the textbook model of the chain of command occur at points *C* and *D*. When a break occurs at *C*, it simply means that the role of the under secretary in the day-to-day management of the department has been abrogated, and the chief of staff has taken over those duties. The traditional role of the under secretary as surrogate for the secretary in official functions remains, but he plays little, if any, significant role in the substantive operations of the department. A break at D, which is almost invariably associated only with an accompanying break at C, is also almost always terminal for the under secretary: Not only is he cut out of the day-to-day management, but he is also no longer tossed the bone of performing ceremonial functions. Typically this sort of double break occurs either because of a sharp personality clash between the secretary and the under secretary or because the secretary has lost confidence in the loyalty or competence of the under secretary.

It might seem that a break at C or at both C and D would require the under secretary to be an idiot or the chief of staff to be a direct descendant of Machiavelli. In fact neither has to be true (although either will expedite matters). Many agencies have constituent interest groups whose goals are diametrically opposed, so it is not uncommon for an administration to appoint as secretary an individual sympathetic to (or at least identified with) one of the groups, while also appointing as under secretary a person whose views are consonant with those of a competing group. This gives both groups high-level access within the agency, and the group that comes out second best is usually smart enough to recognize that half a loaf is better than none. However, when a "split appointment," such as this occurs, it requires an extremely astute under secretary to avoid an unpleasant break at links C or D. The outcome of a double break for the under secretary depends on how close he is to the White House: If very close, he will eventually be moved to some other "laterally comparable" position, either in the White House, another agency of the executive branch, or in some suitable presidential commission. If the under secretary is not particularly close to the White House he will be given an appropriate amount of time to find employment outside of the administration.[3]

The nominal and real chains of command that I have highlighted for the upper echelons of the bureaucracy are generally mirrored at lower levels as well. For example, each assistant secretary generally is equipped with an executive assistant (read chief of staff) and a deputy (read under secretary). Although the nominal chain of command runs through the deputy, it is not unusual for the executive assistant to assume many of the duties that are, on paper, reserved for the deputy. The reason for this is analogous to that at the higher echelon: The selection of a deputy assistant secretary is importantly influenced "from on high," while the choice of an executive assistant is almost always exclusively that of the assistant secretary. This tandem occurrence of two chains of command—one on paper and one

real—continues to proliferate as one moves even further down the bureaucratic organization. At each level, the extent of convergence or diver-
gence between the chains depends on two factors: (1) the extent to which
the principal at each level has control over the choice of the person
immediately beneath him in the paper chain; and (2) the loyalty, integrity,
and usefulness of the parties involved. The relevance of each of these
factors is the subject of subsequent sections.[4]

Wealth in the Bureaucracy

Roughly once a year (typically in September or October), the major
newspapers and wire services covering Washington publish an exposé on
the excesses of senior-level bureaucrats.[5] The focus of these exposés is
usually one of the following: the use of chauffeured cars, extravagant
consumption of office space or accoutrements, or meals purchased in
executive dining rooms at subsidized prices. Although such "perks" are in
fact some of the ways in which senior-level bureaucrats are compensated
for their efforts in Washington, they are only remotely related to the force
that attracts senior people to Washington initially, or induces them to work
hard once they are there. The ultimate aphrodisiac of "Potomac Fever" is
power—the right to control the use and value of economic resources
without the direct discipline of the marketplace. The trappings of power
so often chronicled by the press are (sometimes) manifestations of the
existence of power, but in no way elucidate its sources or functional
expressions. The sources of power in the bureaucracy are threefold: (1)
loyalty, (2) usefulness, and (3) consistency.[6]

LOYALTY

The importance of loyalty in the bureaucracy—both to one's boss and to
one's subordinates—stems largely from the system of property rights
implicit in the system. Most important is the absence of market discipline.
Even though there are periodic elections, the interval between them is
long, the outcomes are usually unaffected by the day-to-day operations of
the bureaucracy, and the results rarely have much impact on the employment of career bureaucrats. Indeed, the career status of most bureaucrats
compounds the problem: Barring illegal workplace behavior, it is almost
impossible, as a practical matter, for a career employee to be fired or
involuntarily transferred. Since a manager's most powerful tools for disci-
plining disloyal behavior are thus stripped, employees exhibiting loyalty
are highly valued and accordingly rewarded with more responsibility, and
thus power. The essential feature of loyalty in this context involves the

subordinate acting *as though* his superior can continuously monitor and easily discipline him—even though the superior can in fact do neither most of the time.

Loyalty toward subordinates is expressed in a different matter. It is a commonplace observation that the bureaucracy is encumbered with a welter of rules and procedures. These are not concocted aimlessly (although it sometimes seems that way), but motivated rather by the absence of market discipline. If an employee in the private sector takes action causing large negative changes in the value of the firm, owners of the firm either halt the behavior to protect their wealth, or the firm goes out of business. In either event, there is a very nearly self-enforcing mechanism that, on average, brings such behavior to a halt reasonably promptly.

In the public sector this discipline is replaced by the ballot box, a slow, relatively crude instrument. Consequently, an elaborate set of rules and procedures has been developed—rules to make sure that many people can review decisions, and procedures to ensure that they do review them. Even trivial regulations and seemingly innocuous correspondence must routinely be approved by as many as twenty people in a dozen layers of the bureaucracy. Indeed, at times the system reminds one of a cluster of Lilliputians attempting to move an elephant whose natural penchant is to remain motionless: Unless (almost) all of the actors agree on a decision and push in the same direction, nothing happens. The analogy is less far-fetched than it might seem at first glance; for example, given the activities the elephant is likely to undertake at various locations, there is a strong tendency for the Lilliputians to cluster at the head and sides, implying a tendency toward backward or at best sideways motion. Similarly, if enough people coalesce at a particular location, implying a decision in direction, those on the opposite side had better move quickly to avoid being squashed.

There is, of course some social product from all of this, for it is almost impossible for one person to do something incredibly stupid.[7] But accompanying this positive result is a considerable cost: inertia bordering on being terminal. Indeed if all of the rules were followed, nothing (as opposed to almost nothing) would get done in Washington. Hence, subordinates are directed to break rules, avoid procedures, and generally render ineffective the subordinates of other bosses who are attempting enforcement. Along the way, egos are bruised, feelings hurt, and anger aroused. This may lead the losing subordinates to appeal to their boss for some form of remedial action. It is at this point that a boss's loyalty becomes critical—for both winners and losers. Even if a losing boss is unconcerned about the outcome, he must *appear* to be concerned and make some effort to reverse it; otherwise his subordinates will be less diligent in the next engagement—one might really matter. Similarly, a winning boss must stand behind the methods and actions of his subordinates—"flying air cover," so to speak—or he too, will find reduced effectiveness in the next encounter. But as long as a boss is loyal to his people and protects them, they will work even more diligently in the future, thereby increasing their boss's effectiveness and power.

USEFULNESS

The second source of wealth in the bureaucracy is usefulness—a combination of anticipation and delivery. The higher one rises in the bureaucracy, the greater the number and difficulty of the issues to be confronted. Even with a work week that increases steadily with one's responsibilities, there is generally less and less time to think about any particular issue. One consequence of this is that "fire drills"—frantic attempts to adjust to unanticipated developments—become more frequent as one moves up the bureaucratic ladder. The key to avoiding fire drills is anticipation. Much of the time spent on this activity is "wasted," in the sense that most low-probability events never happen. However, it only takes a few payoffs for the boss to appreciate the value of being able to concentrate on high-probability events, relying on subordinates to worry about unlikely occurrences. Such reliance generates power for subordinates, who become possessors of information that is costly to obtain in their absence.

The second element of usefulness is the ability to deliver the product requested within the required time period. It is commonplace for two-hour deadlines to be placed on tasks that should have two days or even two weeks devoted to them. Any attempt actually to do a two-day job in two hours is doomed to failure, for no useful product can be delivered; and in a bureaucracy, "delivery" is everything. Since measuring the value of output is difficult in the absence of pricing, simply measuring its *existence* takes on greatly added importance. Moreover, anyone asking for delivery of a two-day job in two hours is either (1) so good that he can make up for deficiencies in a mediocre product or (2) so bad that he will not be able to tell that it is mediocre. In either event, he *will* be able to determine whether or not the product exists.

The problem of never having enough time to do a proper job in the federal bureaucracy is rampant in the upper levels, and explicable by the system of property rights, and thus the incentives, that the actors face. Upper echelons of the bureaucracy are populated almost exclusively by noncareer (usually political) appointees, whose expected tenure on the job is very low—for the top four layers of a typical executive branch agency, expected tenure is less than two years. This creates two types of incentives. First, investment in creating routines is discouraged, since the latest routine will have to be recreated as soon as the next personnel change occurs. Hence, tasks tend to be done on a catch-as-catch-can basis in response to the latest request—which in itself typically appears to be randomly generated, since there is no routine for generating requests. Second, short expected job tenure encourages individuals to create and react to quick-turnaround projects, since the returns from long-term projects will not materialize during their tenure and thus cannot be appropriated by them. Of course, if there were a class of well-defined residual claimants to the "profits" of a bureaucracy, incentive structures presumably could be devised to lengthen the time horizon of senior appointees. However, as noted earlier, the election process makes voters only the most rudimentary claimants to the fruits of the bureaucracy's labors.[8]

CONSISTENCY

The final source of power in the bureaucracy is consistency—in product delivery and in treating subordinates. I previously noted that a mediocre product is better than no product at all. Similarly, knowing ahead of time that a mediocre product is coming is in itself valuable for two reasons. Depending on the ultimate use and the recipient of the work product, there can be a widely varying range of output quality that is desired. Some tasks just don't warrant more investment than is sufficient to yield a mediocre product, and it is wasteful to errantly assign high quality inputs to those tasks. Conversely, if a high quality product is desired, the arrival of mediocre output can necessitate a costly scramble to upgrade the product (this being one of the more notorious causes of having to do a two day job in two hours). Knowing ahead of time what one is going to get thus makes for a more efficient production process; this is true in the private sector as well, of course, but its importance is magnified in the bureaucracy because of (1) the transient nature of employment at senior levels, implying less knowledge about the attributes of specific inputs; (2) the relatively lower quality of internal signals of quality, such as pay and rank; and (3) the previously noted tendency of senior-level people to specialize in quick-turnaround projects, implying high adjustment costs in response to surprises.

Consistency in treating subordinates also takes on added importance in the bureaucracy. In the private sector arbitrary personnel decisions—those not reflecting productivity—impact adversely on the manager's bottom line and thus on personnel decisions made about him. Hence, there tends to be a self-enforcing mechanism in the private sector that protects subordinates from arbitrary personnel decisions. This force is much weaker in the bureaucracy, a fact that goes far to explain the existence of the Civil Service system. Lacking a well-defined bottom line, managers in the bureaucracy have much greater latitude for arbitrary personnel decisions. If they avoid this temptation by making decisions consistent with the output of their subordinates, they will be rewarded with greater loyalty and consequently a higher quality product.

Productive Consumption in the Bureaucracy: Access, Proximity, and Resources

In the course of the senior bureaucrat's quest for power, he quickly learns that there are three commodities that simultaneously facilitate the acquisition of power and signal its existence to other bureaucrats. These are access to one's superiors, proximity to them, and control over the use of human and nonhuman resources.

ACCESS

Access determines the flow of information, and since decisions are made only on the basis of what is known, those who control the flow of information control the decisions. Access can come either from being able to get memoranda into the boss's "In" box or from being able to get oneself into the boss's office. Of the two forms of access, the latter ("rug time") is unambiguously superior. In general, a disagreement between subordinates that pits memos against rug time will be won by the latter if the merits of the differing parties' arguments are even remotely equal. The subordinate who makes his case in person does so without cross-examination, while also conducting an unchallenged dissection of the opposing party's arguments. Similarly, if a meeting with two or more disagreeing subordinates is to be held, and one of them is able to get one-on-one time with the boss before hand, he almost surely will win the battle. Such a pre-meeting enables a subordinate to establish "background" events as a framework for the boss to use in evaluating arguments that will be presented in the subsequent meeting. It also enables the subordinate to destroy straw-man versions of an opponent's arguments, thereby lessening the opponent's credibility.[9] Thus access implies that one's arguments are presented in the most favorable light and opponents' in the least favorable, implying that the course of action preferred by the person with access is more likely to be taken.

The complement of access is the control of access. Indeed, any good chief of staff (or his deputy) will make sure that (1) no paper hits the principal's desk without first crossing his own desk; (2) no meetings take place without his prior knowledge; and (3) no important meetings take place without his presence. There are two reasons for this behavior. First, since the information on which decisionmakers base choices is always a proper subset of the total amount of information available, there is discretion and thus power available to the person who controls the information flow. In effect the "traffic controller" can, within some bounds, control the decisions made by his principal. In an ideal world those bounds would be extremely narrow; the principal would always make the same decisions that he would make if he had all the information available to his second-in-command. As a practical matter the principal can never know everything his deputy knows—if the principal could, then he would not need a deputy. And the deputy cannot always be sure how the principal will decide a particular issue, if for no other reason than he can never be certain about the full information set available to the principal. Both parties recognize these facts, and the result is a set of bounds on the discretion—and thus the power—of the deputy that can be quite broad. The range of the bounds varies predictably with two factors. The more important the decision, the smaller will be the discretion allowed to, or accepted by, the deputy: Only important people can afford to make important mistakes. Conversely, the more complicated the series of events leading up to the decision, the greater the likelihood that the deputy will implicitly or explicitly make the decision: The principal's time is worth more than the value to him of becoming involved.

The second reason that the careful monitoring of information going to the principal is important is that, to the extent feasible, his deputy must know what the principal knows. Otherwise he will make decisions (and thus mistakes) that he shouldn't make, and he will refrain from making decisions he should be making. The combination is one that is a nuisance for the principal and decidedly unhealthy for the deputy.

PROXIMITY

The importance of proximity is twofold. First, being close to one's boss makes it simpler to give him information. This lowers the cost to a subordinate of servicing the boss, as well as raising the value of the subordinate to the boss. For example, physical proximity lowers the cost of face-to-face meetings relative to the cost of telephone conversations, a relevant consideration, since (1) body language is often an important part of communication and (2) the successful assignment or delivery of a job typically requires paper to change hands. Proximity also lowers the cost of having a meeting with a subordinate, hence, a closer subordinate is more likely to be included in a meeting. Further, proximity means that there is a greater chance that the boss will know, as part of the ordinary course of business, whether a subordinate is available for assistance, and if not, when he is likely to be available. These may seem to be trivial considerations, and in some settings (for example, the slow-paced life of academe), they are. But in the short-fuse environment of the upper levels of the federal bureaucracy, even a few minutes can determine whether or not a memo is delivered to a cabinet secretary before he has to leave for a meeting with the president. If those few minutes are important enough often enough, people will go to great lengths to save them.

The second advantage of proximity is that it enables a subordinate to know who is gaining access to the principal. This in turn improves a subordinate's estimates of what other information is reaching the boss and hence what information may be necessary to counteract or reinforce that information. And as already noted, knowing who is talking to whom helps avoid having decisions made by people who should not be making them.

TWO VIGNETTES ON RESOURCES IN THE BUREAUCRACY

Who Is That Masked Man?

Offices can bewilder the uninitiated in the Washington bureaucracy. Holders of exalted titles often reside in windowless hovels that one would not wish on a dog, as do movers and shakers who form the backbone of an agency's power structure. Seemingly lowly minions have 400 square feet of window space providing an unobstructed view of the Capitol, while their superiors in the paper hierarchy are lucky to command a view of the men's room. One's first impression is that a mindless idiot has been put in charge of office allocations and given no rules to follow.

To understand this arrangement, one must keep in mind that office assignments are one of the few fringe benefits of bureaucratic life not rigidly controlled by the Civil Service system. Within fairly narrow bounds, most aspects of personnel compensation are regulated by institutionalized rules almost completely independent of one's performance (at least among career bureaucrats). Thus, one of the most important devices for adjusting total compensation on the basis of job performance is office assignment. Whatever their paper rank in the bureaucracy, people who are more productive than average receive better offices; those who are less productive receive worse. As a result, office allocations assume an important role in both hiring and promotion negotiations, as senior managers try to acquire and retain the best people. This is a simple enough point, but in a system like the civil service, where there are so few ways of adjusting compensation, its importance is magnified.

In the private sector, where people can be fired or demoted in response to poor performance, or promoted at a moment's notice, there are several avenues for managers to encourage superior performance and penalize inferior work. This is much less true in the civil service bureaucracy. The distinction, for example, between (permanent) promotions and (temporary) office assignments in the federal bureaucracy is important. A person promoted from one grade to another for superior performance in, say, the Carter administration is entitled to receive the associated higher rate of pay for the rest of his career. A person who receives a superior office allocation is entitled to that allocation for only as long as his boss is satisfied with his work, whether that boss is beholden to the Carter administration or the Reagan administration. As a result, office assignments provide a much more surgically accurate method of controlling subordinates' work performance than do promotions.[10]

The next point to keep in mind is the importance of proximity in determining access to one's boss and proximity's role as an effective means of determining who else has that access. The value of proximity implies that offices of a given square footage, window space, and privacy are more valuable, the closer they are to the boss. As a result, people will give up more of the other desirable office elements for greater proximity to the boss.

The final factor in assessing office allocations is that offices serve as important signaling devices in a bureaucracy. I noted earlier that the expected tenure of senior-level political appointees is less than two years. Moreover, even during their tenure within a given niche in the paper chain of command, their de facto status in the true chain is likely to change at least once. As a result, it is often difficult, if not impossible, for someone seeking assistance from the bureaucracy to determine who is really in charge.[11] Since successful performers are generally rewarded with more power as well as better offices, the opulence of a bureaucrat's accommodations, *given* his rank and proximity to the boss, is a good indication of how useful he is likely to be.

Of the three factors affecting allocations—rank, performance, and proximity—the first and third tend to dominate. Since they work in opposite directions, the result is a peculiar progression of office opulence as one moves up the bureaucratic hierarchy. Within a given level of the hierarchy, individuals of higher rank tend to have more desirable offices. However, as one gets closer physically to that level's boss, the proximity effect begins to dominate, and offices become progressively smaller—until one reaches the boss's office, which is much larger and nicer than that of any subordinate. The result is the configuration shown in Figure 13.3, where office opulence is a combination of size, window area, and furnishings. The essential point is that, given the rank and proximity of a bureaucrat, the opulence of his office conveys useful information about his importance in the real chain of command only when it is at one of the extremes.

This pattern is repeated across executive agencies, with an interesting overlay that emerges as one approaches 1600 Pennsylvania Avenue. Since the White House is the hub of executive decision making in Washington, office space becomes increasingly desirable the closer it is to the White House. This rise in the (implicit) value of space as one nears the president's venue leads to a general shrinkage in the offices occupied by bureaucrats of all levels—culminating in offices within the White House itself, which are notorious for being the most cramped of all.[12]

Unemployment on the Job

The first Reagan administration had three rallying cries: a defense build-up was essential to preserve national security; government regulations were strangling the private sector; and the size of the government had gotten out of hand. By all public accounts, the defense build-up proceeded rapidly, albeit perhaps less rapidly than the president would have preferred. Moreover, while deregulation proved far more difficult than almost anyone anticipated, the drastic reduction in the size of the *Federal Register* alone suggests that substantive progress was made. Yet on the spending side, the best that can be said is that the Reagan administration managed to slow the rate of growth. Importantly, this disappointing performance in controlling spending was due to the ongoing military build-up and to the fact that the president put Social Security spending off-limits to the budget-cutters. Yet even if one focuses solely on discretionary domestic spending, only the rate of growth was slowed.

There is, I think, a deceptively simple explanation for this disappointing performance on the domestic-spending front, one illustrated by budget requests that the operating agencies of the Labor Department proposed during my tenure there. Almost never did a program manager ask for more office space per employee; only infrequently did a manager ask for additional funding that was not driven by his payroll; however, almost *invariably* managers asked for additional staff. This asymmetry was so striking that individuals evaluating program budget requests throughout the government focused their attention almost exclusively on the size of the staff that managers were requesting, rather than on the number of dollars they wanted to spend. Indeed, by the third year of the Reagan administration, the president's instructions to the Office of Management and Budget regarding domestic "spending cuts" referred only to the number of *personnel* that he wanted eliminated. It seemed almost as if

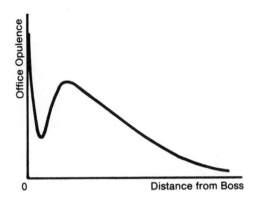

managers were capable of responsible, possibly even efficient, budgetary behavior in all aspects except staffing requests.[13]

This asymmetry in budget requests, and the accompanying upward pressure it puts on the size of the bureaucracy, are, I believe, a direct consequence of the Civil Service system. When a manager in the bureaucracy finds himself with too much office space for subordinates, or too many typewriters or lamps, it is (almost) costless for him to dispose of the excess equipment. But when a bureaucrat has too many subordinates, Civil Service rules make it (almost) prohibitively costly to dispose of them. Barring gross dereliction of duty, a charge that generally takes a *year* of written records and repeated warnings to substantiate and uphold, an individual civil servant simply cannot be dismissed. A transfer to another agency is a possibility, but it requires the acquiescence of that agency's manager, who is likely to wonder why he is expected to receive an employee unwanted elsewhere. Moreover, the proposed transferee can (with a reasonable chance of success) appeal the move, and even if the transfer is accomplished, the net number of bureaucrats is unchanged.

It is possible to dispose of a block of bureaucrats through a "reduction in force" (RIF), in which a number of jobs are eliminated simultaneously. The problem with this course of action is that Civil Service rules (1) treat "jobs" as wholly independent of the people holding them, and (2) give people subject to a RIF "bumping rights" over those occupying jobs "inferior" to theirs. The upshot is that a RIF that eliminates ten "jobs" is likely to dispose of nine valued employees (bumped by those with greater seniority) and only one of the ten worthless ones that one wanted to fire. It is little wonder that managers regard RIFs with as much enthusiasm as they view hostile congressional hearings.

All of this would be academic if the world never changed. But every four years there is a presidential election, and in the meantime it is not unusual for an agency head to depart for greener pastures. Since changes in leadership bring changes in priorities, and thus changes in the talents that are most highly valued, managers would frequently like to alter the composition of their work force. The efficient way to do this would involve replacing the (now redundant) employees with new ones. However, since Civil Service rules effectively preclude disposing of unwanted employees, the only way to "replace" them is to hire new people and cut the old ones out of the process while leaving them in their "jobs."

The outcome of this process is not difficult to imagine: Unwanted employees are shunted aside—assigned to make-work projects or simply allowed to consume copious amounts of on-the-job leisure. Simultaneously, managers press forward with requests for the additional staff they need to get the job done. The result is a system in which many do nothing, at the same time that many more are needed to do anything.

Indeed, one of the most disconcerting aspects of President Reagan's instructions to his appointees was the clash between his mandate to cut budgets and his orders to achieve regulatory reform. When combined with his commitment to increase defense spending, the president's instructions to reduce the rate of growth of total government spending placed severe downward pressure on domestic agencies' budgets. Hiring new employees became almost impossible, and workforce reductions were limited to RIFs and attrition. Since the best people were most likely to leave (because they had the best alternatives), the president's appointees were left with a small cadre of dedicated civil servants and an enormous pool of demoralized employees, many of whom had been buried by previous administrations.

The result was a vexing paradox. True regulatory reform requires an artful blend of fresh ideas from new people and the organizational and institutional knowledge of battle-hardened veteran bureaucrats. Budgetary goals dictated substantial cuts in the workforce. Yet Civil Service rules made it almost impossible to protect staff one wanted to retain, while simultaneously preventing staff reductions to levels that would permit significant numbers of new employees. Thus managers were left with more employees than implied by the president's budgetary goals, and not enough good people to accomplish his regulatory goals. Lewis Carroll had been joined by Joseph Heller.

Conclusion

Most observers evaluate the world, even if implicitly, in the context of a gestalt embodying the notion that decision making is constrained by the existence of competition. Within this context, the behavior observed within the federal bureaucracy seems positively bizarre. Yet once one recognizes that the link between the ballot box and day-to-day bureaucratic behavior is a tenuous, quadrennial event, and that the next best alternatives to our system involve significant reductions in freedom and wealth, bureaucratic behavior emerges as at least comprehensible, if not completely palatable.

Appendix

Almost all of the top jobs in the Washington bureaucracy—some 3,500 of them—are held by political appointees rather than career bureaucrats. These appointees, whose positions range from cabinet secretaries to clerk-typists, occupy positions that are deemed to be politically sensitive, either because of the policy-making nature of the job or because the job requires access to materials with the potential to be politically damaging. They are generally termed Schedule C's—the bureaucratic nomenclature given to the legal authority for their appointments, an authority that exempts them from normal Civil Service procedures for hiring and firing. Therefore such appointees can be hired—and fired—on the whim of the appointing authority, much as in the private sector.

There are two classes of Schedule C appointments—those made directly by the president and those made by the heads of the various executive agencies. All Schedule C appointments are ultimately controlled by the White House, in the sense that all must be approved by the White House Office of Personnel. As a practical matter, presidential appointments are much more closely controlled by the White House, if for no other reason than that they are the proximate responsibility of the president. Should these appointees make a serious error in judgment, the consequences are more likely to damage the president directly.

Most presidential appointees are required by law to be confirmed by the Senate, where they face scrutiny—and opposition—ranging from intense to trivial. The appointment of P.A.S.s[14] is a subject of careful review and strict control by White House personnel. Not only are holders of these jobs—cabinet secretaries, under secretaries, and assistant secretaries, among others—most closely identified with the president; the fact that their appointments must be confirmed by the Senate means that literally their entire life histories (including unsubstantiated rumors) are subject to appraisal by members of the Senate and their staffs. Inasmuch as it is not unknown for Senate staffers to give confidential personnel files of potential appointees to the news services, the White House goes to great lengths to avoid any possible embarrassment to the president.

Presidential appointees not subject to Senate confirmation fall into two broad groups. The first are those individuals who serve in the Office of the President—for example, members of the immediate White House staff or political appointees working for the Office of Management and Budget or the president's science adviser. The second are those occupying jobs that, for technical and legal reasons beyond my comprehension, can be filled by either P.A.S.s or ordinary presidential appointees. Thus jobs that are usually P.A.S. jobs are sometimes filled by presidential appointees not subject to Senate confirmation, because the White House wishes to avoid the scrutiny of Senate hearings (typically because the potential appointee is politically unpopular with the relevant Senate committee). Similarly, jobs that are ordinarily filled by presidential appointees are on occasion filled by a P.A.S. because the appointee demands the additional prestige of having been confirmed by the Senate. As a practical matter, occupants of positions that periodically switch back and forth in this paper hierarchy are treated equivalently by their peers, in no small part because few people know why a particular designation has really been chosen in any given instance.

The distinction between presidential appointees (P.A.S. or not) and other political appointees is artificial in at least two senses: Both are ultimately approved by the White House personnel, and both are presumed to be loyal to the president. Nevertheless, as a practical matter, the distinction is a real one for all parties. First, presidential appointees cannot legally be dismissed by anyone other than the president (although a cabinet member always has the option of dealing with a disfavored subordinate of any rank by cutting him out of the de facto chain of command). Second, presidential appointees are often placed in official situations where they are presumed to speak for the president, in no small part because they are the day-to-day managers of programs that are legally the ultimate responsibility of the president. Lesser political appointees are usually presumed to speak for only the executive agency head who appointed them, because either they are staff minions with no managerial responsibilities, or because their managerial responsibilities consist of coordinating activities of the presidential appointees with the schedule of the agency head who is setting the policy guidelines his managers are to follow. The prototypical model is thus one in which the nonpresidential appointees "move the paper," so that presidential appointees can make the real policy and management decisions needed to run the government.

This simple model is like most simple models: It works some of the time, but not all of the time. Since presidential appointees are visibly implementing programs charged to the president's care, they are selected with a careful eye for their predisposition to do so of their own volition (after all, the president cannot always watch everyone). However, since other political appointees are charged with making sure that the head of their agency gets *his* job done, *they* are selected with that task in mind. This may sound paradoxical, if not wrong; after all, if C wants to do what B wants, and if B wants to do what A wants, does not C want to do what A wants? The answer is *no*—not in Washington, nor in any other bureaucracy.

In this regard, the federal bureaucracy is much like any other. There are an efficient number of Bs to service A and an efficient number of Cs to service each B. Each are chosen on the basis of their comparative advantage in performing each of these tasks. Level A wants level B to do the best it can do to present its views, so that A can make the best decision. To achieve this, level B needs the best information it can get. There are two key elements in this process. First, a given level picks subordinates that have a comparative advantage in doing what that level wants done. Second, given that there are costs to disseminating and processing information, each level of the bureaucracy operates on the basis of what is commonly known as a "need to know." This is simply a shorthand method of saying that superiors do not always tell subordinates everything they know. This is often efficient, but it has the effect of reinforcing the initial comparative advantage of subordinates: Even if they are ultimately loyal to the president, they sometimes act in ways that might *appear* to be disloyal to him because they simply do not know all the facts. The same sort of forces work in the reverse direction, of course; in particular, subordinates often suppress information that might otherwise be passed along to superiors, simply because it is too costly to communicate. This creates some interesting conundrums, including the need to "wire" (that is, prearrange the outcome of) some meetings. The correctly wired meeting is one where a superior makes the same decision he would make if he knew all the information available to subordinates, but does so on the basis of a much smaller (and thus less costly to acquire) subset of information preselected for presentation by those subordinates. An *incorrectly* wired meeting is one where, either through malfeasance or misfeasance, the prefiltering of information results in a decision contrary to what a fully informed decision would have been. For a career bureaucrat, an incorrectly wired meeting may result in a transfer to the Fargo, North Dakota, regional office. For a Schedule C the outcome may be terminal.

Notes

1. My attempt is based principally on experiences at the U.S. Department of Labor (DOL), including events occurring wholly within the DOL bureaucracy, as well as events involving other agencies of the executive branch and entities of Congress. While my perspective is thus colored by my experiences at DOL, I have included no (attempted) generalizations that are inconsistent with observations of other individuals with whom I came in contact in Washington. To the extent that this consonance of experience expands the applicability of my observations, then what follows may be of some use to those who seek to understand a few aspects of bureaucratic behavior.

2. Further nuances regarding different types of appointments in the upper echelons of the federal bureaucracy are discussed in the appendix.

3. A break occurring *only* at D is extremely unusual, since it implies that the secretary has been cut out of the action, an unlikely event, since the secretary generally has closer ties to the president than anyone else in the department. A break occurring between the secretary and his chief of staff may well occur, but is unlikely to be observed by outsiders—since the chief of staff serves at the pleasure of the secretary, a break in their relationship will almost invariably result in a speedy termination of his employment.

4. The lack of market discipline in the bureaucracy is the driving force behind the importance of these factors, and it also helps explain a variety of other personnel-related phenomena. It is commonplace for example, for people to say that they are accepting a political appointment in Washington because they "want to have an impact." However, as discussed in the text, procedural rules in Washington are such that it is almost impossible for a particular individual to alter history significantly. Nevertheless, it *is* possible for an appointee to act in ways consonant with his tastes rather than being constrained to follow a course of action dictated by profit maximization. People have an impact by being able to indulge their preferences in performing their jobs in Washington, for what gets done and the manner in which it is accomplished depend very much on who is occupying a particular job. As a corollary, during the initial months of any administration, people find it inordinately difficult to get the bureaucracy to respond to their requests and have widely varying degrees of success in eliciting responses. In part this is due to the inexperience of new appointees, but importantly it is due to the fact that almost no one knows what the *real* chain of command is during the early days of an administration. Hence, many requests for action languish on the desks of people who *appear* to be the appropriate recipients, but either cannot or will not respond.

5. In even numbered years, it is clear that these stories are timed to coincide with elections. In odd numbered years I believe they are investments made by journalists, so that when stories appear in even numbered years, the reader thinks, "Oh yes, I've heard about this before," instead of thinking "If this is such a big deal, why haven't I heard of this before?"

6. It is sometimes asserted that benediction from above is an important source of power. A necessary condition for the existence of benediction is the imposition by party A (at the upper end of the bureaucracy) on party B of the appointment of party C as an underling of B. Benediction is useful as a source of power only when it arises because party C has demonstrated qualities (1)–(3) toward party A in the past. In this case there is a personal tie between A and C, and B will be foolish to ignore the tie, since if B does, C may bypass B to go directly to A to overturn a decision by B. Apparent (but not actual) benediction arises when C is appointed at the behest of A, but this happens because A owes a favor to some other party, since *that* party has exhibited the qualities (1)–(3) in some other context. This exhibition includes political favors that have helped A to his present position as well as the promise of future favors in a similar vein. This type of benediction does not automatically (or even generally) confer power, since party B recognizes the lack of a direct relationship between A and C. Indeed the lack of such a relationship may often *reduce* the power of C, since B typically resents having C imposed on him and B knows that C must call in chips with his ultimate benefactor to have the latter intercede with A if there is a dispute between B and C—a cumbersome and costly process at best. The upshot is that while benediction is frequently the *proximate* source of power (and thus wealth) in the bureaucracy, the exercise of benediction is almost invariably founded on the existence of demonstrated loyalty, usefulness, and consistency.

7. This is not to say that incredibly stupid things are not done—just that when they are done, a large number of people had to agree to the decision—which in and of itself makes one stop and think.

8. Interestingly enough, senior-level *career* bureaucrats act like "quasi-claimants" because their inherent time horizons tend to be much longer. As a result, they are often the source of much of the stimulus for undertaking longer term projects. This stimulus is, of course, weakened by incentives short-term appointees attempt to impose on them.

9. Best of all for a subordinate is also to arrange one-on-one *post*meeting time—for he can then give a "balanced" assessment of what took place at the meeting, resurrecting along the way straw men for redemolition.

10. Office assignments are not the only means of penalizing or rewarding performance. Disfavored employees can be given difficult, dead-end work assignments and instructed to write and rewrite worthless memoranda. Valued employees can be allowed to attend briefings of one's superiors in the chain of command or given enhanced secretarial or staff support. I focus here on office allocations because they are most visible to the outside observer.

11. The constant churning at the top level of the bureaucracy is a nontrivial source of frustration for people trying to do business with the federal bureaucracy. Phone calls to the same individual can lead to widely differing results even if they are separated in time by only a few months. Similarly calls to the current occupant of a niche in the paper chain often produce different results, depending on who happens to be the current occupant.

Daniel K. Benjamin

12. This phenomenon is best illustrated by a remark President Reagan made on visiting the labor department (located relatively far from the White House) to mark the first anniversary of the Job Training Partnership Act. As the president entered Secretary Donovan's 50 by 30 foot office with floor to ceiling windows overlooking the Capitol, his first remark was, "Gee, Ray, I wish I had an office this nice."

13. In at least two instances of which I am aware, DOL agencies were told that they could actually have *more* money than they were requesting if they would figure out a way of performing some of their activities with more computers and fewer people.

14. A person holding such an appointment is referred to as a P.A.S, a Presidential Appointee confirmed by the Senate.

14

The Anxious Course: Achieving Change in Washington, D.C.

Alan Rufus Waters

And there are some who spread their sail,
   And steer an anxious course in vain,
Who, sport of thwarting tempests fail
   Even an anchorage to gain
Who when at last the currents set
   and heavy clouds of menace form,
Grow weary of the way, and let
   Their vessel drive before the storm.

Louis H. Brindley[1]

Introduction

Anyone of conviction who goes to Washington to manage, administer, or advise a federal government agency will face a test for which there can be little adequate preparation. Whatever the ideological commitment one perceives in the administration, Washington will call for more than the application of reasoned principles. Growth in spending and scale of operations are easy to achieve in the nation's capital: Support comes from all directions. But change that entails reducing the budget and the number of employees of a federal agency will be met with solid resistance. To advocate even a mere reduction in the rate of increase may require tenacity and personal sacrifice of a high order. The Washington experience will sear the outsider who cannot recognize and handle the forces that press on three very basic elements of human life: philosophical beliefs, professional standards, and ability to work effectively.

275

Drawing on my own experience as chief economist for the Agency for International Development (AID), I would forearm the newcomer against the system with advice about some of the barriers and pitfalls, and advocate a method of operation that I now believe is most likely to bring positive results. What I have to say is not intended for those who plan a career in government service and therefore go to Washington to "get in harness" and improve the way the system works. Instead, I hope to reach those who go to Washington to be part of a team that is creating change. In particular I hope to reach those who believe—as I do—that a faceless and overweening federal government is now the greatest threat to our fundamental liberties, and that that government must be constrained, cut back, and allowed to perform only those tasks that unregulated competitors from the private sector cannot perform more effectively and more cheaply. My comrades are all those who want to help dismantle much of the present federal bureaucratic empire, not those who want that empire to operate its bureaucratic structure more efficiently.

I argue that the best way to achieve change in Washington, D.C., is to demand change in clear and simple terms, and to be stubborn in the face of appeals by "reasonable," "practical" people who would rather dicker with the status quo. To take a stand should be applauded as intellectually honest and quite refreshing. Unfortunately, after the first gentle acknowledgment of such a position (qualified instantly by its rejection of the radical), the proponent will be treated as a danger to the operation of the system. Even those claiming to hold similar views about the need for basic analysis and unequivocal choices frequently shrink at the call for decisive action. The proponent of real change will be seen as a mad dog, proposing impossible changes (in terms of the interests of the bureaucracy) in the way things are done. Eventually the mad dog will be destroyed by the system, but in the process, it may be possible to force some recognition of the true evil embodied in the way things are presently done.

Professional Standards and Philosophical Commitment

In his Richard T. Ely lecture, Sir Alec Cairncross describes economics as a business:

> Let's face it. Whatever economics was in the past, it is now virtually an industry. It stretches from the building of new models by the theorists to the supply of advice, forecasts, proposals, and programs by the practitioners, and caters mainly for a market of policy makers in business and government.[2]

Economists share a well-developed body of theory, good analytical tools, and a tested philosophical approach relying on individual people as the key active units. Despite jibes to the contrary in the popular press, we are good at the kind of policy prescription that sells in Washington, and Washington is the predominant market for economic policy. Unfortunately, the money available in the Washington market for policy recommendations has generated a series of problems as well as much prosperity for all the policy-related professions. One visible problem is the degree of product differentiation, as subdisciplines spin off in response to every new opportunity. For example, there are energy economists, transportation economists, health economists, and an increasing multitude of others, usually deriving from some temporary crisis. This problem is to be expected and can be explained quite simply in terms of commercial product differentiation—a standard merchandising tactic in areas of imperfect competition.

There is only one kind of economics, although economic analysis is applicable to numerous problems. Continued growth in the federal bureaucracy gives rise to increasing specialization, which in turn justifies whole new quasi professions. Furthermore, the maintenance of high rewards for increasing numbers of professional people in Washington depends partly on the ability to exclude outsiders. Such exclusion is made substantially easier by erecting professional titles. In the case of the Agency for International Development, for example, the subclass of economists calling itself development economists has carved out a preserve and uses its position skillfully to exclude those with general economic training. Despite a career centered on analyzing problems faced by less-developed nations, I refuse to recognize a separate discipline called development economics. Basically economics is about development: increasing the wealth of individuals and hence the nations in which they reside. Depak Lal, of the World Bank and University College London, put the case well in a recent article:

> seeking to emulate Keynes's iconoclasm (and hopefully renown), numerous economists set to work in the 1950's to devise a new unorthodox economics particularly suited to developing countries (most prominently, Nurkse, Myrdal, Rosenstein-Rodan, Balogh, Prebisch, and Singer). In the subsequent decades numerous specific theories and panaceas for solving the economic problems of the Third World have come to form the corpus of a "development economics." These include: the dual economy, labor surplus, low level equilibrium trap, unbalanced growth, vicious circles of poverty, big push industrialization, foreign exchange bottlenecks, unequal exchange, "dependencia," redistribution with growth, and a basic needs strategy—to name just the most influential in various times and climes.[3]

Rapid growth in demand for policy recommendations has other ramifications. All policy recommendations must be based on some implicit or explicit forecast of future circumstances, and forecasting remains an art. A major pressure on an incoming adviser will be to make short-term forecasts and to produce short-term policies that will have visible conclusions during the tenure of some individual or group, even where it is clear that the only relevant analysis is long term in nature. The pressure is made more extreme because there are always people willing to leap in and produce the required papers if a competent professional protests. Furthermore, the application of scientific reasoning requires us to make assumptions about some elements of complex reality in order to keep models manageable. In policy making, the selection of assumptions (together with the exclusion of elements appearing to be inherently nonquantifiable) can reduce many of our most highly respected activities to mere ritual. The limited evidence available indicates that economists have a poor record in forecasting the short run and medium run under any but the most stable conditions, when almost any projection from the recent past will be satisfactory. The fact that other policy-oriented professions fare much worse is no consolation.

Poor forecasting performance is apparently no barrier, for the demand increases for forecast-based recommendations. Furthermore it appears that the more complex and arcane the analytical technique, the greater the demand for the service. Why? Because federal bureaucrats (who are the predominant consumers of policy recommendations) are likely to be less interested in the ultimate recommendation than in its source and the nature of the process by which it is generated. They also minimize personal risks by taking the prudent man approach to policy, which suggests that one follow the lead of the most respected sources of advice and at the same time keep company with the majority of other forecasters. Bureaucrats have more to lose from commissioning policy studies from new sources—whose conclusions cannot be anticipated—than from continuing to call on those who have provided such services in the past. Also, the more technical and complex (and mathematical) the basis for the recommendation, the easier it is for a bureaucrat to defend its worth before nontechnically trained people.

In Washington there exists a normal distribution of professional people in terms of competence, intellectual interest, and ethical standards. Therefore one will sometimes find people in authority who claim to have studied economics, for example, at some time in the past (and often have a degree to prove the point) but whose intellectual capital has declined with time and involvement in other activities. Such people frequently display an intolerance of their fellow economists and a disdain for professional training more up-to-date than their own.

Another group, not peculiar to Washington but existing there in increasing numbers, consists of those who believe that any professional skill can be mastered at an operational level by reading a few of the "right" books. These individuals are likely to become slaves to some half-baked transient but popular theory. They often master the jargon of some profession and then become willing recruits of a professional subgroup that will grant them a degree of legitimacy. From my observation these people, in their enthusiasm, have played a significant part in leading our foreign aid program down so many false trails in the past.

So what defense is there? To be secure in the basics of one's profession. Before going to Washington there is a natural eagerness to hone the skills that one anticipates will be most useful and appropriate. Most economists try to review the statistical and mathematical tools of their trade or to bone up on some technique, such as project analysis. This is a significant mistake, for the most important requirement in the policy-making world of Washington is methodological rigor: a thorough understanding of what one's profession should and should not try to do. Before going to Washington, then, is a time to stand back and recall what the profession is all about. On the one hand a Washington economist is expected to do many things for which an economist is no better equipped than anyone else; on the other hand it is quite usual to see much economic analysis being done by people who have minimal training, yet are totally unaware that they are quacks. This false assumption of professional competence by nonprofessionals is an added argument for returning to the basics of one's profession and for taking a broader approach than is readily provided in graduate schools or highly rewarded by the profession in general.

For the economist it is a time to read both methodology and the history of economic thought. It is also a good time to recollect that the basic principles of economic analysis apply in less-developed countries to at least the same extent that they do in the more successful market economies. If one has any doubts about this, they should be settled before arriving in Washington. And one should read such works as Buchanan's *What Should Economists Do?*[4]

Knowing the various rationales for market intervention by government officials is good preparation for a world where bureaucratic regulation and intervention are the natural first solution to the symptoms of markets at work. Above all, a sound preparation for Washington requires thinking through the role of property rights in a market economy, for the role of ownership and the formation of incentives are the most totally misunderstood concept among noneconomists in particular and bureaucrats in general. The role of people's rights over property is essential to understanding the nature of development as well as to the effective working of any economic system based on personal freedom. Too often the ignorant

or self-serving in Washington accuse anyone who raises the issue of property rights of being a zealot. A return to methodological roots also arms
one against the tendency to apply arcane and complex theories to inappropriate situations.

Despite all protests to the contrary, the prevailing attitude in Washington
is elitist and paternalistic. It insists that people be regulated because they
cannot make decisions in their own best interests[5] because they are either
denied information or given false information or information too complex
for their limited understanding. People in aid-receiving nations are seen as
children at best, or reluctant and unenlightened peasants at worst. Every
temporary glut or shortage and every change in prices is a special case in
someone's eyes, and social institutions, rather than being created and
revised continuously as human desires dictate, are said to determine
human behavior.

The revival of Austrian economics is a trend worth investigating. Austrians take the market system as a coordinating mechanism, hence they see
the market process as the appropriate focus of attention. This is anathema
to those who use economic arithmetic and statistics to study states of the
market as ends in themselves, but it makes a lot of sense in the light of the
predominant methodology that has justified so much of the antimarket
activity generated in Washington. In particular the Austrians have a valuable approach to the situation in many of the less-developed countries:
They put the entrepreneur at the center of the system. On the other hand
many modern economic analysts, in particular "development economists," have totally excluded the entrepreneur.

The economist has a major advantage in policy analysis, having been
trained to think in terms of systems and alternatives and general equilibrium models. This leads to specific insight into the less obvious implications of policies. The general equilibrium concept should, however, never
lead to a preoccupation with final and static outcomes; it provides only a
framework within which to consider ramifications of any policy. Prior to
arriving in Washington, it is valuable to review general equilibrium concepts. I recommend the late Harry Johnson's *Two-Sector Model of General
Equilibrium* as an unequaled source.[6] Without becoming too enamored of
the model itself, one should read the book with the purpose of reinforcing
one's ability to think in general equilibrium terms.

The growth of the federal bureaucracy has not only given rise to a
proliferation of professional subgroups, it has also led to increasing complexity of underlying economic models as various alternatives vie for
policy makers' attention. The degree to which technical complexity for its
own sake has led to greater acceptance of economic proposals by noneconomists may still be in doubt, but I am firmly convinced that the

greater the complexity of its underlying model, the more likely it is that a policy proposal will be accepted.

The case for major policy change is usually based on fundamental principles and requires little technical complexity. The Washington economist must be able to explain a few basic economic concepts repetitively to successive groups of noneconomists. These fundamental concepts may sometimes be so obvious that the economist is almost embarrassed to explain them.

Markets operate to coordinate the overall economic system in direct response to the actions of multitudes of individual economic decisions. This is our key economic concept. The price system is basically a coordinating system through which society rewards those who produce what people want and penalizes those who do not. Market intervention in one area will produce effects that eventually impinge on prices and quantities in every other market in the economy. The interaction of supply and demand (Marshalian partial equilibrium analysis) is a crucial subset of this approach.

We must continually reiterate that markets will function effectively only where ownership is well defined and hence can be transferred at low cost. The role of ownership is one of the most difficult realities to grasp for the noneconomist or the economist who has been out of touch with the professional literature for the past several decades. It is the block on which every other aspect of a market system rests. If Washington policy makers cannot grasp this, there is no hope of anything but temporary and cosmetic change. We must, therefore, refuse to have the issue of property rights postponed or set aside as too controversial. It is imperative that people in Washington begin to approach every issue by identifying the owners and the degree to which ownership has been attenuated in order to transfer wealth to others. This is important in every application of economic analysis; it is fundamental in the case of the less-developed countries where so much has already gone wrong due to neglect of this basic point.[7]

The concept of opportunity cost is, of course, a shock to those who do not want society to recognize the true cost of what is going on. Every policy proposal must be couched in terms of its opportunity cost or, in other words, what could have been done with the funds and resources had they been used elsewhere. Arguments about dollar values in analyzing projects (particularly with respect to less-developed countries) should always be set in terms of alternative uses for the funds and other resources in question. The best alternative usually emerges from asking how funds would be used in an unregulated and competitive, privately owned activity.

Similarly, the marginal theory of value, which is so totally accepted within the economics profession, is still misunderstood and rejected elsewhere. The economist must be prepared for a continual battle to require that decisions be made on the basis of marginal rather than total or average net effects. What happens to output, price, cost, and demand when we add one more unit? This is the question that must be asked several times daily.

The market system is not analytically simple; its complexities have occupied the best minds over several centuries. But to the layman there is a superficial common sense to the market system that at times causes more problems than all the arcane arguments of economists. For example, noneconomists seldom understand the interaction of supply and demand and how prices are mutually determined in a market economy. The average citizen will usually opt for a political solution to economic problems. Administratively established or fixed prices have a ring of stability and reasonableness to most people that is hard for the economist to comprehend. Officials, too, must continually be forced to recognize that if prices are fixed—making the major assumption that they can be fixed—quantities, qualities, and all of the services that are part of the market process will fluctuate more wildly. One example of this problem surfaced in AID as a struggle to get the senior people to comprehend that an agreement by the Egyptian government to increase the administered price of electricity was not a victory for the market process and did nothing to alter the insane policies that are driving that economy into the ground.

There are many other aspects of basic economic reasoning that a policy adviser will have to propound daily. Perhaps the most significant part of the role we play is insisting that basic economics not be ignored when discussing special cases. Fidelity to basic professional standards requires every professional to know the theoretical framework of the discipline and refuse to be involved in arcane discussions with lay people about the immediate application of complex theoretical approaches that may be of marginal intellectual interest but consume valuable time and energy.

We have mentioned the bureaucracy's delight in complex theoretical analysis: The more obscure the justification, the more it is relished. Even more pernicious is the widespread demand for an essentially consensual method, which is then presented as scientific.[8] Predictably the first demand an insecure bureaucrat makes is for a survey of the literature. Far from being the starting point for a new (and possibly different) conclusion, the survey frequently becomes a head count of published opinions about what is the appropriate basis for a particular policy. While it is useful to understand professional views, it is ridiculous to use this as the sole basis for policy recommendations in a world of rapid intellectual change. The analogy with Copernicus, or other original thinkers, is too obvious: A survey of the predominant Ptolemaic literature would have sustained the pope's rejection of the modern theory of the cosmos without the need for resorting to the doctrine of heresy.

Literature surveys as justification for policy are supported by economists, and others, who can thus keep professionally active. They hopefully gain the respect of their professional colleagues for their apparent understanding of current academic theoretical developments, even when those developments are not yet ready for policy application or are completely inapplicable under the present circumstances. Officials gain from reducing the degree to which their chosen policies can be questioned by people possessing only common sense or basic economic training. In the case of AID there is also the broad and dangerous intellectual constituency that Harry Johnson recognized nearly twenty years ago:

> the urban-centered political philosophical tradition of Western Civilization meshes with the feudal-aristocratic social values of many less developed countries . . . the notion of the inherent inferiority of those who work the land, a notion that prompts and supports the exploitation of the rural primary-producing sector for the benefit of the urban-industrial sector.[9]

Had he lived, Harry Johnson might have also recognized the degree to which it is in the interest of Western intellectuals in general to pander to the pathetic hope that somewhere a touchstone exists, which the economic alchemists will produce, thus removing the grubby need for hard sweat and disruptive entrepreneurial people in the development process.

Professional standards demand that the policy adviser ask simple but profound questions. To do this he must be well trained in his profession and intellectually convinced of the absolute soundness of his arguments. Further, the reaction to objective economic reasoning is frequently the cry that the economist, or other policy adviser, is insensitive to the cruel burdens borne by the poor (but definitely not the government officials and the rich) in less-developed nations. An immediate response to any question about the effectiveness or appropriateness of a particular policy to be followed in giving aid to a foreign country will be met with the assertion (sometimes implied, often explicit) that the economist has no heart and is driven by a mechanistic belief in the efficacy of market solutions under all circumstances. Such silliness must be met head-on with a coldly logical examination of the track record achieved by the alternatives.

If there are heartless economists—which we must assume there are, since we only reflect humanity and our society—they are to be found among those who would continue to pursue the collectivist policies that have already impoverished so much of the aid-receiving Third World.

They are to be found among those with so little intellectual stamina that they have countenanced prolonged food aid, which has destroyed the capacity of so many nations to feed themselves. Economists are as humane as anyone in society and perhaps more so because they think through the long-term effects of popular policies that may ultimately degrade and impoverish those they are intended to help. An economist must often oppose administrative self-interest, and that takes a rare courage. Acquiescence and compromise seem so reasonable when the alternative is to be an outsider or to be ignored. But compromise is the most misused term in Washington; it frequently means relinquishing professional convictions and agreeing not to speak on certain issues that might embarrass one's superiors.

Effectiveness

Effectiveness means attaining the goals that led one to Washington. Unfortunately, the very definition of attainable goals is extremely difficult in the governmental setting of Washington, D.C. It is unusual for anyone to have a sufficiently detailed understanding of what is going on in a particular agency to be able to identify specific issues on which to take a stand. A reasonable goal may therefore be to work toward a change in policy implementation by requiring participants in the present system to acknowledge the full implications of what they are doing, and not to truncate the range of competitive alternatives by saying that this or that will not likely be implemented. This may not sound like a very lofty goal, but it is a sufficient basis for consistency in a typical federal government agency where competitive markets may receive an occasional good word but little serious attention, and undesired alternatives are rejected in terms of "political reality."

There are small engagements to be won or lost in each of the endless meetings that characterize the administrative process. Given the right personality and a degree of tenacity, it is possible to build coalitions and persuade colleagues, thus achieving a consensus able to bring about change in the way things are done. However, what is achieved in one administration can quickly be reversed in another. It is fundamentally wrong to think that lasting changes in human behavior (in this case changes in the behavior of middle-executive ranks of a federal agency) are possible without a fundamental change in the pattern of incentives. Furthermore, to a large extent the structure of incentives is determined by those in Congress and the administration, who alone are capable of changing the civil and foreign service structure and reducing the power of civil and foreign service unions to write their own regulations. The Grace Commission did magnificent work in identifying the scope of distortions that the present overall federal management and personnel system generates. The individual in a particular agency must, in large part, work with the system as it is.

There is another option: the mad dog approach. Instead of trying to alter institutions and human nature marginally, we can find the key pressure points and operate directly on the incentive structure, or at least ensure that less constructive activities of the system are minimized.[10] The danger is that as soon as one is perceived by the career bureaucrats and the career political appointees as actually achieving disruptive change (disruptive because any real change is disruptive), one becomes a lightning conductor, a focus of efforts to discredit and emasculate, a mad dog to be destroyed. Hence, this is not a long-term policy; the person who undertakes it must act and then be prepared for isolation and rejection as soon as the opposition realizes what is happening.

The mad dog approach requires clear understanding of the nature of information and knowledge in any complex organization: "What matters, then, is knowledge actually used at the decision-making point, not the knowledge in process of development or authentication, or even the knowledge clearly apparent to particular individuals or organizations somewhere in society."[11]

The support of the group immediately around one is most important in any position requiring a managerial as well as an advisory role. Before accepting a specific position, it is wise to speak with those who direct the agency in order to gauge the degree to which they share your convictions and philosophical approach to problems. It must be recognized that there are people in Washington who have developed careers as political appointees. They have become part of the professional administrative caste and like to think of themselves as pragmatic or practical in some undefined sense. This usually means that they are maximizing the returns to their own careers by going along with whatever causes the least threat or pain in terms of present and future opportunities. There is nothing unexpected about this, but one must be careful to recognize that their level of commitment to almost any philosophical stand is relatively low.

For example, the terms "conservative" and "liberal" have a meaning all their own in Washington. Many of the executives in various agencies must prosper under several different administrations, and by this I mean the senior tenured bureaucrats as well as the career political appointees in the middle ranks who survive to be reappointed by succeeding administrations. For these people, and for others who hope to emulate them and have a long career in Washington, it is necessary to avoid becoming too closely identified with any particular viewpoint. In this way they develop a certain amorphous approach and an elusive ability to change viewpoint with the times.

One also finds people who attend all the appropriate meetings and loudly proclaim a commitment to a particular view of society, but who in their selection of staff and day-to-day operations, make policy decisions that are anthithetical to what they say they believe. This gives added evidence that the incentive structure is the key and that changes in personnel or leadership (the "throw-the-rascals-out-and-replace-them-with-good-people" approach) are unlikely to achieve much by themselves.

To avoid being embroiled in subsequent and avoidable personnel issues, it is wise to secure prior agreement on the right to recruit deputies and immediate staff. Without this seemingly trivial provision, one is doomed from the start. What often happens is that soon after arrival, an economist or political adviser is either required to accept the deputy of the person being replaced or allowed to select a deputy from a predetermined list of people already in the system. Similarly, one must have prior agreement about hiring a personal secretary. Try to hire someone from the outside, but if that is truly impossible, ensure that it is someone whose track record is vouched for by those one trusts.

A little paranoia is better than an open and generous naïveté. Be acutely aware of the "good-people" justification for the behavior of those who frustrate the policies one advocates. Certainly one finds our society (or at least the intelligentsia) fully represented in Washington, D.C.; one finds both decent people and the malign, all well rewarded for their services and generally content with their role in life. But the assertion that, despite their attitudes and activities, all members of a group such as the foreign service employees are basically "good people" is reminiscent of Patterson's description of another well-traveled group of "good-people": the Swahili of the East African coast at the turn of the last century.

> Their life is spent in journeying to and from the interior carrying heavy loads of provisions and trade-goods on the one journey, and returning with similar loads of ivory or other products of the country. They are away for many months on these expeditions, and consequently—as they cannot spent their money on the march—they have a goodly number of rupees to draw on their return to Mombasa. . . . Nothing ever seems to damp the spirits of the Swahili porter. Be his life ever so hard, his load ever so heavy, the moment it is off his back and he has disposed of his posho (food), he straightway forgets his troubles.[12]

In many agencies substantial power resides in the personnel office. Through detailed understanding of arcane rules, and connections with people who run the civil and foreign service unions, personnel officials can determine hiring practices, distribute assignments, and facilitate or thwart transfers. They are in a position to offer both positive and negative rewards to people throughout the system, and hence have a widespread power base. The only solution for the person seeking change is to have the support of the people at the very top of the agency and to be able to use that support when crucial issues are involved. The head of an agency must be prepared to intervene forcefully, personally, and at low levels if the issue is right.

As an example of the power of entrenched personnel officials, and the bureaucracy for which they are the first line of defense, consider the case of an attempt to alter the pattern of recruiting economists in AID in order to develop a group of economists more representative of the profession. Efforts to open up the system were defeated by refusals to provide adequate information, delays of up to a year between the time a person was contacted and the date of final notification that he would be offered a job, and an interview panel on which economists were a minority and personnel and equal employment opportunity representatives had a deciding vote on economic qualifications. The favored characteristics at the deciding interview were that economists should know a foreign language, preferably have Peace Corps experience, and training in development economics. For a variety of reasons these characteristics did not result in hiring people best equipped for the job. The viewpoint of those chosen was frequently statist, and their lack of competence in the basic economics of the market was seldom compensated for by their enthusiasm and social conscience.

Much policy-oriented work involves writing drafts of position papers. In most cases the permanent staff is asked to prepare an initial draft for editing. Their recommendations are, with few exceptions, favorable to state intervention and direct government involvement in production. Their papers are returned by senior economists as unsatisfactory, with corrections and suggestions for revision. The result of the second round seldom differs much from the original draft, and the final step is for the professionals to write the paper themselves. Policy papers and project appraisals within the federal government tend to be excessively circumspect and demonstrate a proclivity for failed policies of the past.

There are, for example, few ringing condemnations of state economic development planning among the final drafts of policy papers produced by AID. Similarly, state enterprises, marketing boards, and other government monopolies in less-developed countries are handled with kid gloves rather than being damned forthrightly for the economic failures they generally are. And seldom is any state institution, however corrupt or inefficient, rejected outright as a potential recipient of U.S. tax funds. This behavior could be the result of an unstated commitment by AID to fund such activities, but there is a more likely reason. Policy papers may mention an ultimate goal of privatization and competition but emerge from the system so muted that no action is required. This is because the competitive private sector is unknown to most bureaucrats, and they recognize that it often has no role for them. It is hard for a bureaucrat to accept the idea of a totally unadministered entity; it is a disturbing idea. The bureaucratic concept of the private sector is mirrored by a few major corporations that are often protected from the rough and tumble of market competition by government contracts, subsidies, regulations, and other institutional arrangements.

If policy papers have to be approved by every major bureau within an agency prior to becoming official, they are likely to represent consensus rather than change. The accumulation of minor changes and revisions, made to comfort every group in an agency, usually results in bland restatements of current practice with every strong stand modified out of existence. This strange concession to the power of the established bureaucrats gives individuals at the lower levels in the various bureaus a virtual veto over policy for the whole agency. There is also a tenderness toward certain areas and issues in some agencies that more or less ensures that nothing controversial can be done. An example of this within AID is population policy, whose advocates evidently hold a position in AID that precludes questioning their role in accelerating the economic development process. Caution and consensus also come into play when policy and position papers must be politically acceptable to the divergent views of various constituencies both inside and outside an agency.

In reviewing the content of a majority of policy papers, it becomes clear that there is still throughout Washington a pervasive belief in the economics of the Keynesian apostasy. This situation arises not only because Keynes's framework of analysis justified increased roles (and therefore rewards) for the civil service and professional politicians; it also arises because of the substantial inertia created by the training and philosophical commitment of the majority of Washington economists now in positions of influence and authority. Once embroiled in the policy process, there is little time for professional retooling. It is only with attrition and the arrival of a new generation that the intellectual ethos will change. The key is to ensure that the existing establishment does not perpetuate itself by continuing to hire only people in its own image. However, it must be recognized that the main pressure to continue hiring and using Keynesian and post-Keynesian economists comes not from professional economists but from noneconomists within the system.

Attempts to accelerate change in the intellectual climate are likely to be frustrating, but so, too, are attempts to change and improve the nature of management. We are in the midst of an information revolution that is changing the nature of management structures everywhere. It is predicted that information-based management structures of the future will be much flatter than the typical management hierarchy today. The future management system can be thought of as an information-flow and decision-making network. With the growing capacity to handle and communicate information, fewer levels of authority will be needed and greater individuality will not only be a possibility, it will be a requirement.[13] Although this pattern may take longer to emerge in government, it must emerge eventually. In fact the groundwork for such a system is already being laid with the widespread introduction of individual microcomputers and increasing access to central sources of data and information. The immediate effect of the information-based management structure will be totally to alter management as we now know it. Under these circumstances it makes little sense to put too much effort into trying to improve and polish the dying structure of the present. And any attempt to accelerate the process of change will meet tenacious resistance because it will be seen as a visible manifestation of the already pervasive sense that something is horribly wrong with the old basis of bureaucratic power: ownership of valuable information from which others may be excluded.

It is, on the other hand, crucially important to learn the present modes of information and power within the organization. This can only be done through personal contact. Gossip and second-hand descriptions of what makes things happen will not do. In Washington, memos are written after the event, the guts of decision making and policy development result from conversations and meetings that seem at the time to be pointless and peripheral. It has always been so in every form of government from the courts of the monarchies to totalitarian communist systems or pluralistic democracies. George Wyndham, one of the finest administrators of an earlier time, wrote to a friend on taking up his appointment as chief secretary in Ireland, "I find that the Government of this country is carried on by continuous conversation."[14]

Another factor affecting the ability to achieve change is the degree to which congressional influence impinges on activities in the agency. Higher education, due to its close relation with many federal agencies, exerts significant pressure on occasion. The private sector works through Congress and seldom tries to influence general policy (compared to specific implementation issues); unwanted external pressures can therefore be deflected relatively easily by an agency. Congressional influence is nevertheless frequently felt in every agency of the federal government. Sometimes the influence is overt, but more often it is subtle. This is particularly true of AID, which is always visible and usually vulnerable because of its un-popularity with the majority of Americans. But the intrusion seldom comes from elected members of Congress (although occasionally it does); it is more likely to come from congressional staffs on Capitol Hill who hold inordinate power through their ability to influence events. Individual congressmen and senators do attempt to expand their personal power by controlling the actions of bureaucrats within various agencies, but they and their staffs are also responsive to the reciprocal power that the civil service can exert in Washington. [15]

For example, AID faces such problems as the insistence by certain congressmen's staff that ways be found to continue sending funds to Tanzania, Mozambique, and a range of other countries that have failed economically, pursue anti-American policies in every international forum, and are driven by a declared socialist ideology. It is difficult to resist such pressures, but more can be done despite the power of such congressional staff members.

Similarly, since much of our foreign aid goes to universities and insti-tutes in the United States, there is peculiar pressure on AID by congres-sional delegations representing universities in their districts (often in coalition with the governments of client countries). Throughout all agen-cies of the federal government, however, the pressure of congressional staff intrusion is felt in some degree, and the extent to which it is restricted depends on factors beyond the control of the individual adviser or bureau director.

Conclusions

Joining the ranks of advisers or managers in Washington requires a fundamental decision whether one wants to be an adviser who makes policy, or a manager who implements someone else's policies. I argue strongly that even if we choose to become managers, we should think in terms of policy generation at every level. We should not go to Washington solely to manage. There is always the temptation to spend efforts improv-ing the way a flawed system works. We must not become embroiled in attempts to make marginal changes in how things are done; instead we must leave the management to others and get on with reducing the size of agencies and redirecting their roles to those for which they were originally established. There must be a major effort to offset the intense drive that, even under the Reagan administration, goes into increasing every agency's operating budget and the scope of its activities.

Courage, tenacity, perseverance, and controlled outrage are the characteristics required of the person who would attempt the mad dog approach to obtaining change in Washington. But the rewards are high: First, one can look back later with satisfaction at having been more than a timeserver. More tangible are the friendships that develop between those who stand firm in the face of entrenched self-interest and demonstrate there is real substance to our arguments. Finally there is the pure excitement of the contest and the fun of seeing hypocrites forced to discuss issues they would rather not have to defend and would rather take for granted. The mad dog approach is for the participant in life, not the observer.

At the operational level the mad dog approach requires a new appointee in Washington to develop a personal staff, however small, that he can rely on not to subvert his efforts and to interface between him and the system. This will help one avoid becoming tied down by administration or day-to-day management of staff. This is necessary because management within the federal bureaucracy becomes an end in itself and a substitute for the serious work of orchestrating change. In the longer run attempts to manage the system more effectively and produce better results are doomed to failure.

Having set up an immediate staff, send a continuous stream of written suggestions and recommendations (with the necessary supporting argument and evidence) upward to policy makers in the agency. Attend, or have a staff member attend, as many meetings as possible where it is likely that issues of substance will be discussed or decisionmakers will be present. There is a tradition in Washington of decrying the need to attend endless numbers of meetings. Attending many of the meetings is a defensive measure for career bureaucrats who fear that their territory may be encroached on in their absence. The truth is that the meetings would not occur unless someone saw them as valuable, and they were the locus of stopping or initiating action of some sort. Therefore it is prudent to attend meetings.

Washington is a city of caution—no action is taken that can possibly be deferred. Therefore Washington is a city of endless analysis, professional procrastination, and vigorous inaction (nobody would say that bureaucrats are not busy). It is also a city of quantification, for it is much easier to defend action or lack of action if one has data to back oneself up. But for the person who knows the nature and limitations of data, the shield is easily pierced.

The mad dog approach requires one to make major recommendations, always keeping the system on the defensive as it rationalizes inaction and the impossibility of change. Do not try to second-guess, and take into account potential objections to policy recommendations. Develop the analysis in terms of what is best and force the system to demonstrate why it is impossible to implement it. Demand consideration of basic issues and do not become drawn into arguments about why the present system must be taken for granted.

Finally, have a contented private life and enjoy the infinite pleasures of Washington to the full. But be prepared for the time when one is dropped from the official circle and subjected to a kind of sensory deprivation while at work. Plan to use that sudden gift of free time to think constructively, study, and write. Do not dwell on loneliness or think of defeat, for the very fact of eventual exclusion by the system is a measure of your success. This final period is a time for decompression, and should be treated as one of the honorable rewards of the mad dog approach.

Notes

1. "Fate," in *Poems by Louis H. Brindley* (Dublin: Cuala Press, 1945), pp. 41–42.

2. Sir Alec Cairncross, "Economics in Theory and Practice," *American Economic Review* 75, no. 2 (May 1985): 1.

3. Depak Lal, "The Misconceptions of Development Economics," *Finance and Development* 22 (June 1985): 10. Professor Lal goes on:

> for the major thrust of much of "development economics" has been to justify massive government intervention through forms of direct control usually intended to supplant rather than to improve the functioning of, or supplement, the price mechanism. This is what I label the dirigiste dogma which supports forms and areas of dirigisme well beyond those justifiable on orthodox economic grounds. (p. 10)

4. James M. Buchanan, *What Should Economists Do?*, preface by H. Geoffrey Brennan and Robert D. Tollison, (Indianapolis: Liberty Press, 1979).

5. I am fascinated by our constant talk of regulating industries, activities, or institutions. We never talk about the reality, which is that we regulate *people*. It is akin to the way we talk about price supports for commodities, or about tariffs and import quotas on various goods. I have to believe that another generation will refuse to accept such patronizing behavior by their government officials.

6. Harry G. Johnson, *Two-Sector Model of General Equilibrium*, The Yaro Jahnsson Lectures of 1970 (Chicago: Aldine Atherton, 1970).

7. A senior career foreign service bureaucrat dismissed the importance of ownership rights in my presence by saying conclusively that "we do not want a crusade." The nature of ownership rights is the basic and underlying element that differentiates us from a socialist society, such as the Soviet Union. It is ironic that property and ownership cannot be discussed even as purely technical matters

without an immediate assumption by left-wing liberals that the matter is vaguely indecent.

8. The whole issue of the authentication process by which we verify ideas is brilliantly discussed by Thomas Sowell in *Knowledge and Decisions* (New York: Basic Books, 1980). "The method of verification is what distinguishes pure science from pure myth" (p. 5), and "problems arise when one method of verification masquerades as another" (p. 6).

9. Harry G. Johnson, *Economic Policies towards Less-Developed Countries* (London: George Allen and Unwin, Ltd. 1967), pp. 68–69.

10. This suggestion should not be taken to its logical extreme in agencies where the staff is rewarded for idleness. There are those who would like the federal system to achieve nothing and hence avoid doing harm. We might whimsically call this the Stephen Leacock ploy:

> Let me sing to you of the Nothingness,
> > The Vanity of life,
> Let me teach you of the effort you should shirk,
> Let me show you that you never ought to make the least endeavor,
> Or indulge yourself in any kind of work.

(Stephen Leacock, "Idleness," in *College Days* (London: John Lane the Bodley Head Ltd. 1923), p. 125.

11. Thomas Sowell, *Knowledge and Decisions* (New York: Basic Books, 1980), p. 11.

12. Lieut.-Col. J. H. Patterson, D.S.O., *The Man-Eaters of Tsavo,* foreword by Frederick Courtney Selous (London: Macmillan 1907), pp. 118–19. Elsewhere in the book Patterson was less charitable. He suggests that their name came from a corruption of the words *sawa hili,* which mean "those who cheat all alike" (p. 117).

13. For a good and succinct exposition of this argument, see Peter F. Drucker, "Playing in the Information-Based 'Orchestra'," *Wall Street Journal,* 4 June 1985.

14. The Rt. Hon. George Wyndham, letter to Charles T. Gatty from Dublin Castle, dated 17 November 1900. J. W. Mackail and Guy Wyndham (eds.), *The Life and Letters of George Wyndham,* vol. 2, (London: Hutchinson, sometime after 1925), p. 407.

15. On this see Gordon Tullock's discussion of William A. Niskanen, "The Pathology of Politics," in Richard T. Seldon (ed.), *Capitalism and Freedom, Problems and Prospects* (Charlottesville: University Press of Virginia, 1975), pp. 37–38.

Index

holding on depositors' interest, 235–36

Bartel, Ann, 52

Baxter, William F., 90, 121–22, 219

Becker, Gary, 107

Bell Operating Companies (BOCs), 104; first triennial review of, 122–25; in inter-LATA toll markets, 121–22, 127; toll service monopoly of, 107; vertical integration of, 111. *See also* AT & T

Benzene decision, 55, 68*n*

Borg-Warner case, 48

Bread-and-butter antitrust, 93–96

Broadcast regulation, economics of, 22–23

Brown, Charles, 128

Brubaker, Sterling, 139

Brunsdale, Anne, 183*n*

Bubble concept, 58, 69*n*

Buchanan, James, 4

Budget deficit, federal land sale and, 145–46, 152–53

Building codes, economic effects of, 26

Bumpers, Daile, 43

Bureaucracies: operation of, 13; power in, 14; lack of market discipline in, 272*n*. *See also* Federal bureaucracy; Regulatory bureaucracy

Burlington, support of cotton dust standards, 26

Cabinet departments, chain of command in, 254–58

Cable television (CATV), regulation of, 22–23

Cairncross, Sir Alec, 276

Campaign contributions, 229–30

Campbell, Thomas, 46

Canada, trade with, 169–70

Capacity decision, predatory or efficient, 19

Capture regulation theory, 106–7, 109

Cartelization-by-regulation, 226–27

Carter, Jimmy: "midnight" pretreatment regulations of, 57; petroleum price decontrol of, 43–44; reduction of FTC powers by, 71–72

Carter administration: deregulation during, vii, 6–7; economic incentives for environmental improvement in, 37; federal lands in West and, 134; privatization during, 156–57

Cenarrusa, Louis, 157

Cenarrusa, Pete, 157

Chain of command, 254–56; breaks in, 257, 272*n;* function of, 256; mutations of, 256–57

Chevron decision, 58–59

Child labor regulation, 24

Children's product regulation, 212–13; hazards and, 220*n*

Christiansen, Gregory, 44

Chrysler, financial difficulties of, 27

Cigarette television advertising ban, increased consumption with, 25

"City of Boulder" legislation, 49–50

Civil Aeronautics Board (CAB), 21, 186; airline competition and slot market and, 195–99; airline regulations of, 22; demise of, 9, 13; legal problems with ADA of, 189–91; need for regulatory reform in, 186–87; opportunity and demand for reregulation of, 191–95; regulation reforms in, 7; results of deregulation in, 187–89; route moratorium of, 201*n;* rulemaking authority of under section 204, 191

Civil Aeronautics Board Sunset Act, 189, 190–91

Civil servants, new breed of, 16

Civil Service system: bureaucracy size and, 266–68; penalizing or rewarding performance in, 264–266, 273*n;* resource allocation in, 264–66

Clawson, Marion, 138, 139–40

Clayton Act, 101; Section 7 of, 215

Clean air, market forces to achieve, 58–59

Clean Air Act: purpose of, 60; reauthorization of, 55–56

Mattress safety standard, 25
McChesney, Fred S., 105–6
Meat inspection laws, 27
Meetings, attending, 286, 291
Merger Guidelines, Department of Justice, 49, 94–96, 102*n*, 215–17; below-guideline case triggers of, 220*n* under Reagan, 92–93
Mergers: benefits and reasons for, 180; deterrence of, 221*n*; sub rosa regulation of, 215–17
Metzenbaum, Howard, 43
"Midnight" pretreatment regulations, 57
Miles-per-gallon (MPG) regulation, 24
Milker bills, 230
Miller, James C. III, 45–50, 61, 76, 80–83, 87*n*, 90–91, 97, 190, 219
Mineta, Representative, 190–91
Minimum-wage legislation, 226
Monopoly, government-sponsored, 96–97; attack on, 97–98
Monsanto–Spray Rite case, 48
Moore, Thomas Gale, 56
Moore, Winston S., 204*n*
Morrall, John, 52
Morrison, Steven, 43
Multiplexing, 114, 116
Muris, Timothy, 45–46
Muss, Joshua, 153

Nader, Ralph, vii; on FTC failure, 71; on trade regulation, 86*n*
National Highway Traffic Safety Administration, expanded regulations of, 7
Natural Resources Defense Council v. *Morton,* 134
Nelson, Phillip, 76
Netting, 69*n*
New Deal, 9
Niskanen, William, 143–44
Nitrosamines, regulation of, 214
Noerr-Pennington doctrine, 19, 97
Noise Standard compliance, 53

Nonprice competition, regulation of, 22
Nutritional labeling requirements, 82

Occupational noise regulation, 55; proposal to increase levels of, 67*n*
Occupational Safety and Health Act, 51; General Duty clause of, 54; section 6a of, 66*n*
Occupational Safety and Health Administration (OSHA): assessment of performance of, 11; changing enforcement activities of, 51–53; expanded regulations of, 7; focused approach of, 50–55; informal complaint procedure of, 54; inspections by, 54; progress of and special-interest opposition, 60; promulgation process of, 53; under Reagan, 41; Review Commission of, 54–55; targeting program of, 53–54
O'Donnell, Thomas, 53
Office assignments, 264–66
Office of Management and Budget, regulation through, 218
Offsets, 69*n*
Oil industry mergers, 96
Opportunity cost, 281
Ownership: definition of, 281; rights of, 292–93*n*

Packwood, Finance Committee Chairman, 234–35
Pareto optimality, 31*n*
Parker doctrine, 27
PATCO strike, 195
Payola, ban on, 227
PBXs, 116–18
Peltzman, Sam, 201*n*
Pennington case, 19
People Express, 188
Personnel office, power of, 286–87
Pertschuk, Michael, 50, 71, 84–85, 89
Petroleum price decontrol, 43–44
Pfizer doctrine, 78–79
Pigou, Arthur C., 20, 28